Strange Affinities

Perverse Modernities

A series edited by Judith Halberstam and Lisa Lowe

Strange Affinities

THE GENDER AND SEXUAL POLITICS OF COMPARATIVE RACIALIZATION

*Edited by Grace Kyungwon Hong
& Roderick A. Ferguson*

DUKE UNIVERSITY PRESS *Durham & London 2011*

© 2011 Duke University Press

All rights reserved

Designed by Jennifer Hill

Typeset in Arno Pro by Keystone Typesetting, Inc.

Library of Congress Cataloging-in-Publication Data appear
on the last printed page of this book.

Strange Affinities

THE GENDER AND SEXUAL POLITICS
OF COMPARATIVE RACIALIZATION

*Edited by Grace Kyungwon Hong
& Roderick A. Ferguson*

DUKE UNIVERSITY PRESS *Durham & London 2011*

© 2011 Duke University Press
All rights reserved

Designed by Jennifer Hill
Typeset in Arno Pro by Keystone Typesetting, Inc.

Library of Congress Cataloging-in-Publication Data appear
on the last printed page of this book.

Contents

Acknowledgments

This book has been a collective effort from the start and has benefited from the work and care of many. First and foremost, we thank our contributors. We wanted to make the process of compiling the book a truly collaborative one, and we could not have done so without their hard work and dedication.

As a part of this collaborative process, we held a workshop and symposium at UCLA in the spring of 2007 that gathered most of the contributors. We read each other's essays and edited the book together. It was a tremendous amount of work for the contributors in the midst of what were certainly hectic personal and professional schedules, but it undoubtedly strengthened the book and our intellectual community. Although Shirley Lim's essay did not end up in the final version of the project, she played an energetic part in our conversation, and we acknowledge with gratitude her many contributions. For the major funding for the workshop, as well as administrative support, we thank UCLA's Center for the Study of Women, in particular Kathleen McHugh, Jessie Babiarz, Van Do Nguyen, and

Brenda Johnson-Grau. We also thank the Asian American Studies Center, the Women's Studies Department, the Asian American Studies Department, the Chicano Studies Research Center, the Lesbian, Gay, Bisexual, Transgender Studies Program, and the Critical Race Studies Program at UCLA, as well as the University of California Humanities Research Institute for their generous support. Jenna Miller-Von Ah and Samantha Hogan of the UCLA Women's Studies Department provided further administrative support, for which we are immensely grateful. We thank Rafael Perez-Torres, Russell Robinson, and Judith Halberstam for their participation in the symposium. Christina Nagao provided valuable research assistance. In Los Angeles, the LOUD Collective has been an unwavering source of keen intellectual engagement and warm support.

Ken Wissoker has been the most patient, supportive, and generous of editors throughout what has undoubtedly been a much longer process than he first anticipated. We are grateful to Courtney Berger and Leigh Barnwell for their impeccable editorial assistance. We also thank Rebecca Fowler, who ushered this book through the production process, and William G. Henry, for his keen-eyed copyediting prowess. We thank also the anonymous readers, whose careful and rigorous comments only made this book better. Lisa Lowe and Judith Halberstam, editors of the Perverse Modernities series and mentors extraordinaire, offered invaluable good cheer and wise counsel throughout the process and, if truth be told, our entire careers. We owe them more than can be expressed.

This book emerged from a desire to identify and invent analytics through which to compare racial formations, in distinction to comparative race scholarship that simply parallels instances of historical similarity across racial groups in the United States. Such a project entails not only articulating commonalities between communities of color but imagining alternative modes of coalition beyond prior models of racial or ethnic solidarity based on a notion of homogeneity or similarity. This project is necessitated by the changing configurations of race and nation in the wake of movements for decolonization and the social movements of the mid-twentieth century, which have revealed the limitations inherent in nationalist and identity-based forms of collectivity, even or perhaps especially when they are expressed in minority or cultural nationalisms. As we discuss in more detail later, the stakes for identifying new comparative models are immensely high, for the changing configurations of power in the era after the decolonizing movements and new social movements of the mid-twentieth century demand that we understand how particular populations are rendered vulnerable to processes of death and devaluation over and against other populations, in ways that palimpsestically register older modalities of racialized death but also exceed them.

We have found that the greatest potential for producing such alternative comparative methods lies within formations that have emerged to name the shared comparative method of bourgeois and minority nationalisms: women of color feminism, and a related intellectual tradition, what Roderick A. Ferguson has called queer of color critique. We assert that much of what we now call "women of color feminism" can be seen as queer of color critique, insofar as these texts consistently situate sexuality as constitutive of race and gender. Further, not coincidentally and not unimportantly, lesbian practice and identity were central to many of the most foundational women of color feminists, including Audre Lorde, Cherríe Moraga, Barbara Smith, and the Combahee River Collective. We thus narrate queer of color critique as emerging from women of color feminism rather than deriving from a white Euro-American gay, lesbian, and queer theory tradition.

Women of color feminism and queer of color critique profoundly question nationalist and identitarian modes of political organization and craft alternative understandings of subjectivity, collectivity, and power. In situating women of color feminism and queer of color critique in this way, we read these formations as comparative analytics rather than descriptions of identity categories, and we highlight the comparative nature of women of color feminism and queer of color critique that has heretofore been underexamined. Women of color feminism and queer of color critique reveal the ways in which racialized communities are not homogeneous but instead have always policed and preserved the difference between those who are able to conform to categories of normativity, respectability, and value, and those who are forcibly excluded from such categories. As we argue, such a comparative method is immensely important in the current moment, as neoliberal modes of power rely on such valuations to subject the racialized poor to brutal violence *through* rhetorics of individual freedom and responsibility. As Lisa Cacho observes in her chapter in this book: "In a sense, a comparative analytic assumes that in the United States, human value, legally universalized as normative, is made legible in relation to the deviant, the non-American, the nonnormative, and the recalcitrant: the legally repudiated 'others' of U.S. value" (27). This comparative methodology allows us to see moments when certain racial *groups* could articulate a demand for incorporation, albeit unevenly, over and against other racial groups as complexly interrelated to the processes by which subjects, within racial collectivities, are differentially incorporated or excluded from the class, gender, and sexual norms of respectability, morality, and propriety and thus placed on different sides of the dividing line between valued and devalued. For example, Helen Jun's chapter details the ways in which the black press in the nineteenth century cast African Americans as worthy of citizenship by contrasting them to the Chinese, in ways that emphasized gendered and classed values of uplift and respectability that render abject not only the Chinese but also "nonrespectable" African Americans as well.

In this introduction, we describe the dominant mode of comparison underlying modern Western thought and its implicatedness in the legitimation and erasure of racialized, gendered, and sexualized violence. We then delineate poststructuralist methods of comparison, on the one hand, and minority nationalist critiques of racialized violence, on the other, as two important but incomplete critiques of modern Western comparative methods. Finally, we situate women of color feminism and queer of color critique as providing an alternative comparative method that, in its deep critique of the racialized, gendered, and sexualized devaluation of human life, gives us a blueprint for coalition around contemporary struggles. We observe that because the dominant mode of comparison is an epistemological structure, the alternative comparative method of women of color feminism is rendered *illegible* within this dominant schema. We situate culture, defined expansively as being exemplified by works of cultural production, but also inhering in everyday practices of language and relationality, as the site where such alternative comparative modes are imagined and brought into being.

For a description of dominant Western epistemology, we turn to Lisa Lowe, who renders central the comparative method derived from Weberian sociology. Lowe describes Weber's comparative method as one that establishes an "ideal type" of social organization, which is represented by rationality within Western industrial society. Against this ideal, Weber and his social scientific descendants characterized other ("non-Western") modes of social organization as deviant, atavistic, irrational, violent, and so forth. In this way, Lowe notes, "Centering western industrial society as the normative *ideal type* against which 'difference' was conceived mediated a racial epistemology emerging out of an earlier conjunction of European colonialism and slavery in the 'new world' " (Lowe 2005, 410).

This notion of different societies with their own discrete cultures orders a particular spatial imaginary under modern nationalism. Akhil Gupta and James Ferguson write:

> The distinctiveness of societies, nations, and cultures is predicated on a seemingly unproblematic division of space, on the fact that they occupy "naturally" discontinuous spaces. The premise of discontinuity forms the starting point from which to theorize contact, conflict, and contradiction between cultures and societies. For example, the representations of the world as a collection of "countries," as on most world maps, sees it as inherently fragmented space, divided by different colors into diverse national societies, each "rooted" in its proper place. (Gupta and Ferguson 1997, 33–34)

In other words, the spatial imaginary that allows for the division of global space into nation-states situates each nation-state as discrete entities, differentiated by unique cultures, within an abstract and fragmentable world space. In this way, modern nation-state formation presumes the comparability of nation-states.

Poststructuralist theories of space, in particular Michel Foucault's notion of heterotopia, have provided important critiques of the normative spatial imaginary of Western bourgeois nationalism dependent on the notion of discrete, comparable spaces. While most famously elaborated in "Of Other Spaces," Foucault's discussion of heterotopia in *The Order of Things* explicitly relates this concept to the functions of classification and comparison. Foucault bases his theorization of heterotopia on a passage from Jorge Luis Borges that describes the classificatory principles of a Chinese encyclopedia's entry on animals as "(a) belonging to the Emperor, (b) embalmed, (c) tame, (d) suckling pigs, (e) sirens, (f) fabulous, (g) stray dogs, (h) included in the present classification, (i) frenzied, (j) innumerable, (k) drawn with a very fine camelhair brush, (l) *et cetera*, (m) having just broken the water jug, (n) that from a long way off look like flies" (Foucault [1970] 1994, xv). Foucault describes this passage as a heterotopia, or a confounding of classification and comparison that goes far beyond mere juxtaposition. In describing heterotopia, he writes:

> I mean the disorder in which fragments of a large number of possible orders glitter separately in the dimension, without law or geometry, of

the heteroclite; in such a state, things are "laid," "placed," "arranged" in sites so very different from one another that it is impossible to find a place of residence for them, to define a *common locus* beneath them all. Utopias afford consolation. . . . Heterotopias are disturbing, probably because they secretly undermine language, because they make it impossible to name this and that, because they shatter or tangle common names, because they destroy 'syntax' in advance and not only the syntax with which we construct sentences but also that less apparent syntax which causes words and things (next to and also opposite one another) to "hold together." (xvii–xviii)

Heterotopias thus are not exclusively literal spaces (as in Foucault's famous examples of the cemetery, the mental hospital, etc.) but spatial imaginaries that mark epistemological or discursive failure, disjuncture, or dissonance. They emerge at the moment when the epistemological certainties that are required for comparison are undermined. Foucault notes that in this passage Borges does away with the *site* or "common locus" on which comparison is made. He does away with the "table"—both the actual examination table that serves as the common place that unifies the diverse objects that can be placed on it and the table as in a chart that regularizes the data that make it up—that is implied by a utopic mode of comparison. In other words, utopias are *ideal types* against which other kinds of spaces can be compared; they are also spaces of stability (like the table) that allow for comparison. Heterotopias, in contrast, make the basis for comparison impossible. To take this idea back to Gupta and Ferguson's discussion of modern nation-states, we may observe that nationalism generates a utopic comparative method, under which a stable concept of the world, divided up into neatly discrete nation-states, enables the comparison of one nation-state to another.

As valuable as this critique of normative modes of spatial comparison is, however, it is ultimately undone by Foucault's inability to name the material conditions of race that are the disavowed conditions of possibility for the very modes of Western comparison that he wants to undo. In Foucault's exegesis of Borges, comparative incommensurabilities are situated in the Orient as the site of illogic and unreason, or as Foucault puts it, China as the "privileged *site of space* . . . at the other extremity of the earth we inhabit, a culture entirely devoted to the ordering of space, but one that does not distribute the multiplicity of existing things into any of the categories that make it possible to name, speak, and think" ([1970] 1994, xix). Ultimately, Foucault's notion of heterotopia does not undermine Borges's casting of China as the ultimate other to the West; the West still operates as, in Lowe's words, an *ideal type* against which China can be seen as the mirror opposite. While Foucault reads Borges as imagining Chinese epistemology as internally heterotopic (i.e., rendering Chinese animals incomparable to each other), he takes for granted Borges's understanding of China and the West as stable and comparable social formations.

In contrast, minority nationalisms emerged as a part of the epistemological challenge to racist and colonial legacies of Western thought articulated by the social movements of the 1960s and 1970s in the United States. As Mike Murase notes in his essay about the student strikes at San Francisco State University in 1968 and 1969 that established the ethnic studies program on that campus, the protesting students were "part of a larger Third World movement representing the growing awareness of Third World people throughout the world of their *common experiences under colonial domination, within and without the continent of the United States*" (Ethnic Studies Committee 1974, 3; quoted in Murase 1976, 208, our italics). As Roderick A. Ferguson notes in his chapter in this book, C. L. R. James observed that ethnic studies emerged as a critique of the U.S. nation-state as an exemplar of Western civilization. James describes the discipline of African American studies in his chapter "Black Studies and the Contemporary Student" as an intervention into Western civilization as a racial project constituted through the intersecting histories of European slavery, imperialism, and colonization (C. L. R. James 1993, 397). Both minority nationalisms and women of color feminism and queer of color critique are legacies of these social movements, from which many of the theorists most associated with women of color feminism and queer of color critique migrated. As such, both formations pose the history of race in the United States within this more expansive genealogy.

Yet we must distinguish between women of color feminism and queer of color critique and the minority nationalist ideologies also produced out of these social movements.[1] These minority nationalisms advanced comparative analytics that reflected how race-based movements in the United States understood the nature of racial formation. In other words, the question of how to compare the various circumstances of minorities in the United

States was centrally part of the racial projects of antiracist movements among African Americans, Chicanos and Latinos, Asian Americans, and Native Americans. As we can see from the earlier passage from Murase, what became known as the internal colonial model provided the comparative analytic that linked the various nationalist movements in the United States. As the historian Ramon Gutiérrez notes, this model arose in the 1950s in the social sciences as a way to "explain the 'development of underdevelopment' in Africa, Asia, and Latin America" (Gutiérrez 1997, n.p., our italics). While Gutiérrez notes the ubiquity of internal colonial paradigms in the era of the social movements of the 1960s and 1970s, citing Harold Cruse, Kenneth Clark, Stokely Carmichael, and Charles Harris, he observes:

> But it was Robert Blauner who best articulated the theory in relationship to American minorities, maintaining that while the United States was never a colonizer in the 19th Century European sense, it had nonetheless developed economically through the conquest and seizure of indigenous lands, the enslavement of Africans, and the usurpation of Mexican territory through the war. "Western colonialism," wrote Blauner, "brought into existence the present-day patterns of racial stratification; in the United States, as elsewhere, it was a colonial experience that generated the *lineup of ethnic and racial divisions.*" (1997, n.p.)

To refer back to Murase's chapter as an example of the internal colonial model, we see that he historicizes the migration of Asians to the United States as part of a larger narrative of white supremacy and racialized exploitation. He situates the fight for ethnic studies as a project of renarrating history so as to undermine internal colonialist ideologies that posit native peoples as "troublesome savages who impeded the fulfillment of the European settlers' 'divine right' of Manifest Destiny," African slaves as "primitive savages that had to be 'domesticated,'" and Chicanos as "illegal" (Murase 1976, 206). Murase names the ways in which the colonial imaginary is a fundamentally comparative one, a "utopic" comparative method that situates Western civilization as an ideal type and scripts racialized groups as discrete and internally homogeneous types that are differently but equivalently backward, primitive, and eradicable. Against this colonialist history, Murase deploys an oppositional narrative that recalls native rights to the land on which they "lived for centuries in North America before the first white ever set foot," the cruelty and greed of "white men who hunted down 100 million Blacks in the interior of Africa to sell them as slaves," and the usurpation of Mexican territory that absurdly made Chicanos "illegal" on the very lands they once owned (206).

This internal colonial model gave nationalists of color a broad narrative for how the United States produced racial divisions and inequalities. This model provided a comparative framework for understanding those divisions and inequalities at the same time as it furnished a blueprint for coalition. That is, the seizure of Indian lands, the enslavement of Africans, and the usurpation of Mexican territory are, in Murase's account, different but *equivalent* violences enacted by the U.S. nation-state, to which he adds the exploitation of Asian immigrant labor. In this way, minority nationalism uses the exact comparative method of all other nationalisms, as described by Gupta and Ferguson: rather than nation-states being discrete and comparable, it is racial groups that are discrete and comparable in the minority nationalist imaginary. Coalition in this context would therefore mean a confederation of discrete formations.

Murase never considers some of the limitations of this mode of coalition. For example, he never attends to the ways in which these examples of racialized dispossession and abjection might depend, at different historical moments, on differentiated life chances and modes of incorporation for some racialized groups over and against others. Neither does he imagine that differences might exist *within* these groups along the lines of gender and sexuality, differences that women of color feminism and queer of color critique arose to name. In this way, in addition to lubricating ideologies of discreteness, the internal colonial model also helped to establish comparative analyses within ethnic studies as technologies of gender and sexuality. As the internal colonial model promoted comparative agendas based on narratives of underdevelopment, those narratives were oftentimes articulated as those of castration. Hence the lineup of ethnic and racial divisions was frequently figured as the castrated gender and sexual histories of straight men of color. From this position, hegemonic comparative analysis would help to constitute a fraternal politics across race, ethnicity, and nation aimed at heteropatriarchal retrieval.

Women of color feminism and queer of color critique developed an alternative mode of comparison in opposition to the comparative analytic of minority nationalisms that, while themselves critical of the racial violence underpinning modern power, ultimately reproduced its comparative method. In this way, women of color feminism and queer of color critique have something in common with poststructuralist challenges to normative comparative method, as represented by, for example, Foucault's notion of heterotopia. While the comparative method generated by women of color feminism and queer of color critique is heterotopic insofar as it troubles the assumptions of discreteness intrinsic to nationalist modes of comparison, we argue that because this method emerges to name the material conditions of racial and colonial violence, it reveals the particularities erased by Western epistemologies in ways that Foucault fails to do.

The comparative method of women of color feminism and queer of color critique is heterotopic insofar as it refuses to maintain that objects of comparison are static, unchanging, and empirically observable, and refuses to render illegible the shifting configurations of power that define such objects in the first place. Instead women of color feminism and queer of color critique were fundamentally organized around *difference*, the difference between and within racialized, gendered, sexualized collectivities. This deployment of difference has been misread as a form of cultural pluralism and, as Jodi Melamed reminds us in her chapter here, in many sites has been incorporated into a neoliberal multicultural project. However, the mobilization of difference by women of color feminism and queer of color critique was intended not to erase the differentials of power, value, and social death within and among groups, as in a multiculturalist model, but to highlight such differentials and to attempt to do the vexed work of forging a coalitional politics through these differences.

Such a heterotopic mode of comparison can be found in Cherríe Moraga's preface to *This Bridge Called My Back*:

> I can't prepare myself a revolutionary packet that makes no sense when I leave the white suburbs of Watertown, Massachusetts and take the T-line to Black Roxbury.
>
> Take Boston alone, I think to myself and the feminism my so-called sisters have constructed does nothing to help me make the trip from one end of town to another. Leaving Watertown, I board a bus and ride it quietly in my white flesh to Harvard Square, protected by the gold highlights my hair dares to take on, like an insult, in this miserable heat.
> *I transfer and go underground.*

Julie told me the other day how they stopped her for walking through the suburbs. Can't tell if she's a man or a woman, only know that it's Black moving through that part of town. They won't spot her here, moving underground.

The train is abruptly stopped. A white man in jeans and tee shirt breaks into the car I'm in, throws a Black kid up against the door, handcuffs him and carries him away. The train moves on. The day before, a 14-year-old Black boy was shot in the head by a white cop. And, the summer is getting hotter.

I hear there are some women in this town plotting a *lesbian* revolution. What does this mean about the boy shot in the head is what I want to know. I am a lesbian. I want a movement that helps me make some sense of the trip from Watertown to Roxbury, from white to Black. I love women the entire way, beyond a doubt. (Moraga 1981, xiii)

Instead of Foucault's heterotopic *nowhere*, which he places in opposition to the empirically fixed and fixing table, Moraga gives us the heterotopic *somewhere* of the subway, in which the objects of comparison—herself, Julie, the boy on the train, the boy who was shot, lesbian separatists—have an unstable interrelation to each other, because they have changing meanings depending on context. These objects are not merely incongruous, as in Foucault's analysis, and they are not merely uncategorizable under a uniform set of criteria. Their relationality is constantly shifting, as Moraga notes when she contrasts Julie's hypervisibility within a white suburb to her invisibility on the subway and when she then juxtaposes Julie with herself and the boy on the train. Moraga's "unmolested" passage through the city, her "protected" status, is complexly determined by, and determining of, the surveillance and disciplining the boy undergoes, as well as the brutal state repression that ends the life of another racialized boy.

In contrast to Foucault's characterization of heterotopia, which is situated in the mysterious and exotic irrationality of China (with all its attendant Orientalist overtones), the illogic and unreason named by Moraga are the brutal residues of the deployment of "order": the space of the subway is the "underground" of the "law and order" repressive carceral state that, as Grace Hong has argued elsewhere, was a necessary part of Boston's transformation in the 1970s and 1980s into a "global city" organized around finance capital and technology (see Hong 2006, x–xi). Moraga's subway heterotopia is certainly rendered "impossible" and illegible, not because it is an Orientalist symbol of the exoticized other to Western logic but because the incommensurability of categories and subjects—between Moraga, the boy on the train, Julie, the fourteen-year-old shot by a cop—is the disavowed condition of possibility of a city based on capitalist extraction of profit from gendered and racialized labor, the privileging of whiteness as indexed by the creation and protection of suburbs, and the consequent uneven devaluation of racialized life. This is the definition of difference for women of color feminism and queer of color critique: not a multiculturalist celebration, not an excuse for presuming a commonality among all racialized peoples, but a cleareyed appraisal of the dividing line between valued and devalued, which can cut within, as well as across, racial groupings. Difference, for Moraga, has serious, fundamentally deadly consequences, as the boy shot by the police reminds us. Such consequences underscore the urgency and impor-tance of an alternative comparative analytic that would take into account such deadly differences between the valued and the devalued.

Moraga's response to this uneven devaluation of racialized life is decid-edly not the opposite reaction of *valuing* life, of seeking comfort in the pockets of safety where certain forms of racialized life escape such devalua-tion. She frames her ability to ride unmolested in the subway because she passes as white not as a relief but as an insult. In so doing, Moraga under-scores the ways in which such a condition places great strains on coalitional politics. Certainly the minority nationalist rubric of a commonly experi-enced internal colonialism that binds all racialized peoples together falls apart under such strain. A new kind of politics is required, and for Moraga, seeking respite in one's value, no matter how hard-won, is exactly the kind of politics that a women of color feminism must displace; this is exactly why she longs for a different "movement that helps her make sense of." Put differently, Moraga frames the political project of women of color feminism and queer of color critique as a rejection of the ways in which bourgeois and minority nationalisms create idealized identities. Moraga's alternative to these nationalisms, therefore, is *not* to establish "women of color" or "Chi-cana lesbian" as yet another idealized identity, an ideal type that replaces the ideal type of either the nation-state (citizen) or minority nationalism ("Chicano"). Rather, she seeks to undermine the logic of the ideal type entirely. Moraga consistently evades the logic of the ideal type, the idealized subject, by highlighting, rather than obfuscating, her protected and valued status and rejecting that status as the foundation for her politics. An important aspect of the project of Moraga and Anzaldúa's book, then, is to invent a politics, out of something they call "writings by radical women of color," as a comparative analytic of difference. Further, for Moraga, such a politics requires a retheorization of what it means to be lesbian. She frames this entire episode with a rumination on the inadequacy of dominant practices of lesbian politics—that is, as "lesbian separatism"—for understanding the intersection of race, class, and gender. We might thus name Moraga's quest for a "movement that helps her make sense of" as the quest for a queer of color critique, as well as for a women of color feminism.

Lest we imagine that Moraga is unique in the way she defines difference as the line between valued and devalued, life and death, or that this preoccupation with crafting a different kind of politics began with the publication in 1981 of *This Bridge Called My Back*, we now turn to some earlier, equally classic texts of women of color feminism and queer of color critique. In the following section, we closely examine two chapters, one by Frances Beal and another by the Combahee River Collective. Beal, as a very early woman of color feminist theorist, tends to define the gendered racialization of black women as entirely abject and does not explicitly consider the relational privilege that certain racialized subjects accrue in relation to other racialized subjects. Moraga is much more attuned to relational racial and gender formation, and this has to do with the differences between the context of Beal's writing and Moraga's later historical moment. Yet we do believe that a connection can be made between Beal and Moraga and that a genealogy of theorizing exists between these two moments of women of color feminism. We situate the Combahee River Collective's "Black Feminist Statement" as a kind of bridge between the two. While Beal's chapter situates all black women as similarly exploited, because she situates this exploitation as not only racialized but gendered and sexualized, and because for her this exploitation is organized around the devaluing of black lives, Beal's solution is not to raise black women to the status of the new "ideal type" but to try to imagine a new form of relationality that destabilizes conventional roles. The Combahee River Collective further elaborates on the gendered and sexualized nature of racialized devaluation and highlights the ways in which the terms by which people are valued or devalued can cut within racial groups. As such, both of these texts refute the stability of racialized identities and imply that a different kind of comparative model, one that does not take racial groups as discrete, comparable entities, is required.

Beal's essay "Double Jeopardy: To Be Black and Female" (1970) precisely addresses the ways in which race and gender are not essentialist or biological categories but processes of valuation and devaluation. While the essay's title seems to refer to an identity category or ontology ("to be black and female"), the text begins not with a description of black women as a group or an identity formation but with a discussion of capitalism, patriarchy, and racism as processes that create normative categories.

> In keeping with its goal of destroying the black race's will to resist its subjection, capitalism found it necessary to create a situation where the black man found it impossible to find meaningful or productive employment. . . . The black woman likewise was manipulated by the system, economically exploited and physically assaulted. She could find work in the white man's kitchen, however, and sometimes became the sole breadwinner of the family. (Beal 1995, 146)

National culture in the United States, however, renders abject the very gender roles produced within black communities by an economic situation produced by capitalism. Capitalism constitutes black men and women as nonnormative and then punishes them for this deviance:

> America has defined the roles to which each individual should subscribe. It has defined "manhood" in terms of its own interests and "femininity" likewise. Therefore, an individual who has a good job, makes a lot of money, and drives a Cadillac is a real "man" and conversely, an individual who is lacking in these "qualities" is less of a man. . . . The ideal model that is projected for a woman is to be surrounded by hypocritical homage and estranged from all real work, spending idle hours primping and preening, obsessed with conspicuous consumption, and limiting life's functions to simply a sex role. (Beal 1995, 146–47)

For Beal, capitalism is centrally structured around the construction of norms and values. These normative categories are racialized, gendered, classed, and sexualized at the same time. Those who do not fit these norms of respectability are dismissed and demonized and are thus subject to all manner of material and social marginalization. However, as Beal notes, black women's conditions belie these normative precepts: "It is idle dreaming to think of black women simply caring for their homes and children like the middle-class model. Most black women have to work to help house, feed, and clothe their families. . . . Black women were never afforded any such phony luxuries" (147). For Beal, the result of this disciplining of black women through the construction of hypocritical norms is their more efficient economic exploitation as well as their subjection to eugenicist sterilization campaigns.

As such, challenges to these relations of rule must happen at the level of norms. Beal asserts in an oft-quoted passage:

> We must begin to understand that a revolution entails not only the willingness to lay our lives on the firing line and get killed. In some ways, this is an easy commitment to make. To die for the revolution is a one-shot deal; to live for the revolution means taking on the more difficult commitment of changing our day-to-day life patterns. This will mean changing the traditional routines that we have established as a result of living in a totally corrupting society. (154)

Linking this thought to her earlier discussion of the creation of racialized, gendered, and sexualized middle-class norms as the basis for this "totally corrupting" capitalist society, we may read her prescription for "changing the traditional routines" as a call to abandon the politics of respectability and thus to interrogate the desire to be valued, and therefore safe, within a system that punishes devaluation with death.

As Beal implies with her discussion of sterilization campaigns, these processes of valuation not only determine economic status or life chances but, at a more basic level, constitute the dividing line between life and death. The Combahee River Collective, a Boston-based black lesbian feminist organization that emerged in the 1970s, invokes a similar analysis that even more pointedly gestures to the necropolitical implications of the racialized and gendered processes of valuation. A pamphlet written and distributed in 1979 by the Combahee River Collective in response to the unsolved murders of twelve black women in the Boston area is titled "Why Did They Die?" The collective's answer to this question gestures at the determination of valued and devalued as the dividing line between life and death. Because the twelve women were murdered in different ways and in different contexts, the murders were understood as unrelated and thus were rendered invisible within conventional meaning-making practices that bestow significance on deaths. The women were not the victims of a serial killer or even an industrial accident, and so these dead black women were not seen in aggregate. Their deaths were understood as random individual deaths, rather than societally determined ones. Indeed, the deaths were narrated not only as individual but as inevitable or even deserved: "The mother of a 15-year-old girl, one of the first two victims, says that when she reported the disappearance of the girl to the police they hesitated to file a report claiming that the girl had probably gone off with a pimp" (Combahee River Collective 1979, 41). Mobilizing racialized and gendered notions of black female sexual immorality that, as many scholars have noted, date back to the era of chattel slavery, the police articulate black female life as valueless and thus definitionally unprotectable.

As a corrective, the Combahee River Collective mobilizes an alternative meaning-making practice that identifies the causes of these deaths: "Our sisters died *because* they were women just as surely as they died because they were black" (1979, n.p.). In linking these deaths and insisting that race and gender are the names for the processes that ushered these women to their untimely deaths, the Combahee River Collective maintains that the twelve black women were killed because their lives were not valued and, in this way, were outright extinguished. While race and gender are the names they give to the processes by which these women are rendered alien to respectability and propriety, it is the deviant sexuality attributed to them that makes their deaths "acceptable." In this way, the Combahee River Collective highlights the differences *within* black communities, challenging assumptions of racial uniformity, discreteness, and comparability.

In so doing, women of color feminism and queer of color critique situate *culture* as the site for the production of alternative modes of comparison and affiliation. Cherríe Moraga attests to the need for a movement that "helps her make sense of." That is, Moraga does not articulate, for example, stopping police brutality or ensuring economic security for people of color as the organizing principles of the movement she wants, although assuredly these are struggles that such a movement may encompass. For Moraga, at base, the radical potential of such a movement comes in its ability to produce alternative meanings, alternative understandings about the nature of power. This intervention is one that lies in culture. Similarly, Frances Beal emphasizes the need to rethink "day-to-day life patterns" as a revolutionary practice. For Beal, revolution is not merely an economic or political transformation but a transformation that happens at the level of subjectivity: "A people's revolution that engages the participation of every member of society, man, woman, and child, brings about a certain transformation in the participants as a result of this participation. Once you have caught a glimpse of freedom or experienced a bit of self-determination, you can't go back to old routines established under a racist, capitalist regime" (Beal 1995, 154). In the introduction to their pamphlet, the Combahee River Collective likewise describes their activism in the following terms: "A Boston Black Feminist group, the Combahee River Collective, *provided an analysis* of the murders that helped Third World women *understand* what was happening to them" (Combahee River Collective 1979, n.p., our italics). In Moraga's words, the collective helped to "make sense of" these murders in their larger historical context. The project of women of color feminism and queer of color critique, in other words, is to create a language to describe what has been rendered unknowable through normative comparative method. Yet in creating this language, these women of color feminist text must emphasize what cannot be known, what escapes articulation: Moraga's desire for a movement that has not yet come, Beal's "glimpse of freedom," or the Combahee River Collective's description, in their foundational "Black Feminist Statement," of "a *clear leap* into revolutionary action" that black feminist activism demands (Combahee River Collective 1981, 213). If, as Lowe argues, the dominant mode of comparison exemplified by Weberian social science depends on an empiricist mode that claims the knowable, we can see why an alternative comparative method must traffic in the unknowable and the devalued.

These earliest iterations of women of color feminism and queer of color critique offer us important optics for present-day mobilizations of power. In women of color feminism and queer of color critique, we find an analytic for understanding how the creation of categories of value and valuelessness underpins contemporary racialized necropolitical regulation. The decolonization movements that inspired striking Third World students in the 1960s and 1970s have necessitated changes in the operation of global capital.[2] Neocolonialism and globalization produce new racial formations and thus demand new methodologies for the study of race.[3] This violent reorganization of the world economy exacerbates established modes of exploitation, creates new conditions of dispossession, and produces new displacements alongside new forms of immobility. As Roderick A. Ferguson reminds us in his chapter in this book, the influx of Asian, Latino-Chicano, and African migrants into the United States since the Immigration and Nationality Act of 1965, for example, has demanded the recognition of the histories of colonialism, decolonization, war, and structural adjustment in Africa, Asia, and Latin America as part of understanding these migrants' racial formations. And again, the development of the "prison-industrial complex," which incarcerates African Americans en masse, cannot only be narrated in relationship to the long history of the U.S. nation-state's dispossession of African Americans but, as Ruth Gilmore has observed, must also be understood as one of the many effects of a global economic transition after World War II (Gilmore 1998–99).

In the contemporary era, ascriptions of value and valuelessness are unevenly detached from overt reference to race, yet their deployment provides for extreme racialized violence. In her chapter in this book, Jodi Melamed delineates the post–World War II era as a moment when "white supremacy entered a phase of permanent crisis" (87) occasioned by the vilification of racism and fascism as the ideological justification for war, and by the emergence of movements for decolonization. As a result, a new racial formation emerged, one that "organizes the hyperextraction of surplus value from racialized bodies and naturalizes a system of capital accumulation that grossly favors the global North over the global South" (83). Yet the same neoliberal formation mobilizes multicultural rhetoric "as the key to a post-racist world of freedom and opportunity" (78). It does so by "engender-[ing] new racial subjects as it creates and distinguishes between *newly privileged and stigmatized* collectivities" (our italics) while "cod[ing] the wealth, mobility, and political power of neoliberalism's beneficiaries to be the just desserts of 'multicultural world citizens'" (83). Contemporary regimes of power naturalize brutal racialized, gendered, and sexualized violence, labor exploitation, and the rendering of subjects as redundant and disposable by creating new, nominally nonracialized categories of privilege and stigma, or, in other words, valuation and devaluation.

We can identify these processes as a novel deployment of comparison that creates new ideal types. In other words, while in an earlier era, categories such as race, gender, and sexuality stood as the dividing line between those who were protected from "premature death" and those who were not, today these categories are unevenly sutured to older categories of race, gender, and sexuality (Gilmore 2007, 28). Thus we see racialized, gendered, and sexualized subjects accruing previously unimaginable access to capital and citizenship in formations such as a global Asian technological and professional class (Ong 2006), elite global South nationalist state managers and bureaucrats (Alexander 1994), and an African American middle class that exists as a conduit for state violence against, and disciplining of, the African American poor (Cohen 1999). Yet at the same time, such an organization of power enables *exacerbated* conditions of brutality, social and physical death, and violence—indeed, the relegation of billions of racialized, gendered, and sexualized lives to disposability and valuelessness—the world over. The unequaled worldwide increase in imprisoned populations and in practices of criminalization and incarceration is one, though by no means the only, haunting example of this exacerbated dismissal of lives (See Sudbury 2005; see also A. Davis 2003; Schneider and Amar 2003). Other examples of necropolitical practices and their effects include the utter abdication of state protection of black life in New Orleans in the wake of Hurricane Katrina, the largely unsolved "feminicides" of hundreds of working-class Mexican women along the U.S.-Mexico border, particularly in the Ciudad Juárez region (see Fregoso 2003), and the emergence after 9/11 of the category "terrorist" as the name for those whose lives cannot be recognized as lives, a category that legitimates U.S. wars in Afghanistan and Iraq. Older modes of struggle organized around the presumption of homogeneity within racial groupings fail to address these differences.

Yet we do have a "usable tradition" from which to create a new politics of struggle for our current moment. Insofar as theorists like Moraga, Beal, and the Combahee River Collective have already begun to identify and critique such a mode of governance and to theorize alternative understandings of the political, we submit that we can find in these writings, and in the models of comparison developed within them, inspiration for a politics for the present. Lisa Lowe encourages us to "consider a *genealogical* study that would *both* situate 'difference' within the modern apparatus of comparison *and* attempt to retrieve the fragments of mixture and convergence that are 'lost' through modern comparative procedures" (Lowe 2005, 412).

In that spirit, we the editors and contributors have collectively endeavored to articulate how racialized, gendered, and sexualized difference has been produced and understood through comparison, as well as to produce new analytics through which to apprehend coalitional possibilities, or in other words "strange affinities." While some of the chapters in this book

(Ferguson, Hong, Keeling, Melamed) explicitly take up women of color feminism in its myriad incarnations, all offer relational analyses that unsettle received categories and modes of comparison in ways that share a kind of kinship, or a strange affinity, with the relational comparative analytic of women of color feminism and queer of color critique.

The chapters in part 1, "Alternative Identifications," describe and sometimes even enact new modes of connection through the deployment of a relational comparative analytic. We begin with Lisa Cacho's meditation on the difficulties in mourning the death of her cousin Brandon. Cacho's chapter thematizes its own failure to articulate alternative modes of subjectification in the face of pathologizing definitions of racialized and gendered subjects by highlighting the impossibility of finding a language to valorize and memorialize the life of her young male cousin without replicating such pathologizing narratives. This impossibility, Cacho observes, lies in a long material history of racialized and gendered evaluation of Latino men's lives, a history that undergirds a system of value in which her own position as an educated, upwardly mobile professional is valuable only *because* Brandon's position is devalued. When Cacho, despite these seemingly insurmountable epistemological challenges, finds a way to value Brandon in his own terms, we see the creation of a new form of relationality and coalitional possibility. In a different context, Kara Keeling's analysis of new-digital-media social movements similarly describes a different model of relationality. Keeling delineates the ways in which these digital-media social movements mobilize identity politics that radically disrupt a discrete and coherent notion of subjectivity. Keeling uses Gilles Deleuze's theorization of "I = Another" as a description of subjectivity that refuses the normative identity politics of "I = I." That is, rather than connecting through similarity (the "I" can be equivalent only to another "I"), the formulation "I = Another" can imagine a connection through difference. Keeling observes that the new-digital-media social movements find a way to forge such connections. Likewise, Jodi Melamed identifies two different deployments of identification in texts, both of which are characterized as women of color. Yet one, Azar Nafisi's *Reading Lolita in Tehran*, uses a form of identification based on similarity (much like "I = I") that underwrites neoliberal multiculturalism, while the other, June Jordan's poem "Moving towards Home," uses a form of identification organized around difference ("I = Another") that challenges neoliberal multiculturalism.

Having seen these elaborations of new modes of connection, we move in part 2, "Undisciplined Knowledges," to chapters that attend to the epistemological erasures of normative comparative models. Roderick A. Ferguson critiques the narrative trajectory of African American studies by examining the African migrant. Ferguson details the ways in which the discipline of normative African American studies implicitly creates an ideal type: the African American subject narrated through the usual historical trajectory of enslavement, emancipation, and civil rights struggle, against which the African migrant can only be seen as deviant. Centering the African migrant in African American studies, Ferguson argues, demands a complete reorganization of the foundational assumptions of the field. Ruby Tapia's chapter shifts the focus to a certain kind of liberal feminism by detailing the ways in which feminist viewing pleasure relies on spectacularized racial violence. Quentin Tarantino's *Kill Bill* films, Tapia observes, have been read as providing feminist agency to women who are subjects, as well as objects, of violence. However, this version of feminist agency is predicated on older modes of viewing that take for granted that racialized violence is pleasurable, and ultimately and not coincidentally valorizes the white woman as mother. Chandan Reddy takes on the ways in which the modern pro-gay-marriage movement likewise erases racialized histories when it uses analogy as a mode of comparison of race and sexuality. He does so by tracing the residues and incommensurabilities that haunt the use of the landmark antimiscegenation case *Loving v. Virginia* by the pro-gay-marriage movement. Finally, Sanda Lwin's chapter takes on literary disciplinarity by examining the ways in which W. E. B. Du Bois's attempt to narrate an international racial solidarity through the allegory of mixed-race union in his novel *Dark Princess* requires the disruption of the generic conventions of romance.

Part 3, "Unincorporated Territories, Interrupted Times," moves from examinations of the contradictions of disciplinary norms to explorations of the ways in which alternative comparative modes require the reorganization of time and space. These chapters examine a figure or concept that troubles certainties of time, place, space, and nation. We begin with Victor Bascara's chapter on the documentary film *Kelly Loves Tony*, which details a year in the life of two Mien refugee teenagers in the San Francisco Bay Area. By tracing the different ways in which the film treats Kelly, a straight-A student longing for upward mobility, and Tony, a high-school dropout with a criminal record who fights a deportation hearing, the film situates the refugee as both confirming and disrupting the progressive temporality of U.S. modernity. Bascara's chapter underscores one of the implications of women of color feminism and queer of color critique: that taking the intersection of race, class, and gender seriously means understanding that differently gendered racialized immigrant subjects (Kelly, on the one hand, and Tony, on the other) can be considered different racial formations that can be subjected to comparison. Martha Chew Sánchez's chapter traces the figure of the Chinese as undermining the certainties of Mexican national identity, which has long been organized around erasing the complex histories of migration to Mexico. Chew Sánchez retrieves the presence of the Chinese in Mexico in fragments, out of such unlikely archives as a poem by her sister remembering her Chinese grandfather. Grace Hong traces the ways in which the comparative method of minority nationalism is undermined and reinvented through ambivalent or ironic treatments of nationalist sentiments in Chicana/o literary texts. Identifying the ways in which nationalism articulates itself as a proscribed form of mourning, Hong observes that the ironic or even outright humorous depictions of death seen in Oscar Zeta Acosta's novel *The Revolt of the Cockroach People* and Ana Castillo's *So Far from God* are aesthetic strategies that provide alternatives to nationalist affect. Bianet Castellanos attends to the ways in which Mayan migrant workers undermine the constitution of the urban as the ideal type, against which the rural migrant is rendered abject. Through their deployment of the word *chingar*, a Spanish word recast with indigenous connotations (both negative and positive) of bravery, autonomy, and aggressiveness, Mayan migrant workers narrate and negotiate their working conditions and establish the boundaries of their communities. Helen Jun's study of the black press explores the ways in which African American claims to citizenship relied on establishing African American respectability over and against the heathen Chinese. The book ends with Cynthia Tolentino's examination of a short story by the contemporary Puerto Rican writer Ana Lydia Vega. Tolentino situates the figure of the English governess in Vega's short story as an allegory for the ambiguity of Puerto Rico's status as unincorporated territory and observes that because gendered norms of respectability create a multiplicity of nonnormative subjects—from the liminal class position of the governess to the deviant sexuality of enslaved peoples—tenuous alliances between such subjects can be imagined, albeit briefly and contingently.

While these chapters demonstrate the complexity and variety of projects inspired by comparative race analytics, we hope that we do so in a way that does not institutionalize comparative race studies as yet another hegemonic discourse that suppresses the internally contradictory and heterogeneous nature of new social formations. In contrast, we suggest a comparative race project that centers these contradictions and heterogeneities as a political practice and intellectual methodology that is not definitive but instead serves as a basis for all of us to continue to endeavor collectively.

Notes

1   In defining women of color feminism in this way, we are distinguishing the formation from women who, from within nationalist movements and through a nationalist idiom, articulated their own interests and proved themselves agential subjects, a formation Emma Perez (1999) has called "feminism-in-nationalism."

2   For an analysis of the effects of decolonization and Third World liberation movements on U.S.-based social movements, see Young 2006.

3   For a discussion of the changes in racial formation in the wake of the social movements of the 1960s and 1970s, see Omi and Winant 1994, especially chap. 6, "The Great Transformation." See also Melamed 2006.

1 Alternative Identifications

Racialized Hauntings of the Devalued Dead

The ghost is hungry and selfish . . . and lost and bearing all the weight of the world it carries. *And no one understands.*
—Avery Gordon, *Ghostly Matters*

This story is about a road that never ends. It begins with a car crash.—Rubén Martínez, in performance, April 22, 2000

On March 24, 2000, my cousin Brandon Jesse Martinez died in a car accident in San Diego, California.[1] He was nineteen. When Brandon was alive, he frustrated teachers, counselors, employers, and even his friends and family. He took drugs sometimes, drank sometimes, and sometimes slept all day. He liked low-rider car culture and Tupac Shakur. He was quick witted and too clever, thoughtful and impulsive, well intentioned and reckless. His teachers thought he was lazy and a troublemaker; he proved them right by never graduating high school. He lied on job applications and didn't pay his bills on time. He believed that one day he would go to prison even though he never planned to commit a criminal offense. He didn't donate his free time to religious or social activism; instead he smoked, drank, and joked a lot. These were the memories Brandon left me, his parents, his sister, and the others who loved him. It made it hard to share stories about him that didn't also characterize him as a "bad kid," a "deviant subject," or an "unproductive citizen."

Our conflicting memories and feelings about Brandon's "deviance" evoked deeply felt tensions at the memorial service and the gatherings afterward as we struggled but failed to ascribe value to Brandon's life and life choices. We were nostalgic for the days of his childhood, and we were upset over losing his future and the person that he would never become. We shared our most recent memories of him as a teenager and young adult in carefully crafted fragments thick with anger and anguish. For some of us, his death became the pretext for teaching moral lessons: Don't drink and drive. Go to school. Listen to your parents. Pray. These lessons attributed meaning and purpose to Brandon's death. His death could be instructive for his friends and cousins because for those he left behind, "it was not too late." But these lessons also taught us to devalue his life because they depended on understanding Brandon as an example never to emulate or imitate. His life was narrated as important because he provided us with a constructive model to evaluate, judge, and reject. The first line of a poem written by his sister Trisha Martinez echoed loudly, persistently, and honestly in the space of his haunting: "You just don't know how much he meant" (T. Martinez 2000). In many ways, we didn't, because we didn't know how to valorize the choices we warned him not to make or how to value the life we told him not to live. How could we explain to others and ourselves how much he meant when his most legible asset was his death?

We couldn't translate his value into language. We couldn't talk about Brandon as valuable not only because he was marked as deviant, illegal, and criminal by his race and ethnicity but also because he did not perform masculinity in proper, respectable ways to redeem, reform, or counter his (racialized) deviancy. Even if we had attempted to circumvent the devaluing processes of race and gender by citing other readily recognizable signs and signifiers of value, such as legality, heteronormativity, American citizenship, higher education, affluence, morality, and respectability, we still would not have had evidence to narrate him as a productive, worthy, and responsible citizen. Ascribing (readily recognizable) value to the racialized devalued *requires* recuperating what registers as deviant and disreputable to reinterpret those devalued beliefs, behaviors, and bodies as misrecognized versions of normativity who deserve so much better. Value is ascribed through explicitly or implicitly disavowing relationships to the already devalued and disciplined categories of deviance and nonnormativity.

Lindon Barrett theorized that value needs negativity; the "object" of value needs an "other" of value as its "negative resource": "For value 'negativity is a *resource*,' an essential resource. The negative, the expended, the excessive invariably form the ground of possibilities for value" (Barrett 1999, 19, 21). In other words, the act of ascribing legible, intelligible, and normative value is inherently violent and relationally devaluing. To represent Brandon as the object of value, we would need to represent ourselves as the devalued other. On some level, the *violence* of Brandon's death was perversely and disconcertingly a "source of value" for us because it valorized the life choices that each of us made that he did not; it naturalized how and why he died while simultaneously reaffirming our social worth and societal value. His violent death validated the rightness of our choices and the righteousness of our behaviors: "The relativities of value [are] ratios of violence" (28).

Because value is made intelligible *relationally* and violently, it makes sense to employ a comparative method to analyze the "not-value" of Brandon's short life and long haunting. A comparative analytic centers relational, contingent, and conditional processes of devaluation, which makes it particularly useful for examining the ways in which interconnected processes of valuation, valorization, and devaluation (i.e., race, gender, sexuality, class, nation, legality, etc.) work interdependently to reify value and relations of inequality as normative, natural, and obvious. Although it is informed by the differential devaluation of racialized groups, this approach does not necessarily entail an explicit comparison of two or more racial groups because relations of value are not always explicit. Oftentimes processes of differential devaluation work invisibly and implicitly, or they may be referenced abstractly (i.e., we are not "illegal aliens," "terrorists," or "criminals"). On the other hand, because race is rarely the only and certainly not a necessary signifier for devaluation, sometimes a comparative analytic obliges us to examine the ways in which gender, sexuality, nationality, citizenship, and class function to differentially devalue people *within* aggrieved groups as well as between and among them. In a sense, a comparative analytic assumes that in the United States, human value, legally universalized as normative, is made legible in relation to the deviant, the non-American, the nonnormative, and the recalcitrant: the legally repudiated others of U.S. value.

Examining how value and its normative criteria are naturalized and universalized enables us to uncover and unsettle the heteropatriarchal, legal, and neoliberal investments that dominant and oppositional discourses share, which work to render the value of nonnormativity illegible. We could not disentangle the various intersecting, differential, contingent, and relational processes of valuation and devaluation that made the value of our lives and the choices we made to become valuable dependent on the devaluation and violent invalidation of Brandon. Although he was devalued by legally protected norms and disciplined by many of us many times, we never disowned, abandoned, or rejected him—his death was too painful for us to realize that it also validated our social value. The empty space he left behind in each of us *necessarily destabilized* the value binaries and hierarchies that formed the foundations for each of our lives; still empty, the space of his absence still holds ruptural possibilities.

He was profoundly valued, but we could not tell you why.

Drinking Suspected

When Brandon died in a car crash with his two friends, Vanvilay Khounborinh and William Christopher Jones, news media coverage of their accident criminalized them and the racial masculinities that they each embodied. They became part of the preexisting news narrative that had devalued their lives when they were alive. As Isabel Molina Guzmán reminds us, "News media draw upon routine professional practices and socially available and widely circulated narratives to tell their stories . . . stories that perform beyond the function of information" (Molina Guzmán 2005, 182). To apprehend how such widely circulated narratives about criminalized men of color function beyond disseminating information, it is productive to also examine the inundation of stories about white men and women in positions of power. Ruby C. Tapia argues that such news stories are never inconsequential because the media does not just honor the memory of public figures; it also passes on social values, "immortaliz[ing] ideologies of patriarchal capitalism and white supremacy." Tapia encourages us to read the erasure of "non-spectacularized lives" in relation to or against "hypervisible *whiteness*, along with its haunting figures and social consequences" (2001, 263). These representations aid in constructing the "norms of gender, sexuality, and domestic space" that Nayan Shah contends are necessary to prove one's "worthiness" of political rights and social resources, which means these stories too form and inform the representational and narrative violences that make discipline and punishment of the racialized unreformed seem natural and necessary (2001, 254).

For these reasons, the erasure of Brandon's, Vanvilay's, and William Christopher's nonspectacular lives and devalued deaths in print media might best be understood through a comparison with the haunting figures and social consequences of white masculinity. By juxtaposing the *San Diego Union-Tribune*'s representations of Brandon's accident alongside the fatal accident of the San Diego Padres' fourth outfielder Michael Darr, we learn that the "facts" of people's behaviors have little significance for determining whose deaths are tragic and whose deaths are deserved. The detailed descriptions of these drunk-driving accidents provide us the shortcut ideological codes used in deciding which human lives are valuable and which are worth-less. In effect, the articles written about Michael Darr evoke public sympathy by representing his embodiment of straight white masculinity as socially valuable and by depicting his friends' and family's grief as a universal experience, while the article about Brandon, Vanvilay, and William Christopher activated racial anxieties over criminalized youth and young men of color.

On March 25, 2000, the *San Diego Union-Tribune* printed an article about Brandon's car accident titled "Three Men Killed When Speeding Car Hits Trees; a Fourth Walks Away" and subtitled "Drinking Suspected; Auto Was Traveling Without Headlights." Joe Hughes, a journalist who often reports on local crimes and drunk-driving accidents for the *San Diego Union-Tribune*, described Vanvilay's driving as reckless and irresponsible joy riding, claiming that witnesses corroborated police officers' suspicions that the car was "speeding and may have been racing other cars" (J. Hughes 2000, B1). Vanvilay was driving Brandon's 1984 Mustang, which was not a racing car and in fact was not even a car that ran very well, but in San Diego, "racing" alludes to a racialized car culture, predominately practiced by young Asian men in high school.[2] Along these lines, it seemed not to matter to police, witnesses, or Hughes whether or not the examiner's report would reveal alcohol in Vanvilay's blood; even if he was not legally intoxicated, he was represented as definitely recklessly driving (if not, then as if) drunk. The accident was framed as inevitable and deserved through construing their illegal behaviors (underage drinking and driving) as a daily pattern, connoting both immorality and criminality: "In addition [to detectives learning that the four had been drinking that evening], alcoholic containers and mixing beverages were found in the car's mangled remains" (J. Hughes 2000, B1).

In contrast, even after the examiner's report was completed on Michael Darr and police had confirmed that his blood alcohol level was ".03 above the legal limit [of .08]," the Highway Patrol officer on duty still doubted that Darr's accident would be considered a result of drunk driving: "Did alcohol play a role? . . . It may have. We described the cause as inattention. He was driving in the flow of traffic. He was not speeding. He was not weaving."[3] Although Darr was intoxicated and not wearing a seat belt, he was still portrayed as a good driver on the night of his fatal accident ("not speeding" and "not weaving"). The Padres' second baseman Damian Jackson was also quoted to distance the drunk driver from drunk driving:

> "I can't justify the amount of beer that he had," Jackson said. "But I believe that alcohol was not a factor.
>
> "Mike had the tendency to pay attention to other things while he was driving, just like myself. He'd be changing a radio station, or putting CDs in while driving. Carelessness like that I think had something to do with getting off track and trying to overcompensate."[4]

Although Darr had been drinking and driving, the cause of his death was determined to be neither intoxication nor reckless driving but rather "inattention," "carelessness," or "trying to overcompensate."

Sports staff writers, rather than the local-crimes journalists of the *Union-Tribune*, reported Darr's accident, which is important because sport has become a crucial site for resecuring, as Kyle W. Kusz contends, "the central and dominant cultural position of White masculinity." Because white men are no longer perceived as athletically dominant, sport "enables the fabrication of a crisis narrative about the precarious and vulnerable cultural position of White males" (Kusz 2001, 412). Baseball, in particular, as "America's national pastime," has been "associated with whiteness in the West for centuries" (Nowatzki 2002, 83). Darr's death was thus also empathetically representative of the "tragic" position of white men in contemporary U.S. society.[5]

When alive, Darr received little media attention because he was only a fourth outfielder, but in death he was transformed into a would-have-been-great ballplayer:

Darr, 25, was the Padres' minor league Player of the Year in 1997 and again in 2000, when he shared the award with Jeremy Owens. He ran faster than the average ballplayer, threw farther and harder than the average outfielder and as a minor leaguer posted on-base and batting averages well above the norm.[6]

In death, Darr can be idealized. The various news articles about Darr's life and death draw on testimonies by his trainer, manager, and colleagues (not his wife or family), which idealize him as well as the men he represents. As Dana Nelson has argued, "national manhood" as an imagined white fraternity works best with "absent or dead men" (1998, 204). As a relatively young white athlete, Darr symbolizes (an innocent) white male victimization; his death activates these anxieties while his professional, fraternal relationships tell the *shared* story of loss: "[Manager Bruce] Bochy said he told the players: 'Let's make every day count, with our family, our friends and what we do on the field. Do it for Mike's sake. . . . We all should count our blessings. Every one of us. Really, it could have been any one of us.'"[7] In other words, Darr's death not only mobilizes national manhood ("Do it for Mike's sake") but also mobilizes an imagined white fraternity over and against the absent bodies of women and the abject bodies of racialized others, such as Brandon, Vanvilay, and William Christopher.[8]

This is most evident when we compare how the two accidents were represented to readers of the *Union-Tribune*. Krasovic often quoted the Padres, all of whom continually reference fraternal belonging: "Every one of us. Really, it could have been any one of us." Staff writer Nick Canepa directly facilitated public identification with the Padres, so that the reader figuratively experiences Darr's death as a member of the Padres fraternity:

> What can you say?
> You get the call early in the morning, just before heading over to the Padres complex to examine the rites of spring. It is a terrible, terrible thing. Darr was married (Natalie) and was the father of two sons.
> What can you say?
> You can say nothing. You can say you're sorry. It never seems as if it's enough. Because it isn't enough.[9]

Among other examples, the articles I have cited tell us that losing a loved one is a universal experience—"a terrible, terrible thing" that happens to "every one of us."[10] But this supposedly universal experience is not invoked in the article about Brandon.

In Hughes's article, not only are first- and second-person pronouns and referents never used, such as "we," "you," "everyone," "our," and "us," but the terms employed to refer to Brandon and his friends detach them from their *own* personal connections to communities, friends, and families as if they were already merely another statistic: "the four had been drinking," "three men died," and a "fourth occupant walked." Readers were not encouraged to empathize with the car crash victims or with those who survived them.

On the other hand, the news articles about Michael Darr construct death as a universal experience. People of all colors and genders are encouraged, if not expected, to identify with Darr's family and empathize with his fraternity. We can all relate to losing a loved one, but the universal experience of sudden loss and unexpected death is represented through a particular and specific dead body—a body reconstructed and idealized to mobilize the interests and investments of an imagined white fraternity to resecure its cultural, political, social, and economic dominance (see Kusz 2001; Lipsitz 1997; Nelson 1998; and Wiegman 1999). Perhaps the most illustrative example of the (particular) Padres fraternity as representative of the (universal) American nation is when Bruce Bochy associated the tragedy of Darr's death to the tragedies of September 11, 2001: "I think we experienced as a club something akin to what the nation felt after 9–11."[11]

The social value of particular lives and specific deaths, like Michael Darr's, continue to be immortalized through familial relations as well. When the Padres played their last game at Qualcomm Stadium on September 28, 2003, players Phil Nevin and Gary Matthews Jr. took turns carrying Mike Darr Jr. onto the field with the theme song from the movie *Field of Dreams* playing in the background. Fittingly, *Field of Dreams* is about the living ghosts of fathers and baseball players, not so subtly conjuring Darr Sr. to participate in the postgame ceremony.

> The sight of [Ken] Caminiti and Darr's son on Nevin's shoulder were also the moments that seemed to strike the strongest chord with the fans staying long into the evening.
>
> "The reaction of the fans was very special," said Matthews. "They remember. I think they'll always remember. It's easier for me to deal with now. Seeing Junior is a positive thing. I don't feel sad anymore."[12]

While "seeing Junior" felt healing for Matthews, what evoked tears from the fans was the sight of Darr Jr. growing up without a father. In this way, Darr Sr.'s social value is reproduced and passed on not just through, but also because of, his familial relations (Tapia 2001, 268).

But not all familial relations can script social and human value onto the dead. It is telling that in the death and funeral notices, my aunt and uncle connected Brandon to the nationally sanctioned and sanctified institutions—family and sports—that ascribed social value to Michael Darr: "Beloved by all who knew him, he left a large family and many friends behind. Brandon was active in youth sports and played baseball in Mira Mesa" (Martinez and Martinez 2000).

Because racialized deviancy is rendered as gender and sexual distortion, many of our efforts to be included within the populations deemed worthy, deserving, and valuable are spent trying to conform to the norms of gender, sexuality, and domesticity considered "universally American" and crystallized as the "national family." Sport affiliations and family relations are ideological codes for normative (socially valuable) masculinity, as evidenced through the narrative strategies deployed by the sports writers of the *Union-Tribune* to rework Darr as an idealized victim of social change. But these codes work only incompletely for Brandon because ascribing societal value to the devalued dead requires narrating their lives through the same ideals, morals, and ethics that disciplined them while they were alive.

Mourning without Words

The *San Diego Union-Tribune* depicted deaths by drunk driving in very different ways, which determined whether or not the dead deserved to be mourned. Oftentimes official accounts of death and dying such as news media or police records do not acknowledge particular racialized tragedies as collective loss. Brandon's, Vanvilay's, and William Christopher's deaths, in fact, were represented as not-losses and not-tragedies through the journalist's "performance of explicit non-caring" (Taylor 2003, 147). Public sympathy for them was not just not evoked but explicitly refused. This refusal makes it necessary to juxtapose the limited official archive of the written, recorded accounts of their deaths with the ephemeral performances of their friends' and relatives' mourning, explicit performances of love, care, and grief beyond words.

Privileging "anecdotal and ephemeral evidence," as José Muñoz explains, "grants entrance and access to those who have been locked out of official histories and, for that matter, 'material reality.' Evidence's limit becomes clearly visible when we attempt to describe and imagine contemporary identities that do not fit into a single pre-established archive of evidence" (1996, 9). Brandon's friends and relatives created what Ann Cvetkovich calls "an archive of feeling," an archive constituted by the lived experiences of mourning and loss, ephemeral evidence that is now anecdotal (2003). It is an archive of the felt traces and sticky residue their deaths left behind in everyone's chests. These feelings temporarily incarnated took various visual forms, a roadside memorial, T-shirts, and the wrecked car. When the story about the value of lives cannot be told, the visual can be an alternative mode of expression. It is akin to the way in which Karla Holloway examines performances of mourning as central to African American culture: "visual excess expressed a story that African America otherwise had difficulty illustrating—that these were lives of importance and substance, or that these were individuals, no matter their failings or the degree to which their lives were quietly lived, who were loved" (2002, 181). Witnesses would be left with fleeting imprints etched in their memories, raw material their unconscious might use for dreams.

In this archive, value is ascribed to Brandon, Van, and Chris through their friends' and relatives' public mourning, their performances of explicit caring, profound pain, and deeply felt depression, desperation, and despair. I situate these ephemeral traces alongside the news article to illustrate how people ascribe value to the devalued through visual languages. While the official, limited archive of Brandon's death functioned primarily to repudiate him, this archive of feeling documented a different way to measure value. Unlike the news articles, there was no attempt to make this grief universal, and in fact, the particular and specific were all that mattered. His name was Brandon. He died in this car on this road. Brandon's, Van's, and Chris's family and friends created their own publics to witness their grief. By doing so, they resisted the erasure of their loved ones and made a statement: these were valuable young men, and they are missed. Their audiences were not given the opportunity to ask why.

Soon after the crash, on the median of Calle Cristobal, friends and relatives erected a roadside memorial overflowing with flowers, brightly lit by candles, and replete with personal messages, mementos, tributes, and items the deceased might need, such as rosaries, oranges, water, boxes of their favorite cigarettes, and cans of menudo. Brandon's sister, Trisha, attached her poem to the site's tree, the memorial's center, reminding us all of the need for alternative meaning making at the base or the core of the tragedy: *you just don't know*. Noticeable from both sides of the road, the makeshift memorial mourned and remembered Brandon, Vanvilay, and William Christopher, but it also functioned to reactivate the scenario of their deaths, forcing roadside spectators to become witnesses and participants (Taylor 2003, 32). According to Diana Taylor, a "scenario places spectators within its frame, implicating us in its ethics and politics" (2003, 33). This particular memorial was staged in such a way that pedestrians and drivers would have to actively and consciously not notice it. Because the memorial was located on the median of Calle Cristobal, you had to run across the road that claimed the young men's lives to maintain it. It was not a safe crossing, but it protected the site from intentional and accidental vandalism.

The young men's best friend Shawn Essary, who had declined to go out with them on the night of the accident, created four hundred T-shirts and fifty caps in their memory. In his design, three open roses are connected by thorny vines, symbols of love and death connected by the pointed pains of suffering, violence, and redemption. The shirts bear their pictures, birthdays, and death day, and all the clothing is boldly underscored by "R.I.P." Worn in public by the young men's family members and friends long after the funerals were over, the clothing unerased our racialized dead as our other/ed bodies all helped Brandon, Vanvilay, and William Christopher transgress another border, the one between the living and the dead.

The roadside memorial and clothing were especially important means by which Brandon's, Van's, and Chris's friends could participate directly in honoring their dead with dignity. Their friends had limited resources to express their grief, had no control over the mourning rituals or funeral preparations, and needed to negotiate the pain of losing three people all at once. Fusing three distinct religious and cultural backgrounds, they held their own ceremonies in the middle of the road: it happened *here*. They used their own bodies to display the communal tombstone that they would have written, walking around in silent protest: our chests hurt *here* where Brandon, Chris, and Van rest in peace. They carried their grief heavily on their backs, like living altars with so much symbolism: I got your back.

Front of T-shirt. Photograph by David Coyaca.

The visual performance of explicit caring was also vital for my aunt and uncle, Christine and Jesse Martinez Jr., who made brief appearances on the news and gave speeches at high schools. Saving the car in its wrecked form, they towed it to, and displayed it on, several San Diego high school campuses. Their activism in encouraging teenagers not to drink and drive narrated Brandon's death as illogical and preventable, as tragic and avoidable.

Rather than warning people *of* young men like Brandon, Van, and Chris, they cautioned young adults *like* Brandon, Van, and Chris. They recognized that life can be unforgiving, but those moments never have to be all-determining. Directing their anger and heartache into anti-drinking-and-driving activism ensured that Brandon's death had a purpose. They refused to let him die in vain, speaking their story and leaving behind his name like an echo. Here is the car, and this was his name. At the next party their teenage audiences would attend, fleeting imprints of a wrecked car and a parent's tears might be resurrected, a reminder, a remainder, to hand over the keys.

This archive of feeling evidences the human, familial, and social value of Brandon, Vanvilay, and William Christopher as their friends and family publicized their private pain. They were important alternative representations that helped us to mourn and work against Brandon's absolute erasure. But his picture on a T-shirt, a poem by his sister, the red box of cigarettes he smoked, and a lonely funeral card were not enough pieces of his lost life to reassemble into a proper eulogy to tell you why he mattered, to tell you why you lose out too because the life he led and the future he would have had were your losses too. I began to forget what his voice sounded like, and couldn't remember the exact brown of his eyes. The emotive power of this archive of feeling was also limited precisely because it relied on feeling; it depended on grief and survival guilt. And it was all we had to ascribe value to Brandon—how much we hurt determined how much he was valued.

Driven and Disciplined

What we wanted to tell you was why Brandon was a valuable human being who did not deserve to die so young, and lacking a narrative that could convince others why Brandon mattered hurt us all. When he died, it seemed as if he did not hold the attitudes, values, desires, or work ethic that would eventually have enabled him to have a decent-paying job that could provide for a future wife and future children in a nice suburban neighborhood. This American dream framed how our middle-class mixed-race families grieved. Because our parents, aunts, and uncles wanted this dream and this future for their children, Brandon was narrated as a bad example to follow, but a good lesson to learn. Either we devalued his life by demonizing the same deviant qualities we missed and mourned, or we unduly disciplined ourselves for not diverting his delinquency early enough.

We all wanted a better life for Brandon, but no one could guarantee it, so his death also became understood and talked about as everyone else's private failure and the rational but humanly incomprehensible "will of God."[13] I found myself wanting to argue with my family that the "inevitability" of Brandon's "justifiable" death could not be attributed solely to his decisions, my aunt and uncle's parenting, the personal moments we each failed him, or God's will. Brandon could not be blamed completely for his decisions because there were so many options he never had and so many second chances that he was never given. How could Brandon, his parents, or his friends and other relatives be held accountable for making the wrong choices when the right opportunities never arose?

Weren't most resources withheld from Brandon, Vanvilay, and William Christopher? Economic restructuring and capital flight eradicated the blue-collar jobs that these young men did not have to go to the next morning (see M. Davis 1990, 208; Castells 1991, 308; Miyoshi 1996, 255). Poorly funded schools in segregated communities provided them with inadequate educations to attend a four-year college.[14] Gang profiling marked them as potential criminals and gang members in the eyes of law enforcement (see Miller 1997; Escobar 1995; Rodríguez 2000). The widespread exploitation of both professional and unskilled immigrants makes it more profitable for companies to hire immigrants than train the racialized working class (P. Martin 1994, 94; Reddy 2005). The long history of U.S. militarism and imperialism in Asia, Latin America, Mexico, and Africa makes it more profitable for companies to relocate to countries economically devastated by structural adjustment policies because it is more profitable to exploit, abuse, and dehumanize racialized women and children in the global South than it is to pay decent salaries, provide insurance, and follow health and safety regulations domestically (Bello 1994).

Brandon, Vanvilay, and William Christopher were surplus labor, not needed for the time being but presumably always desperate enough to take a job should one have opened. What they did in the meantime was live with their parents and sleep late in the morning. They drank beer when everyone else was sleeping and talked about dreaming their way out of their respective depressions, about how the day would come when their lives would be different. Socializing over a few beers can be imagined as either an innocent, harmless recreational activity (e.g., after a long day at work) or an indicator of criminality. Which one is evoked depends on the color of your skin, your

gender, and your age, your drinking company, where you live, where you drink, and whether or not you have a job to go to the next day. Brandon, Vanvilay, and William Christopher were a racially mixed group of unemployed and insecurely underemployed young men of color (Mexican American, Laotian, and African American, respectively), who were fostering their own homosocial relationships with each other in a predominately middle-class suburban neighborhood. The recreational practices that they shared, as well as the individual work activities that they lacked, marked them as lazy and immoral, potentially criminal and always illegal. At the time that they died, their lives were not on the way to middle-class status, marriage, property ownership, or white-collar careers, and their (in)activities already fit a media and law enforcement profile that criminalizes racial masculinities—especially when embodied by Latino, African American, and Southeast Asian young men (Gray 1995; Miller 1997; Escobar 1995; Rodríguez 2000; Tang 2000; R. Martinez 2002). Read and represented as irresponsible and reckless, their social practices are rendered deviant, understood as needing discipline by the military or punishment by and containment within the prison-industrial complex. Could he really be blamed for not making better decisions when the only institutions recruiting him were prison or the military?[15]

I thought that if I explained the ways in which racialized economic hierarchies governed Brandon's life, I could give my family a different story for why he died that did not center on his or their personal failures. I felt compelled to make sense of the ways in which structural conditions can constrain people's lives. Brandon was an English-only-speaking American citizen; he was a high school dropout, who lived in a middle-class neighborhood and came from a middle-class family. No one in my family would have been convinced that he was destined for tragedy, and no one would have believed that his life choices were so limited that he could only choose between "bad" and "worse." And because I didn't have concrete evidence or cousinly intuition that Brandon *wanted* the options that would have made it possible for him to have higher education, job stability, and a decent salary, even I didn't believe the story I spun for myself—though telling it made me feel better most of the time. In other moments, the subtext unsettled me because it suggested that some people are not afforded the opportunity to become better people or to make better decisions, implying that some people are fated to die young. I had to take away his agency to represent him as a victim manipulated by his own desires; I had to take away his decision to not make decisions and erase his talent for choosing non-options.

Before Brandon died, the story of racial exclusion and racial exploitation always seemed so sensible. For me, its primary purpose was to evoke sympathy for the people that many Americans are quick to devalue. This is not at all an easy task though it seems as if it should be. To evoke public sympathy, we need to appeal to American norms and values, and doing so requires us to mitigate all the evidence that might suggest a person or population deserves devaluation if evaluated by those norms. This means re-presenting young men of color who lead unsympathetic lives (such as gang members, drug users, or risk takers) as latent law-abiding, hard-working, family-oriented men, who have unfairly been excluded from the resources and opportunities that would lead them to make responsible, normative choices.[16] And if we concede that economic opportunities will not necessarily integrate marginalized men of color into legal and moral economies, we risk unintentionally validating conservative policies. In other words, the subtext is unsettling because for racial exclusion to work as a sympathetic narrative, it needs to draw on the neoliberal ideologies that work to legitimate global capitalism, naturalize inequality, and stigmatize nonnormativity.

Roderick A. Ferguson argues that contemporary capital requires the people of color it recruits and renders redundant to transgress the normative prescriptions of gender and sexuality that the state works to legally universalize (R. Ferguson 2004, 11–18). In the era of American neoliberalism, the state pathologizes or pities racially marked gender and sexual transgressions and celebrates racialized normativity exemplified by U.S. multiculturalism (Bascara 2006, xvi–xvii; J. Lee 2004, xix–xx). As neoliberal restructuring facilitates the continued integration of unevenly developed world economies, these deracialized and reracialized categories of devaluation are replicated on a global scale, which benefits the wealthy elite of neoliberal states and worsens life for everyone else (Reddy 2005, 103–105; Harvey 2007, 9, 15–18, 31–35, 103–19, 159, 169–70; see also Bello 1994). As a result, people of color around the world have been dispossessed and displaced at alarming rates by the same neoliberal policies that have enabled the elite of the global South to join the world's most wealthy. Jodi Melamed explains that the current contradictions of the global economy are managed by American neoliberalism's inconsistent deployment of race to extend and obscure global capitalism—a racial project she aptly terms "neoliberal multiculturalism." By "sutur[ing] official antiracism to state policy" (Melamed 2006, 16–17), neoliberal multiculturalism manages and disavows the contradiction of a world economic system built and sustained by racialized and gendered violence and exploitation, on the one hand, and free market capitalism as the symbolic epitome of racial and gendered equality, on the other. For instance, by using "the rhetoric of civil rights to portray 'economic rights' as the most fundamental civil right," neoliberal multiculturalism enables the state "to advocate in an absolutist manner for deregulation, privatization, regulated 'free markets,' and other neoliberal measures as the only way to guarantee economic rights" (16–17).[17]

Conflating economic rights with civil rights to justify U.S. intervention extends the ways in which property rights have been privileged in the United States over the human rights of the dispossessed and propertyless populations of color (Lowe 1996, 24–25; Hong 2006, 11, 34, 42, 48). Thus, in the United States, the struggle for civil rights could not really be disentangled from property rights (the right to buy a house anywhere as a sign of racial progress) or consumer rights (affirming dignity through the right to eat at any restaurant in any seat).[18] According to Michel Foucault, this particularly American history created the context for the distinct character of American neoliberalism: "The generalization of the economic form of the market beyond monetary exchanges functions in American neo-liberalism as a principle of intelligibility and a principle of decipherment of social relations and individual behavior" (2008, 243).[19] In other words, American neoliberalism demands "an economic analysis of the non-economic" (246). As deciphered and interpreted through American neoliberalism, human value registers as human capital, and social worth is evaluated from the perspectives of "real" and "speculator" markets—we can attribute value by recounting a person's useful and unique assets, talents, skills, and investments, and we can speculate about a person's future value: what can we expect this person to contribute to society in the future?

When he died, Brandon's value was entirely noneconomic. From what we knew, he didn't have (and so he couldn't capitalize on) a rare talent in high demand; his education was not a low-risk investment that promised a high return. In fact, he was expensive to maintain because he still lived at home, and without skills, experience, or education to improve his chances for a better job, even his future contributions were not worth speculation. Brandon was disposable, redundant, and interchangeable; it did not matter that he embodied the privileged categories of neoliberal multiculturalism (as a biracial, American-born citizen). In this instance, being part of a category of privilege was an asset that offered access to the opportunity to choose to become someone whom America would consider worth something. As both privileged and stigmatized,[20] Brandon was offered opportunity, but it came with obstacles. He was given the chance to become socially valuable— all he had to do was take "personal responsibility" for increasing his social worth and augmenting his human capital by making better (i.e., normative) choices. His value was illegible because he opted out.

Dead Ends and Detours

It would be untrue to Brandon to script him as a victim who was unable to access a better life, and in fact, privileging the American Dream and the financial stability one needs to acquire it devalues the life he led and trivializes the choices he made. So I tried to reimagine how his choices were empowering. I imagined that it was a form of empowerment for him to perform Mexican American masculinity through hip-hop music, low-rider cars, and baggy clothes. Although sometimes his attitudes and his attire could be read as stereotypical, they could also be read as evidence of an "oppositional social identity" because youth of color often take their models of racial authenticity from popular culture (Tatum 1997, 61).

Performing racial masculinity could be read as a form of resistance if we read culture as political: " 'Politics' must be grasped," as Lisa Lowe and David Lloyd assert, "as always braided within 'culture' and cultural practices" (Lowe and Lloyd 1997, 26). Robin D. G. Kelley insists that reserving the category of resistance for activists, organizations, and leaders underestimates and depreciates everyday forms of resistance, such as strategies to subtly subvert exploitation or artistic approaches to reclaim and "redecorate" public space. In fact, not only may we misread resistance as deviance, but in so doing we run the risk of patronizing youth, workers, and communities as childishly disobedient, rather than consciously and deliberately defiant:

> If we are to make meaning of these kinds of actions rather than dismiss them as manifestations of immaturity, false consciousness, or primitive

rebellion, we must begin to dig beneath the surface of trade union pronouncements, political institutions, and organized social move ments, deep into the daily lives, cultures, and communities which make the working classes so much more than people who work. (Kelley 1996, 3–4; see also Viesca 2004)

Kelley admits that many minority cultural practices might be considered " 'alternative,' rather than oppositional," but although leisure activities are created for pleasure, they often become (or can be read as) political in relation to where and when they take place (Kelley 1996, 47, 166). Intention doesn't always matter. Brandon didn't need to be devoted to radically progressive politics to be valued by the kinds of epistemologies that motivate antiracist, anticapitalist projects and scholarship.

Yet like the story of racial exclusion, the narrative of resistance wasn't quite the right analytical framework for making sense of Brandon's life. I wasn't convinced that his clothes, music, and recreational activities could be considered resistant or oppositional evidence for a latent political consciousness. I needed to imagine that he would have become, or at least could have become, a vital and valuable actor in the struggle for social justice. Although this perspective decriminalizes and depathologizes non-normative racial masculinities, it ascribed value to the potential for resistance that racial masculinities signified. In rereading Brandon's actions and attitudes as evidence of his potential to become an anticapitalist, antiracist "revolutionary-to-be," value could only be attributed to him by arbitrarily divorcing the person he was from the imagined, idealized person he could have been. He might have become an activist although it seemed just as likely that he wouldn't; as Viet Nguyen asserts, "The subject who refuses to be hailed by dominant ideology can also refuse to be hailed by resistant ideology" (Nguyen 2002, 157). To narrate Brandon as someone who should be valued, I had to recast who he was into someone he might never have become.

Narratives of resistance sometimes betray an underlying assumption that acts of defiance will lead to (or at least support) progressive politics. For Saba Mahmood, reading resistance in this way can easily lead to a misreading of agency. From this perspective, agency means resisting "dominating and subjectivating modes of power" because it is assumed that disrupting and frustrating norms is an innate need that motivates everyone all the time (Mahmood 2005, 14). Mahmood asks us to think about whether "the category of resistance impose[s] a teleology of progressive politics ... that makes it hard for us to see and understand forms of being and action that are not necessarily encapsulated by the narrative of subversion and re-inscription of norms" (9). Her questions and insights help me understand why calling Brandon resistant doesn't feel right, either. If both dominant and oppositional discourses of value center norms—as either rules to live by or prescriptions for proper behavior to work against—then Brandon, who was nonnormative in many ways but intentionally oppositional to norms in hardly any, could only be evidence for someone else's value. Because he was the "negative resource" of normativity and respectability, he also ascribed value to the activists and academics who protected and defended all the disillusioned members of disempowered communities.

As an academic, I was not just an innocent bystander in these relational processes of valuation and valorization, sharing my time and resources with my disillusioned and disempowered cousin to steer him toward a future I imagined as more valuable than his present. Before we found out that Brandon would not graduate from high school, he asked me to tutor him. We met once a week for a couple of months, but though he was receiving As and Bs on the assignments we worked on together, his overall grades weren't improving. I learned that this was because those were the only assignments he completed. I explained that the tutoring would work only if he did his homework every day, not just once a week with me. He apologized for wasting my time, and our tutoring sessions stopped. It never crossed my mind to ask him why he wanted tutoring. I assumed he wanted to graduate, but I think he just wanted to talk.

He talked about pressures from his parents to graduate, get a good job, move out of the house, and become responsible. He talked about how he thought the students at his high school voluntarily racially segregated them-selves, and how he and his few close friends of different colors didn't have a group to join, a place to fit. He talked about how police were always follow-ing him, and he told me about how he felt left out and left behind when his parents became part of the middle class. We talked about wishing we knew our fathers' languages because we felt there were things our grandparents wanted to tell us that English could not communicate. We talked about growing up with white mothers and growing out of internalized racism. We talked about West Coast rap music, the different car cultures of Mexicans and Filipinos in Southern California, and the best place to buy Dickies. I talked about the future I wanted him to have: community college, universities, student organizations like MEChA (Movimiento Estudiantil Chicano de Aztlán), and ethnic studies classes. He listened.

In the first (and last) essay we worked on together, he told me he wanted to be a lifeguard. The assignment was to pick a career and research a path to achieve his goals. He had a list of questions he was supposed to answer: Why did you choose this occupation? What are the qualifications that you would need? What do you see yourself doing in fifteen years? He decided he would like to be a lifeguard even though it was not an occupation that easily lends itself to becoming a career since lifeguarding is temporary, seasonal, and pays only up to $10,000 a year (B. Martinez 1997, 2). It was an interesting choice because, at least the way I saw it, being a lifeguard would not change his life all that much. He wouldn't have much more disposable income than if he continued to work with his uncle (he'd probably have even less); he'd have to continue living at home, and the only upward mobility the job could offer was becoming a lifeguard II. I didn't dissuade him directly, but I did try to encourage him to think about other options—particularly ones that needed higher education.

He reluctantly obliged me because he thought the teacher would like to read about that too, but he also resisted, probably because going to college didn't sound appealing. He wrote, "After lifeguarding there are several occupations that you could take up such as a paramedic, swimming coach, or a ski patroller, according to *Vocational Biographies*. That's not much to look forward to, but they are not the only options to take. You may have some other skills, so that's where a good education comes in for landing a better job" (B. Martinez 1997, 4). He did not specify those better jobs, possibly because they didn't look better to him. He chose a career that was not a career, and to climb the socioeconomic ladder, he had to drop out of his dreams and go back to school.

This is why contextualizing Brandon's life choices through his exclusion from decent-paying blue-collar work was inadequate; it implies that access to good-paying jobs or higher education would have enabled him to make different choices. But as his essay on the future he would never have suggests, he didn't really want a nuclear family with a house in the suburbs. He might not have taken one of those decent-paying blue-collar jobs even if they were still available. At the same time, Brandon constructed himself not only as someone who was not productive but also as someone who was not useless: "I am not quite sure but when you save a person's life I bet it makes you feel very good inside that is something I could see myself doing. Plus just being around the water and people all the time seems like something good for me" (B. Martinez 1997, 2). He didn't want to work to pull himself up a corporate ladder; he wasn't interested in raises or promotions. He wanted to spend his time on the beach, feeling good on the inside if someone needed help, feeling good on the outside when everyone was safe. He wanted to be accountable to everyone and responsible for everyone.

There's nothing necessarily revolutionary in wanting to live this life, but choosing a seasonal career that would ensure downward mobility is not quite normative, either. He had a talent for choosing life's non-options, and because he often didn't make decisions according to American neoliberal logic, his decisions were usually illogical or unintelligible (but not necessarily wrong) when evaluated through a cost-benefit or supply-and-demand analysis. He seemed to think of himself as someone who didn't fit into the life he had inherited, and while his efforts to redesign, evade, and defer the American dream might not provide us with blueprints for redistributing resources, perhaps they can help us to think about the importance of redistributing dignity.

A Politics of Deviance

Sometimes his age makes it difficult to ask the questions I have been asking because who he was at nineteen is an unreliable predictor for the adult he might have been at age thirty-eight or sixty-two. But the expectations for the adult he was supposed to become disciplined him for most of his life and provided a way to measure his (real and speculative) value after he died—as if " 'living' is something to be *achieved* and not *experienced*" (Holland 2000, 16). So much of life and its supposedly seminal moments is organized according to the universalized expectations of the family and its gendered roles in naturalizing private property (buying your first home), wealth accumulation (passing down inheritance), and the pleasures of domestic consumption (planning weddings and baby showers)—all of which repackage reproductive labor as the unpaid but rewarding labor of love. The milestones of heteronormative and homonormative life that Brandon would never be able to experience rendered his life tragic. He would not have children to carry on his family's name, and his death deprived his parents and sister of their own significant life moments with him. Our sadness sometimes even precluded our capacities to mourn his passing according to the life experiences he might have wanted for himself, which may not have included ones we imagined for him. We needed to disconnect the life he experienced from the life he had been failing to achieve.

It is difficult to value Brandon by the quality of his life experiences when time and space are organized through heteronormativity and dictated by capital accumulation,[21] but by situating him in a "queer time and place," we can find ways of being and frameworks for valuing that "challenge conventional logics of development, maturity, adulthood, and responsibility" (Halberstam 2005, 13). As Judith Halberstam argues, "Queer subcultures produce alternative temporalities by allowing their participants to believe that their futures can be imagined according to logics that lie outside of those paradigmatic markers of life experience—namely birth, marriage, reproduction, and death" (2005, 2). Denaturalizing (hetero)normative time, space, and the life achievements they universalize enables us to extend value to— or at least suspend judgment of—all kinds of people who live outside the logics of capital accumulation and bourgeois reproduction.

> All kinds of people, especially in postmodernity, will and do opt to live outside of reproductive and familial time as well as on the logics of labor and production. By doing so, they also live outside the logic of capital accumulation: here we could consider ravers, club kids, HIV-positive barebackers, rent boys, sex workers, homeless people, drug dealers, and the unemployed. Perhaps such people could productively be called "queer subjects" in terms of the ways they live (deliberately, accidentally, or of necessity) during the hours when others sleep and in the spaces (physical, metaphysical, and economic) that others have abandoned, and in terms of the ways they might work in the domains that other people assign to privacy and family. (Halberstam 2005, 10)

In some ways, Brandon lived in a "queer time and place," and in others, he might even be considered a "queer subject" (Holland 2000, 178–80). Although his experiences weren't necessarily comparable or similar to queers of color, a queer of color analysis "makes some sense" of his life without condemning or celebrating who he was or could have been.[22] Queer of color analysis, as defined by Ferguson, extends the "theorized

intersections" of women of color feminism "by investigating how intersecting racial, gender, and sexual practices antagonize and/or conspire with the
normative investments of nation-states and capital" (R. Ferguson 2004, 4).
Put another way, both women of color feminism and queer of color critique
stress that sometimes "it may be necessary to overcome resistance in order
to achieve resistance" (Pile 1997, 24). For Brandon, the failure to meet
heteronormative and neoliberal expectations (and his reluctance to even
try to attain them) was compounded by his racial background as Chicano/
Mexican American because he was not just a lazy kid without a high school
diploma who drank too much and lived off his parents. When Brandon
defied normative investments in heteropatriarchy and American enterprise,
he gave credence to racial stereotypes, which is partly why he also could not
be fully valued through a politics of racial normativity.[23]

Brandon was always confusing me in ways I couldn't name. Trying to
figure out the motives for his choices often eluded me because his actions
and his attitudes were simultaneously neither complicit nor resistant as well
as both at the same time. Imposing a normative framework onto his aspirations made his goals and desires difficult to decipher because he wanted to
be unremarkable and live his life a little on the lazy side. He was only
lackadaisically defiant, but we all read him as rebellious because he kept
diligently deferring or sabotaging what was supposed to be his American
dream. It was as if he followed a logic all his own, and maybe that was the
tutoring lesson I was supposed to learn. Maybe I failed because I looked in
all the wrong places to find methods, narratives, and strategies for ascribing
social worth to his personhood, trying to make him fit into my overre-
searched reasons and rationales rather than making an effort to remember
what he might have been trying to teach me.

I think he wanted to teach me how to make sense of what Cathy Cohen
terms "a politics of deviance" (Cohen 2004, 3–4). A politics of deviance
would neither pathologize deviance nor focus most of its energies on trying
to rationalize why people choose deviant practice over proper behavior.
Instead we would read nonnormative activities and attitudes as forms of
"definitional power" that have the potential to help us rethink how value is
defined, parceled out, and withheld (38). Both Cohen and Kelley resist
spinning a normative narrative that ascribing value to the devalued often
demands; in different ways, they give us a language of value that translates
"the cultural world beneath the bottom" into lived practices and living

alternatives to American norms: "Ironically, through these attempts to find autonomy, these individuals, with relatively little access to dominant power, not only counter or challenge the presiding normative order with regard to family, sex, and desire, but also create new or counter normative frameworks by which to judge behavior" (Kelley 1996, 12; Cohen 2004, 30).[24] Of course, sometimes defiant or deviant practices critique the rules of normality (purposely or inadvertently) but don't necessarily break them; they might direct us toward necessarily nonnormative criteria for recognizing social worth even if they don't model or theorize alternative ways of living.

Brandon's unintelligible ethic of deviance might not be unapologetically normative or radically transformative, but it is definitely a way of living that interrogates and elucidates the ways in which dominant understandings of morality and ethicality may sometimes mitigate oppositional politics and scholarship. When we take Brandon and others like him seriously, we are expected to suspend judgment of those who choose to drive down fatal roads because there is value as well as fear in taking risks and living differently—even if it means actively and accidentally leaving the rest of us behind, empty and haunted. As Rubén Martínez reminds us, "The road may kill us in the end, but it's also the only way to get to where we're going."[25]

Notes

I would like to thank Trisha Martinez for her willingness to share not only materials for this article but also her feelings and insights about her grief and that of others. I also thank Christine and Jesse Martinez for the many ways in which they inspired this project. I am especially grateful to the other contributors to this book for their careful readings of my chapter, in particular Jodi Melamed and Grace Hong. I owe much appreciation to many conversations with W. David Coyoca, Helen H. Jun, Fiona I. B. Ngô, Isabel Molina Guzmán, Eileen Díaz McConnell, Richard T. Rodríguez, George Lipsitz, Yen Espiritu, Lisa Lowe, Ruby C. Tapia, Gregory Lobo, Kent Ono, Angharad Valdivia, Chandan Reddy, and Roderick Ferguson.

1 "Wreck in the Road" is the title of a song written by Rubén Martínez, which he performed with Los Illegals on April 22, 2000, at Expresso Mi Cultura in Los Angeles. Text provided by author; see also Rubén Martínez 2001.

2 Although Calle Cristobal is not far from a possible racing strip (the roads changed weekly or daily), American cars like Brandon's 1984 Mustang—big, clunky, old, and slow—were not part of this particular racing culture, which raced late-model

Hondas and Toyotas, most of which were modified to maximize speed and performance. Vanvilay, however, as a young Asian man, fit the profile of a racer, though the car he was driving did not.

3   Arizona Highway Patrolman Frank Valenzuela, quoted in Tom Krasovic, "Darr Legally Intoxicated, Says Examiner's Report," *San Diego Union-Tribune*, March 14, 2002, D1.

4   Damian Jackson, quoted in Krasovic, "Darr Legally Intoxicated," D1.

5   The media usually represents athletes of color in less sympathetic ways. See, e.g., Cole and Mobley 2005. For a specific examination of the history of Latinos in baseball, including how Latino ballplayers have been racialized, see Burgos 2002; and Regalado 2002.

6   Tom Krasovic, "Padres Crushed by Loss of Darr; Teammates Speak of Personality, Potential," *San Diego Union-Tribune*, February 16, 2002, D1.

7   Bruce Bochy, manager of the San Diego Padres, quoted in Tom Krasovic, "Bochy Hopes Team Can Learn from Tragedy," *San Diego Union-Tribune*, February 23, 2002, D3.

8   Because Dana Nelson's analyses focus on "the era of 'universal' white manhood suffrage" (1780s–1850s), the imagined white fraternity she examines literally refers to white men (1998, xi). The way in which "national manhood" would still be considered an imagined white fraternity in the contemporary period is probably best understood by defining whiteness as "a possessive investment in whiteness." George Lipsitz defines the possessive investment in whiteness as "a social structure that gives value to whiteness and offers rewards for racism"; a possessive investment in whiteness reinforces and reifies racial inequalities but is not necessarily practiced and possessed only by white people (1997, viii).

9   Nick Canepa, "Padres Crushed by Loss of Darr; Words Just Can't Soften His Passing," *San Diego Union-Tribune*, February 16, 2002, D1.

10   Krasovic, "Darr Legally Intoxicated," "Padres Crushed by Loss of Darr," "Bochy Hopes Team Can Learn from Tragedy." Tom Krasovic, "Darr Tragedy Leaves Team Trying to Go On," *San Diego Union-Tribune*, February 17, 2002, C1. Bill Center, "On a Swing and a Miss, Padres End It at the Q; Rockies Stage Rally to Wrap up an Era," *San Diego Union-Tribune*, September 29, 2003, E1.

11   Bruce Bochy, quoted in Bill Center, "Despite Tragedy, Positives Found; Darr's Death Put in the Past; Team Moves Forward," *San Diego Union-Tribune*, April 1, 2002, C5.

12   Center, "On a Swing and a Miss."

13   For our families, becoming middle-class would not automatically be inherited. Because people of color were subject to redlining and restrictive covenants and were excluded from the programs that enabled wealth accumulation during the New Deal and afterward, many middle-class families of color in the contemporary era are unstable (Massey and Denton 1993, 36–37, 51–58; Oliver and Shapiro 1997, 16–18, 39–41, 87–89; Lipsitz 1997, 5–18; McConnell 2005, 22–30, 36–41). Many lack significant assets to pass down intergenerationally, and racial discrimi-

nation in education and the workforce also makes it difficult to pass down oc-
cupational mobility (Oliver and Shapiro 1997, 90, 157 58). For an analysis of the
ways in which housing policies and homeownership affect Latinos in the contemporary era, see McConnell 2005.

14 For an analysis of particular hardships of urban areas, see J. Lee 2004; Kozol 1992;
Lo 1995; Orfield, Eaton, and Jones 1997.

15 According to Jorge Mariscal, "*The Army Times* reported that 'Hispanics' constituted 22 percent of the military recruiting 'market,' almost double their numbers in the population" (2009, 3). In a separate article, Mariscal explains that
"military service does not close the economic gaps separating the majority of
Latinos from the rest of society but potentially widens them" because military job
training such as "small arms expertise and truck driving" does not translate into
well-paying jobs within the civilian economy (2003). African American men and
women constitute an overwhelming 22.4 percent of the military while constituting only 12.41 percent of the civilian population between the ages of eighteen and
forty-four (Office of the Assistant Secretary of Defense 2004, appendix B-25).
Latinas/os are especially overrepresented in potential combat positions; for instance, over a quarter of Latinas/os in the army and over 20 percent of Latinas/os
in the marines serve in the infantry (B-30). In 2008, Latinas/os constituted 39
percent of the incarcerated population in California prisons (California Department of Corrections 2008).

16 Of course, these are not mutually exclusive; for instance, some men of color might
support their partners or children through illegal economies. See Cohen 2004, 36.

17 I am quoting Melamed's analysis of the Bush administration's 2006 National
Security Strategy.

18 On consumerism and citizenship, see Hong 2006, 88–91.

19 Foucault explains that "liberal type claims, and essentially economic claims" in
the United States "were precisely the historical starting point for the formation of
American independence" (2008, 217). Unlike Germany and France, in America,
"The demand for liberalism found[ed] the state rather than the state limiting
itself through liberalism" (217).

20 Melamed explains that privilege and stigma no longer neatly correspond to racial
categories: "Neoliberal multiculturalism breaks with an older racism's reliance on
phenotype to innovate new ways of fixing human capacities to naturalize inequality. The new racism deploys economic, ideological, cultural, and religious distinctions to produce lesser personhoods, laying these new categories of privilege and
stigma across conventional racial categories, fracturing them into differential
status groups" (2006, 14).

21 As Halberstam explains, "Queer temporality disrupts the normative narratives of
time that form the base of nearly every definition of the human in almost all our
modes of understanding" (2005, 152).

22 I am referencing Hong's definition of women of color feminist practice as a
"reading practice" and a "methodology for comparative analysis" (2000, xi, xvi).

Women of color feminist practice emerges to "make sense of that which is pathologized or rendered invisible by the epistemologies of nationalism" (xii).

23   See Rodríguez 2009 for an insightful analysis of family and nationalism. See Richie 1996 for an excellent analysis of the impossibility of heteropatriarchal investments in poor communities of color.

24   Unlike Kelley, Cohen specifically does not define most acts of defiance and deviance as evidence of resistance because she reserves "resistance" for acts with political intent (2004, 39).

25   Rubén Martínez, performance with Los Illegals on April 22, 2000, Expresso Mi Cultura, Los Angeles.

I = Another

Digital Identity Politics

It was a while before we came to realize that our place
was the very house of difference rather than the security
of any one particular difference.—Audre Lorde

The epigraph, a quotation from Audre Lorde, calls attention to the ways that the knowledges, energies, intu-
itions, failures, and passions that can be collected under the
rubric of women of color feminism or, perhaps, as Roderick
Ferguson suggests, queer of color critique have been directed toward or followed from a sustained engagement
with difference as a politically charged mode through
which to forge bonds of understanding that might support
revolutionary movements for social and economic justice
and liberation more broadly conceived. Lorde's assertion—
that "our place is the very house of difference, rather than
the security of any one particular difference"—itself signals
a transformation within a praxis of collectivity earned
through struggle within and through the categories of black
lesbian and women of color over just one lifetime. What
emerges from that transformation is difference as an animating logic of belonging. Yet difference here does not
simply assume a hegemonic or normative formation from
which particular individuals are dissimilar because of the
various but fixed ways they are positioned collectively out-

side that formation. Rather, it is what holds together "the very house of difference" and is that through which "our place" might cohere.

In this regard, Lorde's notion of difference is another way to describe a logic of collectivity and belonging that Brent Hayes Edwards illuminates in a prior historical moment as characteristic of "the practice of diaspora" (Edwards 2003). Edwards reveals the ways that prior modes of racial solidarity themselves contain subterranean logics of belonging that can be mined to address our present need for what Ferguson and Grace Kyungwon Hong refer to in the introduction to this volume as "alternative modes of coalition" (2). Referring specifically to the African diaspora as it was constituted through transatlantic flows during the early part of the twentieth century, Edwards writes:

> If a discourse of diaspora articulates difference, then one must consider the status of that difference—not just linguistic difference but, more broadly, the trace or the residue, perhaps, of what resists or escapes translation. Whenever the African diaspora is articulated (just as when black transnational projects are deferred, aborted, or declined), these social forces leave subtle but indelible effects. Such an unevenness or differentiation marks a constitutive décalage in the very weave of the culture, one that cannot be either dismissed or pulled out. (13)

Edwards explains *décalage* further as follows:

> Décalage is one of the many French words that resists translation into English. . . . It can be translated as "gap," "discrepancy," "time-lag," or "interval"; it is also the term that French speakers sometimes use to translate "jet lag." In other words, décalage is either a difference or a gap in time (advancing or delaying a schedule) or in space (shifting or displacing an object). . . . Décalage indicates the reestablishment of a prior unevenness or diversity; it alludes to the taking away of something that was added in the first place, something artificial, a stone or piece of wood that served to fill some gap or rectify some imbalance. This black diasporic décalage among African Americans and Africans, then, is not simply geographical distance, nor is it simply difference in evolution or consciousness; instead it is a different kind of interface that might not be susceptible to expression in the oppositional terminology of the "vanguard" and the "backward." In other words, décalage is the kernel of

precisely that which cannot be transferred or exchanged, the received biases that refuse to pass over when one crosses the water. It is a changing core of difference; it is the work of differences within unity, an unidentifiable point that is incessantly touched and fingered and pressed. (14)

Describing décalage as "a different kind of interface," Edwards points to that which is incommunicable, yet perceptible, "the kernel of precisely that which cannot be transferred or exchanged." Along these lines, the insights that Lorde crystallizes in the epigraph gives us difference as an internally structuring logic of belonging wherein difference inheres even within that through which we ostensibly belong—our place is the very house of difference. As such, it is, as Lorde implies, insecure and precarious because it is always open and vulnerable to, rather than constituted in opposition to, others.

Lorde defines difference as "that raw and powerful connection from which our personal power is forged." While Edwards offers décalage to introduce a gap—a changing core of difference—as an enabling, animating force of diaspora, Lorde equates a similarly charged difference with connection. Here it is helpful to think Lorde's "connection" through the terms that Edwards makes available for thinking the articulations of the African diaspora: "Articulations of diaspora demand to be approached ... through their décalage. For paradoxically, it is exactly such a haunting gap or discrepancy that allows the African diaspora to 'step' and 'move' in various articulations. Articulation is always a strange and ambivalent gesture, because finally, in the body it is only difference—the separation between bones or members—that allows movement" (15). Defining difference as connection, Lorde makes a similar point about the conditions of possibility for what she calls "liberation": "Advocating the mere tolerance of difference between women is the grossest reformism. It is a total denial of the creative function of difference in our lives" (Lorde 2007, 111). In ways consistent with Edwards's theorization of the African diaspora, difference, for Lorde, is that which allows movement or creativity.

The dynamic logic of belonging through the work of differences within unity, the "changing core of difference" through which a collective is constituted, opens onto a mode of collectivity that movements and their media makers today are making perceptible and, in some cases, revealing as praxis. In the context of visual media (rather than of the literary texts with which

Edwards works), I suggest that this logic operates according to the indexical relationship posited as "I = Another." This formulation of identity as difference captures the sense of transformation, rather than rupture, that characterizes many liberation movements in their contemporary configurations and describes the processes of identity and identification facilitated through the media that sustain, educate, challenge, and recollect those movements. "I = Another" does not jettison identification as a political strategy but introduces difference into the equation, albeit problematically. As I explain in the following section, "I = Another" also constitutes a contestation of the status and role of the index that emerges before the index trouble that the rise of the digital regime of the image makes perceptible. What becomes perceptible with the spreading influence of the digital regime of the image, then, is a valence of identification and belonging that is part of a longer trajectory of political struggle and cultural production that is in the process of being excavated in work like that of Edwards, Chela Sandoval, and others (Sandoval 2000).

The Digital Regime of the Image and Logics of Belonging

Given the complexity of the relationships between the digital regime of the image and global capitalism, my concern here is to assess what theorists of new media, including myself, have perceived to be a shift within the ways that the image functions vis-à-vis questions of indexicality and identity formation. In particular, I wish to theorize the ways that the digital regime makes perceptible a set of transformations in how notions of identity and belonging are mediated. This chapter explores general transformations in the common senses of coalition and belonging perceptible when attending to the changes in the media through which common senses are elaborated and put into circulation. The transformations I explore here point to a renewed interest in forging dynamic modes of commonality and belonging that exceed the prior logics of identity politics while remaining invested in the workings of difference that some versions of those politics made into politically salient sensibilities and strategies.

Under pressure from the changes in the practices and possibilities of visual culture wrought by the ascendancy of the digital, theorists have recently returned to questions of the index and, specifically, to the ways that various media function in relationship to that which they are understood to mediate. I use the term *index* here to refer to a type of sign that functions through an assertion of its actual connection to the object to which it refers. For my purposes, *index* encompasses both its status as a trace of its referent and its deictic functions in relation to linguistic shifters, such as *I, you,* et cetera.[1] In much contemporary thinking, digital media herald a transformation within the ways that visual data work on and through those sentient beings engaging them. At the same time, studies of practices emergent within digital culture are contending with the shifting ground of the body as a privileged mediator of and site for sociocultural identifications and are revealing the extent to which the body's textual or visual index in cyberspace opens onto new configurations, making possible different insights into processes of identity formation.

A range of theoretical explorations of the potential that digital technologies hold for transforming current understandings of fundamental concepts such as identity, reality, space, time, and signification has recently emerged. I seek here to contribute to this ongoing creative intellectual project by offering an argument about the emergent force of difference as a collective logic of belonging, the mechanisms through which this logic is becoming common sense, and the dangers and possibilities that lie therein.

In what follows, I offer ways to conceptualize the centrality of difference to the logics of identity and identification perceptible when attending to the digital regime of the image. As I stated, Lorde's invocation of "the very house of difference" can be reread in the context of contemporary scholarship to situate what I refer to as "digital identity politics" within a trajectory of thought and struggle that takes flight out of a women of color feminism whose appearance we can locate in the 1970s and 1980s. In my usage of it here, women of color feminism marks a political, ethical, and intellectual project, an articulation, and in Edwards's terms, "a process of linking or connecting across gaps," from a variety of geographic locations within the United States and occasionally outside of it in the face of a neoliberalism gathering strength. The formulation I associate with digital identity politics, I = Another, is an equation in which difference functions in and as the index. To explore the range of possibilities and pitfalls in that formula, at the end of this chapter, I analyze three different digital media projects. The first is a set of advertisements from a recent campaign to raise funds to fight AIDS in Africa, the I Am African campaign. The second is a digital story produced at the Highlander Research and Education Center during a workshop by the now defunct media justice organization, Third World Majority. I end with a discussion of the 2003 documentary by Big Noise Tactical Media, *The Fourth World War*.

Of particular interest to this project are the ways that digital video technologies and, importantly, the digital regime of the image they orchestrate have become part of the communicative strategies of movements for social and economic justice. While much of the work on new media has focused on the Internet, digital art, and Web-based practices, I am concerned most specifically with new-media practices whose logics and genealogies include those that inform prior film, analog video, broadcast media, and photographic practices. The media of specific interest in this chapter are digital video and digital photography, media whose presumed relationship to what they record remains continuous in many important ways with the relationships that have historically been assumed to cohere in photography and film.

The discontinuities within what digital video and digital photography inherit from film photography and celluloid, however, will be my primary focus. Important to my argument is an understanding of the pressure the digital regime of the image puts on the ways images commonly present themselves as an index of what they appear to record. Questions of medium specificity are important to my thinking insofar as they illuminate the ways that particular media not only facilitate but also are enmeshed in a set of socioeconomic relations whose historical force is inseparable from the various ways those relations are mediated and hence communicated. The status of the digital as index is emerging as one of the concerns of theorists of new media. It has been argued that the digital image's susceptibility to manipulation, its reproducibility and thus its resistance to cohering as a discrete and unique tangible object (a characteristic of the medium that poses a substantial challenge to dominant notions of ownership and property rights), and its ability to reduce any data to the seemingly neutral and immaterial status of ones and zeros have undermined any claims that the digital image might make to index "the real."[2] Yet, as did films and photographs before them, digital images continue to index the set of lived and fluid relations into which they enter upon becoming perceptible, material relations I have described elsewhere in terms of the processes involved in the constitution of "common sense."[3]

Although the digital image disturbs the faith previously invested in the image's ability to access and touch the real, a faith on which the cinematic capitalizes, it nonetheless remains connected to material relations insofar as it must work through or against existing forms of common sense to communicate something or become meaningful in any given context in which it is perceived. While it helps to make visible the ways that the relationship of the filmic and photographic image to reality also rests on common sense, the digital regime of the image as we encounter it in digital video and digital photography functions as a bridge between the photographic and filmic images of the nineteenth and twentieth centuries and whatever that regime of the image will reveal itself to be to, for, or as "the coming community" (see Hansen 2006).[4] It is in its current configuration as still cinematic yet extending toward other organizations of perception that I engage the digital image here.

I contend that the digital regime of the image organizes and orchestrates a set of psychosocial relations in ways that signal a transformation within, rather than a rupture from, those relations organized by and through film and photography. With the understanding that others have begun such work, I leave for another time a full assessment of the political economy of digital technologies, even as I emphasize that the digital regime of the image is implicated in (at the same time as it offers a mode through which to challenge) global capitalist exploitation. The relationships between the digital regime of the image and capitalist exploitation include the ways that finance capital itself moves via digital circuits as ones and zeros across the globe; the role of the Internet, cell phones, and other new-media technologies in organizing and managing communication across geographic space, helping to structure shifting temporalities of communication; and the transformation of common senses, their attendant organizations of sociality and belonging, and therefore the hegemonic relations those common senses maintain and challenge.

In the introduction to a special issue of the journal *differences*, the film theorist Mary Ann Doane rationalizes the journal's intellectual project of exploring "the viability of indexicality as a concept, an expectation, and a crucial cultural and semiotic force" arguing that there has been a "massive attack" on the index and referentiality that was possible only through "an enormous reduction of the concept." She locates the genesis of this attack in the 1960s. Referring to the questions raised by the journal's contributors about the status of the index under pressure from the digital, Doane states:

At the heart of all of these questions is the vexed issue of referentiality in representation, a concept subjected to a massive attack from the 1960s on—by structuralism in its centering of Saussurian linguistics, poststructuralism in its emphasis upon textuality, and cultural studies with its notions of social or cultural constructivism. This structuring absence was only possible through an enormous reduction of the concept. The relegation of indexicality to the myth, illusion, and ideology of realism has left critical problems in an impenetrable obscurity. (Doane 2007, 6)

Though an assessment of the merits of Doane's characterizations of the complex, various, and oftentimes nuanced projects of Saussurean linguistics, poststructuralism, and cultural studies regarding questions of representation, referentiality, and realism is tangential to my concerns in this chapter, I offer her formulation to point to the ways that the crisis of faith in the index might be said to have strong tentacles that become most perceptible in the 1960s and 1970s.[5] If this is arguably the case, then it is important to consider that the conditions under which not only the image as index but also "I" as index (if we accept Doane's generalizations of the forces conspiring against a reduced concept of the index) are destabilized include anticolonial struggles in Africa, Asia, and South America; the Black Power struggles that were connected to the anticolonial ones; the destabilization of feminist identity politics, especially as advanced by black and women of color feminisms operating according to their own formulations and understandings of the role of identity in politics; and other efforts to forge collectivity and alliances around commonly held oppositional stances to imperialism, bourgeois nationalism, and state violence. In that context, destabilizing faith in the referentiality of a hegemonic notion of the index can be understood as one of the ways that identity politics worked in the 1960s and 1970s—identity politics was an anti-essentialist project that destabilized the authority of existing articulations of identity and universality. The coincidence between the widespread articulation of identity politics and the context in which Doane locates a certain type of "index trouble" also highlights the tension in the notion of identity as a particular designation (i.e., one's identity) and politics as a collective activity or, at least, as a concept in which a notion of collectivity is meant to matter in some way.[6]

Rather than heralding the triumph of identity as a self-evident equation of the index with its seemingly proper referent ($I = I$), the emergence of identity politics as a logic of collective identification and action strikes a blow to the very confidence with which "I" achieves its coherence.[7] The challenges posed by this attack are taken up in various ways from disparate sociopolitical and geographic locations. Here I am interested in two related, but divergent, innovative deployments of the formula I = Another. The first can be understood as a response to the set of challenges posed to the integrity of the index by various sociopolitical movements from the 1950s to the 1970s. The examples I consider of the first deployment are Gilles Deleuze's discussion of Jean Rouch and Pierre Perrault in *Cinema Two: The Time-Image* and the supermodel Iman's I Am African advertising campaign. The second deployment of I = Another is a recalibration of identity politics from within contemporary movements who are its inheritors. I discuss digital storytelling and Big Noise Tactical Media's documentary *The Fourth World War* as examples. Both deployments of I = Another are problematic; yet the recalibration of identity politics evident in the digital story I discuss and in *The Fourth World War* interests me more than how I = Another functions as a mode of appropriation in the I Am African campaign. The digital story and *The Fourth World War* direct identification toward a changing core of difference as a value and a vehicle through which to transform existing socioeconomic and geopolitical relations. The I Am African campaign attempts to arrest "the changing core of difference" and fix its signification to set it to work in the interests of existing relations, assimilating difference by representing it.

Both of the visual cultural innovations I discuss here can be described as operating according to the equation I = Another, but the ways that each diverges from the others' deployment of that equation offer important insights into the political promises and pitfalls of the formulation I = Another itself. The I Am African campaign operates in ways that are akin to appropriation. The digital story and *The Fourth World War* open onto compelling possibilities for furthering efforts to forge commonalities with and within difference. Both might be said to be consistent with the current operations of the digital regime of the image, which should be understood as an affective and communicative organization of perception saturated with the workings of capital and caught in a dynamic process of transformation that it both expresses and facilitates.

I = Another

The equation itself (I = Another) is one elaborated by Gilles Deleuze in his work on cinema. Deleuze introduces this formula (which he attributes to Arthur Rimbaud [1854–91]) in a discussion of the differences and similarities between the direct cinema of Pierre Perrault and the cinéma vérité of Jean Rouch. Because I seek to engage and trouble this formulation in what follows, it is worth quoting at length:

> For Perrault, the concern is to belong to his dominated people, and to rediscover a lost and repressed collective identity. For Rouch, it is a matter of getting out of his dominant civilization and reaching the premises of another identity. Hence the possibility of misunderstanding between the two authors. Nevertheless each one as a film-maker sets off with the same slender material, camera on the shoulder and synchronized tape recorder; they must become others, with their characters, at the same time as their characters must become others themselves. The famous formula, "what is suitable for the documentary is that one knows who who is and whom one is filming," ceases to be valid. The Ego = Ego form of identity (or its degenerate form, them = them) ceases to be valid for the characters and the film-maker, in the real as well as in the fiction. What allows itself to be glimpsed instead, by profound degrees, is Rimbaud's "I is another." (Deleuze 1989, 152–53)

According to Deleuze, one of the most important characteristics of the cinema in which "I is another" allows itself to be glimpsed is that it "brought every model of the true into question" and by so doing worked to establish a different register of the true, that of Storytelling (1989, 275–76). Though Deleuze focuses here on direct cinema and cinéma vérité, both of which are specific types of documentary filmmaking, what he describes as a radical possibility of filmmaking on celluloid reaches maturity and, it could be argued, becomes the norm with the rise of digital media because the destruction of the true and what Deleuze refers to as "the powers of the false" are built into the digital regime of the image by virtue of the malleability of its images and its consequently widely acknowledged problematic relationship to any notion of a premediated reality.[8] In other words, the equation I = Another is readily available in the digital and is frequently (though not necessarily) deployed in the context of what I am calling a "digital identity politics."[9]

I am using the phrase *digital identity politics* to reference a politically charged set of ethico-political relations that can be characterized by the formulation I = Another and is facilitated and made perceptible by digital technologies. What I am calling digital identity politics can be located within a historical trajectory that includes, as my presentation of Deleuze's use of I = Another indicates, certain direct cinema and cinéma vérité practices, as well as other cinematic practices of the Third Cinema movement, a film movement that began in Latin America in the late 1960s and was taken up elsewhere by other filmmakers who were connected to social movements in different geographic locations and sociopolitical contexts.

Like any politics that seek to make assertions based on identification, digital identity politics are a messy set of claims over, about, and through contested histories, memories, processes, territories, investments, interests, and so on, but they also seek to facilitate a politics and a mode of engagement by drawing on the digital's intimate relationship to décalage. The contrasts between Perrault and Rouch that Deleuze characterizes in the sentence that precedes the long quote I provided earlier as "a big difference in situation . . . which is not simply personal but cinematographic and formal" are significant also because they point to the divergent routes I = Another might take when it articulates a politics and the various interests it might serve along the way.

Deleuze is relatively uncritical in his discussion of the films of Jean Rouch (whose documentary work in Africa is controversial). In addition, Deleuze adopts the formulation I = Another itself from another controversial French figure, Arthur Rimbaud, who claimed famously and problematically, "Je est un negre." As I hope mentioning these examples suggest, there is a danger to this drive to become the other that I think is particularly salient when the I claiming to be another occupies a position of privilege in relation to existing hierarchies of power. The danger lies in the tension between the crucially important insistence on historical specificity and the demand for historical rupture, or, to put this into the terms of political economy, the tension between production and reproduction (see Keeling 2007, chap. 7). This is the more general problem of the emergence of the new and the (im)possibility of creating another world, but it also is a

"We Are All African." Photograph by Michael Thompson.

problem on which politically engaged discussions of new media and the digital might be predicated.

Connected to the trajectory of the formula I = Another of which Rouch is a part, recent digital imagery raises similar problems of appropriation. One example among several is the supermodel Iman's ad campaign to raise awareness about AIDS in Africa. It is to a discussion of this campaign that I now turn, presenting it here as emblematic of the ways that I = Another provides an opportunity and a rationale for a mode of appropriation wherein the needs and interests of an other are assumed to be served by articulating them into the systems and structures of the I who stands in for the dominant group vis-à-vis that for which the other is representative.

As Iman's campaign illustrates, the current configuration of the digital regime of the image facilitates both tendencies identified by Deleuze (which he associates with Rouch and describes as characteristic of Perrault), and each tendency carries a complex relationship to the workings of difference made perceptible through digital imaging. I Am African features many well-known North American and European celebrities, including, among others,

Richard Gere, Elijah Wood, Heidi Klum, Seal, and Gwyneth Paltrow. Part of the Keep a Child Alive effort to provide the medical services necessary to treat AIDS in Africa, the challenging visual imagery of the ad campaign is belied by the rationale for it provided on the campaign's website.

The rationale for the advertisements relies on an appeal to the ways in which Africans are the same as "us." The "About 'I Am African'" page on the website reads:

> Each and every one of us contains DNA that can be traced back to our African ancestors. These amazing people traveled far and wide. Now they need our help. Most Africans cannot afford the lifesaving anti-retroviral drugs (ARVs) that have transformed AIDS in the West to a treatable and manageable disease. ARVs are miracle drugs. We take them for granted here in the West but to an African family they are tragically out of reach because of cost, even by some Governments. Just think for a moment how you would feel if the drugs to keep your child alive were out of reach, knowing that they are available in other countries, but not to you and your family. For just one dollar a day you can help provide these medicines. Help save the life of a child, a mother, a father, a family, "our human family" our first family. Go to www.keepachildalive.org to keep Africa alive . . . before its too late.

While it cannot be denied that it is important to work toward ending the suffering caused by AIDS in Africa and elsewhere, the written plea to do so featured on the I Am African website is predicated on an appeal to the ways that Africans are the same as "us" in the West who have access to treatments for AIDS. Rather than work through and with the complexities of the challengingly mutually dependent relationships on which the Keep a Child Alive effort hinges—problematic relationships referenced by the digital imagery produced for the campaign—the written explanation of the campaign flattens the differences between "us" and "people-in-Africa-with-AIDS" into a notion of sameness rooted not only in our DNA but also in our shared socioeconomic units of reproduction (families) and in an invitation ("imagine how you would feel") to project our structure of feeling in the face of gross and utterly indefensible injustices onto those whose feelings about that situation we are by that very invitation denied access.

It is objectionable that stylized versions of what seem meant to be tribal markings carry the weight of a visual reference to "African" in ways that insist on a static and romanticized version of diverse and complex groups of people on a large continent. Still, the clearly fabricated nature of the colorful markings points to the artifice in the work of the index in the photographs. The unequal relationships indexed in these photographs as common sense could inform a sustained investigation into those relationships. Instead a set of equivalences between "us" and "people-in-Africa-with-AIDS" is produced without destabilizing or providing insight into the processes that perpetuate the unequal distribution of wealth, information, and resources that perpetuate the HIV/AIDS rates in Africa, which are by all accounts exorbitantly high in many countries on the continent.

I = Another functions in the I Am African campaign along the same lines that Deleuze claims Godard attributes to the work of Jean Rouch:

> Godard says this in relation to Jean Rouch; not only for the characters themselves but for the filmmaker who "white just like Rimbaud, himself declares that I is another," that is, me a black. When Rimbaud exclaims, "I am of inferior race for all eternity . . . I am a beast, a negro . . ." it is in the course of passing through a whole series of forgers, "Merchant you are a negro, magistrate you are a negro, general you are a negro, mangy old emperor you are a negro . . . ," up to that highest power of the false which means that a black must himself become black, through his white roles, whilst the white here finds a chance of becoming black too ("I can be saved . . ."). (Deleuze 1989, 153)

Though a sustained discussion of the complexities of the problems raised by appropriation is beyond the scope of this chapter, it is important to point out that the phenomenon Deleuze describes here via Godard's account of Rimbaud is objectionable in part because it is predicated on a construction of "a negro" that denies those who are subjected by the term access to its workings. "Black" here indexes an ethical relationship to history and being in the world that becomes available only to whites or through "white roles."[10] In the deployments of I = Another discussed thus far, that of the I Am African campaign and that Deleuze attributes to Rouch via Godard, the force and potential of the other are appropriated in the service of the consolidation of an "I" whose own access to power and privilege is meant to be contested or disavowed by the power of its declaration to be another. Yet the workings of power and privilege itself, including those through which the "I" claiming to be another is constituted, remain unchallenged.

We are in the throes of a transformation connected to the formulation I = Another, a formulation that, in the examples I have discussed, facilitates a politics of appropriation characteristic of Rimbaud, Rouch, and the I Am African campaign. Yet that formulation and Deleuze's discussion of it also offer a mode that yearns toward possibilities that exceed those of appropriation.

Ya no serás tú, ahora eres nosotros
(You Will No Longer Be You, Now You Are Us)

One of the primary difficulties that the filmmakers in the Third Cinema movement of the late 1960s faced was the cost of production. It is well-known that digital filmmaking is much less expensive than celluloid. Given this, it could be argued that digital films and other creative digital-media productions are in a position to belatedly fulfill aspects of the Third Cinema project. The characteristics and effects that today are attributed to the digital might be perceptible as possibilities within prior politically engaged documentary filmmaking practices and the Third Cinema project. As I stated, I am suggesting here that what today is becoming visible about the image under the regime of the digital is present as potential in prior organizations of the image. Rather than claiming that digital identity politics references a new form of sociopolitically engaged identity production, I suggest that I = Another names the dominant tendency within the digital image regarding questions of identity and, further, that this tendency taps into (but also complicates an assessment of) the differential form as a component of early twenty-first-century social movements under capitalist production.[11]

One practice emerging with and through the newly accessible digital technologies is digital storytelling. It is a practice that has been taken up by some of the organizations whose political genealogy passes through black feminism and women of color feminism. For Deleuze, storytelling is of paramount importance to the creation (via the formulation that he attributes to Rimbaud, "I is another") of what he calls "a people." Theorists and practitioners of digital storytelling help us to push Deleuze's insights even further. Though the parameters of digital storytelling as a method are unclear and still in formation, digital storytelling involves creating a personal narrative using digital technology such as a digital video camera and computer editing software. Third World Majority, a nonprofit organization that was based in Oakland, California, and staffed and directed by women of color, explains that the digital storytelling movement is "a grassroots media phenomenon in which communities are creating their own short, three- to five-minute digital stories from the found material in their lives (digital video, photographs, letters, news clippings, etc.). The principles of the community digital storytelling movement draws from a diverse body of work including: third cinema, popular education, creative writing, oral history, filmmaking, and digital media manipulation." Digital storytelling, especially as promulgated by Third World Majority, is expressly about creating community and forging bonds of solidarity between seemingly disparate groups through sharing personal stories.

In "Movements of Resistance in the South," a digital story created by two staff members at the Highlander Research and Education Center in New Market, Tennessee, during a workshop held by Third World Majority, the personal narratives of immigration and activism offered by each of the two narrators, Ana and Paulina, are presented as moments in broader sociopolitical, economic, and world historical narratives. In their own voices over an image track that includes found documentation of Latino immigrants, maps, and pictures of themselves and their family members, Ana and Paulina describe themselves as "two young Latinas organizing for social change in the South today, ahora." Through her first-person narrative of immigrating with her family from Mexico to North Carolina and her first experiences at the Highlander Center, Paulina insists that communicating one's story in the context of the U.S. South is an activity that involves making the experiences of oppressed and exploited populations resonate within difference. Speaking on the soundtrack together, Ana and Paulina explain, "Stories, encuentros, interconnect with other peoples. We are doing the work of connecting our communities for a broader movement/movimiento."

As politicized by Third World Majority, digital storytelling produces an "I" that might simultaneously produce another that also references oneself. Yet the use of still photos, a staple of digital stories, insists on the validity of the reality they index. The challenge for the digital storyteller becomes one of excavating the collective history hidden in the often highly personal visual information presented to support the story. In Paulina and Ana's digital story, the photos and other visual information such as the maps provide another mode of communication that mirrors the narratives' insistence on the commonality that the Highlander Center's programs might help to produce between groups marked by racial, ethnic, and other differences. The work of their digital story is to make visible the socioeconomic relations indexed by the photos and to politicize those relations by bringing to the surface what is common to them. Within the terms of their story, that commonality is produced spatially, on the grounds of the Highlander Center (in the mountains of Tennessee), and throughout the southeastern United States more broadly. In this way, Paulina and Ana, via their digital story, labor to make visible another history of the U.S. South, one that might contest the notions of the South in common circulation. They do this in the interest of producing a South that is a viable and dynamic house of difference in which a renewed radicalism might be forged out of a vibrant history of collective action and struggle, a history to which that of the Highlander Center itself testifies and continues.[12]

Digital storytelling also is a characteristic of another digital production, albeit one on a far grander scale than those produced via Third World Majority's digital storytelling workshops. *The Fourth World War* (2003), a documentary film by Big Noise Tactical Media, presents itself as a film by and for a movement that is still in dynamic formation. The film provides a story of "the movement" for those involved with what has been characterized as "a movement of movements." It achieves its affective power from this goal, reaching those who already agree with its basic premise that the current configuration of power needs to be contested vigorously, and revealing the interconnections between the specific sites of struggle characteristic of what the film makes possible to understand as a global response to empire. As such, the film is indifferent to those for whom the rationale for the current configuration of power and the violence that supports it works, and it is uninterested in sifting through the complex and uneven arrangements of exploitation and domination it asserts comprise a coherent "system of violence," empire. Like much contemporary leftist and radical media, the film provides an invaluable document and analysis of ongoing struggle and aids in the construction and circulation of a story about that struggle. Similar to the achievement Deleuze credits to Pierre Perrault's documentary work, *The Fourth World War* creates a legend. It constructs a "we" that is a myth as well as a promise.

In the film, issues of geographic specificity are elided in the interest of producing a common sense that might support a coherent alternative globalization. Like Paulina and Ana's digital story, the voice-over by Suheir Hammad and Michael Franti introducing *The Fourth World War* is a personal one that bleeds into the narratives of others. It does so in the interest of forging connections between geographically disparate struggles against corporate globalization to produce in the film's viewers a common sense of solidarity, a desire for an alternative globalization, and an intuition that its achievement is possible through sustained struggle. It makes palpably present the yearning for change that many of us feel in our bones or our joints. *The Fourth World War* gives a form to that yearning and puts it into circulation, making it available for other projects.[13]

The film claims that "everywhere there is war," a war without an end or boundaries and that this, the Fourth World War, is a war between "a system of terrifying violence" and "all of us who will stop this war." *The Fourth World War* produces this "us" by visually creating a sense of spatial continuity between geographically distant people and places and by providing a personal narrative that begins by admitting to a sense of isolation that contradicts the visual production of connection. The film itself is organized by putting several stories of collective struggle into formal proximity with each other. Each story is presented as particular to the local history out of which it is narrated, but the stories themselves each take place over the course of the same two years and share a common iconography of protest and the militarized violence that seeks to squash protest or that the protests seek to smash. The iconography and the logic of the film's cuts between different geographic locations produce a sense of historical connection and immediacy between struggles in different places waged by different groups of people over the span of the same two years.

In the story told from Buenos Aires, for instance, in the face of the disconnection and fear characteristic of the "system of terrifying violence," knowing one's neighbors becomes a political act predicated on refusing fear. In another sequence, in a montage of photographs of Argentines disappeared during the brutal military dictatorship from 1976 to 1983, digital video editing techniques facilitate the presentation of photographs of the disappeared at an increasingly rapid pace until none of the people in the photographs can be distinguished as specific individuals, yet the affective force achieved through the sheer number of the disappeared makes palpable their common situation. That overwhelmingly unjust situation, the equation between each of the disappeared individuals, rather than a document of each individual himself or herself, is what the sequence indexes.

Another of the film's deployments of I = Another that makes perceptible the sense of belonging within difference, in ways that extend such belonging to potentially include anyone who perceives the sequence, can be found in the film's first montage of only some of the different locations and events presented in the film—South Africa in September 2002, South Korea in April 2001, Palestine in July 2002, Argentina in 2001. The logic of the montage is orchestrated by making available a sense of the similarities between the police violence that confronted protesters in each location. Anonymous behind their riot gear, the police look basically the same from place to place, and the protesters also appear to be similar in their tactics, fervor, indignation, and grief. Though they differ from place to place in their language, clothing, complexion, and manner, in this initial presentation of conflict between protesters and police in disparate geographic locations, the police are like the police elsewhere, and the protesters are like their counterparts in other places during roughly the same period. Although complicated at various moments in the film primarily through the use of close-ups that show the similarities between individuals wearing the police uniforms and those protesting state actions, the logic of connection in this early montage is consistent with the assertion made by the voice-over narration that "all of us who will stop this war" are forged in a collective confrontation with "a system of terrifying violence," a contemporary system that is global in scope.

In short, *The Fourth World War* insists that the collective "all of us who will stop this war" is produced in a struggle against a system characterized by fragmentation and fear, rather than in a struggle between peoples, each different from the other in terms of nationality, or religion, or race, or class. Because of this, "all of us who will stop this war" names an irreducible multiplicity that must valorize the least within it in order to survive at all.

Representation is at work in digital identity politics, but the content of that representation is the relationships digital identity politics orchestrate, express, and make perceptible. The political challenge of the digital regime of the image is an ethical one that attends to representation more broadly, but the digital stages that question in terms of responsibility to and for others more clearly and more immediately than did prior regimes of the

"It is the hour of looking and looking at ourselves." Screen grab from *The Fourth World War*, © Big Noise Tactical Media, 2003.

image. Part of the work of *The Fourth World War* is to provide for the viewer a sense of the spirit of the people the film documents and to incorporate the viewer into the mythic "we" the film works to generate. The film ends with a rhythmic montage of where the film has taken its viewers, recollecting a dispersed movement. The montage and its accompanying soundtrack call forth a sense of the ethical force of that movement and hence an intuition that is not yet a glimpse of its triumph. Concluding the voice-over narration that tells the story of this movement of movements, Michael Franti explains:

> We walked and these moments changed us. We saw the buildings burning and the pain in our neighbors' eyes. We rushed bayonets in the mountain and lines of police in the city. We were touched by too much death. We loved and felt alive. We heard the echo of our word in other voices. . . . This is not the whole story or the only story. . . . A much greater story remains to be told.

Suheir Hammad concludes, "A story we will write together."

Over just images of conflict, heroism, and resolve, the last speaking voice on the soundtrack is a call issued in Spanish. Mindful of the complexities of translation and the décalage that attends any translation, I present this call in the English translation offered in the film's subtitles. The speaker does not appear, existing in the film as a disembodied, ethereal voice,[14]

> Brothers and Sisters, it is the hour of dignity. It is the hour of looking and looking at ourselves, without shame and without fear. It is the hour of struggle. Open your hearts, then, warriors. Prepare the feet which we gave you, open your eyes and your ear, which we are, attentive. Become our word once again. You will no longer be you, now you are us. Walk, then, walk the land of the other, walk and speak. Take our face now. Take our voice now. Go with our gaze. Make yourself our hearing in order to listen to the word of the other. You shall no longer be you, now you are us. Go down from the mountain and seek the color of the earth in this world. You shall no longer be you, now you are us.

Issued at the end of the film, this call reaches a viewer who is already implicated as part of the film's production of a mythic "we" forged in struggle. The agency here is with the collective, the "we" and "us." Rather than a celebration of appropriation, this is an invitation to, among other things, "make yourself our hearing" to work in the interest of the "us," "you" who can "listen to the word of the other" with a collectively forged faculty of hearing. Here, I = Another begins to crumble, and something different can be sensed.

The temporal logic of the charge that ends *The Fourth World War*, "Ya no serás tú, ahora eres nosotros"—replete with the impossibilities of translation marked by Edwards's term *décalage*—is rooted in "now" ("now you are us") and declares the end of one history, of one story, and the beginning of another that does not correspond to the logics that precede it. You = us indexes a situation now that depends on the annihilation of a condition in which you = you has a future. When you = us, you = you has no future. It no longer matters whether or not one says I; you = you ends and you = us starts now. Here digital identity politics gesture toward a noncorrespondence between competing regimes and the valorization of something different that can be perceived in the interval, gap, or break between them. ("Become our word once again. . . . Take our face now. . . . Go with our gaze.")

Risking a politics of appropriation and essentialism, the politics articulated here exceed identification and yearn for a type of unity in difference. When articulated most compellingly, such a politics is unafraid of multiplicity, making of it a house rather than seeking the security of any one difference that might be understood as "its own"—its own voice, its own gaze, its own sensibility, its own structures of feeling. This politics is articulated most compellingly when it acknowledges that appropriation and essentialism are the risks it carries, internal logics into which I = Another consistently threatens to collapse before it might gesture toward the radical potential it harbors. Yet, as the call at the end of the film illustrates, the twin risks of appropriation and essentialism are wagered because they disguise therein a radical promise, a present and future responsibility to the other within, to the "us" that is the now of each "you," and to the "we" referenced by each "I."

> I urge each one of us here to reach down into that deep place of knowledge inside herself and touch that terror and loathing of any difference that lives there. See whose face it wears. Then the personal as the political can begin to illuminate all our choices.
> —Audre Lorde, "The Master's Tools Will Never Dismantle the Master's House"

Notes

My thinking about the issues considered here has been shaped by my interactions with several people. I wish to thank the following for offering suggestions, criticisms, and other help along the way: Chandra Ford offered instructive comments on several drafts of this chapter. Miguel Najera helped with the English–Spanish translation. Cynthia Tolentino provided comments on, and suggestions for, revising an earlier draft of this chapter. Versions of this chapter were presented to audiences at the American Studies Association, the Multi-ethnic Society of Europe and the Americas, Northeastern University, and at the Center for Citizenship, Race, and Ethnicity Studies at the College of St. Rose. I am grateful to those audiences for their interested engagement with many of the ideas contained in the present version. Grace Hong offered suggestions and advice throughout the writing process. Christine Balance, Jayna Brown, Erica Edwards, Yogita Goyal, and Jodi Kim offered comments on, and suggestions about, revising a late draft.

1 I have attempted to be mindful as well of the ways that a renewed interest in the work of Charles Sanders Peirce informs a return to questions of the index in ways that complicate the prior deployments of the concept within film studies. For a series of recent interrogations into the workings of the index in relationship to film studies, see the special issue "Indexicality: Trace and Sign" of the journal *differences*, edited by Mary Ann Doane (2007).

2 Lev Manovich's (2002) arguments about these elements of new media have been influential.

3 That what is referenced by the image are sociohistorical relations saturated by the

workings of power and participants in the struggle for hegemony is one of the arguments relevant to the present chapter that I develop in *The Witch's Flight: The Cinematic, the Black Femme, and the Image of Common Sense* (2007).

4   See Hansen 2006. The reference to "the coming community" is to Agamben's book by the same name.

5   In addition to identity politics, but not separate from them, transformations in the realm of visual culture during the 1960s and 1970s also put pressure on the workings of the index. See Krauss 1977.

6   Norman (2007) makes an argument about the ways that the Combahee River Collective statement produced a "we" that, rather than fixing identity, is generative of "a collectivity that is achieved in its ability to travel across identity, time, and place to spark collectivity beyond the specificity of the original group." This recent reassessment of identity politics in relationship to processes of identity formation and, specifically, to essentialist notions of those processes is consistent with my efforts here.

7   It is important to acknowledge that a relationship with the other has long informed philosophical thought about identity. Yet the destabilization of identity's ability to cohere as such and the work it accomplishes by doing so, is what I want to locate in the thought, culture, and politics of the 1960s and 1970s.

8   It is significant, therefore, that Deleuze introduces I = Another in the context of a discussion about documentary film, since that is a mode of filmmaking whose claims on the real are foregrounded insistently.

9   A consideration of Deleuze's theories of difference and their importance to his oeuvre is beyond the scope of this chapter. In addition to Deleuze's work on these questions in *Difference and Repetition* (1994) and elsewhere, see Baugh's essay, published in 2000, comparing and contrasting the notion of difference in Deleuze's work with that of *différance* in Jacques Derrida's.

10   Given Edwards's (2003) discussion of the difficulties involved historically in translating *negre* and *noir* into their English equivalents, it would be interesting to investigate the French words Deleuze uses that Tomlinson here translates as *negro* and *black*. I have not yet undertaken that task.

11   My invocation of "the differential form" here is a reference to Chela Sandoval's theory of it in *The Methodology of the Oppressed* (2000).

12   For more information about the Highlander Center, see http://www.highlander center.org.

13   Such as that of Barack Obama's ascendance to the presidency of the United States. His 2007–8 campaign capitalized on a widespread yearning for change by channeling it into a narrative through which emerged Obama himself, an identifiable image of a widespread yet seemingly earnest hope for connection through difference.

14   For text of a communication from the EZLN, part of which is heard at the end of *The Fourth World War*, see http://www.1worldcommunication.org/wordsofthee zln.htm.

Reading Tehran in *Lolita*

Making Racialized and Gendered Difference Work for Neoliberal Multiculturalism

> Especially because those subjects who produce knowledge
> along the specific axes of their own social difference . . . are
> seen to derive their institutional and epistemic authority from
> merely being who they are, there needs to be a sustained
> critique of the many redeployments of knowledges that
> emerge in the name of women.—Laura Hyun Yi Kang,
> *Compositional Subjects: En/figuring Asian/American Women*

I n their introduction to this volume, the editors assert that the comparative methods of women of color feminism and queer of color critique develop in reaction against, and in difference with, the typical comparative methods of bourgeois and minority nationalisms, as these inform mainstream politics as well as scholarship in American and ethnic studies. Although minority nationalisms were critical of bourgeois nationalism when it came to its methods for valuing and devaluing along the axis of race, they nonetheless reproduced its hegemonic comparative methods when it came to ascribing value and difference along axes of gender, class, nation, and culture. In other words, minority nationalisms rejected racism and its differential schemata without challenging patriarchy, nationalism, and capitalism as normative systems.

Women of color feminism and queer of color critique, in contrast, develop comparative methods to debunk and to jam these interlocking and necessarily reductive normative systems. According to the editors, these comparative analytics "are intended not to erase the differentials of power, value, and social death within and among groups . . . but to highlight such differentials" (9). The primary comparative mode is not to think in terms of parallels and within conventional categories but to think relationally, in a manner that estranges normal categorical terms. Intersectional analysis, for example, is a methodology that recognizes how procedures of race, gender, class, sexuality, and other modes of constituting identity categories as differential interlock in action with one another. These aggregate in exploitative and discriminatory processes targeting women of color, which cannot be grasped or redressed by theories or laws committed to a model of the individual as autonomous or abstract, yet can be grasped readily by epistemological analyses of women of color's varied experiences, what Cherríe Moraga and Gloria Anzaldúa call "theory in the flesh" (Moraga and Anzaldúa 1983, 23). Thus, in contrast to how difference structures normative systems (and in contrast to how hegemonic comparative methods understand it), women of color feminism and queer of color critique use and define difference as "a cleareyed appraisal of the dividing line between valued and devalued" (Hong and Ferguson, this volume, 11).

The epigraph by Laura Kang reminds us that "knowledges that emerge in the name of women" are deployed just as readily within normative systems and by hegemonic comparative analysis as they are deployed for oppositional purposes or by critical comparative analysis. One of the central dilemmas this volume addresses is the degree to which women of color feminism and queer of color critique have been misapprehended and misconstrued, often in an antithetical manner (which has led scholars to overlook their innovative comparative models). Specifically, their objects of concern—women of color, sexuality, lived experiences of subject formation—have been reinscribed within scholarship that shares the ideals (or metanarratives) of the big normative systems, such as the primacy of the individual, esteem for capitalist democracies, the unity of culture, and the framing concept of the nation. Kang hints at the most common result of such disfiguring reinscriptions: the reducing of women of color feminism's theory of embodied knowledge to a notion of knowledge in bodies, which allows a mode of analysis to be mistaken for a method of identity consolidation. Ironically, this misreading leads to the frequent mischaracterization of women of color feminism as "identity politics" when, as Roderick A. Ferguson demonstrates, the main thrust of women of color analysis is not only to repudiate identitarianisms but also to repudiate the very concept of a fixed identity (R. Ferguson 2004, 110–38).

My scholarship identifies successive formations of multiculturalism as influential normative systems for ascribing value and valuelessness in the period after World War II. I argue that the permanent crisis of white supremacy did not end racialization as a procedure that privileges some and stigmatizes others, but instead inaugurated a revision of the terms of these procedures under the sign of antiracism. In particular, I am interested in the establishment of official or state-sanctioned antiracisms. In a larger manuscript project, I examine how official antiracisms ratify specific articulations of the U.S. state, international political order, and global economy, consistently resolving conflicts involving race on liberal political terrains that conceal the economic inequality that global capitalism generates (Melamed, forthcoming). In addition, I center literary studies as a primary cultural technology for assembling and disseminating the normative regimens of successive official antiracisms.

Here I focus on neoliberal multiculturalism, which I identify as a recent form of official U.S. antiracism. I examine how neoliberal multiculturalism redeploys "knowledges in the name of women" in a manner antithetical to, yet often mistaken for, women of color feminism. I also argue that neoliberal multiculturalism has used literary studies to promulgate its discourse of racialized and gendered difference in ways that further obscure and (mis)appropriate the intellectual space carved out by women of color feminism and queer of color critique.

I will define neoliberal multiculturalism presently. (Briefly, neoliberal multiculturalism portrays an ethic of multiculturalism to be the spirit of neoliberalism and posits neoliberal restructuring across the globe to be the key to a postracist world of freedom and opportunity.) First, I want to emphasize how neoliberal multiculturalism contains the radical potential of specifically gendered ways of knowing expressed in literature and instead teaches us the political use value of female bodies of knowledge. To do so, I look at two quotations from works that contemporary university teaching in the United States sometimes treat as transposable examples of "women of color" writing and might be taught together under rubrics such as "critical perspectives in women's studies" or "studies in race and ethnic literatures." The first is from June Jordan's "Moving Towards Home" (1985), and the second is from Azar Nafisi's *Reading Lolita in Tehran* (2003), which I will subsequently study in depth, taking it as my example of a neoliberal multicultural literary project (Jordan 1989, 142–43).

What is at stake in both quotes are the politics of literary identification or, more precisely, the political allegory that we may interpret from the troping of literary identification. The first quote comes from Jordan's "Moving Towards Home." The occasion for Jordan's poem is the Phalangist-Israeli massacre of Palestinian refugees in Sabra and the Shantila camps of Lebanon in 1982. The poem begins with an epigraph taken from a *New York Times* article on the massacre, which cites a speaker who is identified only by gender: " 'Where is Abu Fadi,' she wailed. / 'Who will bring me my loved one?' " The poem then narrates multiple scenes from the massacre (a bulldozer covering bodies, the rape of a nurse), each framed by the assertion of the poem's "I" narrator that she "does not wish to speak about" each incident. After reviewing the language of "extermination" used by the perpetrators to speak the atrocity, the narrator states a "need to speak about living room," where such events do not happen and where Abu Fadi is not missed "because he will be there beside me." The quotation I want to examine is the poem's final stanza group:

> I was born a Black woman
> And now
> I am become a Palestinian
> against the relentless laughter of evil
> there is less and less living room
> and where are my loved ones?
> It is time to make our way home.

Typical of women of color feminism's analytical project, the poem is anti-identitarian; it performs an act of excessive identification on the part of the narrator that defies the protocols that make identitarianisms coherent (a first-person singular "I" having been "born a Black woman / ... am become a Palestinian"). The passage exemplifies the conjoined epistemological-political project of women of color feminism: it works as politics in the first place by innovating ways of knowing that abrogate normal politics. Arjun Appadurai has described a similar process as the use of "the imagination as a social practice" (Appadurai 1996, 31). As the impossible appears in literature (a black woman is made over as a Palestinian), a thinking of justice opens up that necessarily flouts the ordinary mandates of national borders and fixed identities.

The excessive identification that the passage declares is, in the context of the poem, in the first instance a *political* (not psychological) identification that emerges out of *intersectional analysis*, a core epistemological project of women of color feminism, which analyzes race, class, gender, sexuality, religion, location, and other factors as intersecting (not discrete) processes crossing domains of practical consciousness and macrosocial institutions. The two positions "Black woman" and "Palestinian" are bridged by analytical and experiential juxtapositions, including a practical consciousness of the past and present of divergent but interlocking state racisms (in Israel and the United States) within (neo)colonial capitalism. We are made to see how racialized, classed, and militarized forms of occupation connect the national occupation of Israel-Palestine to the economic, urban, and cultural circumstances that crowd and confine many African American women (i.e., urban segregation, trapping poverty, confining cultural images).

The poem does not privilege gender as a sort of universal transfer point for identification among women; the narrator is made over, or made also, a "Palestinian" unmarked by gender. Because the poetic performance is called into being in response to the wail in its epigraph that is identified, only semianonymously, as female, Palestinian, refugee, "woman" as a category of difference is preserved. The poem's troping of the politics of literary identification, "a Black woman . . . am become Palestinian," thus remains answerable to the trace of the female Palestinian subaltern.

We can interpret the passage as an expression of an oppositional politics that grounds transnational solidarity in a shared vulnerability to violence, by attending to the passage's play on the idea of "living room." *Lebensraum* was the watchword for German imperialism. "Living room" in Jordan's poem, in contrast, is a watchword for a "homely" politics based on the minimal demand that the people you love cannot be removed violently from your home. Along these lines, in the poem's concluding call for the reader to participate in "making our way home," "home" is an open figure for a secure life, in contrast to the violences that link Sabra-Shantila and black urban poverty. Literary identification thus allegorizes a process of building strange affinities beyond identitarianism, using the framework for nourishing life envisioned by subjugated classes for whom "the world is a ghetto" (see Winant 2001).

The second quote comes from Azar Nafisi's *Reading Lolita in Tehran: A Memoir in Books*. A transnational migrant between Iran and the United States (the U.S.-educated daughter of a former mayor of Tehran under the reign of Reza Shah Pahlavi), Azar Nafisi was a junior professor of English literature at the University of Tehran during the Islamic Revolution and continued to teach in Iran after the revolution. Since leaving Iran for the United States in 1997, Nafisi has been integrated as a New Immigrant intellectual into centrist and neoconservative policy and academic circles. *Reading Lolita in Tehran* tells the story of Nafisi's experience as an upper-class woman, mother, wife, and professor of English literature from the beginning of the Islamic Revolution to her return to the United States. At the heart of the memoir is a secret class, something like a book group, which she organizes in her home for her most dedicated female students. According to the book's narrative protocol, the idea is that great literature can help women achieve self-actualization within the confines of severe gender oppression in the Islamic Republic of Iran. The passage I want to look at describes her students' reaction to Henry James's *Daisy Miller*:

> Daisy was the character my female students most identified with. Some of them became obsessed. Later in my workshop, they would come to her time and time again, speaking of her courage, something they felt they had lacked. Mahshid and Mitra spoke of her with regret in their writings; like Winterbourne, they felt they were bound to make a mistake about her. (Nafisi 2003, 333)

In contrast to Jordan's excessive act of identification that shakes up the foundations of identitarianism, Nafisi's passage values literature as a means of shoring up a psychologically coherent female identity modeled on James's "American Girl." In further contrast to Jordan's poem, a feminist cultural universalist idea of woman has everything to do with identification in the passage from Nafisi. The only heterogeneity the category of woman maintains in this passage is assimilationist: Iranian woman seeking to become (like) woman in the West. Represented as marginal subjects to U.S.-European women, Nafisi (the textual figure) and her female students—elite postcolonials and once and future migrants to the metropole—efface for readers in the United States those marginalized or cut off from social mobility in Iran, especially rural women and the urban poor.

Where Jordan's poem crafts the literary text as something that lets us reread the social text (letting intersectional analysis ride on the literary imagination), Nafisi's passage relies on a literary formalism to evacuate the material histories that join Europe and the United States to the Middle East. Finally, in contrast to Jordan's "living room," a desired domain of security for people made chronically insecure, Nafisi's "living room," the location of her book group, is an unspoken and unspeakably bourgeois space, where Western cultural and political supremacy are taken for granted, and "home" is part of a moral and affective code that legitimates a politics of privatization.

While both passages may appear superficially to be examples of multicultural women of color writing, I argue that *Reading Lolita in Tehran* appropriates the cultural authority of women of color feminism while hollowing out its epistemological and political project. Where Jordan's poem exposes racialized, militarized social and epistemological orders that confine African American women and Palestinians in ways that resonate, *Reading Lolita in Tehran* depicts Iranian-Muslim women desiring to become more like James's "American Girl" in a way that manufactures a will for U.S.-sponsored "liberation" of women in Iran. In place of women of color feminism's anti-identitarianism and intersectional analysis, we get the molding of women as self-possessed, possessive individuals and native informants who validate ideological truths about the desires of Iranian women to be more like American women. Thus we can distinguish the critical comparative analysis enacted in Jordan's poem, which lets us think the unevenness of the biopolitics of global capitalism, from the hegemonic comparative method Nafisi's memoir performs, where codes for racialized and gendered difference compose an assimilative multicultural order that makes U.S. global hegemony appear just and fair.

Neoliberal Multiculturalism's Deployment of Racialized and Gendered Difference: Producing the Global Multicultural Citizen as a Privileged Racial Subject

Let us begin by considering neoliberal multiculturalism as a signifying practice in which a language of multiculturalism dissimulates the racialized social and economic structure of neoliberalism. Race continues to permeate capitalism's economic and social processes in neoliberalism. It organizes the hyperextraction of surplus value from racialized bodies and naturalizes a system of capital accumulation that grossly favors the global North over the global South. Yet a kind of multicultural rhetoric portrays neoliberal policy as the key to a postracist world of freedom and opportunity. Neoliberal policy engenders new racial subjects as it creates and distinguishes between newly privileged and stigmatized collectivities. Yet a kind of multiculturalism codes the wealth, mobility, and political power of neoliberalism's beneficiaries to be the just desserts of "multicultural world citizens." A language of multiculturalism consistently portrays acts of force required for neoliberal restructuring to be humanitarian: a benevolent multicultural invader (the United States, multinational troops, a multinational corporation) intervenes to save lives, give basic goods or jobs, and promote limited political freedoms. In all these expressions, an idea of the ethic of multiculturalism appears as the spirit of neoliberalism.[1]

In a previous essay, I tracked the development of official antiracism in the United States from racial liberalism to neoliberal multiculturalism and examined neoliberal multiculturalism in depth as a global racial formation (Melamed 2006). My argument here follows from the larger argument of that essay. To understand the significance I accord Nafisi's memoir, I focus on how neoliberal multiculturalism constructs the global multicultural citizen as a privileged racial subject by using specifically racialized representations of women (women of color, Third World women, Muslim women) and by fashioning for its own ends the knowledge-making and subject-forming powers of American universities and literary studies.

Since the previous essay and today, the global recession has led to a mainstream reassessment of neoliberalism for the first time in thirty years. The crisis has cast doubt on the drive to deregulate, the superiority of free markets over governments, the increasing emphasis on speculative capitalism, and the capacities of global regulatory institutions. It is not clear how the crisis will be managed and whether or not such management will deepen, displace, or revise neoliberalism. In any case, neoliberal multiculturalism as a racial formation will not soon disappear from the scene. This is because it is written on the ground, as it were, in the processes of valuation-devaluation and internalization-externalization that drive social reproduction and in the subject formation of persons.

Let me give a brief genealogy of neoliberal multiculturalism and discuss some of the key modes of valuation and devaluation it operates as a racial formation. Neoliberal multiculturalism represents the latest configuration of a new articulation of racial ideology and capitalism that arises with U.S. hegemony in the post–World War II period and with what Howard Winant calls "the racial break" (Winant 2001, 31–33). Previous articulations of race, geopolitics, and capitalism relied on white supremacy to ideologically unify colonialism and its corresponding capitalist relations. After World War II, however, white supremacy entered a phase of permanent crisis, spurred initially by the casting of the war as a fight against racism and fascism and by the numerous and overlapping postwar anticolonial and antiracist movements. As the United States rose to global prominence after World War II and became the agent of transnational capitalist expansion, it had both to manage the racial contradictions and antagonisms that gave rise to anticolonial and antiracist movements and to counter Soviet propaganda that decried racial violence in the United States as proof that American-style democracy and capitalism were hopelessly compromised by white supremacy.

In doing so, the United States rearticulated relations between racial ideology and capitalism: whereas before World War II, white supremacy justified the nongeneralizability of colonial capitalist wealth, after World War II, with global decolonization and the Cold War, the United States deployed an official or state antiracism to legitimate its geopolitical ascendancy and the transnational capitalism it led. Articulated within a liberal symbolic framework of abstract equality, market individualism, and inclusive civic nationalism, official U.S. antiracism, initially articulated in the Cold War as racial liberalism, maintained that the integration of African Americans as equal citizens of the United States would morally legitimate U.S. global leadership, especially in the eyes of formerly colonial nation-states in Asia and Africa.

Official or state antiracism in the United States, as it emerged first in the form of racial liberalism, recognized racial equality as a national social and political goal. However, it also narrowed the scope of antiracist thinking and goals to those that were compatible with or privileged the nation-state, national security, and other goals compatible with "Americanism." While expanding some liberal freedoms and inventing a racially inclusive nationalism, official liberal antiracism also modernized racialized privilege and discipline and adapted these to postcolonial conditions and the demise of legal segregation. By binding antiracism to U.S. nationalism, as this bears the agency of transnational capitalism, it also depoliticizes the links between race and economy (a relationship critical to 1930s and 1940s antiracist thinking in the African American public sphere and movements from Pan-Africanism to the Popular Front) (see Von Eschen 1997). Because the scope of the political in the postwar United States precisely shields matters of economy from robust democratic review, official forms of antiracism *depoliticize* capitalism by collapsing it with Americanism. This results in a situation where official antiracist discourse and politics actually limit awareness of global capitalism.

When the subsequent civil rights movement revealed the limitations of the racial liberal framework, liberal multiculturalism emerged as an ascendant form of official antiracism that seemed to provide greater (cultural) recognition and (representative) equality but continued to function as a nationalist antiracism that associated Americanism with the benefits of capitalism. It depoliticized economic arrangements by decisively integrating individualism, property rights, and market economies into what racial equality may signify or what may signify as racial equality (for example, equal opportunity to compete, abstract equality before the law, and the right to own and dispense of property without covenants or other restrictions). Liberal multiculturalism's framework for racial equality, which focused on cultural integration and full recognition of multiracial and multicultural identities, cohered well with post-Keynesian times in the 1980s and 1990s. Its pluralist framework took for granted the primacy of individual and property rights at the cost of collective and substantive social rights. This made it possible not to recognize as race matters the downsizing of state responsibility for social welfare and the growing power of concentrated wealth and capital to diminish human life and to escape accountability from the diminishing regulatory powers of government.

Like racial liberalism and liberal multiculturalism, neoliberal multiculturalism provides a restricted sense of antiracist equality and codes U.S.-led global capitalist developments as beneficial. Yet in contrast to the earlier official antiracisms, which are in the weave of nationalist discourses that dissimulate capitalist development as part of racial equality *for people*, here a multicultural formalism is abstracted from anything but an ideal relation to concrete human groups and instead directly codes an economic order of things. It represents a certain set of economic policies as multicultural rights and portrays the equality of the free market as the most fundamental

expression of equality. In addition, it remakes categories of racialized privilege and stigma beyond color lines, representing the advantages enjoyed by
neoliberalism's winners to be the just desserts of global multicultural citizens. Since the civil rights era, liberal individualism has limited the ability
of dominant antiracist thinking to grasp the economic, legal, political, and
epistemic structures that anonymously produce racially unequal outcomes.
With the apotheosis of the individual in neoliberal rationality, it has become
even easier for seemingly antiracist or multicultural thinking to misrecog-
nize systemic failures in social and economic relations to be the result of
individual characteristics, choices, and personalities.

After the racial break, liberal race procedures are unevenly detached
from a wholesale white supremacist logic of race as phenotype, yet they
remain deeply embedded in a logic of race as a set of "historic repertoires
and cultural, spatial and signifying systems that stigmatize and depreciate
one form of humanity for the purposes of another's health, development,
safety, profit or pleasure" (Singh 2004, 223). Privileged and stigmatized
racial formations no longer mesh perfectly with a color line. Instead new
categories of privilege and stigma determined by ideological, economic,
and cultural criteria overlay older, conventional racial categories such that
traditionally recognized racial identities—black, Asian, white, or Arab-Mus-
lim—can now occupy both sides of the privilege-stigma opposition.

I see neoliberal multicultural racialization as operating along with what
Aihwa Ong calls "differentiated citizenship" (2006, 89–92). According to
Ong, the dictates of global capitalism have entered state administration, so
that to maximize profitability and to minimize doing what is unprofitable,
governments subject populations to different treatments according to their
worth within (or their connection to, or isolation from) neoliberal circuits
of value. This leads to the dis- and rearticulation of citizenship rights,
entitlements, and benefits into different elements whose exercise is then
associated with neoliberal criteria. Mobile individuals with human capital
exercise citizenship-like claims in diverse locations, while other citizens are
devalued and vulnerable, in practice unable to exercise many rights and
subject to the state's disciplining and civilizing or disqualifying regimes
rather than the pastoral care bestowed on the state's supposedly more worthy
citizens (14–21). Neoliberal multiculturalism as a racial formation helps to
make the internalization-externalization procedures Ong describes appear
fair by innovating new systems for ascribing privilege and stigma and laying

these over previous racial logics. Neoliberalism scripts its beneficiaries as worthy multicultural global citizens and its losers as doomed by their own monoculturalism, deviance, inflexibility, criminality, and other attributes.

The unevenness of neoliberal racialization is often what gives it its power to racialize without seeming racist. As neoliberal calculations in governance produce differential citizenship, with subjects of value for neoliberal circuits able to exercise citizenship-like entitlements beyond national borders and unvalued subjects losing elements of citizenship in situ or as migrants, a certain moral calculus normalizes these everyday relations of difference and inequality. These neoliberal codes, which fix human potentials and justify different social fates, interact with preexisting ethnoracial schemes that "can be reinforced and crosscut out by new ways of governing that differentially values populations according to market calculations" (Ong 2006, 79). In the United States, this means a new flexibility in racial procedures, such that racism constantly appears to be disappearing according to conventional race categories, even as neoliberal racialization continues to justify inequality using codes that can signify as nonracial or even antiracist.

I take the definition of race as a set of "historic repertoires and cultural, spatial and signifying systems that stigmatize and depreciate one form of humanity for the purposes of another's health, development, safety, profit or pleasure" from Nikhil Singh. Singh reminds us in *Black Is a Country* (2004) that color lines became meaningful in Western capitalist modernity as they overlapped with other criteria used to represent those who are cut off from capitalist wealth (or exploited for its accumulation) as outsiders to liberal subjectivity from whom life can be disallowed to the point of death. We must now ask how, in an era of economic globalization, historic repertoires and cultural, spatial, and signifying systems have shifted to include and exclude on the basis of being an insider or outsider to neoliberal subjectivity and its moral calculus. As neoliberalism's social relations of production interpellate and order subjects within managerial and professional regimes or regimes of labor and incarceration, terms of privilege accrue to individuals and groups—attributes such as multicultural, reasonable, feminist, and law-abiding—making them appear fit for neoliberal subjectivity, while others are stigmatized as monocultural, irrational, regressive, patriarchal, or criminal and ruled out. Such individualization disappears structural and material relations that position persons within modes of production and structures of governance.

Importantly, "multicultural" signifies as antiracist even as it becomes a way of ascribing racialized privilege to some forms of humanity. As economic citizenship becomes more central to racial procedures, I suggest that while the idea of whiteness as property still holds, globalization also creates "multicultural" as a new form of whiteness, or rather, the category of whiteness and its privileges are displaced into the category of multiculturalism. Traditional white privilege still comes into play in the United States even as some white people are left behind or left unprotected as government shifts from service to (its historically favored white) citizens to capital maximization within globalization, which requires and produces a multiracial, multilingual, multicultural elite. At the same time, neoliberal racialization can intensify technologies for disqualifying, civilizing, and disciplining people of color without class privilege, renewing older racial schemata.

American universities have become a key site for racializing individuals of value to neoliberalism as multicultural and for teaching them the codes of privilege and stigma that naturalize contemporary biopolitics and its uneven distributions. Aihwa Ong notes, "American universities have attracted a multicultural, multinational and mobile population, the very kind of educated, multilingual and self-reflexive subjects now considered to be the most worthy individuals" (Ong 2006, 155). According to Ong, under the aegis of self-care, university training inculcates individuals with attributes that teach them to bear the agency of neoliberal capitalism, egoistic individualism, self-enterprise, and calculative practices, qualities that are then taken to distinguish multicultural global citizens. Students most often learn the racializing codes for vulnerable or exploited groups through so-called leadership training and discourses of mission, benevolence, and reform. As students learn to do good, to feed the poor, to uplift women, and to assume responsibility for near and distant others, they learn to play their parts in the civilizing and disqualifying regimes that target populations disconnected from circuits of neoliberal wealth and value.

Conversely, one of the key elements of citizenship being lost by those who do not win under neoliberalism is access to higher education. Those without college educations are racialized as lacking, monocultural, backward, inept, unambitious, and incapable, with these codes overlapping conventional phenotypical racial categories and meanings, adding flexibility to white, African American, Asian American, Latino, and American Indian racialization. Such racialization prepares one socially to be governed by technologies of labor and incarceration, rather than the pastoral technologies that nurture multicultural citizens. While whites continue to receive preference based on skin color alone, the lack of access to higher education for poor and working-class students has intensified to become the most pressing civil rights issue in higher education. Class remains racialized, and the racialized fixing of human potential by class keeps large pools of temporary and vulnerable workers available. One striking example of how neoliberal multicultural racialization intensifies conventional racialized exclusion by denying access to higher education is the passing and enforcement of the Immigration Reform Act of 2006. Contradicting the equal-protection clause and reversing long-standing denizen rights, the act states that illegal aliens cannot be considered residents of a state for purposes of assessing tuition at public universities. Denying undocumented students mobility through higher education is just one strategy that racializes immigrants as fugitive populations, contributing to a matrix of laws, informal social customs, economic systems, and symbolic systems that keep abandoned and unvalued populations—immigrant and citizen—more vulnerable to isolation and exploitation. Recognizing a fundamental coherence between such strategies and those that maintained slavery and a Jim Crow social order, Rachel Buff has coined the term "Undergraduate Railroad" to refer to the covert and often illegal work of administrators, faculty, and communities to provide in-state tuition to undocumented students (see Buff 2008).

Literature also enters into the training of transnational professional-managerial classes as an element of the technologies of subjectivity, which influence the self-making of elites, and technologies of subjugation, which elites learn to exercise to manage less-profitable populations. On the one hand, the idea that literature has something to do with antiracism and being a good person enters into the self-care of elites, who learn to see themselves as part of a multinational group of enlightened multicultural global citizens and to uphold certain standards as (neoliberal) multicultural universals. On the other hand, the idea that engaging with literature helps one to come to terms with difference ethically prepares elites to administer differentiated citizenship across the globe. In other words, literary training prepares them for the part they will play within disciplinary and civilizing and disqualifying regimes that manage populations cut off from (or exploited within) circuits of global capitalism.

In the last ten years, much excellent scholarship has examined the retool-

ing of American universities to produce a transnational managerial-professional class for global capitalism and how this has impacted the teaching of
literature. Gayatri Chakravorty Spivak wrote presciently in the early 1990s
of a "new orientalism" of Third World literatures (Spivak 1993, 56). David
Palumbo-Liu (*The Ethnic Canon*), Inderpal Grewal (*Transnational America*), and others have analyzed the recruitment of U.S. ethnic literatures to
represent marginality according to the requirements for constructing globalizing metropolitans as the new center (Palumbo-Liu 1995; Grewal 2005).
The recent emergence of the rubric "global literature"—a category so broad
that it seems to call for theme-based (i.e., ideologically driven) teaching
rather than rigorous transnational literacy—would seem to prove the accuracy of their analysis.

How does neoliberal multiculturalism seek to fashion literary culture,
practices of reading, and literary value? In line with literature's centrality for
nineteenth- and early twentieth-century European liberalisms, which
helped to provide the social organization and ideological legitimation for
European colonialism, literature after the racial break has been integrated
into the forms of liberal race hegemony that organize post–World War II
American society and global ascendancy. I argue in other work that the
functions literature fulfilled within colonial knowledge-power processes
have been displaced into and revised within the era after the racial break
(Melamed 2008). High cultural ideas of literature continue to assert the
excellence and universalism of the West (now led by the United States) and
to distinguish between superior and inferior forms of human life. Postwar
liberal antiracism and the need for antiracist social transformation also
continue to cathect to an idea of literature as a tool for information retrieval
and for entering into a sympathetic relation with a culturally distant other.
First with the race novel of the 1950s, and today with multicultural literature, literature by writers of color or about race is defined as a medium
uniquely able to express the intimate truths of racial conditions and consciousness and to powerfully communicate these across race lines to arouse
sympathy in white audiences. Within a paradigm that understands race
chiefly as prejudice or a matter of white attitude, the idea of literature as a
powerful tool for arousing white sympathies assigns it a leading role in
ending racial inequality.

Neoliberal multiculturalism continues to pose literature as a solution to
problems of knowledge and relation. Where racial liberals in the 1950s once

read African American literature as native informant texts to bolster the idea of a racially inclusive liberal nationalism that could morally legitimate U.S. Cold War hegemony, today a managerial-professional class for global capitalism reads multicultural, ethnic, and postcolonial novels as native informant texts to learn good global citizenship. We can see this in the new relevance of world literatures, often the work of Anglophone postcolonial diasporics, justified as an effective tool to help Americans get to know diversity. As mentioned previously, Gayatri Chakravorty Spivak has noted the importance of literary culture to socialize and legitimate a professional-managerial class in the United States as multicultural-savvy agents for global capitalism. Spivak warns that the institutionalization of world and multicultural literatures through a diversity-requirement approach has been made necessary by the financialization of the globe and the corre-sponding imperative for U.S.-based readers to (think that they) know the world (Spivak 1993, 277). For Inderpal Grewal, this translates to U.S. read-ers of world or postcolonial literature being trained to extract preconceived information about "female oppression in the Global South" from literature as diverse as Bharati Mukherjee's *Jasmine* and Nawal El Saadawi's *The Fall of the Imam*, a move that reinforces the hegemonic rendering of female em-powerment as the mission of the global North and helps to ideologically consolidate the economic restructuring required by capitalism as the duties of good global citizenship.

As Grewal suggests, the cultural politics of literary culture often intersect with the global symbolic politics coalescing around the figure of "woman in the South." Supplementing Grewal, I suggest that literature written by or about woman in the South (or woman in the Middle East) gets recruited not only for discourses of legitimation but also, importantly, for discourses of information and rationalism that have become key to sublating problems of knowledge and relation, which global interventions by the United States might otherwise evoke. Given the need to produce and disseminate infor-mation about the Middle East to American audiences to make U.S. inter-ventions in the region legible, women's writing, cast as transparent and easily accessible "evidence," functions in place of or alongside scholarship.

While dominant reading practices in the United States after 1945 subject *all* racialized women's writing to presumptions of authenticity and truth telling, women's autobiography and memoir are particularly so construed. The international controversy over the facticity of *I, Rigoberta Menchú: An*

Indian Woman in Guatemala is a case in point (see Burgos-Debray 1998). First, it demonstrates the degree to which women of and in the global South are set up to be native informants for U.S. audiences. As Mary Pratt notes, *I, Rigoberta Menchú* was a key text for multiculturalism in American universities in the 1980s and 1990s (Pratt 2001). In line with multiculturalism's agenda to decenter a Eurocentric curriculum, *I, Rigoberta Menchú* was positioned as a representative and authentic text about contemporary Mayan life and culture, about the recent political history of Guatemala, and much more. Although sometimes taught as *testimonio*, a genre that implies representational complexity—a hybridization of oral interview, mediated transcriptions, situational transmission, and composite accounts—the fact that the book's prestige could be undermined by factual errors demonstrates the degree to which its value lay in its treatment as truth-telling autobiography.

We can evaluate David Stoll's *Rigoberta Menchú and the Story of All Poor Guatemalans* (1999) to be an early neoliberal multicultural attack on Menchú's status. In contrast to U.S. liberal multiculturalists, Stoll recognizes and would subvert Menchú's testimonio as a political document (not transparent truth) meant to focus attention on the "scorched-earth warfare" of military governments in Guatemala against leftist movements in the late 1970s and early 1980s.[2] Although his interest is mostly in the Culture Wars, Stoll's text, in fact, in the contemporary geopolitical context appropriates indigeneity to support a neoliberal agenda. Claiming that the more "authentic" (i.e., less educated, less traveled, less left politicized) tribal members of Menchú's village just wanted to be "left alone" by the leftist movements, Stoll construes indigeneity as nonengaged, desiring privacy and self-sufficiency; this cultural-values language is key to the code that construes neoliberalism as a moral good. The politics of representing "what Indians want" takes on increased urgency in light of the extraordinary movement, since the publication of Menchú's testimonio, of pan-indigenous movements in Central and South America into national politics, especially the election of Evo Morales in Bolivia, and their often trenchant critique of neoliberal goals and agendas.

If *I, Rigoberta Menchú* is a political text woven in the fabric of left resistance to Cold War military oligarchy in Guatemala, which liberal multiculturalism appropriates as the authentic cultural expression of an indigenous Mayan woman, then Azar Nafisi's *Reading Lolita in Tehran*, however much it touches on the fabric of political resistance to gender oppression in the Islamic Republic of Iran, has been appropriated by multicultural neo-liberalism as a cultural text that provides the truth of "woman in Iran" for the war on terror and helps to ideologically consolidate an assimilationist multicultural neoliberal universalism.

Reading Tehran in *Lolita*: Seizing Literary Value for Neoliberal Multiculturalism

Why would a major foreign policy institute appoint a professor of literature to direct one of its key projects? At first glance, Azar Nafisi might seem an un-likely choice to head the Dialogue Project at the School of Advanced Inter-national Studies at Johns Hopkins University. But when we grasp neoliberal multiculturalism and how it links geopolitics, literary value, and racialized gender, Nafisi's appointment as director makes sense, especially following her rise to prominence with the success of *Reading Lolita in Tehran*.

The Dialogue Project's website initially describes its goal as being "to promote—in a primarily cultural context—the development of democracy and human rights in the Muslim World."[3] But it soon becomes apparent that the real target is not "them" but "us": "The Dialogue Project seeks to educate those in non-Muslim communities—whether they be policy mak-ers, scholars, development professionals, members of the media or ordinary citizens—in the complexities and contradictions that govern both Western relations with and life in many predominantly Muslim societies." In other words, the Dialogue Project seeks broad-based influence over the political conversation in the United States about the relationship between the West and "the Muslim World."

In *The Twilight of Equality?* (2003), Lisa Duggan persuasively argues that the rhetorical strategy of forging a "Third Way" is central to neoliberal cultural politics (Duggan 2003, 48–50). We find such a strategy at work in the Di-alogue Project, which positions itself as an alternative to both Huntington-style "Clash of Civilizations" thinking and "Islamism." It then associates left-progressive U.S. scholarship with Islamism and goes on to make its central point:

> Unfortunately, whether consciously or unconsciously, many in the West have become complicit in imposing the Islamist discourse on interna-tional relations. Among the expert and policy communities, people have

adopted a language and a mindset that encompass concepts such as "Western cultural imperialism" and "cultural relativism"—deploring the former as they applaud the latter. In this way, the worst claims of Islamist rhetoric are accepted as fact, and this apologist thinking imposes on the peoples of the Muslim-majority countries a repressive form of cultural determinism.[4]

How does left-progressive thinking—dehistoricized, abstracted, and caricatured as cultural relativism and Western cultural imperialism—get allied with Islamism? Apparently what unites these two positions is a "cultural relativism" that "encourage[s] a conception of culture and ethnic heritage as essentially static and closed, and which see[s] the change that results from cultural interaction as a culturally corrosive and unwelcome development."

Distinguishing itself from such a closed and unified conception of culture, the Dialogue Project defines its putatively commonsensical position as one that grasps the multiplicity of all cultures. But instead of a robustly integrative sense of the heterogeneity and dynamic nature of *every* culture, the Dialogue Project emphasizes that so-called Muslim-majority countries and cultures are open to transformation. Its distinctly assimilationist view assumes that Muslim-majority countries and cultures would change and adapt to resemble the United States but for the influence of local Islamists and their progressive-left U.S. academic collaborators. These academics mislead Muslims with their ideology of "Western cultural imperialism," the idea that "the growing influence of Western—primarily American—culture throughout the world [is] a damaging, callous, and morally reprehensible imposition on other societies and traditions." In contrast, the Dialogue Project's vision is multicultural in the sense that it insists that all the world's multiple cultures are or should be free to become America.

The Dialogue Project's depiction of an American academy unknowingly permeated by Islamism functions in the first place to delegitimate postcolonial studies and any scholarship that situates U.S. geopolitics in the history of colonialism and neocolonialism. More broadly, it works to undermine the authority of the academy as a whole.[5] Importantly, it constructs an idea of a virtual (neoliberal) public in support of its own putatively commonsensical position, a strategy to seize the terms of public debate that resembles Nixon's "silent majority" strategy.

Azar Nafisi herself, in her capacity as the Dialogue Project's female and

Iranian director, stands as evidence for the inclusive nature of the neoliberal multicultural consensus the Dialogue Project envisions. Yet Nafisi's own *Reading Lolita in Tehran*, I argue, is an infinitely more successful example of multicultural neoliberal cultural politics, one that refashions seemingly progressive (i.e., antiracist) and conservative (i.e., family values) ideologemes into a presumed consensus position, which appears nonpolitical, neutral, and universal as it secures consent for neoliberal processes and agendas. With *Reading Lolita in Tehran*, we see that the politics of literature and race have moved into a distinctly post–Culture Wars phase: multiculturalism is no longer opposed to a "vital center" or "common culture" (imagined as global and Eurocentric simultaneously); rather, the former serves as proof of the latter's inclusiveness.

I do not analyze *Reading Lolita in Tehran* in terms of authorial intentions or interpretations. In contrast to Hamid Dabashi, who has denounced Nafisi as "the Fox News anchorperson of Western literature" and accused her of "seeking to recycle a kaffeeklatsch version of English literature as the ideological foregrounding of American empire," I disclaim all ad hominem attacks.[6] Rather, I consider how the particular system of signs at work in *Reading Lolita in Tehran* shores up axiomatics of neoliberal multiculturalism, even as neoliberal multiculturalism "produces unquestioned ideological correlatives for the narrative structuring of the book" (Spivak 1999, 133).

My reading throughout is attentive to the special purchase that comes with the weaving together of the genres of memoir and "great books literary criticism," signaled in *Reading Lolita in Tehran*'s subtitle, *A Memoir in Books*. On the one hand, the authority of memoir rests on the *particular* identity and experience of the author, who, according to convention, is collapsed with the memoir's narrator. Authenticity, which is how literary value is construed for memoir, relies on particularity. In American literary history, this is associated with the role of literature in liberal race reform, with race novels and memoirs by authors of color conceived as vehicles for the transmission of racial consciousness and conditions. The authority of great books literary criticism, on the other hand, relies on the presumed *universality* of great literature and on the critic's ability to communicate and, indeed, to wield the power of the universal. In American literary history, great books literary criticism accompanies canon-building projects that use literary value to secure the perceptions, beliefs, and experiences of elites as the norm, or what is to be desired or esteemed.

Reading Lolita in Tehran merges these two traditions of literary value in a narrative that we can reduce to the following equation: an Iranian woman tells her personal emotional and true story of the Islamic Revolution in Iran and its aftermath as the story of how she harnessed the power of great literature as an instrument for the self-liberation of women in Iran. *Reading Lolita in Tehran's* hybrid genre, memoir-literary criticism, enables a powerful and intertwined politics of identity and politics of knowledge. It guarantees its representation of women's oppression by the Islamic Republic of Iran through the narrator's (Nafisi's) expertise in harnessing the universal and transhistorical standpoint of great literature. At the same time, it uses the lens of "great books for women" to redact the total complexity, contradictions, and historicity of Iran to bits of moralistic knowledge that align easily with neoliberal ideological codes for what counts as free or unfree, fair or unfair, good Muslim or bad Muslim.

Many critics have commented on the cover of *Reading Lolita in Tehran*: a sepia-toned photograph of two young women in dark hijab looking down with modest expressions at something cropped out of the image. In keeping with the work's title, perhaps we are to imagine that they are reading a volume of Nabokov together. It turns out, as Hamid Dabashi has scandalously uncovered, that the image is actually an extreme alteration of part of a photograph, which presents two very modern, young Iranian women reading a newspaper article about the election to the presidency of reform candidate Mohammed Khatami in 1997. According to Dabashi, the transformed photograph symbolizes *Reading Lolita in Tehran's* neo-Orientalizing tendencies: it transforms an image of women involved in, and absorbed by, internal politics in Iran into a titillating representation of two young Iranian Lolitas for American audiences.[7] My reading of the text as one that offers Nafisi and her female students to American readers as candidates for assimilation to a global multicultural public leads me to offer another take on the photo. When we blur our eyes, their hijabs seem to become the head scarves of that archetype of U.S. citizenship, the Ellis Island immigrant, and their eager expressions and glowing pale skin seem to come not from their excitement over *Lolita* but from eager anticipation of joining the American project. Just as whiteness embodied the ideological coordinates for conferring U.S. citizenship during the Ellis Island era, the global citizenship that neoliberal multiculturalism confers has its own ideological requirements. These are now embodied not only as white but also as multicultural and overlap with cultural and economic criteria to ascribe privilege and stigma, internalizing some into the neoliberal project while externalizing others as unfit for (neo)liberal subjectivity.

Reading Lolita in Tehran's narrative arc tells the story of the self-making of Nafisi and the students she refers to as "my girls" into First World approximate versions of "empowered women" through the agency of Western literature and against the gender apartheid of Khomeini's regime. At the center of the story is a woman's consciousness-raising book group. Nafisi gathers together her most dedicated students from the University of Tehran and Allameh Tabatabai University in her living room on Thursday mornings. She approaches the "great books" on her reading list as tools for the self-development of her "girls" and their emotional survival of gender apartheid; her goal is to see "how these great works of imagination could help us in our present trapped situation as women . . . to find a link between the open spaces the novels provided and the closed ones we were confined to" (Nafisi 2003, 19).

The text appears to endorse a feminist cultural universalism, even referring to the book club as a "communal room of our own" (19). But as the individual stories of Nafisi and her students demonstrate, what is most important in the text's construction of women's self-actualization is that the terms of female emancipation are absolutely bound up with codes for cultural values that dissimulate neoliberal measures as good, natural, and right. In other words, feminist cultural universalism serves as the form of appearance of a neoliberal multicultural cultural politics; it naturalizes a necessary relationship between women's freedom, freedom of the imagination, and free markets. *Reading Lolita in Tehran* reworks conventional narratives of female entrance into individualism such that the individualism Nafisi's students achieve is a distinctly neoliberal brand. Nafisi, for example, teaches her girls that Austen's heroines are "rebels," who "risk ostracism and poverty to gain love and companionship and to embrace the elusive goal at the heart of democracy: the right to choose" (307). This "right to choose," in line with neoliberal discourse, collapses the language of economic and individual freedom and is equal parts consumerist and liberal.

We also see the acquisition of a distinctly neoliberal individualism in the arc of one of Nafisi's students, Nassrin, a young woman from a religious family. Gradually, through the agency of literary reflection, Nassrin evolves from a taciturn young girl who keeps her hijab on during the living room sessions to an outspoken young woman who wears jeans and revealing T-shirts and chooses to move to London. Before her departure, Nassrin explains her decision to the book group: "I don't want to be secret and hidden forever. I want to know, to know who this Nassrin is. You'd call it the ordeal of freedom, I guess" (323). The "ordeal of freedom," reminiscent of Cold War rhetoric, in fact, serves as a shibboleth for capitalism coded as freedom of the individual, narrated here as the success of feminist consciousness-raising. (Because the memoir does communicate, with some power, the terrorizing of women in the Islamic Republic of Iran and their experience of the regime's relentless political manipulations of the female body, the language of individualism as neoliberal "freedom" and "choice" often sounds hollow.)

Luxury items and Western-identified consumer goods provide the mise-en-scène for *Reading Lolita in Tehran*'s narrative of female self-emancipation through books. The reader is provided with affect-laden descriptions of the flowers on Nafisi's coffee table, the beautifully wrapped sweets her "girls" bring to the sessions, and how the women dress and groom themselves. Superficially, this mimics the nineteenth-century bourgeois realism of Jane Austen and Henry James, whose novels the women read. But in the contemporary context of global economic citizenship, where the ability to consume defines membership in a transnational elite and counts as a form of political power, it is significant that women's ascension into individualism is played out through their manipulation of, and affinity with, consumer goods. It creates a symbolic relation where consumption indexes female liberation, which attaches emancipatory and affect-laden value to consumer goods themselves. This, in turn, reinforces the presumed legitimacy of a transnational, multicultural consuming class to presume its own universality.

In a further example of the resonance between *Reading Lolita in Tehran*'s protocol and the axiomatics of neoliberal multiculturalism, the book deploys the trope of love to consolidate an ideologeme that appears contradictory outside the framework of a neoliberal cultural politics: the linking of women's power and agency with conservative gender roles and "family values." The narrator Nafisi is repeatedly teased by her students and family for her obsession with love. Furthermore, the memoir invests heavily in love as an expression of female agency. For example, Nafisi teaches her students that the heroines of Jane Austen's novels were, in the social context of the time, "rebels" who "refused to marry men they did not love" (194). The narrative repeatedly contrasts such freedom-in-loving to the Islamic Republic of Iran's "outlawing of love," the repressive, postrevolution laws governing intercourse between men and women, which, according to the memoir, have fostered a political obsession with sex and, correspondingly, diminished personal capacities for love. In line with the memoir's theme of Iranian women achieving self-actualization through reading great books, Austen's novels putatively teach Nafisi's female students that love is a form of resistance to gender oppression in the Islamic Republic of Iran and an effective expression of women's social power.

Making love a sign for female agency makes acceptable the conservative gendering that the protocol of *Reading Lolita in Tehran* takes for granted as normal. The character of Nafisi herself is the best example of this gendering. Although sometimes shown in the classroom as a professional educator, Nafisi is mostly staged in a happy domestic sphere, as a wife and mother, somewhat subservient to her architect-engineer husband, who comes across as the true professional in the family. More disconcertingly, the character Nafisi comes across as distinctly girlish in her obsession with love, in a certain whimsicalness of character, and especially in her relations with "her magician," a close male friend and advisor who regularly chides her for her childlike sensibilities, calling her his Alice in Wonderland.

The heterosexist gendering and romanticization of family life we find in *Reading Lolita in Tehran* is a predominant motif of the cultural politics of privatization. From 1970s neoconservatism through contemporary neoliberalism, policies of upward redistribution that rely on the privatization of public resources and the shifting of social maintenance costs from the government to individuals have ideologically cast the heteronormative family as the locus of responsibility, desire, and relationality (see Reddy 2005). What at first appears to be a paradox in *Reading Lolita in Tehran*'s narrative structure—the combination of seemingly incompatible themes of female self-actualization and individualization with heterosexist gendering and a sentimentalization of family life—makes sense according to neoliberal multicultural axiomatics that have recourse, on the one hand, to the family values talk that casts privatization as a moral good and, on the other hand, to a neoliberal multiculturalism that would legitimate itself on the basis of the freedom it secures for Muslim-Arab women.

Let us now consider *Reading Lolita in Tehran* as literary criticism and the politics of knowledge encoded in its construal of literary value. Although there is no explicit discussion of literary critical methodology in *Reading*

Lolita in Tehran, we can identify it as an innovative work of great books
literary criticism: modern Western classics provide its principle of organization; it models a formalist reading practice; and throughout, it accepts as
necessary and true the methodological and ideological precepts of great
books literary criticism, such as the separation between aesthetics and
politics, the idea of the special moral purpose of literature, and the positing
of a general reader as the addressee of the text. In the history of American
literature, great books literary criticism and its accompanying canon-building projects have secured epistemes of dominance and consent for hegemony as the expression of the best values and traditions of the past and
present.[8]

What is unique in *Reading Lolita in Tehran* is that its aspect as multicultural memoir to some degree disguises it as a new formation of great
books literary criticism. Moreover, the dissonant combination of multicultural memoir and great books literary criticism allows for a new project
of literary canon making, in line with a multicultural neoliberal universalism to be mistaken for a new formation of "embodied knowledge" in the
tradition of critical multiculturalism or women of color feminism. In other
words, by casting the great books as encompassing the truth of Iranian
woman and an instrument for their best development, *Reading Lolita in
Tehran* fortifies the presumed inclusiveness, universality, and excellence of
great literature and thus Western high culture as it is being remade into
global high culture.

In line with great books literary criticism, *Reading Lolita in Tehran* the-
matically secures a separation of spheres between aesthetics and politics,
first by deriding the Khomeini regime's politicization of literature (its fierce
censorship of books and authors), and second by construing the literary to
be a refuge from politics, a private space of personal self-cultivation (a
binary that coheres well with neoliberal castings of the moral value of
privatization). This allows *Reading Lolita in Tehran* to cast its discussion of
great books as politically neutral, even as its literary formalism yields highly
politicized truths about the Islamic Republic of Iran. For example, in the
following passage, the book group reads Nabokov's *Lolita* to reflect on their
personal conditions of unfreedom. In terms of knowledge production, reading *Lolita* for *Reading Lolita in Tehran* allows the total social text of life in
Iran to be absorbed into the literary text of *Lolita,* to produce from the event
of reading a political formalism that categorically condemns the Islamic

Republic of Iran: "I [Nafisi] added that in fact Nabokov had taken revenge against our own solipsizers; he had taken revenge on Ayatollah Khomeini. . . . They had tried to shape others according to their own dreams and desires, but Nabokov, through his portrayal of Humbert, had exposed all solipsists who take over other people's lives" (Nafisi 2003, 33).

In another example, summary judgment is passed on the Iranian Revolution through the lens of *The Great Gatsby*: "[Our] fate [was] similar to Gatsby's. He wanted to fulfill a dream by repeating the past. . . . Was this not similar to our revolution, which had come in the name of a collective past and had wrecked our lives in the name of a dream?" (Nafisi 2003, 144). Through literary formalism, which construes great books as neutral vehicles of higher truths, American readers are presented with a moralism that occupies the place of—and is taken to be as good as—informed analysis of the varieties, purposes, and stages of the Iranian Revolution and Khomeini's rule. The strategic use of literary refraction to make highly politicized knowledge appear objective can be labeled "Reading Tehran in *Lolita*."

Importantly, as part of its politics of knowledge, *Reading Lolita in Tehran* renews the old colonial trope of literary sensibility as a means of distinguishing between those fit or unfit for (neo)liberal subjectivity. In this way, it recruits literature for racializing processes that work beyond the color line, separating good from bad Muslim according to presumably cultural criteria. This comes through distinctly in the Fitzgerald section. Here Nafisi describes how she turned the epidemic of public prosecutions in postrevolutionary Iran into a teaching moment by putting Fitzgerald's *The Great Gatsby* on trial for immorality. She assigns the role of prosecutor to a young man called Mr. Nyazi, a soldier in the Revolutionary Guard and a working-class student leader of the Islamic Student Association, who is an outspoken critic of the text as an "immoral" influence on "our revolutionary youth" (Nafisi 2003, 120). Although *Gatsby* is presumably on trial, *Reading Lolita in Tehran*, in fact, constructs a show trial against Mr. Nyazi and the political, theological, and class fractions he represents, indicting them for dogmatisms and insensitivity to the pain of others. In doing so, it constructs the pro-revolution poor in Iran as unfit for membership in the neoliberal multicultural global community the text conjures.

The key evidence *Reading Lolita in Tehran* offers is Nyazi's dogmatic practice of reading. He prosecutes Gatsby as a bad book that "preaches illicit relations between a man and a woman" with a hero who is "an adulterer, a charlatan, and a liar" (Kaplan 1993, 126). (Indeed, the text captures something of the Khomeini regime's own project of instrumentalizing culture to separate good Muslims from bad Muslims in Nyazi's closing statement that "as a Muslim, [he] cannot accept Gatsby" [Nafisi 2003, 125].) To be *The Great Gatsby*'s defense attorney, Nafisi appoints Zarrin, a stylish, upper-class female student. Her defense makes it clear that Mr. Nyazi's failure as a reader in fact indicts him on the level of identity: "Mr. Nyazi has demonstrated his own weakness: an inability to read a novel on its own terms. All he knows is judgment, crude and simplistic exaltation of right and wrong" (128). Continuing to apply a highly racialized language of moral value to distinguish bad from good Muslims, Zarrin declares that the "carelessness" of the rich in Gatsby "is a reminder of another brand of careless people. Those [typified in Mr. Nyazi] who see in black and white, drunk on the righteousness of their own fictions" (131). *Reading Lolita in Tehran* constructs Mr. Nyazi and Zarrin as oppositional personas, not only in terms of literary sensibility but also in terms of class (poor or wealthy), location (rural or urban), and religion (devout or pragmatic). In this way, racializing codes overlap, so that literary sensibility forms a chain of associations that humanize and privilege rich, cosmopolitan, nominally religious Muslims and, in turn, dehumanize and stigmatize those who are working-class, rural, and devout.

Nafisi appears in the role of defendant, that is, as *The Great Gatsby* itself. Her testimony makes the comprehension of "great literature" a sign for the morality of the reader. As she explains to the jury (her literature class), "A great novel heightens your senses and sensitivity to the complexities of life and of individuals, and prevents you from the self-righteousness that sees morality in fixed formulas about good and evil" (133). The motif of "great books" here serves Nafisi as a kind of social litmus test. Those who say yes to them are candidates for the neoliberal multicultural global community the text imagines on the basis of their capacity for feeling and moral comprehension. Those who say no rule themselves out as inferior, less universal, less fully humane and human persons.

The memoir's narrative arc—its story of female empowerment—converges with its exegesis on the great books at the end of *Reading Lolita in Tehran*, where Nafisi all at once becomes a writer, a liberated woman, and a migrant to the United States. On the cusp of her departure from Tehran, she sits outside in the glow of the late afternoon sunshine to pen her thoughts "for [the] new book" she will write in the United States:

> I have a recurring fantasy that one more article has been added to the Bill of Rights: the right to free access to the imagination. I have come to believe that genuine democracy cannot exist without the freedom to imagine and the right to use imaginative works without restrictions. . . . To me it seemed as if we had not really existed, or only half existed, because we could not imaginatively realize ourselves and communicate to the world. . . . I went about my way rejoicing, thinking how wonderful it is to be a woman and a writer at the end of the twentieth century. (338–39)

In keeping with the neoliberal multicultural tenet that not only is America the whole world ("a nation of immigrants") but the whole world is America, the Bill of Rights need no longer be identified specifically with the United States; it expresses the ideal moral center of the entire world. Collapsing Nafisi's textual moment of self-authoring with the moment when she is about to become a diasporic in the United States, *Reading Lolita in Tehran* equates going to the United States with becoming a participant in the cocreation of the world. As for "the right to free access to the imagination" that sets off the passage's reverie, the very vocabulary and syntax of the phrase mirror neoliberal linguistic codes that use a language of moral values to make its logic of privatization, commodification, and market rule appear just. Free access, with its connotation of open markets, is taken as a right, while the imagination is treated as a commodity that helps to idealize commodities in general. Between the lines of the passage's fuzzy universalism, a notion of great literature (the highest expression of the imagination to which access is demanded) serves to naturalize economic freedom as the same as human freedoms of thought and speech. *Reading Lolita in Tehran*'s story of female achievement culminates with assimilation into the world, where Nafisi and her students are cast as an elite multicultural female leadership class for a neoliberal global order that legitimates neoliberalism in the name of the emancipation of women.

Obscured Opposition: Foreclosing Postcolonial
Studies and Muslim Feminisms

Reading Lolita in Tehran centers some forms of gender, race, and class politics even as it marginalizes others. Through the decontextualizing machine of literary formalism, *Reading Lolita in Tehran* equates feminism with feminist cultural universalism, antiracism with assimilation into a nonredistributive multiculturalism, and erases class politics altogether, implicitly situating fully realized humanity only in the propertied class subject. Significantly, to have its version of gender, race, and class politics appear inevitable, *Reading Lolita in Tehran* must negate or obscure a myriad of post-1968 literary critical movements that potentially activate textual analysis for gender, race, and class analysis not compatible with multicultural neoliberalism.

While it does so mostly by assuming the givenness of its own great books approach, *Reading Lolita in Tehran* goes out of its way to undermine postcolonial studies. Consider the following straw-man attack on Edward Said in the "Jane Austen" section:

> One day after class, Mr. Nahvi [a student and member of the Revolutionary Army] followed me to my office. He tried to tell me that Austen was not only anti-Islamic but that she was guilty of another sin: she was a colonial writer. . . . He told me that *Mansfield Park* was a book that condoned slavery, that even in the West they had now seen the error of their ways. . . . It was only later, on a trip to the States, that I found where Mr. Nahvi was getting his ideas from when I bought a copy of Edward Said's *Culture and Imperialism*. (289–90)

The cartoonish misrepresentation of Edward Said's work from the mouth of an infantile ideologue, treated as more or less accurate by the narrator, demonizes postcolonial studies, through Said, depicting it as politically dogmatic pseudo-scholarship to make Nafisi's own great books reading practice appear nonpolitical and scholarly in comparison. In seeming alliance with neoconservative attacks on the influence of postcolonial studies on area studies, *Reading Lolita in Tehran* attacks postcolonialism's influence in English departments, where in the last twenty years, it has effectively trained students to recognize the joints between the symbolic and epistemological functions of literature and colonial and neocolonial rule, to read literary texts within social texts, and to recognize how the subjectivizing functions of literature work in tandem with (neo)colonial systems of racial-ization, gendering, and sexualizing.

The attack on Said, in fact, appears to be a red herring to draw attention away from the texts and projects of postcolonial feminisms. In particular, I argue that Said functions in the text to efface the scholarship of Gayatri Chakravorty Spivak. Here I can only indicate the formidable contradictions that Spivak's work, if acknowledged, might make visible in the text of *Reading Lolita in Tehran* by summarizing two of Spivak's major interventions in extremely broad strokes. First, Spivak remains attentive, in a deconstruc-tionist vein, to representations of "woman in the margins." In particular, she probes the effacement of the gendered subaltern in and through representa-tions that appear to disclose the figure as a transparent object in the docu-ments and rational systems of the hegemonic (in the past, the colonial archive; in the present, the knowledge systems organizing the financializa-tion of the globe) (see, e.g., Spivak 1994, 66–111; 1999, 306–11; 1996, 245–69). Complementary to this, Spivak analyzes the tendency for the upwardly mobile postcolonial female migrant to appear in the global North in the clothes of her "home country" class subordinate and to be recruited as a native informant to produce information that allows managers for global capitalism to believe that they are doing right by oppressed women.

Second is Spivak's theory of literary training under the rubric of a "hu-manities to come." Defining humanities teaching as "the noncoercive rear-rangement of desire," Spivak theorizes a role for literary training that would interrupt the reflexes and habits of knowing that the global dominant in-stills through university education—habits of self-centering, sanctioned ig-norance, and strategic exclusion that enable the reproduction of global class apartheid (see, e.g., Spivak 1999, 112–97; 2004; 2003). Against "the demand not for clarity but immediate comprehensibility by the ideological average" that "destroys the force of literature as a cultural good," Spivak theorizes literary training as learning to suspend oneself in the text of the other through the built-in virtualizing powers of the imagination (Spivak 2003, 71). She construes a reading practice attentive to the singular and unverifi-able in literature as a concept-metaphor for an engagement between the First World knowledge producer and those below class lines of mobility in the global South, where the former undertakes the impossible task of trying to grasp a cultural inscription that is not her own, with the intention of eliciting an (unverifiable) response from the other.

Shirin Ebadi's memoir *Iran Awakening: A Memoir of Revolution and Hope* (2006) brings into high relief what *Reading Lolita in Tehran* conceals when it is read as a disclosure of the Iranian-Muslim woman on the margin (see Ebadi 2006). Recipient of the Nobel Peace Prize in 2003, Ebadi is a lawyer who fights for the rights of women and children in Iran and is committed to postcolonial principles of self-determination, as well as the idea that a positive interpretation of Islam, democracy, and gender equality can be aligned. Although Ebadi became well-known in the United States after receiving the Nobel Peace Prize, and her memoir was published by a major press (and prominently endorsed by Azar Nafisi), *Iran Awakening* never achieved best-selling status and is seldom taught in American universities.

In contrast to *Reading Lolita in Tehran*'s story of great books as the nurturing medium for female self-development in private life, Ebadi's memoir chronicles her political consciousness-raising as a Muslim feminist and her entrance into public political struggle in Iran. The history of feminist activism in Iran after the revolution that the memoir recounts makes visible the complete absence of both an organized women's movement and a positive vision of Muslim feminism in *Reading Lolita in Tehran*. Furthermore, while Nafisi depicts women to be either violated by the revolution or cynically complicit with it (for example, becoming members of the Morality Police), Ebadi posits a dialectical relationship between the Iranian revolution and Iranian feminism: "In the end, the Iranian Revolution has produced its own opposition, not least in a nation of educated, conscious women, who are agitating for their rights" (215). She cites figures that place women, as of 2006, at 65 percent of all university students and 43 percent of the workforce, noting that after the revolution, traditional parents had no excuse to keep their girls out of schools, now officially Islamic institutions.

Ebadi's life appears representative not through homogenizing the category "Iranian woman" but because others grant her the right to represent them by claiming her political work as their own. In contrast to the end of *Reading Lolita in Tehran*, which narrates Nafisi's departure from Iran as her entrance into freedom as "a woman and a writer" in the United States, Ebadi's memoir ends with her return to the Islamic Republic of Iran after receiving the Nobel Peace Prize. A spontaneous mass demonstration of thousands of women greets her at the Tehran airport, bearing signs such as "This Is Iran" and "We Are United for Peace and Humanity." Disrupting neoliberalism's supposedly feminist geopolitics, Ebadi asserts that "women in Iran must be given the chance to fight their own fights, to transform their country uninterrupted," and underscores throughout her memoir that oppression of women comes from patriarchy, not Islam (205). In contrast to Nafisi's idealization of women's freedom in the West, which renders the U.S. domestic scene utopic, Ebadi's arguments—as she casts patriarchy as a global phenomenon and poverty as a human rights violation—have a potential political force in the United States and in local contests over justice and distributions of socially produced wealth.

Finally, Ebadi's epilogue, which deals with her fight to get the memoir published in the United States, strikingly disaggregates "freedom of expression" from neoliberal platitudes, revealing the narrow scope of "free access to the imagination" in *Reading Lolita in Tehran* and of "open exchange" in the School of International Studies' Dialogue Project. Ebadi's epilogue recounts her legal battle against a little-known but disconcertingly powerful Treasury Department provision that forbade the importation of intellectual or informational material from embargoed countries and thus barred the publication of *Iran Awakening* in the United States. Although offered an exemption by the Treasury, Ebadi joined forces with a number of other embargoed authors and their publishers and filed a lawsuit declaring the measure to violate the rights of Americans under the First Amendment of the U.S. Constitution. Faced with the prospect of a federal court striking down its policy as unconstitutional (and exposing the issue more broadly to the American public), the Treasury Department voluntarily revised its regulations on December 16, 2004. Against the idealization of "free access to the imagination" as the spirit of U.S.-led neoliberalism, Ebadi makes visible the insidious prepolitical censorship exercised routinely through the bureaucratic powers of the U.S. government. In contrast to the tepid call for conversation in the Dialogue Project, Ebadi worked in an activist way from Iran to secure an infrastructure to make possible broader knowledge and education about Iran in the United States, thus freeing U.S. citizens from a rights-violating constriction to which most had been unconscious.

So what does the prominence of Azar Nafisi's *Reading Lolita in Tehran* indicate about the stakes of literary practice in neoliberal times and the deployment of multicultural signification to make neoliberal arrangements appear just? As the foregoing discussion indicates, the answer to the question must be broached by considering the literary and literary critical work that *Reading Lolita in Tehran* pushes aside when it is taught alongside June

Jordan's poetry as a comparable expression of women of color feminism, when it replaces *I, Rigoberta Menchú* as a preeminent example of multicultural autobiography, or when it elbows out Shirin Ebadi's account of Muslim feminist activism. We see that despite the idea, inherited from the role of literature in liberal race reform, that the purpose of Nafisi's memoir is to tell American readers the truth of what goes on *over there*, the real target of the memoir, as it functions within the weave of neoliberal multicultural discourse, is what we comprehend *here*.

Neoliberal multiculturalism does not (or not yet) dominate reading practice or the norms of literary culture. In fact, the scope of the projects that *Reading Lolita in Tehran* would either appropriate or displace—the work of Jordan, Menchú, Spivak, and Ebadi—instead suggests that literary forms of knowledge and reading practices continue effectively to expose the absolutisms, alibis, and ellipses that allow neoliberal arrangements to appear in the disguise of global multicultural justice.

Notes

I deeply appreciate the encouragement, sweat, and patience of Grace Kyungwon Hong and Roderick Ferguson. I am also especially grateful to Lisa Cacho, my chief reader and interlocutor at the "Strange Affinities" symposium at UCLA in May 2006. I benefited enormously from the symposium, and I would like to thank and acknowledge all its participants, that is, the authors of this collection. Finally, as ever, I thank Chandan Reddy for his important contributions to the work.

1 *Neoliberalism* now most commonly refers to a set of economic regulatory policies including the privatization of public resources, financial liberalization (deregulation of interest rates), market liberalization (opening of domestic markets), and global economic management. See McMichael 2000. In defining neoliberal multiculturalism, however, I work with a more expansive understanding of neoliberalism as a term for a world historic organization of economy, governance, and biological and social life. It involves a paradigm shift in governance in its demand that nation-states act in the first place as subsidiary managers of the global economy and rationalizes biological and social life often on the basis of the violence that individuals and communities have had to absorb with social and economic restructuring for neoliberalism. Multiculturalism, too, has a long usage history, beginning in the 1970s, when it named grassroots movements in education for community-based racial reconstruction to its current deployment as a policy rubric for business, government, and education. Neoliberal multiculturalism, as a racial project and ideology, represents an effort to secure consent for neoliberal policy and agendas within the United States and around the globe.

2 The original, Spanish-language edition of Menchú's book makes its status as a political document clear, first with the Marxist connotations of the title, *Me llamo Rigoberta Menchú y asi me nacio la concienca*, or *My Name Is Rigoberta Menchú and This Is How My Consciousness Was Born*, and second by including in an appendix a pamphlet from the leftist Comite de Unidad Campesina (Committee for Peasant Unity).

3 School of Advanced International Studies, Johns Hopkins University, "Dialogue Project," http://dialogueproject.sais-jhu.edu/aboutDP.php.

4 School of Advanced International Studies, Johns Hopkins University, "Dialogue Project," http://dialogueproject.sais-jhu.edu/aboutDP.php.

5 On the tendency of neoconservative politics to sidestep academic knowledge production through the activity of dedicated think tanks and non-peer-reviewed publications, see Lapham 2004.

6 Hamid Dabashi,, "Native Informers and the Making of the American Empire," *Al-Ahram Weekly On-line*, http://weekly.ahram.org.eg/2006/797/special.htm.

7 Fatemeh Keshavarz picks up on Dabashi's critique by choosing an image of two smiling Iranian women in sunglasses and hijab holding protest signs for the cover of her own memoir, *Jasmine and Stars: Reading More than Lolita in Tehran*.

8 For example, we can map the relationship between the American Renaissance's ambition to forge a national literature in the 1850s and U.S. contiguous colonialism. We can also correlate the institution of a Western Civilization curriculum in the United States in the early and mid-twentieth century to the imperative to consolidate a new modern whiteness on the eve of U.S. global ascendancy. On the social history of American literature within U.S. hegemonic process, see Kaplan 1993.

2 Undisciplined Knowledges

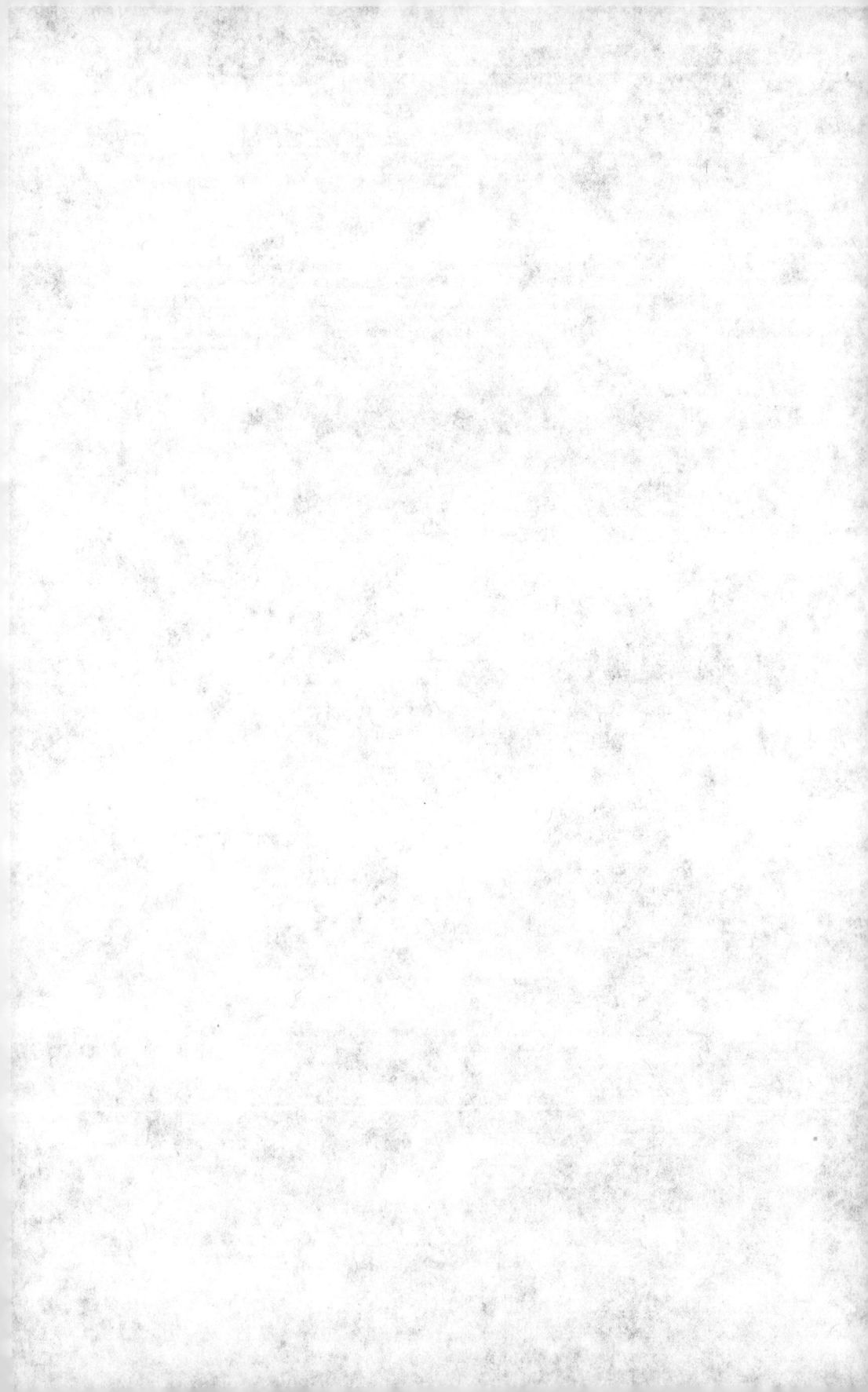

The Lateral Moves of African American Studies in a Period of Migration

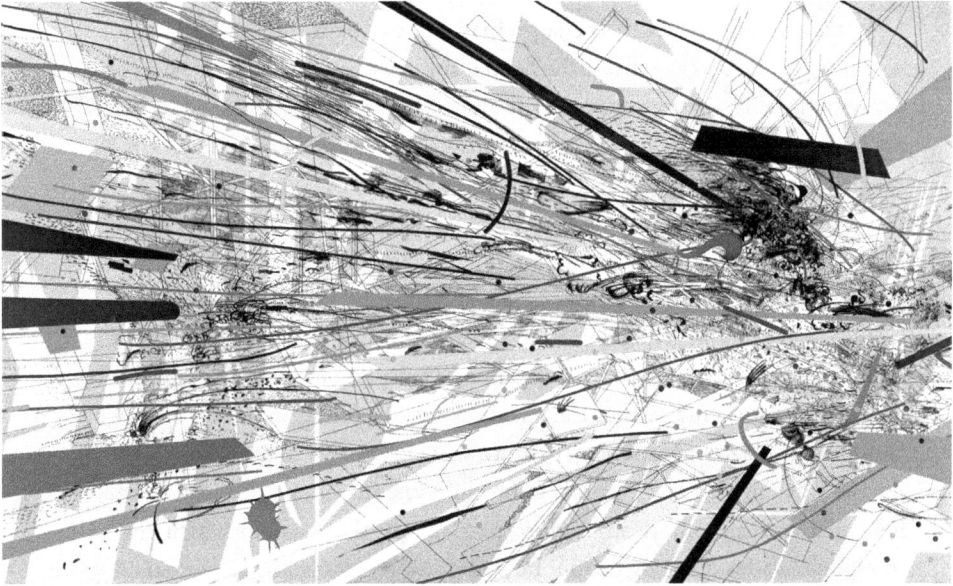

This painting by the Ethiopian American artist Julie Mehretu is titled *Suprematist Evasion*. On the surface, the painting seems dense and chaotic, with lines running everywhere, sometimes straight, sometimes bending, and often crisscrossing. To most viewers, this nonrepresentational piece defies description, never seeming to arrive at a point. The elements of the painting explode on the canvas. The result is as beautiful as it is tumultuous. The details— the lines, the colors, the points—are infinitesimal, and yet as a whole the painting is overwhelming. But for Mehretu the painting is much more than visual dissonance. Describ-

Julie Mehretu, *Excerpt (Suprematist Evasion)*, 2003. Ink and acrylic on canvas, 32 x 54 inches (81.3 x 137.2 cm). Collection Nicolas Rohatyn and Jeanne Greenberg Rohatyn. Photograph by Erma Estwick. Courtesy of the artist, © Julie Mehretu.

ing her work, Mehretu says that issues of globalization, power, history, identity, and culture preoccupy her. She is interested in the "multifaceted layers of place, space, and time that impact the formation of personal and communal identity."[1] For Mehretu, the painting represents more than an assemblage of random colors and errant lines. The painting depicts geographic spaces—cities, even—as the products of global forces. As an artist whose personal history is shaped by migration, it would not be improbable to suggest that the painting refers to the ways in which East African migrations have changed the composition of social formations in the contemporary era.

While the title refers to the suprematist movement, the painting converges with, and diverges from, the formal and epistemological properties of suprematism. Theorizing suprematism as a painterly effort designed to free art from the "dictatorship of representation," the Russian painter Kasimir Malevich created a purely nonobjective artistic piece, symbolized by the black square on a white background (Malevich 1968, 341). In doing so, Malevich offered suprematism as a radical disruption of painting's presumption that it could faithfully and accurately depict reality.

Following in and departing from the tradition of Malevich, Mehretu's *Suprematist Evasion* disturbs the presumed transparency of reality and our alleged ability to convey that transparency by "depicting" how the heterogeneities of black migrations constitute that reality. We might also read it for the ways in which it comments on the evasions of an epistemological field like African American studies, particularly the ways in which that discipline evades questions about how migrations compel us to reorganize knowledge within that field. To begin with, let's say that the lines, rectangles, squares, and dots in Mehretu's painting depict the communities and identities constituted out of black migrations to the United States. With this in mind, we might say that the painting, therefore, symbolizes the emergence of new African American communities and identities, which are formed out of heterogeneous migrations from East Africa. Using the painting as our hermeneutic, we could say that these are communities and identities that are nonrepresentational, defying straightforward descriptions and expectations of homogeneity, linearity, and transparency, descriptions and expectations that typify nationalist ideologies and the hegemonic mode of plotting African American racial formations—that is, from transatlantic slavery, to Jim Crow, to civil rights, Black Power, and on to integration.

Mehretu's *Suprematist Evasion* might then be understood as disturbing the plotline that has come to define African American racial formations. Indeed, we might imagine the painting as a meditation on how contemporary black migrations, in general, and ones from East Africa, in particular, reshape our narration of African American racial formations and redefine the objects of African American studies. To underline this point, we might begin with African immigrants like the Ethiopian-born activist Abdulaziz Kamus.[2] Immigrants like Kamus are well aware of the constructed nature of transparent, homogeneous, and linear articulations of identity. In a *New York Times* article from August 29, 2004, Kamus recalled the rebuffs that he encountered when he suggested that campaigns to address prostate cancer within African American communities should focus on African immigrants as well. Kamus stated, "The census is claiming me as an African-American. . . . If I walk down the streets, white people see me as an African American. Yet African Americans are saying, 'You are not one of us.' So I ask myself, in this country, how do I define myself?" (Swarms 2004).

Mr. Kamus and migrants like him seem to be what the painting is trying to address. Indeed, Mr. Kamus's question—"In this country, how do I define myself?"—seems to echo Mehretu's interest in the identities and communities that emerge in this global moment. What would it mean to make the painting's interest and Mr. Kamus's question about the circumstances of African migration and the possibilities of African American identity the basis of a reinvented African American studies, one that does not take our now canonized geohistorical origins to be the only way of depicting and narrating African American racial formations?

More pointedly, contemporary black migrations pressure African American studies to reconsider its assumptions about African American racial formations.[3] In light of such migrations and the election of President Barack Obama—a child of East African migration—we can no longer assume that African American racial formations trace their line of descent to the middle passage or are punctuated simply by certain historical junctures like Reconstruction, Jim Crow segregation, civil rights, and Black Power. Like the painting, African American racial formations *and* African American studies are undergoing a type of explosion, no longer containable within a single geopolitical terrain or history. Indeed, what this moment requires is an African American studies that is organized not around transparency, linearity, and homogeneity but around lateral maneuvers and strategies that permit identifications and analyses across and through differences of ethnicity, religion, history, culture, gender, sexuality, class, and language.

Put simply, contemporary black migrations are more than demographically significant. They are epistemological formations that compel critical ruptures within African American studies, demanding significant and unprecedented paradigm shifts. The contours of globalization, generally, and global migration, specifically, provide an opportunity to fashion an African American studies organized around the heterogeneity and radical nonidentity of black racial formations. By "heterogeneity" and "nonidentity" I do not mean to suggest that African and Caribbean migrants are nameless, faceless, historyless people. I only mean to suggest that the dazzling diversity of black racial formations in this moment, especially, provides the most recent and glaring justification for our insistence that African American racialization cannot be reduced to a single identity, issue, or national history. In doing so, those formations exceed the nationalist presumptions of the U.S. nation-state and the field of African American studies, presumptions that attempt to negate and manage the critical possibilities of black migrations to the United States.

Contemporary black migrations productively derail the project of African American history. By "derailment" I mean that new African American subjects question the utility of grounding African American history within a line of descent that starts with the middle passage, moves to slavery, proceeds to Emancipation, stops briefly at Reconstruction, passes through Jim Crow segregation, and arrives at civil rights. I do not mean to suggest that these formations do not matter or should become secondary in any way. Indeed, a troubling process is at work within the academy that commodifies the question of migration, making it cohere with the university's interest in contemporary globalization and subsequently producing slavery, civil rights, Jim Crow, and Black Power as the other to that interest—as formations whose presumed banality pales in the face of migration's stylishness. In contradistinction to the commodifying logic of this ideology, we might promote a critical appreciation for the ways in which past formations of American slavery, Jim Crow, and civil rights were and are in conversation with prior and existing forms of migration.

Migrations from Africa, the Caribbean, and Latin America eschew these origin narratives and instead demand engagements with diverse histories of colonization, war, national and economic decline in Third World countries, the maneuvers of the World Bank and the International Monetary Fund, and immigration. International black migrations demand that we decenter African American history as the origin of African American racial formations and as the purpose of African American studies. Another way of stating this would be to say that contemporary black migrations to the United States call for a genealogical analysis of African American racial formations, an analysis that would permit myriad origins, one origin never being more important than the other. In his theorization of origins, Michel Foucault wrote:

> The purpose of history, guided by genealogy, is not to discover the roots of our identity but to commit itself to its dissipation. It does not seek to define our unique threshold of emergence, the homeland to which metaphysicians promise a return; it seeks to make visible all those discontinuities that cross us. (Foucault 1977, 162)

Contemporary black migrations call for a genealogical analysis that can make visible the discontinuities that constitute African American racial formations. Genealogy is much more than a philosophical matter. In this case, it is a matter of how social formations presume epistemic shifts in the study of race.

Queer and Feminist Genealogies of the Study of Migration

In the terrain of culture, we might find precedents for the kind of lateral maneuvers that this essay desires. The work and theorizations of artists and scholars of color have insisted on regarding processes of migration as formations constituted by heterogeneous discourses of race, gender, and sexuality. Specifically, the heterogeneous foundations of black migrations were never really intended to be simple observations but were deployed to rearrange knowledge and rebut essentialist narratives about black racial formations. Discussing the ways in which the heterogeneous and intersectional constitution of black racial formations in the British context compelled observers to alienate "the essential black subject," Stuart Hall wrote in his essay "New Ethnicities" (1996):

> The end of the essential black subject also entails a recognition that the central issues of race always appear historically in articulation, in a for-

mation, with other categories and divisions and are constantly crossed
and recrossed by the categories of class, gender, and ethnicity. . . . [The]
question of the black subject cannot be represented without reference to
the dimensions of class, gender, sexuality, and ethnicity. (Hall 1996, 444)

Hall's remarks have considerable bearing on how we interpret the epistemic
pressures of global migration. Hall points to the ways in which the critique
of essentialism had its genealogy not in a poststructuralism disinterested in
racial formations but in black queer and feminist critical and artistic work
rising out of the harrowing circumstances of British neoliberalism, work
conducted by artists like Ajamu, Rotimi Fani-Kayode, Isaac Julien, Kobena
Mercer, Sonia Boyce, Pratibha Parmar, and others.

The context of migration and cultural politics lead to the end of an
essential black subject and toward the "extraordinary diversity of subjective
positions, social experiences and cultural identities which compose the
category 'black.' . . . What this brings into play is the recognition of the
immense diversity and differentiation of the historical and cultural experience of black subjects" (Hall 1996, 443). Recognizing this diversity necessarily means alienating the presumed innocence that accompanies the essential black subject. In the context of black subjects within the United
States, it means questioning the innocence of the hegemonic plotline of
African American history.

We may think of the end of the essential black subject as a conclusion
brought about by the emergence of black feminist and black queer critical
production. We might also apprehend Hall's remarks about how the question of black social formations is produced out of "dimensions of class,
gender, sexuality, and ethnicity" as arising out of feminist and queer intellectual and artistic work. As Cornel West argues in his now classic article
"The New Cultural Politics of Difference":

> In the diaspora, especially among first world countries, this critique
> [of "homogeneous national communities" and "positive images"] has
> emerged not so much from the Black male component of the left but
> rather from the Black women's movement. The decisive push of post-
> modern Black intellectuals toward a new cultural politics of difference
> has been made by the powerful critiques and constructive explorations
> of Black diaspora women (e.g., Toni Morrison). (1994, 73)

Like Hall, West points to the fact that observations about the gender and sexual heterogeneity of black racial formations are part of a long tradition of feminist (and queer) insights.

Elsewhere I have argued that contemporary globalization is constituted through regimes of gender and sexual normativity and the disruptions to those regimes (see R. Ferguson 2004). In addition to that, contemporary migrations to the United States take place within a context that is explicitly gendered and (hetero)sexualized by the state. Discussing this point, the Asian American theorist Chandan Reddy argues, "The re-organization of U.S. immigration policy in the 1990s through the 'Family Reunification Act' reconstitutes state power through the deployment of 'family,' constituting the conditions of possibility for the juridical recognition" of migrants of color, generally, and queer migrants of color, particularly (Reddy 2005, 103). In a report on the condition of queer of color immigrants in New York that Reddy cosubmitted for the Audre Lorde Project, Reddy and Natalie Bennett write:

> With the effective dismantling of welfare benefits of non-citizen racialized workers, workers brought in through family reunification have increasingly been forced to be dependent on family ties for access to room and board, employment, and other services, such as (what amounts to) workplace injury insurance, healthcare, child care, etc. In other words, federal immigration policies such as Family Reunification extend and institute heteronormative community structures as a requirement for accessing welfare provisions for new immigrants by attaching those provisions to the family unit. In sum, the new federal structure has increased immigrants' exposure and structural dependence on heteropatriarchal relations and regulatory structures. Many queer immigrant interviewees spoke about the impossibility of "being gay" in a context in which one's dependence on "family"—broadly defined—is definitional to living as an immigrant in the City.[4]

Reddy and Bennett's argument reveals the ways in which immigration laws in this moment act as technologies of race and sexuality, pressing migrants into regimes of gender and sexual normativity. Thus migrations to the United States cannot be understood apart from complicated formations around gender and sexuality.

Indeed, it has been a nationalist unconscious that has tended to interpret black migrations apart from investigations of gender and sexuality. Providing a necessary caution about such analyses and how they often use the category of diaspora to suppress discussions of gender and sexuality, Gayatri Gopinath argues, "Nationalism and globalization do indeed constitute the two broad rubrics within which we must view diasporas and diasporic cultural production. However, the concept of diaspora may not be as resistant or contestatory to the forces of nationalism or globalization as it may appear" (2005, 6). According to Gopinath, diaspora loses its potential for critical contestations inasmuch as it becomes an alibi for heteropatriarchy. Accordingly, we must constantly scrutinize the various ways in which the category "diaspora" is deployed, recognizing that not every deployment can or will illuminate the gender and sexual crosscurrents that form black social formations. For our purposes, it means that a lateral African American studies must see contemporary black migrations not only as a racialized class articulation, for instance, but as a gendered and sexualized one as well. Whatever the points on the plotline of black social formations, each one is constituted heterogeneously. Thus the project of this essay is not simply to argue for the global imperative of African American studies but also to say that globalizing African American studies will not necessarily insulate it from nationalist ideologies that end up disciplining black social formations that deviate from the profiles most familiar to the discipline.

Migration and the Challenges to Nationalism

As it attempts to use migration to push against taken-for-granted assumptions about racial identity, diaspora, and shared histories, this essay deploys migration not simply as a historical phenomenon but as an epistemological lever for moving certain fixed historicizations concerning black racial formations. In a similar vein, Hall situates migrations to Britain within the diverse phenomenon known as contemporary globalization, a moment in which culture and identity lose their coherence as national formations and are ultimately unhinged from national moorings. As Hall states, "One has also to remember that Englishness has been decentered not only by the great dispersal of capital to Washington, Wall Street, and Tokyo, but also by this enormous influx that is part of the cultural consequences of labor migrations, the migrations of peoples, who go on at an accelerated pace in the modern world" (1997a, 176). Hall implies here that the study of migration is a way of reframing and *rehistoricizing* contemporary globalization and the limits of national identity and culture. English identity could no longer insulate itself from forces outside the nation. Indeed, migration represented the moment in which English identity was being reconstituted by black immigrant cultures from Pakistan, Ghana, Jamaica, Barbados, and elsewhere. Heterogeneous migrations in the British context, coupled with the internationalization of capital, helped to promote the relative decline of those authorities associated with the nation-state, authorities that had previously determined the itineraries and possibilities of culture and identity. In the moment of explosive migrations and the mobility of transnational capital, culture and identity were often blasted out of the reach of nationalist historiography.

As culture and identity fell out of the grip of nationalism, black British intellectuals and artists theorized black racial formations as heterogeneous and anti-essentialist. In the context of this epistemological intervention, Hall wrote:

> What is at issue here is the recognition of the extraordinary diversity of subjective positions, social experiences and cultural identities which composes the category "black"; that is, the recognition that "black" is essentially a politically and culturally constructed category, which cannot be grounded in a set of fixed trans-cultural or transcendental racial categories and which therefore has no guarantees in nature. (1996, 443)

Migration thus provided the impetus to analyze the declension of the nation-state form under globalization and to observe the denationalization of identity and culture: whereas identity and culture once reflected the primacy of the nation-state, under the conditions of contemporary globalization, identity and culture ceased to be beacons for the national and became the traces of the global. "Black" in the British context became the material trace of transnational migrations and diverse histories of colonization and decolonization, histories that would disrupt the coherence of English identity and culture and the presumed benevolence of the British nation-state. Black British cultural studies is what scholars and artists like Stuart Hall, Pratibha Parmar, Paul Gilroy, Hazel Carby, Isaac Julien, Kobena Mercer, and others offered as a critical enterprise that might accommodate that heterogeneity and put it to antinationalist purposes.

This aspect of black British cultural studies proves particularly beneficial for a similar undertaking in the American context. Migrations from East Africa blast black racial formations out of the neat campus that begins with slavery and ends with freedom. Joseph Takougang and Bassirou Tidjani note, for instance, that while African immigrants to the United States immigrated for educational and professional purposes with the assumption that they would take that knowledge back to their newly independent nations, contemporary migrants are compelled to migrate and are more than likely to stay because of "the failure by African states to provide economic opportunities for their citizens and the prevalence of corrupt and highly repressive regimes that have suffocated a vast range of individual freedoms" (Takougang and Tidjani 2009, 32). This applies especially to migrants from war-torn countries such as Ethiopia, Somalia, and Sudan who came to the United States in the 1980s and 1990s through the U.S. Refugee Resettlement Program (35). As East African migrants do not hail from the historic dispersions of transatlantic slavery but emerge from the complexities and failures of national liberation, they require plotlines that exceed the canonical course for black racial formations—one beginning with the middle passage and ending with some version of independence or national liberation.

Women of Color Feminism and the Challenge to Comparison

A critical project of the sort I undertake in this essay implies a critique of comparative methods and ideologies, a critique of the modes under which we compare different types of black subjects. Discussing the genealogy of comparison, the sociological theorist Craig Calhoun writes:

> From very early on, European thinkers approached human diversity with a vision of differences among types, not a ubiquity of cross-cutting differentiations. . . . Especially under the influence of nationalist ideas, they developed notions of societies as singular, bounded, and internally integrated, and as realms in which people were more or less the same. On that basis, a great deal of modern social theory came to incorporate prereflectively the notion that human beings naturally inhabit only a single social world or culture at a time. (1995, 44)

As Calhoun notes, ideas of discreteness are foundational to modern social thought and nationalism, particularly to notions of national identity. As those ideas imply a common and shared story line, they secrete hegemonic plotlines that are presumed to be the ingredients for identity.

Inasmuch as the canonical story of African American history marginalizes the histories and experiences of new African Americans who are formed out of histories of international migration, that plotline risks unwittingly deploying the hegemonies of comparative ideologies by canonizing a plotline that would pertain to some but not to all. We can see this canonization at work in certain currents within African American studies. For instance, Maulana Karenga's *Introduction to Black Studies* makes African Americans the center of that field and its conception of diaspora:

> Just as a point of departure and sound procedure, does not logic demand a thrust which is not over-ambitious, but begins where it is, in the U.S. among African Americans, and then as it grows stronger, expands outward? In other words, is not the study of African Americans the core of Black Studies in the U.S., the study of an African people neglected more than any other, certainly more than the study of Continentals or Caribbeans? (quoted in Edwards 2001, 57)

Karenga here insists on a plotline for black studies that begins with African Americans and uses that as the starting point of all interrogations of black racial formations. The passage, moreover, implies that the narrative arc that pertains to African Americans is more important than the storylines of "Continentals or Caribbeans." While certain versions of nationalism assert a harmony between different black cultural groups, this early definition of black studies—inasmuch as it works to make African Americans the diasporic hegemon—formalizes a conflict between those groups. We can think of Karenga's maneuver not so much as a discrete and bygone citation, an ideology that the field has overcome. We might approach it instead as a genealogist would—that is, as an insistence on "the rude memory of . . . conflicts" (Foucault 1977, 83). In other words, this articulation can help sensitize us to the ways in which apparently innocent theorizations of African American studies might in fact engender conflicts between various black ethnic groups.

Touching on Karenga's vanguardism and opposing it to C. L. R. James's argument that "Black Studies require a complete reorganization of the intellectual life and historical outlook of the United States, and world civilization as a whole," Brent Edwards notes the constitutive nature of this contradiction in his essay "The Uses of Diaspora": "The discourse of diaspora . . . is both enabling to black studies, in the service of such an 'intervention' [like James's] and inherently a risk, in that it can fall back into either racial essentialism or American vanguardism" (Edwards 2001, 57). In relation to migrations to the United States, an African American vanguardism would thus attempt to discipline the epistemic possibilities of black migrations and their implications for African American studies—either ignoring those migrations or incorporating them as subordinates to a primarily American intellectual and historical center. In either case, those migrations would be prevented from the "complete" reorganization for which James called.

As an alternative, we might read women of color feminist formations as calls for a reorganization of knowledge within African American studies, a reorganization that gets at the very heart of ideologies of discreteness and singularity, ideologies that are so foundational for comparative thinking. For instance, in her essay "Age, Race, Class, and Sex: Women Redefining Difference," Audre Lorde identifies this aspect of modern social thought and defines women of color feminist work as deliberately disruptive of this aspect:

> Much of western European history conditions us to see human differences in simplistic opposition to each other: dominant/subordinate, good/bad, up/down, superior/inferior. In a society where the good is defined in terms of profit rather than in terms of human need, there must always be some group of people who, through systematized oppression, can be made to feel surplus, to occupy the place of the dehumanized inferior. Within this society, that group is made up of Black and Third World people, working-class people, older people, and women. (1993, 114)

Here Lorde suggests that to redefine difference means interrogating the ways in which producing difference is also a way of producing comparisons and contriving hierarchies of classification.

In her essay "Insufficient Differences," Lisa Lowe discusses the material effects of the oppositions that Lorde addresses. Locating the institutionalization of these oppositions within Max Weber's theory of ideal types, Lowe writes:

> Rational action within modern western industrial society constituted the ideal type, a heuristic proposition that founded Weber's Verstehen,

or "interpretive" sociology, against which that difference, variance, or convergence of specific social and historical instances were measured.

. . . We might understand Weber's comparative method as the institutionalization of "difference" as a modern apparatus for apprehending and disciplining otherness, or what Michel Foucault . . . would term a governmentality, according to which other groups, societies and formations were studied either as analogues destined to assimilate western classifications, or as "pathological" deviants to be eliminated or suppressed. (2005, 410–11)

As Lowe suggests, comparative analysis has also been a way to smuggle racial discourses into the philosophical chambers of modern social thought and identity, to discipline modes of difference, and to forestall their potential for epistemic reorganization.

The historic occasions for comparison—imperial voyage, slavery, migration, the Protestant Reformation and its overturning of Catholic orthodoxy —generated the conditions as well as set the parameters for interpretation (see Calhoun 1995). More specifically, those moments were the material terrains that constructed modes of differences as discrete and monolithic. Lorde engages the long legacy of this construction, demanding that we see such articulations as contingent rather than necessary:

Certainly there are very real differences between us of race, age, and sex. But it is not those differences between us that are separating us. It is rather our refusal to recognize those differences, and to examine the distortions which result from our misnaming them and their effects upon human behavior and expectation. (1993, 115)

For Lorde, the real question of difference involves asking what discursive trappings have typically attended our understanding of difference as inherently discrete and antagonistic, and how we might understand those trappings as contingent rather than necessary. This question for Lorde requires a new and urgent interpretive and comparative agenda. As she writes, "The future of our earth may depend upon the ability of all women to identify and develop new definitions of power and new patterns of relating across difference" (123).

As women of color feminism, in general, and black feminism, in particular, have tried to devise nonhierarchical ways of understanding difference, these feminist formations have not only insisted on the heterogeneity of racial formations but have implied alternative modes of comparison as well. We might then say that inasmuch as women of color feminist formations attempted to disrupt this constitutive element of social thought and nationalism, those formations attempted to break radically with the course of modern thought and communal forms. Indeed, black feminists were at the lead of such developments. As Grace Hong writes, "[Because] black feminism envisions 'African American' not as essential and unchanging, but as always already a coalition of different, sometimes competing formations, it implies the possibility of alliances among a variety of racial, gendered, sexualized and national differences" (Hong 2006, xxvii–xxviii). Indeed, this particular aspect of black feminism provides the foundation for a lateral articulation of African American studies.

We might therefore read Bernice Johnson Reagon's classic speech "Coalition Politics: Turning the Century" as yet another provocation to think beyond African American studies' hegemonic plotline for black racial formations. Reagon begins by discussing the ways in which forms of nationalism consecrate homogeneous notions of belonging and identity through the figure of home. That figure promotes separatist politics that Reagon addresses through the metaphor of the barred room. "Sometimes you get comfortable in your little barred room, and you decide you in fact are going to live there and carry out all of your stuff in there. And you gonna take care of everything that needs to be taken care of in the barred room" (1983, 358). The barred room suggests comfort and stability to its occupants, but as Reagon argues, nationalism's barred room exists in tension with coalitional practices. "Coalition work is not work done in your home. Coalition work has to be done in the streets. . . . Some people will come to a coalition and they rate the success of the coalition on whether or not they feel good when they get there. They're not looking for a coalition; they're looking for a home!" (359). For Reagon, coalition connotes a constant defamiliarization of categories that suggest the comforts of home. In the context of Reagon's speech at the 1981 West Coast Women's Music Festival, "woman" was the familiar and deceptively transparent category. We might think of "African American"—particularly as it is populated by the subjects of migration—as a category ready for defamiliarization as well.

African American Studies, Migration, and the Critique
of Western Civilization

In general, migrations to the United States after World War II are typically
the outcome of processes of U.S. neocolonialism. The sociologist Rubén
Rumbaut argues in his article "Origins and Destinies: Immigration to the
United States since World War II":

> Migration patterns are rooted in historical relationships established be-
> tween the United States and the principal sending countries—that is, the
> size and source of new immigrant communities in the United States
> today is directly if variously related to the history of American military,
> political, economic, and cultural involvement and intervention in the
> sending countries. (Rumbaut 1994 588)

This fact obtains for black migrants from Africa and the Caribbean. These
historic conditions account for the migration of peoples from Egypt, Ethiopia, Somalia, Nigeria, Ghana, and elsewhere. As such, black migrant and
refugee communities within the United States bear the trace of U.S. neocolonialism.

In addition, such migrations have produced an unprecedented diversity
among black communities within the United States. For instance, the 2000
U.S. Census reported 36,216,207 African Americans within the United
States. Of that number, 6.7 percent were foreign born. That percentage of
foreign-born blacks represented a 1.9 percent increase from 1990. In New
York City, the number of foreign-born blacks increased 4 percent from 1990
to 2000. In Boston the number increased 7 percent in that time; in Minneapolis it increased 12 percent (Swarms 2004, 11).

The types of African American racial formations emanating from black
migrations to the United States take place within the moment after the civil
rights movement and during the period in which the nation-state must
negotiate with supranational entities in the form of multinational corporations, the United Nations, migration, and so forth. These migrations neces-
sitate certain lateral procedures at the level of epistemology, procedures
that can illuminate histories of war, neocolonialism, and structural adjustment—histories that exceed the taken-for-granted plotlines of African
American history.

Rather than being foreign to black studies, these procedures are actually implied in the most classic formulations of African American studies. For example, in his speech "Black Studies and the Contemporary Student," James refused an ethnic absolutist theorization of black studies in which the discipline focused singularly on black folks to the exclusion and occlusion of social forces and the political struggles of other peoples.

> Now to talk to me about black studies as if it's something that concerned black people is an utter denial. This is the history of Western Civiliza-tion. I can't see it otherwise. This is the history that black people and white people and all serious students of modern history and the history of the world have to know. To say that it's some kind of ethnic problem is a lot of nonsense. (1993, 397)

Through this passage, James points to what we might think of as a tension within African American studies—that is, the articulation of African Ameri-can studies as an identity politics organized around a people or nation and an African American studies poised as an oppositional enterprise that crit-ically engages social formations globally. Such an engagement, for James, meant that Western civilization, rather than the nation, was the condition of, and the conceptual nucleus for, black racial formations. Another way of stating the point would be to say that contemporary migrations call into question the identity of African American studies and its summary of black social formations.

   After 9/11, immigration controls and American nationalism threatened the lives of immigrated African Americans and compromised their U.S.-born counterparts. The sociologist and legal scholar Elizabeth Heger Boyle and the sociologist Fortunata Ghati Songora discuss the broad procedures of the war on terror—procedures that expanded bureaucratic procedures and restrictions around immigration and promoted informal racist prac-tices against East African immigrants and refugees in Minneapolis and Saint Paul. They contend that East African immigrants, Somali immigrants especially, dealt with the war on terror and the subsequent fear of deporta-tion by keeping a low profile and also by petitioning for citizenship in hopes that it might protect them from further abuses (Boyle and Songora 2004). By using citizen status as a bulwark against repressions enacted in the very name of American citizenship, new African American migrations point powerfully to the dialectic of freedom and unfreedom that has always struc-tured U.S. citizenship. That dialectic took on new resonance in the contemporary moment. Implying the interaction between freedom and unfreedom, the Asian American legal theorist Leti Volpp argues, "September 11 facilitated the consolidation of a new identity category that groups together persons who appear 'Middle-Eastern, Arab, or Muslim.' This consolidation reflects a racialization wherein members of this group are identified as terrorists, and are disidentified as citizens" (Volpp 2001–2, 1576).

African immigration, in particular, also points to the dangers of reducing African American identity, whether immigrated or U.S. born, to American identity. It was the conflation of American identity with African American that led one of Boyle and Songora's respondents, a Somali woman, to tell the following story: "It was . . . two days after September 11 at Lake Street when a Black American man driving a car wanted to hit us right in the middle of the street—the car my friend and I were in. 'Bullshit Islam! You stinking Muslims that burn our buildings and our country!' Thank God, God brought us people, otherwise he wanted to kill us right there" (Boyle and Songora 2004, 329–30). As this story and other instances of U.S.-born African Americans endorsing state practices like racial profiling illustrate, we might say that African American ethnicities after September 11 were differentiated not only by religion, culture, and country of origin but also by how well one could approximate the citizen ideal and insulate oneself from charges of terrorism, a negotiation that depends greatly on whether one is immigrated or U.S. born. Put plainly, after September 11 the ethnic differences that make up contemporary African American racial formations emanate from various negotiations with the citizen-terrorist dialectic, causing tensions and conflicts between immigrated and U.S.-born African Americans. In the name of coalition, a reinvented African American studies must deliberate seriously about the heterogeneous plotlines of black racial formations. This is not an occasion to retreat to the sanctity of canonical narratives of African American identity but a moment to refuse the restrictions of the sacred in our difficult preparation for a more democratic tomorrow.

Notes

1   Julie Mehretu, "Drawing into Painting," Walker Art Center, St. Paul, Minn., April 6–
    August 3, 2003, http://www.walkerart.org/archive/2/AF7361E991C363206165
    .htm.

2   I have chosen to refer to African and Caribbean migrants as "migrants," "immi-

grants," and "refugees." I do so informed by an observation by Nicholas Van Hear in his article "Locating Internally Displaced People in the Field of Forced Migration": "[While] outward movement may be forced, precipitated by persecution, conflict, war or some other life-threatening circumstance, inward movement might involve more choice—of destination, for example—and may be shaped more by economic, livelihood or life-chance considerations. At some point, forced migration may transmute into economic, livelihood or 'betterment' migration. Similarly, return or outward movement might involve more choice than the outward movement. Conversely, migration that initially involved choice may transmute into forced migration, as is the case with the expulsion of migrants from the countries in which they are working or have settled, or with the forced displacement of returnees after they have come home" (Van Hear 2000, 91). I thank Linda Vo for pushing me to think about the limits and utilities of categories like "immigrant" and "refugee" in the context of African and Caribbean migrations to the United States.

3   Conceptually and linguistically I am indebted to Lowe 2001.

4   See the interviews with LGBT immigrants of color collected for this study; all archived at the Audre Lorde Project.

Volumes of Transnational Vengeance

Fixing Race and Feminism on the Way to *Kill Bill*

D ubbed Quentin Tarantino's homage to the kung-fu movies of the 1970s, *Kill Bill: Vol. 1* (2003) and *Kill Bill: Vol. 2* (2004) represent what would appear to be a radical defamiliarization of women's relationship—as both victims and perpetrators—to violence. In the two-volume Hollywood journey toward killing Bill, the revenge fantasy of Uma Thurman's white female character, known alternately as "Bleep," "the Bride," "Black Mamba," and "Beatrix," drives the narrative. In the first film, we learn that she is a former member of the world-class, predominantly female, racially integrated Deadly Viper Assassination Squad (the DIVAS) who, along with her husband and wedding guests, is shot by her former boss, Bill, on her wedding day. She survives a bullet to the head and, after a coma of five years, awakens to the reality that the unborn child she was carrying on the day of the massacre did not survive, as well as to the reality that a hospital orderly has raped her repeatedly and has sold the rape of her to an unknown number of other men. The film's graphic revenge action begins before we know anything about its tragic and violent inspirations, however. It begins immediately after the film's opening credits, with the Bride killing Copperhead (played by Vivica Fox, an African American actress) in front of her four-year-old daughter. As Tarantino's signature temporal back-and-forths have taught us, though, every such jolting moment and every such jolting order of things has its own (non)reason.

In the extradiegetic historical time of the Bride's vengeance, her first victims are actually the hospital orderly and one of his "clients." In the film's time, however, they comprise her second set of kills, after her fight with Copperhead and the time stamp that lands us "four years earlier." Having just risen from her comatose state, clutching and sobbing at the fact of her empty womb and the flashback visions of bullets and bloodied bodies on her wedding day, the Bride hears two men approaching her hospital room. Confused and frightened, she frantically gathers herself back into the appearance of coma and overhears that she is about to be raped as she has apparently been raped countless times before. When the paying rapist climbs on top of her and tries to kiss her, she leaps into merciless action and rips out his tongue with her teeth. With atrophied muscles and her rapist's blood soaking her hospital gown, she manages to pull her body along the floor, stopping when the orderly suddenly returns to call time on the sexual violence. She slashes his Achilles tendon, then repeatedly slams his head between the room's metal door and the doorframe. Thus freed, she moves on to the now-justified business of killing Bill and every member of his Deadly Viper Assassination Squad.

Bill is the last on the Bride's hit list, and therefore audiences waited until *Vol. 2* was released—one full year after the first vengeance kill—to meet Bill and to see the promise of the films' title realized. DiVA O-Ren Ishii, a.k.a. Cottonmouth, played by Chinese American actress Lucy Liu, is first on the list. The Bride finds her in Japan, where Cottonmouth has moved on from her position as assassin-for-hire to become a Tokyo gangland leader. The visualized sequencing of the film, however, is out of chronological order: the battle we *see* first (though it occurs as the second) is the fight between the Bride and Copperhead at Copperhead's home in Pasadena, California. Discussing this particular instance of infamous Tarantinian visual time twisting, one reviewer suggested that Copperhead's death early in the film is a humorously critical commentary on the Hollywood convention of offing black characters first.

Indeed, stock Hollywood maneuvers such as this, when they appear in

Tarantino's films, are often read as purposefully critical social commentary, executed for the purpose of defamiliarizing the place of racialized characters in dominant patterns of filmic narrative. This is indeed an intriguing interpretation, but it depends on an attribution of progressive race politics to an artist whose work, I argue, ultimately offers little basis for it. This interpretation depends, also, on a faith that Tarantino's massive audience consumes his sampling and hyperbolizing of popular cultural narratives as antiracist critics rather than as hip voyeurs to Tarantino's overzealous projections of everything he himself loves to consume, everything "black" about which he fantasizes, and every narrative of cool he can weave into a signature style that Miramax Studios has financed—perhaps quite appropriately—with carte blanche.

In this chapter, I interrogate what some have read as the critical social commentary on relations of race, gender, and violence within *Kill Bill* to reveal its intertextual—indeed, comparative—racialization of feminist vengeance. Whereas my critical interpretations here conform to a visual culture approach—one that examines *Kill Bill* as a racialized revenge narrative that substantially exceeds its cinematic frame—I nevertheless incorporate close readings of particular scenes in my analyses. Between *Kill Bill*'s translations and appropriations of its textual and generic influences, on the one hand, and certain feminist projections of and upon Tarantino's violent sexual and gender politics, on the other, race emerges as a site of radical critical occlusion.[1] At the same time, however, racialized bodies—corporeal, geographic, and cultural—are the radically visible, material preconditions for *Kill Bill*'s widely lauded feminism.

For better or worse, Tarantino's films scream for the application of auteur theory to their analysis, and a large part of what follows assumes exactly this approach. Unapologetic and hyperbolic mixes, samplings, projections, and insertions with regard to visual texts, social identities, and cinematic types constitute Tarantino's unmistakable signature. The extreme pastichic performances of his films, however, never disrupt the personality at their center, which is that of Tarantino himself. Rigorously interrogating the relations of race, gender, and violence in *Kill Bill* brings into relief Tarantino's films' social and political, as well as stylistic, productions. Decoding the vengeful feminism of Uma Thurman's character reveals not only the masterful mix of filmic techniques, narratives, and genres characteristic of Tarantino's films or the violent cross-race inhabitation fantasies that inspire his constructions of masculinity. Indeed, the setting, circumstances, and victims of the Bride's bloody rampage add to Tarantino's artistically generative jumbles of genre and text a cross-gender inhabitation that wreaks a violently masculine, racial revenge from a different angle.

It is no secret that Tarantino's entire oeuvre is in deliberately exploitative conversation with historically racialized visual discourses. Examining Tarantino's projections at the intersection of these discourses with those of violent masculinity, Sharon Willis observes that through their identification with black men, the white male characters of Tarantino's films produce black men as "icons, gestural repertoires, and cultural artifacts, as the threads of cross-racial identification are wound around a white body that remains stable. Perhaps more important, these fantasmatic identifications maintain an aggressive edge: the white subject wants to be in the other's place, without leaving its own" (Willis 1997, 210). To support these observations, Willis cites the characterization and dialogue of key characters in Tarantino's scripts. A combination of her and my list of such characters reads thus: the white-wannabe-black, dreadlocked, drug-dealing pimp played by Gary Oldman in *True Romance*; the white kung-fu-film geek (also in *True Romance*) played by Christian Slater who works in a comic book store and sees Elvis as his mirrored reflection, embraces him as his superego, and at the urging of Elvis himself, Elvis as himself, shoots the white-wannabe-black, dreadlocked, drug-dealing pimp in the crotch and then in the head; *Pulp Fiction*'s Jimmy, the white man played, interestingly enough, by Tarantino himself, who compulsively uses the N-word and protests the making of his home into what he calls a "dead nigger storage"; all the white male members of the Reservoir Dogs gang, each of whom responds to their boss's announcement that they will be named after particular colors with the desperate hope to be "Mr. Black" and then with extreme lament when they must instead assume lighter shades. Many more such characters appear in the growing body of Tarantino's work, but the foregoing list should suffice to make the point. Tarantino's films are literally teeming with crises of white masculinity.

In neither installment of *Kill Bill* do we see these relationships between white and black masculinity visualized overtly in the way that they are in his other films. Rather, in this two-volume crisis, the white boy's identification with and desire for blackness and what Tarantino himself has said that this blackness represents and performs—a natural relationship to violence—are appropriated and acted out through a white *female* revenge narrative (Willis 1997, 210). With the code name Black Mamba, however, *Kill Bill*'s heroine never diverges from the racial and masculinist projects that mark the Tarantinian aesthetic. In fact, this woman—white, but christened with a lethal blackness—achieves what the Reservoir Dogs gang and company only dreamed of. Sampling dialogue, imagery, and recognizable pieces of story lines from samurai and kung fu movies, blaxploitation flicks, and spaghetti westerns of the 1970s, *Kill Bill*'s narrative coheres only and precisely because its leaps of time, space, race, and gender reflect the privilege of white male subject formation to incorporate and reject objects according to what consolidates this formation. Tarantino recounts that he told *Kill Bill*'s cinematographer Bob Richardson, "Look, I want each reel to play like it's a reel from a different movie, all right? You take this reel from *Death Rides a Horse* and this reel from *Zatoichi's Revenge* and then that reel from a Shaw Brothers film. We didn't need one look to bring the movie together. What will bring the movie together is one voice—my voice, my personality—and Uma's image, all right?" (Ansen 1994, 66).

What Tarantino's personality does with Thurman's image is perhaps in part what spurred the creative energy he exercised in coming up with the film's hospital sequence in which she and the audience learn that she has been raped while comatose. Tarantino comments, "Once I got this idea in my mind, I couldn't get it out. It would be a lot easier if I didn't go down that road, but then that would just be cowardice to me. Because there have been reports about, you know, comatose patients being raped. And my feeling is, if Uma Thurman was in a coma for four years, and she's a Jane Doe, nobody knows who she is, nobody's visiting her, she's just a plant—I could imagine guys selling her. And once I came up with that thought, I couldn't let it go" (Ansen 1994, 66). Later in the same interview, he reiterates that this is a movie about "the passions in [his] life." "If you're working from a true place as a writer, I always feel you should be just a little embarrassed when you hand it in, because you will be revealed." (Note he says that you *should* be a little embarrassed.) To continue with the quote: "All that stuff isn't on the surface of this movie. It's buried inside of it. All I can say is, if I went and saw *Kill Bill*, I wouldn't be able to even think about seeing another movie until I saw *Kill Bill* again. I'd feel like, 'That's a movie like sex. That's a movie like drugs,' you know? I can't even think of another girl until I've had another piece of that pussy. I've got to get high on that drug again, like, tomorrow"

(66). Thus, buried not so deep inside the filmic narrative as Tarantino might suggest is the rape fantasy he can't get out of his mind, the rape fantasy turned real for the hospital orderly whom the Bride punishes with death, and who involuntarily bequeaths to her his yellow truck that screams "Pussy Wagon" in pink letters across the door to its bed. Incidentally, this is the same wagon that carts her to murder the black Vernita Green, a.k.a. Copperhead.

Parking and dismounting the Pussy Wagon in front of Copperhead's suburban home, the Bride steps her long, determined legs over a mess of scattered toys on her way to the doorbell. Copperhead answers the door, and her startled appearance triggers a visually and sonically jarring flashback that we experience inside the Bride's mind. A high-pitched, metallic siren slices through their eye-lock as the Bride's translucent face frames the historically distant, rerunning episode for which she seeks vengeance: a fast fist launches the Bride's lacily clad, pregnant body across a room; bloodied, she looks up to see Copperhead standing over her and staring at her, deadly-sporty and remorseless in her assassin's uniform. The fade-out of this mini-film-within-a-face actually fades *into* Copperhead's coldly triumphant stare, the Bride's threatening eyes piercing the flashback for all of its ten seconds. Her enraged punch slams us back to the present day, sending Copperhead's body flying backward in the same arc that the Bride's own body traced five years earlier. The woman-on-woman violence thus comes full circle, shattering Copperhead's domestic haven the way it shattered the Bride's domestic dream. They begin their fight to the death in the living room, smashing and striking at one another with coffee table legs, shards of fine china, and fireplace pokers. Their sweat and grunts make the would-be radical feminism of the scene all the more vivid.

The moment of feminine, maternal truth within this violently gendersubversive context arrives when a school bus pulls up to the house to deliver Copperhead's five-year-old daughter. The women exchange knowing looks: to kill a mother in front of her child is incomprehensible, but to kill a mother who killed one's own child is perhaps an assimilable, if complicated, response in the vein of maternal love. They take a timeout, hide their kitchen knives behind their backs, and greet little Nikki. The soundtrack bleeps out the Bride's self-introduction, but not her creepily loaded pondering at how she would have had a little girl the same age as Copperhead's, if only. Nikki stares, stunned silent at the broken house and bloody mamas,

Copperhead's face triggers the Bride's memory and her vengeance. Screen grab from *Kill Bill: Vol. 1*, directed by Quentin Tarantino (Miramax Studios, 2003).

until Copperhead sends her to her room with a finger snap and a forceful command. She offers the Bride coffee, and they move to the kitchen, where they reminisce with unquellable anger (the Bride) and toughly pleading remorse (Copperhead) on the history that brought them to this moment. The Bride gives no clear answer to Copperhead's question as to whether she plans to continue the fight in front of her daughter until Copperhead breaks the fragile peace by shooting a gun that she's concealed with a box of KABOOM! cereal at the Bride. The Bride blocks the bullet with her coffee mug and launches a knife through the splatter at Copperhead's chest. Her perfect aim kills instantly. She turns to see little Nikki standing in the kitchen doorway, shocked still and quiet, staring at her dead mother. The Bride wipes Copperhead's blood from her knife with a kitchen towel and explains, "It was not my intention to do this in front of you. For that, I'm sorry. But you can take my word for it: your mother had it coming. When you grow up, if you still feel raw about it, I'll be waitin.' " She takes crunchy steps over the cereal on the kitchen floor and leaves the house while a male voice-over recites in Japanese the relevant passages—on revenge and its requisite suppression of compassion—from an unknown text that parodies Sun Tzu's *The Art of War*. Yellow subtitles translate this ancient wisdom into English, and the Pussy Wagon drives off into the California sunshine.

Kill Bill's comedic, parodic inversions of traditional gender roles are thus packed and layered within a hybrid structure of hyperbolized cinematic forms: Copperhead and the Bride negotiate their bumpy history and their maternal investments within a syncretic mix of kung fu, samurai, western, melodrama, female revenge, and exploitation genres. As formally and narratively disruptive as this mix is, there is comfort to be had in the coherence of its ridiculousness. Tarantino's prediction that no one "look" was needed to bring the film together banked on the certainty of his beloved postmodern personal mark and the idea that his audience would see it, wholly, as his. It banked, also, on the appeal of Uma Thurman's statuesque execution of a long-awaited revenge on the reign of the racialized cool in cinema and popular culture.

Each volume of the film plays its own role in these filmic narrative and extracinematic social dramas. *Kill Bill: Vol. 1* stages *Vol. 2*'s background as a merciless rampage, one scripted by the Bride's kill list. She crosses off names as she methodically makes her way through it, traveling the globe to track down her victims. *Vol. 1* enacts an additional rampage, however, a rampage on and through the artistic forms and cultural symbols that threaten Tarantino's white and fragile masculinity. Lining up the revenge narratives of both the Bride and the director in this way, our critical imaginations might conjure a second kill list, one that includes those filmic genres and cultural characterizations with which Tarantino has such deep love-hate relationships. While this parallel is not a seamless line, of course, we can almost see Tarantino crossing "bad-ass blackness and blaxploitation" off his list as the Bride crosses Copperhead off hers, and then "sword-fighting Japanese gangsters and samurai" disappearing simultaneously with Cottonmouth's name.

After the Bride kills Copperhead—actually, before she kills Copperhead; recall that the filmic sequencing of events is out of chronological order—she travels to Okinawa, where a former samurai-turned-sushi-chef, played by Sonny Chiba, makes her a custom sword. She travels with it to the House of Seven Leaves in Tokyo to kill O-Ren Ishii, a.k.a. Cottonmouth, played by Lucy Liu, and every member of her Japanese gang, the Crazy 88s.

This scene is a quite extended one of highly choreographed and stylized violence, with much limb flying, blood spraying, and head chopping. In the end, the Bride is standing, soaked in blood, still wielding her sword, and close to a hundred Japanese bodies lie mutilated all around her. She finds the white-kimono-clad Cottonmouth in a beautifully enchanting garden, where it is silent and snowing. Cottonmouth compliments the Bride on her "impressive instrument" and asks—in Japanese—where she acquired it. She spits disbelief when the Bride tells her that it is a Hattori Hanzo sword and proceeds to smugly threaten her. Cottonmouth then makes quite a production of preparing for their imminent duel, slowly removing her white flip-flops, bowing, and unsheathing and readying her sword across an excruciatingly long thirty seconds. They begin their dance. When Cottonmouth slices open the Bride's back, bringing her to the ground, she directs a wicked laugh downward, musing, "Silly Caucasian girl likes to play with samurai swords." This is not the end, however, for the Bride rises, now speaking her own challenges to her opponent in Japanese. Hobbling in pain, she manages to slice open one of Cottonmouth's legs. Stunned still and incredulous at the sight of her own blood, Cottonmouth apologizes for her ridiculing behavior of a few moments earlier. Indeed, this silly Caucasian girl knows exactly what to do with samurai swords. They exchange more quipped challenges in Japanese and recommence their fight. The fast flurry of arms and shiny metal blurs the final blow such that a slicing sound and the top of Cottonmouth's head flying to the snow-covered ground are its only signs. Standing perfectly still, with an exposed brain and wide eyes, she speaks her last words in Japanese: "That really was a Hattori Hanzo sword." The theme song from Toshiya Fujita's *Lady Snowblood* (1973), "Flower of Carnage," sets a beautifully sad tone as the Bride walks her weary body to a bench in the garden, putting her head in her hands. The snow continues to fall.

Cottonmouth's appearance and surroundings at the House of Seven Leaves give a delicately feminine stage to the Bride's violently contrasting mission of vengeance. Like the apparently traditionally feminine spaces of Copperhead's living room and kitchen, Cottonmouth's aesthetic domain comically fails to rewrite the history, as well as the ever-present threat among the ex-assassins, of woman-on-woman violence. The racial dramas projected and played out through the film are inextricable from—in fact, they are constitutive of—the intricate web of prototypes and parodies, inversions and reproductions, with regard to traditionally ascribed gender roles and capacities that make suspect *Kill Bill*'s feminist agenda. Nevertheless Tarantino himself has described *Kill Bill* as a feminist story, and many published reviews and commentaries on the film cite the large number of women who saw it and shared this interpretation.[2]

A review in the *New York Times* observed that "In *Kill Bill* (which opened

The Bride's snowily enchanted showdown with Cottonmouth. Screen grab from *Kill Bill: Vol. 1*, directed by Quentin Tarantino (Miramax Studios, 2003).

three days after the election of Arnold Schwarzenegger as California's governor), women rise to a level of brutality previously reserved for men like Mr. Schwarzenegger. Where women go in this movie, limbs fly. Heads roll. Blood spurts in three shades of red. It is just the latest in a growing body of movies and television shows featuring wild women wielding weapons." According to this and other reviews like it, the film's inversion of traditional gender roles, particularly as they relate to the execution of extreme violence, strikes a ready chord with our current popular culture, as well as with the feminist sensibilities of a good many women.

However, at the same time that one female interviewee talks about how she's looking forward to bringing her fifteen-year-old daughter to see *Kill Bill*, because it is so empowering and because everything else out there is so silly, other published commentaries remind us of the fantastic nature of the film's representations. Three months before the film's release, the *New York Times* quoted its publicist pre-empting critiques of its relentless blood and gore: "The violence is stylish. It's cartoonish. It is a mythical movie, not realistic." Indeed, headless bodies that spurt many-feet-high streams of blood do instill a sense of un- or surreality within the filmic experience of killing Bill, or killing lots of people of color on the way to kill Bill. But what gets to—what needs to—be relegated to the realm of the ultimately fantastic? Is it how the decapitated, mutilated bodies bleed, in a manner that defies physiological fact, not to mention physics? Or does how these bodies bleed, in a manner so unbelievable, so over the top, render the female executers of the deadly blows dead to the possibility of delivering these blows? Is Tarantino a feminist? Can his cool, creative display of woman-on-woman violence make him one? Who cares? Whether he is or isn't doesn't need to have any bearing on a feminist reading of the film. So let's focus on the film itself, and leave Tarantino out of the discussion for the moment.

Unfortunately we can't. Even if it were possible to separate the general spectacular experience of *Kill Bill* from that of Quentin Tarantino, the person, this possibility is deliberately foreclosed by how he punctuates *Vol. 1*'s opening scene. The frame centers the Bride's brutalized and terror-stricken face, and we hear the voice of Bill, played by David Carradine, saying: "Do you find me sadistic? I bet I could fry an egg on your head right now if I wanted to. You know, Kiddo, I'd like to believe that you're aware enough, even now, to know that there is nothing sadistic in my actions. Maybe toward those other jokers, but not you. No, Kiddo. This moment, this is me at my most masochistic." The Bride manages to respond to him with "Bill, it's your baby" a split second before he shoots her in the head. A black screen with white letters announces: "This is the 4th film by Quentin Tarantino." If this is *him* at his most masochistic, it would follow, then, that his first three films were him as a sadist. Whatever the sense or nonsense of this announcement—its purpose cannot be to remind us of who directed the film, as it was the director himself who drew in millions of dollars on the film's opening weekend—it is meant, without question, to be part of the narrative. Opening thus, the film merges Tarantino with the first spoken words of the film, making him as much Bill's masochistic "personality" as he is Uma's body.

Because the violence around which the story is based and justified is comprised of many unstomachable acts of violence against Tarantino's beloved object—an object/figure he describes as Uma Thurman's body and his personality—it makes sense that Bill/Quentin would himself "feel" the wounding of this revered female character with which he identifies. And it also makes sense that his masochism is at play *beyond* the narrative wounding that his script and direction inflict on Thurman's/the Bride's body. Her revenge against the racialized others who have attempted to murder her and have murdered her future as wife and mother, and with whom Tarantino also identifies in complicated ways in his desire to perform his hipness, is also a visual, vicarious masochism that he enacts, a punishment that he inflicts on the parts of himself that wish to *be* other although he should have only ever despised the other. His sadism and masochism would thus appear to be the perpetually alternating, recuperative arms of his attempted wholeness.

In his review of the *Kill Bill* films, Chuck Stephens discloses what in Tarantino's phenomenally lucrative filmic "soul searching" most touched him: the surprisingly moralistic message about the universal compulsion to protect the birth and life, and to avenge the death, of white purity and innocence at all costs. Of course, Stephens doesn't express it quite this way. Rather, he says: "Strange is the realization that what is patently designed to be the most monomaniacally, involutedly, hermetically sealed movie-about-movieness in the entire cineQT catalog turns out to be the first of Tarantino's films that didn't invite me in only to luxuriate in the fixtures of its cozy culture crib; *Kill Bill*'s super-determined surfaces also managed to act on me as a mirror, and as I watched it, I also found myself looking back out at life. Not a small part of that had to do with my seeing my own three-and-a-half-year-old daughter—whom my ex-wife first nicknamed, during her fourth month of pregnancy, 'Coming Soon'—in the face and circumstances of *Kill Bill*'s battled-overt B.B." (B.B. is the child of Bill and Uma Thurman's character, the Bride) (Stephens 2004, 47).

Thus we have a crucial clue as to how we might finally interpret the narrative arc, if not the clearly not-to-be-taken-seriously individual scenes, of these films. *Vol. 2*, after all, does end with the reuniting of the Bride with the child, and with an unwavering declaration of sorts, with a naming. Specifically, a final naming of the deadly heroine: "a.k.a. Mommy."

The journey of vengeance ends in this way with the restoration to wholeness of three most important fantasy objects in the American historical visual drama of white self-making: the white mother (who we thought was dead, but has risen), the white child (who we thought was dead, but has risen), and their indestructible bond. The simplicity of it—after the intricacies of the film's violence and its jolting rescripting of gender roles in relationship to violence—offers a clean and comfortable narrative closure. Still, could it really be that all this intricately stylized, homagistic violence was for this, this rediscovery of these most universal truths? Is it possible to dabble in and sample from such otherworldly texts and terrains as China, Japan, and Mexico and emerge on the other side of the adventures still pure

The Bride is reunited with her daughter.

The heroine's self is fulfilled, and named.
Screen grab from *Kill Bill: Vol. 2*, directed by Quentin Tarantino (Miramax Studios, 2004).

and whole? In the hands of an amateur director, perhaps not. But as the sheriff who discovers the bloody Bride and the wedding party says of the murdering mastermind behind it all: "This ain't no squirrelly amateur. This is the work of a salty dog. You can tell by the cleanliness of the carnage. A kill-crazy rampage though it may be, all the colors are kept inside the lines. If you was a moron, you could almost admire it." Still, qualifying the pleasure in consuming such a spectacle doesn't disappear the pleasure for the highly specific, if not necessarily moronic, demographic that Tarantino targets.

In an interview with Lisa Kennedy, Tarantino recounts that "someone said to me at Sundance when *Reservoir Dogs* was there, 'You know what you've done, you've given white boys the kind of movie black kids get.' You know like *Juice*, and . . . *Menace II Society*. Blacks have always had those movies. . . . Being bad, looking cool being bad, with a fuck-you attitude. The only time white guys could ever duke it out with black culture when it comes to being big and the coolness of being big is in the 50s, the rockabilly days, when guys would walk around with big ole houndstooth coats and big ole hair. That was as big as black culture in the 70s, and it's all based on looking cool, looking like a badass."[3] The Bride fits rather remarkably seamlessly into Tarantino's arsenal for "duking it out with black culture," and so I have to wonder: Is *Kill Bill* really a film by, for, and about feminists, abandoning a primary engagement with filmic technologies of race and racialization to consider and perform filmic inversions of gender roles? Can it, does it, advance from Tarantino's obsessive representation of racial codes in its revision of women's relationship to violence? And if it does not, can it be a feminist text? What are the implications of a feminism that emerges against the cinematic backdrop of mass violence—cartoonish though it may be—in the "otherworldly" locales of predominantly Mexican-populated El Paso and an utterly foreign Japan? It is against this backdrop, and within the problematic, racialized context of American postfeminism, that the heroine, as Uma Thurman's body and Quentin Tarantino's personality, emerges as white female kung fu master.

In an article on *Kill Bill* titled "Day of the Woman," the renowned feminist film critic B. Ruby Rich writes: "In a wonderfully old-fashioned way, KB2 is focused on the body, its suffering, and its mortality. At a moment when movies are fixated instead on special effects, CGI, cyborgs, aliens, hobbits—in short, everything except human beings—it's downright refreshing to find a film that makes us care about the battered and fatally flawed bodies subjected to its narrative" (Rich 2004, 27). It is significant that Rich's assessment of this film as one that depicts suffering and mortality, the fragility and beauty of the human body, references only *Vol. 2*, where the only bodies killed, except for one (the Bride's Chinese martial arts teacher, whom Elle Driver, played by Daryl Hannah, poisons), were white. Indeed, the "colored" backdrop of a black mother, blood, and Asian limbs that was the entirety of *Vol. 1* is forgiven, if not forgotten, with the emergence of the white characters, including Elle, Bill, and Bill's brother Bud (Michael Madsen), and the slow and careful telling of the real story. The real story, the one that makes sense of all that happened before and after, is the story that takes place in the desserts of Texas and Mexico, the story of the white family, its disruption, and the avenging of its disruption. The final credits in *Vol. 2* visually recount the racially embodied sources of this disruption—with stills depicting characters and scenes from *Vol. 1*—right after a full-screen intertitle assures us, "The lioness has been reunited with her cub and all is right in the jungle."

There was ample mortality in the first volume of *Kill Bill* and ample reminders of it at the end of the second, but not a whole lot of suffering was rendered in either presentation of it. Nor were we made to care about the battered and, if not fatally flawed, then *racially* flawed bodies that were, in Rich's words, "subjected to the film's narrative." We were made, instead and consistently, to care only about the Bride's body and its radical ability to negotiate its violent feminist imperatives with its more traditional maternal imperatives. Perhaps nothing in the film brings this into relief like the juxtaposition of the scene in *Vol. 1* where the Bride kills Copperhead in front of her daughter with the scene in *Vol. 2* where the Bride convinces the Asian American woman assassin who comes to execute her for abandoning Bill and the DIVAS to let her live. She does this by pointing her to a positive home pregnancy test that she's just taken. Maternal identification appears to have strategically racial (non)limits: Copperhead dies and Black Mamba lives. "Revenge is a dish best served cold" (as *Vol. 1*'s epigraph declares) by a white mother.

Given the foregoing textual, intertextual, and extratextual material of *Kill Bill*, how can we move away from an "angry woman of color" position and make a smart critique of something that, because of its overwhelmingly complex, postmodern, intertextual, reverential, and self-referential mazes, cannot possibly be as simply racist as it appears? Perhaps we do what many others have done and call it feminist. But at what cost?

The problem in fantasizing about the Day of the Woman is that this day is one that would necessarily honor and be accountable to both a category (woman) and a movement (feminism) that have yet to sufficiently find their way around the racial silences that they produce. If we begin our efforts to theorize images of violence—and perhaps, as Judith Halberstam encourages us, to radically theorize and exercise our imaginations *toward* violence—then we have to begin with the fact long recognized by antiracist feminists, that the very category of woman does not exist, and has never existed, independently of race (Halberstam 1993). If we start and stay here, in this place of rigorous acknowledgment of intersectionality, our Day of the Woman would have to look—even in our most creatively violent imaginations—different from what it looks like in *Kill Bill*, and different from what it looks like in the feminist critical readings of it that I've encountered so far.

To be clear, I do not discount the possible play and pleasures of our subjective experiences of this or any other image-text. I am really not at all interested in the good-versus-bad game of visual culture critique. I *am* interested in and committed to asking how our theorizations of resistant practices of imagined, perhaps real, violence that occur in, or are inspired by, images can be accountable to the intersectional perspective from which feminist critics aspire to read culture. If and when we cheer the emergence of the white Black Mamba as kung-fu-assassin-turned-mommy, we do so because we're smart enough to get the ironies and the commentaries on race and gender that this defamiliarizing characterization of our heroine performs, regardless of the fact that Daddy-o Tarantino's politics are problematic. We know this. But I want to ask what, if any, disavowals of the racial work of women's violence in *Kill Bill* are necessary for feminist pleasure? And I want to ask the knowingly provocative question: when is feminist pleasure feminist precisely because of how it engages with, and not necessarily in a challenging way, racial logics, racial knowing? A radically different, radically critical Day of the Woman is at least as far away as our willingness to answer this.

Notes

This chapter is a substantially revised version of work that benefited greatly from the generous feedback and insights of a number of colleagues in a wide variety of venues—far too many to name here. I want especially to thank the editors of the special section of *Visual Arts Research* in which a shorter version of this work was first published in 2006, as well as the participants at osu's Visual Culture Gathering that same year. Very special thanks are due Grace Kyongwon Hong and

Roderick Ferguson for including this chapter and for their crucial feedback on its various revisions. I also thank Raphael Pérez-Torres and the anonymous reviewers of the Strange Affinities series for their insights and suggestions.

1   My interrogation of the racial politics of *Kill Bill*'s would-be feminism works in the vein of addressing Lisa Coultard's observation in her essay "Killing Bill: Rethinking Feminism and Film Violence." Coultard notes that *Kill Bill*'s employment of pastiche "should not be excised from the constructions of race, class, violence, and gender at work in intertextuality, self-referentiality, or genre hybridity" (2007, 161).

2   Victoria Ward, "*Kill Bill* a Feminist Statement, Says Tarantino," *Press Association*, October 2, 2003.

3   Lisa Kennedy, "Natural Born Filmmaker: Quentin Tarantino Versus the Film Geeks," *Village Voice*, October 25, 1994, 32.

Time for Rights?

Loving, Gay Marriage, and the Limits of
Comparative Legal Justice

> Only that historian will have the gift of fanning the spark of
> hope in the past who is firmly convinced that *even the dead*
> will not be safe from the enemy if he wins. And this enemy has
> not ceased to be victorious.
> —Walter Benjamin, "Theses on the Philosophy of History"

> The document is not the fortunate tool of a history that is
> primarily and fundamentally *memory*; history is one way in
> which a society recognizes and develops a mass of documen-
> tation with which it is inextricably linked. To be brief let us say
> that history, in its traditional form, undertook to "memorize"
> the *monuments* of the past, transform them into *documents*,
> and lend speech to those traces, which, in themselves, are
> often not verbal, or which say in silence something other
> than what they actually say; in our time, history is that which
> transforms *documents* into *monuments*.
> —Michel Foucault, *Archeology of Knowledge*

Permit me to ask what it means to remember, indeed to
commemorate as anniversary, *Loving v. Virginia*, the
landmark U.S. Supreme Court case that invalidated state-
based antimiscegenation laws.[1] What kinds of critical and
political possibilities do such commemorations make possible? What do we desire when we desire to commemorate
and look back on *Loving v. Virginia*? Indeed, as a paradigmatic text of desire in the United States today, what kind of
desires does *Loving* enable?

On June 12, 1967, the U.S. Supreme Court, in a unanimous vote, struck down Virginia's Racial Integrity Act of

1924, which declared marriage between a white and "colored" person a felony offense.[2] Falling three years after *McLaughlin v. Florida*,[3] which invalidated anti-interracial cohabitation and intimacy laws, *Loving v. Virginia* is credited with invalidating and abolishing all remaining state-based forms of racial discrimination in marriage contracts. This past year marked the fortieth anniversary of that decision. Perhaps an anniversary that would have passed unnoticed by all but legal scholars and a few constituencies (those caught one way or another in the effects and aftereffects of modern anti-miscegenation laws), this anniversary has become a matter of some concern for a majority of American society. In particular, the coincidence of this anniversary with the current legal, legislative, and, to some degree, electoral campaigns for gay and lesbian marriage has drawn *Loving* into an expanded arena of meaning and application.[4] Most subjects would have seen in *Loving* nothing more than the story of the nation's racial morality tale, among the last of the major civil rights jurisprudence that began with the Supreme Court's decisions in *Brown v. Board of Education*[5] and *Bolling v. Sharpe*[6] thirteen years earlier on May 17, 1954. That *Loving* might be a symptom of social relations and forces determining their own lives in the present would surely not have been front in their minds.

And yet all of this changed with the emergence of gay marriage as a central issue of electoral politics and judicial culture at both the state and national levels. All of a sudden, *Loving* became a touchstone of comparative history, politics, and identities. What were the legacies of *Loving* for homosexuals? What are the analogies between racial and sexual difference? Is racial discrimination in marriage contracts arbitrary in a way that sexual-orientation discrimination is moral? And are both forms of discrimination, then, necessarily invidious? Questions such as these have been preoccupying diverse scholars, historians, and lawyers such as Janet Halley, Andrew Sullivan, George Chauncey, Evan Wolfeson, and Randal Kennedy, to name just a few.

How we remember *Loving* and why we remember it at all might be as interesting an endeavor to undertake as answering the questions I just laid out, in part because such an itinerary of investigation will help us see some of the animating fields of force within which those questions are posed, comparisons made, and answers sought.

Janet Halley has argued convincingly that "like race" analogies abound in legal discourse, especially in antidiscrimination claims, in part because nearly every equal-protection claim cannot but cite the race-based jurisprudence for which the Fourteenth Amendment was crafted (2000, 40). This can explain to some degree the reason for *Loving*'s popularity at this moment. As advocates of gay marriage press their claims in the law, they cannot but analogize their claims to those of race-based claimants of discrimination who found in the Fourteenth Amendment an apposite discursive context for their own claims. Indeed, this has generated what Siobhan Somerville richly calls the "miscegenation analogy" in legal communities, policy circles, and media culture, one that argues that sexual-orientation discrimination in the form of sodomy laws and in the restrictive recognition of heterosexuals only by the state in marriage contracts constitutes, like antimiscegenation laws, an indefensible exclusion of a suspect class (2005, 337). Both the like-race similes and the miscegenation analogies thus propel *Loving* into the public light for the purpose of revealing not ongoing racial domination by the state or the failure of legal equality to achieve substantive equality but the invalidity of state-based homophobia and sexual discrimination.

It is important to note here that the desire to remember *Loving* at this historical moment in the interest of furthering the gay marriage movement, for example, is ultimately circumscribed by that interest. This interest first analogizes the discursive productions of sexuality and race in the law and in the broader social formation for which this law is devised, reducing and effacing the specificity of each production as well as their linked and relational coproduction, as Halley and Somerville each separately argue. Somerville, like Darrel Hutchinson and Mary Eaton before her, is particularly acute in revealing how this desire for the "miscegenation analogy" effaces and occludes gay, lesbian, and queer people of color, in particular, as a compound class with distinct experiences of domination and subordination not captured, comprehended, or articulated by prevailing legal and cultural epistemologies founded on so-called single-issue oppression or "suspect class" subordination (Somerville 2005, 345–46; see also Hutchinson 1997; Eaton 1995).

In addition, Somerville argues, analogical thinking of the sort promoted by the miscegenation analogy also effaces the linking of the nonequivalent histories of stigmatized homosexuality and formal racial equality within the law that *Loving*, during the era of its decision, in fact more tightly fastened. Examining the law's codification of homosexuality as a legitimate ground for exclusion in the 1950s and 1960s, in domains such as citizenship and immigration policy, as a precursor to its affirmation in *Loving* that the individual's right to marriage cannot be constrained by state-based racial restrictions, Somerville argues that what is significant about the intersection of race and sexuality is not their analogical relation but the manner in which race depends on sexuality for its normalization.[7] To the degree that law through the *Loving* decision universalizes in its domain the virtue and right of marriage for "all" without restrictions of race at the same time that the law stigmatizes homosexuality as a legitimate ground of exclusion from membership in the state suggests that analogies constructed between miscegenation and homosexual marriage promote the omission of this heterosexualization of race and the racial construction of homosexual practices that *Loving* helped advance. Somerville writes:

> What activists fail to see when using *Loving* as a precedent for same-sex-marriage rights is that the case is not parallel to a history of homosexuality as it is represented in the law; rather, it is embedded in the same history of sexuality that has determined the status of gay men and lesbians as the excluded others. By establishing a fundamental right to marriage regardless of race, the federal state in effect shored up the privileges of heterosexuality through a logic that was on the surface antiracist and anti-white supremacist. (2005, 357)

Following on Somerville's insights that formal equality generated a new organization rather than the abolition of structuring power in the lives of those interpellated by the law, perhaps we can ask a different kind of question about those in our current moment who seek—indeed, desire—the miscegenation analogy. It appears that the desire for the miscegenation analogy among legal activists and gay-marriage-rights advocates is a desire ultimately for formal equality before the law, one that in being withheld constitutes a "dignity assault" for lesbian and gay citizens. But here we run into a paradox: it was *formal* equality—the mode by which the state addressed, absorbed, and sought to neutralize the disruptive demands of the civil rights movement—that created the social and representational conditions that naturalized heterosexuality and homophobic violence, entrenching the law's power to delegitimate gay, lesbian, bisexual, and transgender lives. What then enables at this moment a faith in that very form of equality —abstract formal equality—not to further entrench in the law contemporary forms of social and normative illegitimacy as it promotes and extends formal equality now as a solution for gays' and lesbians' subordination, inequality, and cultural domination? Might we see in this desire for formal equality not just hopes for better terms of living and intimacy but an identity with the law itself, one that imprints gay rights as the leading edge of formal equality? And what of the forms of illegitimacy that formal equality not only refuses to address but surreptitiously further estranges from rights itself? I suggest that even the most single-minded of gay-marriage-rights advocates have not been immune to these questions. Rather, I see in the promotion of the miscegenation analogy the symptom of their penetration by these questions. In fact, the analogy becomes the *form* by which the symptom is structured and temporarily "resolved." Is there not a second analogy desired by gay and lesbian advocates who promote the miscegenation analogy, one that seeks to supplant the miscegenation analogy with something like the "gay marriage" analogy for others seeking to emerge from the shadows of legal illegitimacy that the assertion of formal equality casts?

To be concrete, the demand for gay and lesbian marriage rights as a means of gaining formal equality before the law has intersected, for example, with broad demands by Latino/a, Chicano/a, and Asian immigrant communities and their supporters, for citizenship and an end to the legal delegitimation, harassment, violence, incarceration, and criminalization of twelve million undocumented workers in the United States. That is, gay and lesbian demands for marriage rights and protection under formal equality have intersected with the movements of undocumented workers and their kin who have challenged the juridical state's authority to establish what Hannah Arendt terms "the right to have rights" (1958, 296). How have advocates for gay marriage engaged this critique, which interrogates the moral basis of citizenship exclusion (breaking a law they cannot but break as evidence of their moral degeneracy for citizenship), at the very moment that gays and lesbians seek inclusion into the moral universalism promoted by the law, the law's supposed foundation on the universal and "fundamental right of marriage"? Considering the foregoing argument, we should not be surprised by statements such as those made by the Angeleno Jasmyne Cannick, a lesbian writer and member of the National Association of Black Journalists. In appraising the demands and the public debate constituted by the unprecedented marches for immigrants' rights, Cannick argued in a widely circulated essay for the online edition of the gay and lesbian magazine the *Advocate* that gay marriage rights must first be achieved before U.S. citizens, their representatives, and the Left champion the rights of undocumented workers. Cannick suggests that however compelling the justice claims of "illegal immigrants"—conceding that it "might even be the *next* [italics mine] leading civil rights movement"—this "new" claimant for rights needed to wait until "we . . . [have] finished with our current civil rights movement" (2006). She writes, "[I] recognize the plight of illegal immigrants. I do. But I didn't break the law to come into this country. This country broke the law by not recognizing and bestowing upon me my full rights as a citizen." And she concludes, "Immigration reform needs to get in line behind the LGBT civil rights movement, which has not yet realized all of its goals" (2006).

There is much to say about such symptomatic language, of the way in which rights are construed as goods, the nation as recipient of *its* subjects' labor and lives, and the state as little more than a disperser of those desired goods. But permit me instead to focus on the blurred analogy that is being constructed here. Cannick's discourse fuses two different ideologies. The first produces the law as unfaithful to its own principles, for which African Americans once stood as, but for which gays and lesbians now stand as, the representation of that breech. The second produces an appropriation of a neoconservative ideology that rhetorically effaces the *worldliness* of the civil rights movement by turning that movement into an *American* exceptionalist drama of the nation's repeated betrayal of black equality. In the second ideology and rhetorical argument, that betrayal is most often manifested and figured as a contest between "immigrants" and "African Americans" for social mobility in civil society but is now figured as one between "gays and lesbians" and "immigrants" in the domain of law for legal recognition.[8] If Cannick's statements gained widespread popularity, it did so not only because of her analogizing of black civil rights and the gay and lesbian so-called civil rights movement, but also because of her turn to analogy itself as the narrative and logical form for discussing, reasoning, and thinking through the multidimensional crisis and conflicts that, far from being resolved over time, seem only to reanimate as new contradictions.

It is worth remembering that, as a class of metaphor, analogy is the creation of resemblance or likeness between unlike subjects that is permitted by their "govern[ment] by the same general principle." In the law, analogy expresses an "identity or similarity of proportion, where there is no precedent in point."[9] If analogies draw their rhetorical, affective, and apparent logical force from the resemblance or likeness they constitute between unlike subjects, they also regulate what we understand as the essential matter and meaning of those subjects by their reduction to the principle supposedly shared between them. Here each subject is vulnerable to the principle that supposedly constitutes them. But equally, in linking unlike subjects through a single principle or set of principles, that principle must sever or cut off what cannot be relevant matter to the principle. Thus the principle is also vulnerable, in the form of a failed analogy, to the accumulating forms of unlikeness not just between the subjects compared but equally between each individual subject and the principle to which that subject is reduced. In this way, far from stabilizing both historical and contemporary contradictions (those of the civil rights era of the 1950s to the 1970s and those of our contemporary moment), analogies like Cannick's risk multiplying the unlikeness of subjects not only to each other but to the seemingly stable principle for which they must stand as representative.

Analogy, as a *form* for legal reasoning, generates its own vulnerabilities, ambiguities, and instabilities. Perhaps this is why Cannick must fuse, through appeals to affect and interest, the imperatives of the civil rights movement and the gay marriage movement. Yet in doing so, she must estrange the links between the civil rights movement and the immigrant rights movement, promoting the principle that will relate the likeness of the former comparison (gay rights and civil rights) while simultaneously nullifying the relatability of the latter comparison (civil rights and immigrant rights). To the degree that she makes appeals to the civil rights subject (African Americans), via discourse most closely associated with that subject ("It is this country that broke the law in denying me full rights"), she reopens rather than resolves the contradictions generated by the state's attempt to neutralize and rearticulate the meanings of the black freedom movement. If analogical reason such as that expressed by Cannick or other advocates for gay marriage have import and purchase for the law and legally constituted subjects at this historical moment, they do so because they posit a fundamental identity between unlike subjects otherwise incommensurate. They promise to reduce the terrain of conflict to a single contradiction (the principle found within the analogy), and they promote the resolution of that contradiction as resolving not just the tensions of the present but those of the past as well, which continue to roil our present and the law's legitimacy within it. Analogy screens off incommensurability and heterogeneity, positing instead a principle to which each contradiction constitutes a more or less identical segment of a single line, for which immigrants "must get in line behind" the other segments. For Cannick, if the law is to remain legitimate, it must prosecute the nation, like any other offender, just as it did before, with decisions such as *Loving v. Virginia*. And equally, while the nation must suffer this prosecution from the law, Cannick's analogy offers to it the status of principle or framework for the linking, indeed straightening into a single line of continuity, unlike differences that threaten the transparency and self-evidence of that framework. In the case of analogies like Cannick's, the nation and its bind to liberal law are the supposed deep principle connecting the unlikeness of each claim. Indeed, in making immigrant rights the "next" civil rights movement "behind" that of the gay marriage movement, Cannick argues that enshrining gay marriage "first" "in line for rights" promises the limitless continuity of the nation as analogical principle. It is marriage equality that realigns "our" past (the civil rights era), "our" present (gay rights), and "our" future (immigrant rights), where the first-person plural possessive is none other than the nation form. That is, the nation form, while critiqued for its transgression against the law, is simultaneously offered the chance to "rise again" to the degree that it accepts this indictment and recognizes its accuser. And to the degree that both national law and the nation form are at this moment more vulnerable to displacement, inquiry, reduction, and reappraisal, perhaps we see here the appeal of gay marriage for both representatives of the law and cultural nationalists. If it comes as a surprise that many gay and lesbian groups not only find alliance with cultural nationalism and liberal legalism at this moment but also find in gays and lesbians just recently so reviled cherished comrades as well, this is the shock of recognition that some seek to understand with the coining of the terms "homonormativity" or "homonationalism" (see Duggan 2003; Puar 2007). However much these might look like strange bedfellows, perhaps we are now in the position to grasp analogy as precisely the form that enables these coincidences. In fact, to drive the point home, we might say that in our contemporary modernity, analogy is the logic on which the nation narrates its relation to the differences it constituted but now threaten the revelation of its own incoherency. The nation-state as the promise of analogy between forms of difference is precisely the revelation of its incoherency, of its struggle to remain the principle of differences.

Keeping this vulnerability of the liberal nation in mind, we can better grasp the promise that gay and lesbian marriage advocates make to "remember *Loving*" through analogy as compelling to cultural nationalists and liberal-rights advocates precisely for the way in which it reinstitutes the bond between the nation and liberal rights at the very moment at which they are most threatened by an irrevocable sundering. But I hope I have also explicated how this homonormativity in fact reveals the precariousness of the very vehicles, cultural nationalism and liberal rights, to which they seek identity. In fact, we might be in a position to ask something other than why gays and lesbians desire formal recognition from national law.

Rather, let us ask: Why does national law in this historical moment desire gay and lesbian desire for recognition? Why does it recruit this desire? What vulnerabilities and instabilities are opened when national norms such as the law desire GLBT desire? And might we see in these vectors of desire, between the gay and lesbian subjects' desire for formal rights and the norm's desire for that desire, a nonequivalence between the two desires such that the latter does not merely have the status of that which can fulfill or thwart the former's stated desire, but rather both are vulnerable to the incompletion and exposure that desiring can produce?

To understand why national norms might desire GLBT desire for formal equality through marriage, permit me to return again to the current interest in *Loving*. If we suspend the desire for analogy, for the miscegenation analogy as the import of *Loving*, what other stories might we tell about this decision and its historical value?

Let us begin with this: of the many legal decisions delivered by the Supreme Court at midcentury, *Loving* is possibly the only text (and if not, then one of the only texts) in which the Supreme Court declares in writing that the norm to which state marriage laws assented before *Loving* was one of "white supremacy." The Supreme Court of Appeals of Virginia upheld a lower court's decision that the Lovings broke Virginia's antimiscegenation laws by citing its own decision in *Naim v. Naim*, in which the Virginia Supreme Court upheld a lower-court ruling voiding the marriage between a white woman and a Chinese immigrant who married outside the state of Virginia but later resettled in Virginia as a violation of the state's Racial Integrity Act.[10] And though the immigrant defendant in *Naim* petitioned the U.S. Supreme Court for an appeal, subject to deportation after the voiding of his marriage, the U.S. Supreme Court declined to hear the case.

Thus, in its reversal of the Virginia Supreme Court's decision in *Loving*, the U.S. Supreme Court directly referred to the Virginia court's own citation of its position in *Naim v. Naim*, a position the Court implicitly shared and in either case allowed to stand just a decade earlier. The U.S. Supreme Court writes in *Loving*:

> In *Naim* the state court conclude[s] that the State's legitimate purposes were "to preserve the racial integrity of its citizens" and to prevent "the corruption of blood," "a mongrel breed of citizens," and "the obliteration of racial pride," obviously an endorsement of the doctrine of White Supremacy.[11]

What compels such speech, especially when the U.S. Supreme Court only a decade earlier demurred even to give *Naim* a hearing in its own hallowed hall?

Loving, as document, enacts a performative representation of state-legalized racism and its own self-invalidation of that racism into state-legalized antiracism. How did a state that once used its constitution to uphold anti-miscegenation laws now find in that very document the means not only to invalidate that constitution but to uphold it as well? To what did the law turn, and how did it present itself, so that it could uphold and invalidate itself in the same act?

Loving is part of the historic shift, what Howard Winant refers to as the "racial break," in which the state apparatus moved from being officially white supremacist to officially liberal "antiracist" (2001, 133–36; see also Melamed 2006). And yet, as critical race theorists and historians of the civil rights movement have argued, it is only a willful neglect to remember and hear race-based social movements' actual claims and demands against U.S. racial capitalism that could make those claims and demands synonymous with the legalized formal remedies to racism that the capitalist state offered as an "address" and "response" to those demands (Crenshaw 1995, 110–15; see also N. Singh 2004, 15). That is, as the state shifted from white supremacist to officially liberal antiracist in this period, it distilled from the changing and unstable meanings of both race and racism generated by a society rife with antiracist contestation a meaning specific to its framework. In particular, race is *analogized* either as a private particularity or as a mark of membership in a group, like creed, nationality, and religion, both of which are then protected from invidious state action. Indeed, *Loving* produces an account of race that seeks to organize the meaning of race and racism in a manner consistent with the state's liberal theory of individual liberty, formal equality, and right of property.

Gay marriage advocates who repeatedly interpolate *Loving* into the public sphere by producing like-race similes and miscegenation analogies in their pursuit of marriage contracts ironically only affirm the *Loving* Court's original and unstable analogizing of race itself as a mark or visible sign of membership in a social group. In affirming the legal decision we know as *Loving* as the basis on which they press their claims, gay and lesbian advocates either deliberately or inadvertently further extend a state-based juridical analogy of race itself, displacing the contest of racial meanings produced by the civil rights movement and other social agents contemporary with the decision. In reopening the *Loving* decision, then, we might seek instead to observe the way in which the legal understanding of race and racism is in fact a performative act, one that attempts a conquest over the social contest of racial meanings being produced at that historical moment in U.S. society.[12]

In what follows, I examine different commemorations of *Loving v. Virginia* to tease out the consequences of how *Loving* is remembered. I argue that how *Loving* is remembered can tell us much about both the period of the racial break and our own moment, as well as about the way the state reasserts its legitimacy (now as antiracist) at the very moment of its own self-invalidation (as historically white supremacist). I argue that it is perhaps this function of declaring the law both invalid and legitimate at the same moment that has made *Loving* a touchstone and symptom of our times.

What enables the law to succeed in such a strategy? In upending this strategy, I argue that it is only through temporalizing racial experience into a past, present, and future that the state can both invalidate itself and maintain its legitimacy. To this end, I argue that what legal decisions of this period, such as *Loving*, reveal is the law's unique dependence on historical narrative, on narrating the history of a social group as an inextricable aspect of the justice it promotes. Examining how this is true, I then ask what kinds of instabilities might issue from such a strategy, and how those instabilities might be exploited for further transformation of the state.

For gay marriage advocates who commemorate *Loving*, legal victories, whether against the antimiscegenation laws of forty years past or against the contemporary legal codification of marriage as exclusively heterosexual, indicate less the arrival of a particular social group, African Americans or homosexuals, into hegemony than they do these groups' efforts to free modern norms and the state produced by those norms from the petty restrictions and blockages that prevent their innate development. In this instance, then, to remember *Loving* is to reconnect with the goals of the *Loving* warriors, to see in those goals the image of a modernity, both originally and presently constricted, in an effort to dispatch oneself and others for battle yet again, perhaps for one last battle, to unfetter the norms already at our door. Indeed, if the writings of William Eskridge, an advocate for the legalization of gay marriage, can stand as an example of this mode of commemoration, both *Loving* and contemporary gay marriage struggles are merely protracted stages of cultural development in the full expression of a specifically American nation-state liberalism.[13] Eskridge writes,

> Liberal premises do not require the state to recognize any two people's marriages, nor to attach legal obligations and benefits to such interpersonal commitments, but once the state has made a policy decision to recognize and even encourage marriages, the state may not arbitrarily deny that recognition and bundle of regulations. For example, the state presumptively cannot give marriage licenses to same-race couples but deny them to different-race couples. The United States Supreme Court elevated this liberal principle to a constitutional rule in *Loving v. Virginia*, which held that the state could not bar different-race marriages. . . . Today, the Court's liberal jurisprudence considers sex a quasi-suspect classification, namely, one that is presumptively arbitrary and requires strong justification when deployed by state policy. . . . By analogy to miscegenation, state recognition of same-sex marriage is required by this liberal sex discrimination jurisprudence: just as it is race discrimination for the state to deny marriage licenses to black-white couples because of the race of one partner, so it is sex discrimination for the state to deny marriage licenses to female-female couples because of the sex of one partner. (2001, 855–56)

Here Eskridge defines the contours, relevant for his argument, of a specifically U.S. liberalism, one shaped by the state's active participation in the social definition and recognition of marriage. In his normative reading, Eskridge argues that it is this specifically American-style liberalism that generates the contradictory force of both *Loving* and contemporary gay marriage. Eskridge offers no account or hypothesis for *why* the U.S. government became involved in, or continues to involve itself in, the regulation of marriage.[14] Rather, he seeks merely to suggest that the unity of national culture with liberal universalism *requires* the substantive equality of homosexuals, defined for him by the universal extension of marriage rights to same-sex couples. To commemorate *Loving* in accounts such as these is to commemorate a future in which the law, signified by a state founded on liberal precepts, is unified with American culture and social life, signified by the apparent historical choice to involve the state in the recognition of marriage. If *Loving* is firmly an event in the past, it is worthy of remembering because it signals the origin of a substantive American liberal modernity.

Commemorations can also house a second seemingly opposite position from the one taken by Eskridge and many gay marriage advocates in relation to the anniversary of *Loving v. Virginia*. It is a position that has been voiced most powerfully by scholars, activists, and historians interested in remembering the social and cultural history of specific oppressed social groups, whether they be African Americans or homosexuals. They argue against using commemorations to universalize or normativize a single political position or perspective, particularly one determined by present needs or desires. They argue that such a mode of memorializing misrepresents the uniqueness of social histories of difference that intersect at one point or another with the law. Against the position of Eskridge and others who seek to remember the past as a milestone in the gradual development of a singular quasi-liberal legal subject of U.S. modernity, this position advocates for social histories of difference as the subject of commemoration.

For this group, to remember *Loving* is thus to remember the history of African American struggles for equality and dignity in all spheres of life, including intimacy, as well as the history of the African American civil rights movement's contributions to the meaning of equality and dignity that "we" now inherit as a newly revamped modern society. It is through an engagement with this social history that one can ethically conduct important political comparisons between African American civil rights struggles and the legal movement for gay marriage.

Randall Kennedy's Leary Lecture "Marriage and the Struggle for Gay, Lesbian, and Black Liberation" can emblematize this important mode of commemoration. Remembering *Loving* in our contemporary moment, Kennedy says, cannot but demand an engagement with the drive for gay marriage, a drive against what Kennedy terms "the heterosexual—'straight' —majority." Yet he cautions against what he and others term the "*Loving* analogy*," which argues that "prohibitions against interracial marriage and prohibitions against same-sex marriage are the same" (2005, 788). And he concurs with the social historian George Chauncey that such an argument in fact "does no justice to history and no service to the gay cause" (2004, 161). Moreover, Kennedy argues, such analogizing tells us next to nothing about *why* heterosexual majoritarianism persists and most especially, for his concerns, *why* there are traces of that heterosexism in African American communities as well, despite their formal position in the law as historically oppressed and against majoritarianism. Kennedy argues that we must instead look in the domain of American history to discover repeated instances of "victims victimizing" so that we might work against both our and the previous victims' complacency and righteousness (2005, 797–98). Hence, commemorating *Loving* by remembering African American social history can help us better understand both the past and current forms of oppression, racial, sexual, and otherwise. Indeed, it is through the encounter with, and remembering of, African American social history that we might

> remember that history unfolds in mysterious ways that are difficult (if not impossible) to anticipate. The ugliness of the reaction to *Brown*, the Civil Rights Act of 1964, and other progressive racial reforms helped to awaken the country to the need for a larger, more determined, and ongoing confrontation with past and present racial injustices. A similar chain of events may assist in prompting society to confront and overcome its deeply ingrained oppressions of gays and lesbians. (2005, 801)

Here, remembering actual African American social history through commemorations of *Loving* enables the important understanding of history not, as Eskridge would like, as a normative schema. Rather, social history reveals the power of unexpected (from the perspective of the norm) agents of society. Social history (from below) of the type that Kennedy, Chauncey, and others advocate repopulates political life with *minoritized* social actors and their collective efforts that are left out of the normative accounts such as those produced by the *Loving* analogy and often excluded from the privileged domains of the political sphere and policymaking. And engaging actual African American social history during *Loving* commemorations enables the use of history to contraindicate acts of African American homophobia coded as righteousness, as well as serving as evidence for gays and lesbians that the confrontation against dominating norms, however difficult and apparently failed in their own time, can serve as a moral beacon for a future generation not immune, as the current one appears to be, to the brutalizing agency of exclusion.

For those who hold this position, commemorating *Loving* is (as it is in the previous position) an act of remembering an event that is firmly in the past and fully completed. The event is more or less knowable (what is important about it at least) for the subject who seeks to commemorate and remember it. And, most important, it is an event and representation of the past whose meaning for the present is vital. However, unlike the former position, the past, in this case the social world of which *Loving* is merely representative, is seen as distinct from the present. Precisely because we are the inheritors of that past, despite its seclusion from the time of our present, commemorations, for those who adhere to this position, enunciate a promise to remember the past that brought us here but is no longer, however much remnants or repetitions of that past persist in the present.

To commemorate *Loving* in this instance is at once to highlight the apparent difference between our own contemporary society and that of the past. The imperative to remember this past comes not merely because it can serve as an important negative example for contemporary subjects of society, lest we are destined to repeat the mistakes of the past, though it most certainly does perform this function as well. More importantly, we commemorate this past out of a moral commitment to remember the victims of the society of which we are members.

Whereas from the standpoint of norms and normative accounts of society, such as the one offered by Eskridge, the past is merely an early and primitive moment of national development, this other position, while not entirely contesting that schema, grips on to the past as well to remember the social histories of the groups that had once been excluded from the norms and normative society of which those who remember are a part. Within this temporal logic, commemorations are precisely tools of memory, non-site-specific monuments to the past that settle for us, in the sense of placing, revealing, and representing, the otherness of the past that is both produced and threatened by our very desire for, and experience of, modernity as the universalization of once exclusive norms.

This is demonstrated most vividly by the numerous injunctions of social historians and legal scholars of all political stripes to remember the past "correctly," warts and all. Such activities for the modern citizen and historian demonstrate the *historical and ethical capacity* of the modern subject to appraise the past just as it was, suppressing the apparent modern or postmodern desire for identity, affiliation, congruence, or even juxtaposition and contiguity (see Kennedy 2005). At stake is the valuing of those others, now firmly lost for the present, whose lives and meaning could be grasped by the subject who seeks to remember them through the practice of history. For this subject, to commemorate *Loving* is to gain the opportunity to once again remember national kin who are subject to, and violated by, racism and state-based forms of segregation, and specifically to remember the group particularly ravaged by such legal and extralegal violence: African Americans. Central to the logic, however, that upholds this mode of commemoration and memory is the notion that the historical subjects of the past are themselves whole and unique, sharing a positive essence. Thus within this logic of commemoration, emphasizing African American differences of gender, sexuality, and so forth is beside the point, for such differences are merely an expression of the organized plurality within a unified and positive (in the sense of empirically real) black human community. It is this community that is commemorated, its struggle for survival and equality in the face of repeated enactments of material and symbolic forms of violation and subordination remembered and its enduring self-dignity honored.

This latter mode of commemorating *Loving* has importantly revealed the real disregard for African American history that many gay and lesbian marriage advocates who supposedly seek to commemorate *Loving* evidence. As Randall Kennedy has pointed out, the antihistorical legal formalist mode of comparison and commemoration that many advocates of gay and lesbian marriage rights pursue when they "remember" *Loving* tends to disregard or forget critical differences. For example, while gay and lesbian marriage is not legally recognized, it does not constitute the criminal offense that black-white marriages such as the Lovings' in their time did. That is, the desire for state recognition by gays and lesbians misremembers or forgets not only gay history before the Supreme Court ruling in *Lawrence v. Texas*[15] but also the history of African American survival and struggle precisely against the state, at that time formally white supremacist. Indeed, seen in this light, a more historicized formalist analysis of *Loving* would suggest that the genealogy of which it is a part is definitively not gay marriage rights, with its desire for recognition by the state, but rather something like the contemporary dis-proportionate sentencing guidelines for crack and cocaine possession that further ballooned the disproportionate incarceration of black and Latino men and women in the United States over the last two and a half decades. For in both cases, de jure in the former and de facto in the latter, "the criminality of an act depend[s] upon the race of the actor," to cite Justice Stewart's concurring opinion in *Loving v. Virginia*.[16]

Additionally, critical gay and lesbian historians such as George Chaun-cey have argued that the drive for gay marriage must forgo the logics of dehistoricized comparison with *Loving*, lest we forgot the specific, unique, and historical forms of discrimination that lesbian and gay people experi-enced for most of the twentieth century. Just as African American history, to be commemorated on the anniversary of *Loving*, remembers a people's past, so too gay and lesbian history must be a memory of another people's past. And while gay and lesbian history is neither experientially nor historically separate from African American history (for as Chauncey argues, the segre-gated logics that produced Harlem also made it a refuge of survival and space for self-expression for a number of black and white gays and lesbians in the early twentieth century), each tells the story of a unique people and identity, however racially or sexually plural each people and identity might be (2004, 16).

We see that in the case of African American history, commemoration suggests a past continuous with our own time, while in the case of gay and lesbian history, the past is, while sequentially and chronologically linked, nonetheless discontinuous with the present. It is the place where, for some, our generational kin are now lost, but not forgotten. In the case of Esk-ridge's liberal legal formalism, the substantive difference of the past is de-nied in the interest of establishing an identity between the past and the present within a single continuum of modernity. In the case of Chauncey's and Kennedy's critical liberalism and social historicism, the difference of the past is preserved and engaged to some degree; indeed, modernity, with its care only for the present and the future, is diagnosed as generative of a loss not of historical consciousness as such but of a certain *people's* history as their future, and generational kin are otherwise absorbed into the singu-lar and continuous modernity of which they were originally excluded.

Commemorations, then, in Chauncey's and Kennedy's model, offer the opportunities to remember not just the past but, more importantly, a pre-

viously excluded people in their wholeness, who are the historically important subjects of this past. Remember that this people operates as a reminder
that our modernity, understood as singular, continuous, and expansive in its
contemporary promise of nearly universal inclusion, can easily inspire a
letting go of the past that has nothing to tell us about who we are in the
present, one with devastating consequences for remembering the lives of
those who had originally been excluded from that modernity. This latter
model appreciates the disheartening irony that a people who have been the
victims of a particular modernity, such as African Americans in the making
of an American modernity, must not be forgotten, lest they suffer yet another injustice, however inadvertently, this time at the hands of a new
national unity for which they become the unremembered other.

Both modes of commemoration share a sense of modernity as singular
and continuous. Both divide time into units called past, present, and future.
And both seek to remember the murky origins and discontinuities within
modernity through that very prism of past, present, and future.[17] While
legal formalism commemorates the past as the beacon of a liberalized
modernity still incomplete, promising oneself for the completion of that
modernity, critical liberalism commemorates the past as the figure of an
otherness no longer with us, committing oneself to a vigilance directed
toward the modernity of which one is a part but which historically denied
some of our past kin belonging.[18] And the latter mode of commemoration
acknowledges what the former is anxious to deny: that American modernity, particularly that produced by the nation-state, has had the dual tendency of both recognition and inclusion of certain forms of difference, on
the one hand, and violence and exclusion of other forms—namely, racial
difference—on the other. In the case of critical liberalism, however, commemorating *Loving* as the means to remember black survival of hyperexploitation and violent subordination by the nation is, if not atonement, a
gesture of reparation, one that inserts in the space and time of commemoration (as a conference, a special issue of a journal, or a social history) a
people for remembrance and deliberation.

In the case of the legal formalism, history is little more than formal
memory, a pure means to reveal the demanding truths of a developing
universal norm, such as the universal recognition of marriage as a fundamental right. For critical liberalism, history is a revered and deeply re-
spected site of social agency, one triggered by cultural memory but irreduc-

ible to the particularistic attachments associated with memory. This is in part why the gay social historian and critical liberal George Chauncey argues that in using the *Loving* analogy to pursue its agenda, gay marriage advocacy "does no justice to history" (quoted in Kennedy 2005, 788). History for the so-called critical liberal is not simply a means of representing the past. It is, in fact, the only means by which "we" who share a modern set of norms, a normative modernity, can address and reconcile the ghostly otherness that haunts the borders of those norms, those others among us who were not, in the past, fully included in those norms. While in the case of legal formalism, historical memory merely reinforces an already developing abstract norm, such as the universal right to marriage, in the case of critical liberalism, historical memory, in the form of producing and receiving social history, is a central aspect of the work one does to make the universality of the political sphere just. Unlike legal formalism, here history is not merely a means or a transparency for viewing the norm at work, embracing all forms of difference by its apparently universal or universalizing character and capaciousness. Indeed, if "we" must take care to do justice to history, this is because history plays a central role in the making of a just society governed by legal norms that were once exclusive but are now universal. History has both a redemptive and an explanatory force in relation to the legal norms that were once exclusionary. It is redemptive in the sense that it is a promise not to forget those communities that were once excluded from the very norms to which the remembering subject belongs, lest the injustice of their historical exclusion be redoubled by the injustice of their erasure within social memory. And it is explanatory in the sense that these histories detail the specific social relations that denied a people protection and recognition by those norms. But it is also explanatory in the sense that it relates the distinct meanings encoded in those norms by a people or marginalized community originally excluded from those norms, such as the right of marriage, such that the norm is itself, in our present moment, a monument of sorts to the once historically excluded community or people. The irony, of course, is that the social history of the excluded community now depends for its conditions of representational existence on the popular affirmation of the norm from which it was excluded. Moreover, what is socially remembered of that community is governed by the framework of the norm or norms themselves, such that the social history of the excluded people is told only through the prism produced by that norm or set of norms.

The legal norm, such as the right of marriage, becomes both an abstraction universally valid for members of present society and simultaneously a metonym in the present for the past exclusion and for the people excluded. In this situation the perpetuation of the legal norm is now paradoxically the very means, seemingly, by which a society promises never to forget the historically excluded. Here disavowal operates *through* the representation of subaltern exclusion. It is only when the norm arrives and is received in and through its reified face that it is supposedly cleansed of its social and cultural heteronomy. In our moment of modernity a legal norm stands as a monument of the "defeated" past and the oppressed of that very norm. Far from crumbling under contradiction, the norm attaches itself to the representation of the subaltern communities that it constitutively excluded as a demonstration of its ultimate elevation from heteronomy. By representing its own constitutive exclusions, contemporary juridical norms promise freedom from social history, from the need to historicize themselves by promoting paradoxically the face of excluded juridical history. Ironically, then, society redeems itself and its norms of their exclusionary origins through the universal extension of that norm. To the degree that the norm exists, and because the norm presents itself as transhistorical, it promises temporal perpetuity, the argument goes, the other, the excluded people of the norm will always be the face of that norm. Cast in this way, of the historically excluded other with the very norm from which it was excluded, a certain ambivalence is generated from the standpoint of the subjects excluded by that norm. If the memory of the excluded community, of its otherness in the present, depends on the perpetuation and universalization of the very norm from which that community was excluded, then any desiring of the norm cannot but at once also be the desiring to remember the history of exclusion, perhaps even the social history of the excluded. This ambivalence makes any articulation of the norm by either generational kin of the excluded community or by contemporary communities that are also denied recognition by the norm necessarily difficult to decode, for it is unclear if what they desire is the norm or the face, the historically excluded people in which it also arrives, generating a contemporary subject who might possess both rage against and desire for that very norm.

It is only through history, the careful work of representing and remembering the particularity of the past, that the universalization of the norm in the present is made legitimate. It is only through social history that the excluded are made an inextricable part of the norm from which they were originally and otherwise severed. Thus U.S. legal norms, to the degree that they are foundationally exclusionary (in particular from racialized communities), require social histories of the excluded as the face of those norms as the governing precondition of their abstract universality and universalization. And yet, if the representation of these histories of exclusion is constitutive for the contemporary extension, circulation, and universalization of these norms, they are also regulated by the framework of the norms to which they are constitutively attached. These norms powerfully contour what we seek to know when addressing the excluded face of the norm, of how we apprehend that excluded face, indeed of what gives that face its unity and representational coherence for us. To the degree that the norm has this regulative force in shaping the excluded face, it has been difficult to desire that excluded face, the histories of the excluded and marginalized, without also at once internalizing the norms that both preserve the excluded past in our present and contour what one or we desire from this past. If the norm mediates our access to the excluded past that haunts our present, to the otherness of the past, it powerfully shapes both us and the past. Thus we might ask what it would mean to remember *Loving* in a manner that did not pass over the mediating function of the norm, in a manner that sought out the particularity of the norm that wishes to dissimulate itself both in us and in the excluded history that is now the face of that norm. How might we do this? From what location? And what might it look like? In other words, what kind of critical subjects emerge from the contradictions of critical liberalism and its normative affirmation of difference?

Walter Benjamin (1968, 256) reminds us that "there is no document of civilization which is not at the same time a document of barbarism," and that the historian's task is to retrieve the past for contemporary struggles, lest the past too be surrendered as yet another of the victor's spoils: "Even the dead will not be safe from the enemy if he wins. And this enemy has not ceased to be victorious" (255). Indeed, as Benjamin argues, "the danger [of oblivion] affects both the content of the tradition and its receivers. The same threat hangs over both: that of becoming a tool of the ruling classes" (255). Benjamin reminds us that a social history shorn of its cultural remainders, of the historicity that disrupts formal comparison, jeopardizes both the past and present social struggles, producing instead representations of both that operate in the interest of the victor. It is only those of us willing to fight in the unrefined, underdeveloped, and crude spaces present in our ambiguous times who might seize hold of the past as it flits by the empty, homogeneous time of our present.

What I'd like to do, then, is repose the question thus: What are the other legacies of *Loving* for our contemporary moment? Or perhaps, more appropriately, what legacies of *Loving* does our moment make available, legacies that can be seized against the victors' histories? What kind of past is opened up for collective memory in this moment? And what kind of legacy is *Loving* within this condition? What I would suggest is that *Lovings v. Virginia* is not just the record of the break in the racial state against miscegenation, one of a number of precedent-setting cases in the making of the United States an officially liberal nationalist, anti-white-supremacist state. It is also the record of the way in which that emergent order sought to incorporate substantively black life into its legitimate domain. Katherine Franke has written articulately about the first aborted attempt of the state to do so in the aftermath of the Civil War in the short period we know as Reconstruction. And in many ways, *Loving* is part of a genealogy that might include the numerous petitions for cohabitation rights that Franke brilliantly unearthed as an archive of forgotten and perhaps nearly unrecognizable intimacies among African American slaves both during and after slavery.[19] Engaging *Loving* as a genealogy, then, or from the perspective of a Benjaminian historical materialist, we might read it as the anniversary of both the beginning of the end of the white supremacist state, as well as the beginning of our new times, of the norms that replaced white supremacy as the new socially and ethically reasonable social violences. Let us turn for a moment to the decision. In a rather remarkable passage, the majority opinion begins its reversal of the *Loving* decision handed down by a Virginia State trial judge by quoting the state judge:

> Almighty God created the races white, black, yellow, malay and red, and he placed them on separate continents. And but for the interference with his arrangement there would be no cause for such marriages. The fact that he separated the races shows that he did not intend for the races to mix.[20]

The majority opinion cites this reason only to replace it with an emerging dominant reason of state: liberal racial humanism. Citing *Korematsu v. United States*,[21] the Court averred that the state of Virginia's antimiscegenation statutes cannot prove that there is any longer an abiding state interest in racially regulating marriage. Arguing that it cannot pass muster under the "most rigid scrutiny" review demanded by the Fourteenth Amendment and affirmed by *Korematsu*, the Supreme Court struck down the Racial Integrity Act as abrading both due process and equal-protection rights.[22] Note the mode by which the knowledge of difference as a social and economic force is understood comparatively through racial typology by a Virginia judge, most surely the contemporary descendant of the slavocracy of the nineteenth century. In refuting the state of Virginia's argument for the racial separation of intimacy as a compelling state interest, the Supreme Court issued the following proclamation, one perhaps just as outlandish as the one that they refute, but one that I fear would be passed over as little other than "reason" and hardly as the anachrony that catches one's attention when reading the Virginia State judge's opinion. Here is the Court:

> These statutes also deprive the Lovings of liberty without due process of law in violation of the Due Process Clause of the Fourteenth Amendment. The freedom to marry has long been recognized as one of the vital personal rights essential to the orderly pursuit of happiness by free men.
>
> Marriage is one of the "basic civil rights of man," fundamental to our very existence and survival. To deny this fundamental freedom on so unsupportable a basis as the racial classifications embodied in these statutes, classifications so directly subversive of the principle of equality at the heart of the Fourteenth Amendment, is surely to deprive all the State's citizens of liberty without due process of law. The Fourteenth Amendment requires that the freedom of choice to marry not be restricted by invidious racial discriminations. Under our Constitution, the freedom to marry, or not marry, a person of another race resides with the individual and cannot be infringed by the State.[23]

What is remarkable about this passage, and just as worthy of our historical curiosity, is that racial typology and its comparative logic of racial differences are preserved and even extended in the very decision founded on a new liberal state humanism.[24] What we see here is that although the Supreme Court, the late modern descendants of the agrarian industrialists and the modern industrial elite, provided a new rationality to refute the reason of the Virginia State judge, the modern descendant of the slavocracies—figures, then, of two different modernities—both share a larger singular racialized gendered modernity, one defined by the organization of social differences into racial typologies. Indeed, that modernity is both made ambiguous and reaffirmed by the majority opinion. It is made ambiguous by the fact that racial typology is apparently invalidated as proper science, that is, as legitimate knowledge for the production of state reason: as the court avers, racial classifications are "so unsupportable a basis" of state action that such knowledge is "subversive" to equality, making state action a violation of individual liberty. Yet the negation of racial classification is not, as the court opinion shows, the destruction of racial typology. Rather, racial typologies are preserved, in the discussion of white men, black women, Indians, and so forth, and made coincident with both equality and liberty through the legal subsumption of heterosexual marriage, through heterosexuality and heterosexual gendering as the metonym for marriage, through, that is, marriage as a right.

Further, we could say that the late modern subsumption of marriage into a form of right is simultaneously the cultural production of race and gender as both the remainder *and* paradoxically the formal units for the state's notion of abstract equality and personal liberty structured through marriage. It is also, then, only through marriage as right that the ambiguities present as race and gender are deferred in the perpetuation of a singular modernity, of which the U.S. modern state and its juridical liberalism are a part. As a consequence, we can also say that marriage as a right, which demanded at its time hetero-gendering, but may not need to anymore, is the means by which racial typology is preserved despite the ambiguities generated by a state science founded on racial typology, named here as racial classifications.

Indeed, it is this longer modernity that is refashioned and advanced in the majority opinion and now operated through a rational state liberal humanism where it turns out that marriage (that most modern of things) is in fact one of the "basic civil rights of man" (who knew?) fundamental to the very existence and survival of an "orderly" humankind. And it turns out that the freedom to marry or not marry a person of another race (and let's just note here the sad reality that we are indeed almost at the point at which to not marry will have to be a "right" one exercises) is in fact presumed by that long modern political document we call the Constitution. Indeed, it was precisely this right to marriage on which the modern American suburbia was founded, the promise of marriage, real property, and commodities aplenty, the shifting of the welfare state's resources to the production of suburban infrastructures that resulted in the devouring of almost emancipated urban racialized neighborhoods into suburban highways and on-ramps, and in the creation of the single largest force of natural environmental planetary death, the restrictively reproductive, 2.5-member, middle-class nuclear family. To say this is to say as well that race and gender are the critical cultural remainders of a modernity forcibly made ambiguous and temporarily resolved through the substantive subsumption of marriage into a right.

It is the history of the severing of white supremacy from liberal property that *Loving* is a part of and that activists for gay and lesbian marriage rights now champion. Indeed, whatever other legacy *Loving* might have, it tells those of us who are trying to catch the past as it flashes up in this moment of danger that the universalization of the right to marriage is the very means by which the law forecloses other, perhaps more radical articulations of antiracism. Perhaps we can read in the desire to further extend marriage as a right the preservation of a modern feeling of personhood founded in racial typology. To this degree, we could say that the desire for the universal right of marriage is above all the preservation of an episteme that, moving beyond a debate about its utility, organizes the contemporary failure to describe what is.

Notes

1 *Loving v. Virginia,* 388 U.S. 1 (1967).
2 Id. at 1824.
3 379 U.S. 184 (1964).
4 It is perhaps not accidental that the Supreme Court of Massachusetts delivered its decision affirming gay marriage in *Goodridge v. Department of Public Health* on May 17, 2004, fifty years to the date of the U.S. Supreme Court's decision in *Brown v. Board of Education,* often seen as the precedent-setting modern civil rights case.
5 347 U.S. 483 (1954).
6 347 U.S. 497 (1954).
7 On the extension of normalization to African Americans and its creation of nonheteronormative differences of race, see R. Ferguson 2004.
8 On the worldliness of the civil rights movement *dissimulated* and appropriated as American exceptionalist drama, see N. Singh 2004, 1–57.
9 *Black's Law Dictionary,* 6th ed. (1990), 84.
10 *Naim v. Naim* 197 Va. 80.
11 388 U.S. 1, 7 (1967).

12   Both Patricia Williams and Kimberlé Crenshaw have, in different contexts (one in relation to property law and the other in relation to antidiscrimination law), argued a similar point. Both, as exemplars of critical race theory, suggest that it is not enough to simply unmask the ideology of the law as a guarantor of capitalist social relations and capitalist hegemony, as critical legal theory seeks to do; rather, we must also address the legal sphere as actively producing, constraining, and shaping racial identities and meanings as well as being shaped by those meanings. Here the state is not just a site that sits above or separate from racial struggle but a central domain or terrain of conflict over racial meanings. Both authors stress that the legal remedy of racism within U.S. racial capitalism from the 1970s onward, formal equality, is limited to what Crenshaw (1995) calls "symbolic oppression," failing to address "material oppression." Yet neither author suggests that formal equality is the only manner in which race can be adjudicated in the law. Rather, current law and legal norms concerned with "racial remedy" have rarely championed the racial meanings promoted by race-based social movements or intellectuals of those movements, such as critical race theorists. See P. Williams 1991, 216–38; Crenshaw 1995, 114.

13   See Eskridge 2001, 855–56; William Eskridge, 64 Alb. L. Rev. 853.

14   That is, Eskridge circumvents any account of the history of slavery, continental genocide, and racialized immigration as the primary conditions of determination for the state's regulation of marriage. Rather, the regulation of marriage by the state, and the practices of racial marking and ascription of which it is a part, is re-presented in Eskridge's normative account as, instead, the unequal state recognition of its subjects via marriage regulation. For an account that reveals the centrality of these conditions of determination for the writing of marriage law and jurisprudence in the state of Virginia, see Wallenstein 1994.

15   539 U.S. 558 (2003).

16   388 U.S. 1, 13 (1967).

17   Foucault (1972) offers the term "discontinuities" to discuss ruptures, transformations, or changed arrangements within a modern social formation.

18   This is, of course, the logic and mode of relation that undergirds the (white) liberal institutional desire for Black History Month or any other month or week dedicated to the public recognition of groups historically marginalized by the inheriting institution's (coded as "our") modernity.

19   By unrecognizable intimacies, I mean that they are forms of intimacy that are undesirable to us as intimacies. See Franke 1999, 251.

20   388 U.S. 1, 3 (1967).

21   323 U.S. 214 (1944).

22   388 U.S. 1 (1967).

23   388 U.S. 1, 12 (1967). It is worth asking if the Supreme Court would have ratified *Loving* in the way that it did if the plaintiff had been a black man or a black woman; that is, if in adjudicating the case of a black man's or black woman's right

to marry the Court would have placed the same emphasis on one's fundamental "right" for the orderly pursuit of "happiness." Indeed, if we take the "man" seriously in this statement, we see that *Loving* overturns white supremacy only by affirming the liberal theory of the male prerogative for private life as the precondition for formal equality in the public sphere; what would happen to that right if it had been seized by a black woman or a black man, one wonders?

24 In fact, what is interesting about the majority opinion is that the justices are not working with a white-black or white-nonwhite racial economy so characteristic of most of their civil rights decisions in this period. Rather, they refute the reason of the racial segregation of intimacy by pointing out that the law only prohibited black-white interracial marriage and not marriage between these groups and other racial groups.

Romance with a Message

W. E. B. Du Bois's *Dark Princess* and the
Problem of the Color Line

W hen W. E. B. Du Bois famously predicted, "The problem of the twentieth century is the problem of the
color-line," he described it as "the relation of the darker to
the lighter races of men in Asia and Africa, in America and
the islands of the sea" (2007, 3). Although the centenary
of *The Souls of Black Folk* has come and gone, his prescient
vision continues to be one of the most provocative observations of racial politics today. Readers of Du Bois have
considered, for the most part, his concept of the color line
in terms of a problem of race relations—usually coded as
black and white—in the United States or in transatlantic
Anglo-American contexts (see Edwards 2003; Gilroy 1992;
Hartman 1997; A. Singh 1976). Indeed, this prophetic ut-
terance, articulated in the wake of the failure of Reconstruction, would describe the long civil rights era in the
United States with profound accuracy. Yet if we look more
closely at his extended definition of the color line, we can
see how Du Bois gestures not only to a problem of race
relations organized around the regime of black-white
segregation in the United States but also toward a *global*

problematic organized around relations among and within various geo-political locales.

In 1906, a few years after the publication of *The Souls of Black Folk*, in an essay in *Collier's Weekly*, Du Bois noted:

> The tendency of the great nations of the day is territorial, political, and economic expansion, but in every case this has brought them in contact with darker peoples, so that we have to-day [sic] England, France, Holland, Belgium, Italy, Portugal, and the United States in close contact with brown and black peoples, and Russia and Austria in contact with the yellow. The older idea was that the whites would eventually displace the native races and inherit their lands, but this idea has been rudely shaken in the increase of American Negroes, the experience of the English in Africa, India and the West Indies, and the development of South America. The policy of expansion, then, simply means world problems of the Color Line. (1995a, 42)

In other words, as he phrased it more concisely in that essay's title, "The Color Line Belts the World." We see here not only a reworking of the color line as it appeared in *The Souls of Black Folk* but also an explicit mapping of the United States as part of a global dynamic of imperialism.[1] Moreover, Du Bois argues that anti-imperial resistance movements in Africa and Asia were necessarily linked to struggles for racial justice in the United States, an argument that became a central concern in much of his later work. The image of a color line that belts the world signals not only the global dimensions of competing and overlapping imperialisms but also the potential and possibilities of an alliance of the "darker" against the "lighter" races.

Du Bois's global depiction of the color line allows us to investigate further the phenomenon Lisa Lowe has called "the intimacies of four continents," the interdependencies and "particular connections" between Europe, Africa, Asia, and the Americas (2006, 191).[2] In this context, "intimacy" connotes not merely romantic or sexual relations but also the "spatial proximity or adjacent connection" between colonizer and colonized that is intrinsic to imperialism (193). The "world problems of the Color Line" that Du Bois warns against are a direct effect of the legacies of such global intimacies brought about by the practices of empire. For Du Bois, the four continents are intimately linked through the *close* contact (sometimes sexual, always political) between "whites" and "darker peoples" that emerges out of the European, Russian, and U.S. "tendency" for "territorial, political, and economic expansion."

Du Bois concludes the essay with the following pronouncement:

> The awakening of the yellow races is certain. That the awakening of the brown and black races will follow in time, no unprejudiced student of history can doubt. Shall the awakening of the sleepy millions be in accordance with, and aided by, the great ideals of white civilization, or in spite of them and against them? This is the problem of the Color Line. Force and Fear have hitherto marked the white attitude toward darker races: shall this continue or be replaced by Freedom and Friendship?

The final lines of "The Color Line Belts the World" gesture toward a new potential revolution—but not only or not necessarily of yellow, brown, and black uprising, though that is clearly one option. His ominous closing question proposes another, alternative revolution to the yellow, brown, and black awakenings described earlier. Du Bois locates the potential for another transformative awakening within what he calls "the white attitude"; using the language of "freedom" and "friendship," he gestures to the possibility of multiracial solidarity across color lines. Embedded in this powerful critique of imperialism is another way of thinking about the consequences, and the possibilities, of empire—the potential for nothing less than an international multiracial alliance, a planetary revolution of radical democracy.

It is necessary to take into account that in 1900, when Du Bois publicly introduced his famous concept of the "problem of the 20th century" at the first Pan-African Conference in London, he could not yet imagine—or rather, could only *imagine*—the fall of racialist imperialisms and the rise of subsequent decolonization movements in Asia and Africa (1995b, 639).[3] That is, the international dimensions emerge but do not play a significant role in his discussions in *The Souls of Black Folk*. Almost three decades after Du Bois first introduced his formulation of the color line, he published his fantastical novel *Dark Princess: A Romance* (1928), in which he indeed does *imagine* the possibility of an end to white imperialism and elaborates, albeit allegorically, on the global dimensions he alluded to at the dawn of the twentieth century. Describing the novel to his publishers as a "romance with a message," Du Bois envisions a resolution to the problem of the color line that is forged across national and ethnic lines as well as configured through an interracial and international romance.[4] Set in the early 1920s, *Dark Princess* fantasizes about the fall of European empires in Asia and Africa and the overthrow of systems of racial subordination in the United States. The novel foregrounds the personal relations—alliances, affinities, friendships, and intimacies—between people of color to critique the legacy of white imperialism and racism through the genre of romance. *Dark Princess* reworks the notion of "close contact" through its narration of an international and multiracial coalition among people of color as well as through the intimate friendship between brown and black—the telling of a love story between a South Asian woman and an African American man.

This chapter considers the political prophecy Du Bois first published in *The Souls of Black Folk* alongside the fictive prophecy he sets forth in *Dark Princess*, of the end of Western imperialism. While *The Souls of Black Folk* has long become a part of the American literary canon, *Dark Princess* has only recently received the serious attention of scholars. As Gayatri Spivak has observed, at the time of *The Souls of Black Folk*, Du Bois was "writing as a member of the metropolitan minority," but by the 1920s (when *Dark Princess* was written) we see him "writing as a member of the global colonial world looking forward to postcoloniality" (2003, 98). Indeed, as some scholars have noted, he is also eerily prophetic of what many now regard as a pivotal postcolonial moment, the 1955 Bandung Conference of Afro-Asian nations.[5] The novel's titular dark princess predicts, "In 1952, the Dark World goes free" (297). In *Dark Princess*, Du Bois not only looks forward to postcoloniality and decolonization but also places the "American Negro" as an active and central agent in bringing about that potential.

Matthew Towns, the African American hero of *Dark Princess*, leaves America for Europe—the New World for the Old World—when, despite being an exceptionally talented student, he is expelled from medical school because of his race. In Berlin, he meets a beautiful Indian maharani, Kautilya, who is fighting to save her state of Bwodpur from the clutches of the British Empire. She inspires him to join her international anticolonial coalition of people of color, a "council of the darker peoples of the world." It is the potential of "Black America's" role in this international coalition to overthrow colonialism globally that first unites Kautilya and Matthew in a political alliance and later inevitably evolves into a romantic coupling. Du Bois's lengthy "romance with a message" spans the globe, "from Banares to Chicago and from Berlin to Atlanta," culminating in the messianic birth of

Kautilya's and Matthew's son, the royal heir who is destined to be the future leader of "all the Darker Worlds," at the novel's end (Aptheker 1974, 18).

Dark Princess is a compelling text to examine for a project on the sexual and gender politics of comparative racialization, not merely because of the Asian-black interracial romance that unfolds in its pages. Du Bois foregrounds the differential experiences of Matthew and Kautilya along the lines of race, gender, class, and power. Matthew, the talented man of science, the son of a single black mother who grows up on a farm in Virginia, is barred from graduating from medical school because he is disallowed from taking a course in obstetrics—a course in which as a black man he would necessarily cross the social taboo (and in many parts of the United States at that time the legal taboo) of touching the body of a white woman. Kautilya, the maharani of Bwodpur, despite her political power as a royal head of state and leader of a global council, must defend both her state and her body against the humiliation and exploitation of British imperialism. Moreover, while a reading of the novel necessitates an examination of issues of comparative racialization through the romance between the two protagonists, my chapter focuses on the critique of democracy that emerges out of that intersection.

Dark Princess explores the wavering tension between what we might call Du Bois's dual romances—the strange affinity between internationalism and democracy. Recently scholars have looked to *Dark Princess* as being representative of Du Bois's "internationalist turn." Alys Eve Weinbaum has posited a link between what she sees as Dubois's fictional fascination with interracialism and his political turn toward internationalism (2007, 97).[6] Brent Edwards has suggested that Du Bois's forays into the genre of fiction might even signal a "romance" with internationalism itself (2007, 128). Typically understood as a fictional narrative that tells a love story, the notion of a romance can also connote a fascination with something or someone, the act of wooing and courting someone, or a love affair—but can also indicate a relationship that is not necessarily (or not yet) a commitment or engagement to another person or, in this case, to a political ideology.

Certainly we see hints of this in *Dark Princess*: the fictional Matthew Towns is conflicted—tormented—by the uncompleted work of American democracy and enamored by internationalism, just as, perhaps, Du Bois himself may have been at this time. By 1927 Du Bois had returned from his first visit to Russia, by way of Italy and Greece, and most likely began writing *Dark Princess* during his travels, energized and inspired by his grow-ing intrigue with Bolshevism as well as his disillusionment with capitalism as a recourse to racial justice.[7] But in 1928, when *Dark Princess* was pub-lished, we can trace in the novel not only a turn toward internationalism but also a continued enchantment with democracy—an as of yet unrealized democracy that we might understand as, to borrow a phrase from Jacques Derrida, a "democracy to come" (2005, 86).[8]

Whereas the novel opens with Matthew's dramatic exodus from the United States and follows the two lovers and their coalition as they—like the color line—belt the world in their quest for racial justice, aiming to combat "racism at home and colonialism abroad," the narrative resolution to the quest returns Matthew and Kautilya, as well as the reader, to the terrain of America, waiting for the promise of a democracy to come in the form of their messianic son, Madhu.[9] The geography of the novel is telling: Why is *Europe* the site that serves as the meeting place for Princess Kautilya and Matthew Towns, for the romance between these two expatriate, raced subjects, as well as perhaps between Asia and (African) America, to begin? And why is *America* the site not only where their romance is ultimately consummated but also where their union produces a racially mixed baby, a royal heir both to Kautilya's throne and to Matthew's legacy of African American double consciousness, on whose tiny shoulders the future rests?

Perhaps one reason Du Bois locates Matthew's political awakening in Europe is to return to the site of democracy's birth. In *The Gift of Black Folk*, he noted that "democracy was not planted full grown in America. It was a slow growth beginning in Europe and developing further and more quickly in America" (1924, 136). In *Dark Princess*, Du Bois suggests that the seeds for a new kind of "democracy to come" are planted during Matthew's sojourn in Europe but can only come to fruition in the United States.

Du Bois's own ambivalence between anticolonial politics and American exceptionalism propels the plot of *Dark Princess*. As he so powerfully argued in *The Gift of Black Folk*, the experience of African Americans is intimately and inextricably bound to the development of democracy in America:

> One cannot think then of democracy in America or in the modern world without reference to the American Negro. The democracy established in America in the eighteenth century was not, and was not designed to be, a democracy of the masses of men and it was thus singularly easy for

people to fail to see the incongruity of democracy and slavery. It was the Negro himself who forced the consideration of this incongruity, who made emancipation inevitable and made the modern world at least consider if not wholly accept the idea of a democracy including men of all races and colors. (139)

For Matthew and Kautilya, as well as for Du Bois, the very model for a radical democracy that explodes the color line is the struggle of the American Negro.

Dark Princess

Dark Princess was published when Du Bois was sixty. Looking back on his prolific publication history, he curiously dubbed this novel his "favorite" work (1969, 270). Yet by the late 1920s, as Claudia Tate argued in her 1995 introduction to Dark Princess, "Du Bois' political effectiveness and influence as a cultural leader of Black America was waning" (x). Dark Princess would, on the one hand, serve as Du Bois's message to the younger writers of the Harlem Renaissance about the need to create political art—he firmly believed in the inextricability of aesthetics and politics, or more explicitly, as he famously stated in "Criteria of Negro Art"—that "all art is propaganda."[10] On the other hand, the novel also seems to offer an allegorical resolution to the problem of the color line that Du Bois had introduced almost thirty years earlier.

Dark Princess, as a work of literary fiction, is admittedly flawed. Its initial mainstream reception reflects this—the novel did not even sell enough copies to warrant a second printing in the publisher's eyes. At over three hundred pages, it is often heavy-handed and cumbersome—not exactly what one would call "a quick read." A reviewer for the New York Times summed the novel up this way: "The book is well written, but there is enough material in it for several novels, and the plot is flamboyant and unconvincing."[11] Described by various reviewers as "bewildering," "sentimental melodrama," "sour grapes," and "a strange book," the novel seemed to baffle Du Bois's usual audience (Aptheker 1974, 21–29). But, as Herbert Aptheker noted in his 1974 introduction to Dark Princess, the black press offered a more enthusiastic response. The novelist George Schuyler exclaimed, "Dr. Du Bois is at his best," and the writer and political activist

Alice Dunbar Nelson called the novel "eminently soul satisfying" (Aptheker 1974, 26). Alain Locke, editor of the groundbreaking anthology of African American writing *The New Negro* (1925), commented, "It is to be regretted that, as a novel, 'Dark Princess' is not wholly successful. As a *document* [italics mine], however, it should be widely read" (Aptheker 1974, 28). In later years, scholars of American literature would reconsider Du Bois's novel more generously; as one literary critic noted in the 1970s, "*Dark Princess*, although a poor novel, is socially, psychologically, and politically significant" (A. Singh 1976, 126–27). In the 1990s, Claudia Tate urged, "But if his critics had judged the novel according to the values of an eroticized revolutionary art instead of the conventions of social realism, they probably would have celebrated *Dark Princess* as a visionary work" (1995, ix). Over the years, *Dark Princess* has also generated "interest as an early example of Third World anticolonial fiction" (Sundquist 1993, 619). Often considered alongside fiction of black internationalism (for example, novels by George Schuyler and Claude McKay), *Dark Princess* was published around the same time as F. Scott Fitzgerald's *The Great Gatsby* (1925), Ernest Hemingway's *The Sun Also Rises* (1926), and E. M. Forster's *A Passage to India* (1924), novels that would go on to define the so-called Lost Generation and, in some ways, romanticize empire. What happens if we place *Dark Princess* on the shelf alongside these novels today? Politically significant, important, visionary, but, at least to some critics and its contemporary readers, aesthetically unsatisfying, *Dark Princess* offers an unapologetic critique of the colonial and racial politics that so entranced Du Bois's more commercially successful colleagues.

The novel's scathing critique of American democracy begins with the flight and self-imposed exile of the protagonist from the nation itself. Du Bois does not mince words here: part 1 of *Dark Princess* is titled "Exile," and the sense of disillusionment and alienation is palpable from its first lines. As the novel opens, Matthew Towns is standing on the deck of a ship headed for Europe, looking down at the sea in a "cold white fury" while "in the night America had disappeared and now there was nothing" (1995c, 3). At this point, Matthew has left the United States after having been insidiously barred from completing medical school because of racial, sexual, and gender politics. The school's trustees decide to no longer admit "colored" students, yet Matthew, a prize-winning student who is already at the top of his class, poses a problem. The dean's solution is to deny Matthew admission to a mandatory course in obstetrics, in which he would have to come into physical ("close") contact with a white woman—a social taboo, as well as a legal one, in much of the United States at the time—and without which he would not be able to graduate. As Matthew later explains to Kautilya, "I threw my papers in his face and left. All my fine theories of race and prejudice lay in ruins. My life was overturned. America was impossible— unthinkable" (14). Significantly, he does not say it was impossible or un- thinkable to *live* in America, but rather that *America*—the idea itself—was impossible or unthinkable. The concept of the American nation—and the "fine theories of race and prejudice" that Matthew believed were, or indeed should be, its founding principles—had become no longer tenable. Here Du Bois's fictional hero encounters the very stumbling block of American democracy itself—how to reconcile the legacy or, in Du Bois's words, the *incongruity* of New World slavery with these founding principles—the very conundrum that, as Michael Hardt has suggested, stumped Thomas Jeffer- son himself (2007, 44).

Matthew hops on the first boat traveling abroad and sets sail for Europe, thus beginning his quest for racial justice by leaving the geographic and conceptual borders of America. That his Atlantic crossing is the reverse of both the *Mayflower*'s voyage and the middle passage in terms of both direc- tion and voluntarism is an irony that underscores Matthew's status as an exceptional figure. He crisscrosses the founding journeys of both black and white America. His exile will be self-imposed, his crossing voluntary and his migration temporary.

Once he arrives in Europe, he takes refuge in the Viktoria Café on the Unter den Linden in Berlin. As he ponders the differences between the politics of race in New York and Berlin, he considers how in Europe "he was treated as he was dressed and today he had dressed carefully. . . . He had walked into this fashionable café with an air. . . . Yes, in Europe he could at least eat where he wished so long as he paid." His social mobility appears less hindered by his race in European cafe society, where his entry is seem- ingly secured by the possession of capital, style, and "an air," rather than the color of his skin. Ross Posnock has commented that "Du Bois identifies Matthew with one of modernism's most glamorous icons: the expatriate aesthete abroad, in contemptuous rebellion from provincial America" (2002, 161–62). However, unlike, for example, the fictional expatriates who people the stories of Hemingway or Fitzgerald, or even the real-life American artists and writers who filled the salons of Alice B. Toklas and Gertrude Stein, Du Bois's expat is contemptuous not because America is provincial but because it is *racist*. This is the absolute reason for his exile—he leaves America because it has become "impossible—unthinkable." He has reached the limit of American democracy, the impossibility, the incongruity, of thinking democracy and racism together.

Despite the increased mobility—albeit conditional—that Matthew seems to enjoy in Europe, he remains dissatisfied: something is missing. Du Bois explains:

> Oh, he was lonesome, lonesome and homesick with a dreadful home-sickness. After all, in leaving white, he had also left black America—all that he loved and knew. God! He never dreamed how much he loved that soft, brown world which he had so carelessly, so unregretfully cast away. What would he not give to clasp a dark hand now, to hear a soft Southern roll of speech, to kiss a brown cheek? To see warm brown, crinkly hair and laughing eyes. God—he was lonesome. So utterly, terribly lonesome. And then—he saw the Princess! (1995c, 7–8)

That Matthew suffers from a dreadful homesickness, a longing for his native land, a painful yearning for the wholeness of home, is revealing. It is in the throes of homesickness—incredible nostalgia for his homeland and the shocking realization of the inseparability of black from white America—that he first sets eyes on Kautilya. It is American speech he longs to hear, but it is brown skin that he desires. Du Bois posits this longing for the nation as inextricably linked to the desire for darker peoples—a physical desire for the thick communality that he has left behind.

The passage concludes, "And then—he saw the Princess!" Here Du Bois employs an em dash, conventionally used to indicate a break in thought, as a visual cue to the reader to pause. One almost expects to hear a drumroll dramatically signal the arrival of the princess on the scene. (This quoted passage is a prime example of the occasionally extravagant and heavy hand of Du Bois's writing in the novel.) The novel's heroine, Her Royal Highness, the Princess Kautilya of Bwodpur (a fictional princely state in India), is described as "radiantly beautiful," with "a glow of golden *brown* skin. It was darker than sunlight and gold; it was lighter and livelier than *brown*. It was a living glowing crimson, veiled beneath *brown* flesh" (8; italics mine). The repetition of the word *brown* serves both to emphasize Matthew's utter thrill at seeing another person of color and to elucidate that there are indeed multiple hues of brown. Du Bois paints a spectacular portrait of Kautilya, whose luminous complexion becomes the living embodiment of the "soft brown world" Matthew had been longing for just moments before. Later Matthew notes, "She was 'colored' yet not at all colored in his intimate sense" (14). In this sentence, the word *colored* first appears in quotes and then, the second time, stands alone, suggesting that there are different ways of being colored. To be colored had social and legal ramifications in the American context that Matthew, as an "American Negro," intimately understood. Du Bois hints here at the social and legal complexities of a color line in the United States that does not readily accommodate those who are "other nonwhites."[12] How might this vision of Kautilya as " 'colored' yet not at all colored in his intimate sense" allow us to think comparatively about Asian and African American racial formations?[13]

Matthew's chivalric response to Kautilya's distressed damsel initiates their relationship: they meet because he saves her from the unwanted advances of a lecherous white American. The rescue narrative has long been the catalyst for the genre of the historical romance (see Kaplan 1990, 659–90). Like so many heroes in Arthurian romances, Matthew "saves" Kautilya from the clutches of a dangerous villain and, by rescuing her, appears to inhabit the role of hero from the start. We must bear in mind that Kautilya is no ordinary damsel in distress—she is a princess who is the head of state of Bwodpur, runs a global council of darker peoples, and on several occasions will save Matthew in return. In fact, upon first meeting him, not only does she save him from the depths of homesickness and racial longing, but also, by offering him a new way to reconsider his role as a "member of the global colonial world," she rescues him from the depths of despair over the impossibility of America itself. (Later in the novel, Kautilya saves Matthew not only from corruption in the wheels of the political machine of Chicago but also from a loveless marriage, as a result perhaps ultimately saving the future of America itself.)

When the princess thanks him for saving her—in flawless French, no less—Matthew stammers a response in English, to which she exclaims, "Ah—you are English? I thought you were French or Spanish." Matthew corrects her and explains, "I am an American Negro." Upon hearing this, Kautilya bends forward with sudden interest, stares at him, and exclaims, "An American Negro! How singular—how very singular. I have been thinking of American Negroes all day!" And indeed she has—the two bond over tea in the Tiergarten as Kautilya interviews Matthew about U.S. race politics. Matthew's declaration of his national *and* racial identity as an "American Negro" is critical—neither a swarthy European nor an African, he asserts both his Americanness and his blackness as a member of a "singular" group. He basks in the glow of her "steady full radiant gaze. . . . [fully aware that] It was evidently not of him, the hero, of whom she was thinking, but of him, the group, the fact, the whole drama." He experiences a heady rush from being regarded as the metonymic representation of black America. It is in her presence that "for the first time since he had left New York, he felt himself a man, one of those who could help build a world and guide it" (18). Seeing himself through Kautilya's eyes, Matthew imagines that he can finally assert his masculinity and feels transformed from powerless object of racial oppression to a potentially powerful world leader.

Significantly, this formative moment of politicization for Matthew echoes the oft-cited formative moment in *The Souls of Black Folk* that inspired Du Bois's understanding of double consciousness. Du Bois recounts his first memory of racial exclusion when, as a young boy, a white girl refuses to exchange calling cards with him at school. He writes, "The exchange was merry, till one girl, a tall newcomer, refused my card,—refused it peremptorily, with a glance. Then it dawned upon me with a certain suddenness that I was different from the others; or like them mayhap, in heart and life and longing, but shut out from their world by a vast veil" (2007, 8). This seemingly simple rejection by a glance is the catalyst that sparks the young Du Bois's awareness of racial difference. It is this childhood event that inspires the adult Du Bois to articulate the meaning of "double consciousness," the "sense of always looking at one's self through the eyes of others, of measuring one's soul by the tape of a world that looks on in amused contempt and pity." Both of these formative encounters involve being looked at by an other who is racialized and gendered differently—the white girl who sees the young Du Bois's blackness and rejects his token of friendship, and the Asian princess who looks at Matthew Towns and calls on him to live up to his potential as a world leader. This rewriting of the event that inspired Du Bois's understanding of double consciousness offers a reconciliation of sorts to the "two warring ideals in one dark body" that Du Bois powerfully and aptly described as the experience of being "an American, a Negro." In *Dark Princess*, he articulates a vision of a fuller ontological potential of the "American Negro," refracted off of Kautilya's glance of approval and into Matthew's very soul.

For Matthew Towns—and perhaps for Du Bois as well—Europe is both an escape from the racial politics of the United States and a site of political awakening (see Lewis 2000, 203). In Europe, Kautilya introduces him to the "secret international" of which she is the leader, "a great committee of the darker peoples; of those who suffer under the arrogance and tyranny of the white world" (1995c, 16). The personal rebellion that incited his exodus from the New World to the Old does not merely result in individual enlightenment but evolves into the potential for global revolution. Under Kautilya's tutelage, Matthew has an awakening and sees that "American Negroes are not an amorphous handful"—indeed, the princess confers nationhood on black Americans, telling him upon their first meeting, "You are a nation!" Although "America"—as a concept, an ideology, a place of residence—may have become unthinkable, in Europe Matthew begins to imagine the possibilities of "black America."

Upon meeting the multiethnic and multinational members of the "Great Council of the Darker races," Matthew is challenged to take up their global mission back to the United States. The council consists of representatives from China, Egypt, India, and Japan, an erudite, cosmopolitan lot for whom *belles-lettres* and *beaux-arts* are their lingua franca, and who debate contemporary art and politics in English and French with interchangeable ease. While the other members of the council are skeptical about "the ability, qualifications, and real possibilities of the black race in Africa or elsewhere," Kautilya firmly believes in the necessity of an alignment with "Black America," and together the hero and heroine persevere to eliminate "the shadow of a color line within a color line" (21–22). To become a full member of the coalition, Matthew must demonstrate the "worthiness" of the "American Negro"—and by doing so will prove his loyalty and love to his race, his nation, and ultimately the princess.

Romance with a Message

Why does Du Bois choose the genre of romance to tell a story of anti-imperial internationalism and radical democracy? Before even reading a word of the narrative, his readers are signaled to expect a romance or, more specifically, a "Romance." He calls obvious attention to his genre of choice through the novel's title and subtitle, *Dark Princess: A Romance*. What are the limits and the possibilities of Du Bois's deployment of this particular racialized, sexualized romance? Moreover, what exactly is the message of Du Bois's "romance with a message?"

Throughout *Dark Princess*, Matthew's romantic quest is intricately and intimately bound up with his political mission: "The World was one woman and one cause" (210). His political desire to join the secret international and to combat "racism at home and colonialism abroad" is impossible to disentangle from his physical-sexual desire for the princess herself. Indeed, it is never entirely clear whether he is inspired by the greater mission of the coalition or by the "luminous radiance of [Kautilya's] complete beauty" (14). Doris Sommer, in her influential work on Latin American fiction, has argued that the genre of romance is often used to narrate allegorically the intertwining of erotic fantasies with the desire for a new state—that is, romantic love and patriotism always seem to go hand in hand. Accordingly, the romantic couple's desire for each other is amplified by an urgent desire for "the kind of state that would unite them" (1992, 47). I want to suggest that in *Dark Princess*, the political desire of Matthew and Kautilya is not for "a kind of state" per se but for a global or planetary coalition of darker races, anticipating, if not quite a post-nation-state world, then a postcolonial world that is ultimately materialized in the figure of their son. While Matthew and Kautilya's romance is forged across an internationalist vision, it is significant that the relationship is finally consummated in the New World, America (rather than Europe, where they first meet)—and, moreover, that the child is conceived on U.S. soil. In *Dark Princess*, can the desire for the internationalist vision then ever be uncoupled from a desire for a brand of democracy that is rooted in the idea of America itself?

Messenger and Messiah to the World

The final scene of the novel brings us to the American South—Matthew's birthplace, his mother's "little 40 acres" in Hampton Roads, Virginia (11). His mother's farm both literally and symbolically represents the promise of postemancipation compensation for African Americans as well as the failures of Reconstruction—and one of the enduring failures of American democracy itself.[14] *Dark Princess* ends by recentering the American South as the center of the world—Princess Kautilya describes it as "halfway between

Maine and Florida, between the Atlantic and the Pacific, with Europe in your face and China at your back" (1995c, 286). It is at this auspicious site that we witness the novel's extravagant closing spectacle, in which Baby Madhu (or, as Kautilya notes, "Matthew in our softer tongue") is initiated into his role as "messiah" among a multiracial, pantheistic coalition. Jesus, Allah, Brahma, Vishnu, Siva, and Buddha are all called on to sanctify this moment, suggesting that a pantheon of gods has invested the tiny baby with divine power. Madhu is swayed "up and down and east and west" and proclaimed to be the "Messenger and Messiah to all the Darker Worlds!" This outrageously messianic spectacle is the grand finale Du Bois leaves us with, yet what is sacrificed seems to be any clear program of radical democracy.

As some critics have suggested, Madhu is "reminiscent of the lost son immortalized in 'the Passing of the First Born,'" Du Bois's moving account in *The Souls of Black Folk* of the early death of his first child, Burghardt.[15] Twenty-five years later, in this imaginative work of fiction, Du Bois reimagines that lost child as a domestic and international messiah, the exceptional heir to both aristocracy and democracy, who is both Asian and black, Indian royalty and American-born U.S. citizen, and finally both Asian American and African American. This exceptional (and fictive) child promises to be (or is invested with the potential to be) the solution to the problem of Du Bois's prophecy that "the problem of the twentieth century is the problem of the color-line." Madhu's interracialism and illegitimacy are ultimately made legitimate by his coronation and the subsequent marriage of his parents—according to Matthew's mother, they must make him "an hones' chile." This relentlessly heteronormative narrative, like all good romances, seems to find its narrative resolution in a marriage, typically signifying the wish fulfillment of the hero and heroine—the happily ever after of fairy tales.

It would be easy to dismiss the spectacle and pageantry at the novel's end as Du Bois's attempt at a happy ending, to write it off as one of the novel's many formative flaws. However, the closing union gestures beyond the written narrative of the novel. In a bedroom scene, as Kautilya is recounting to Matthew the meeting she called in London of the leaders of a "thousand million of the darker peoples," she tells him, "We organized, we planned, and one great new thing emerged—your word, Matthew, your *prophecy* [italics mine]: we recognized democracy as a method of discovering real aristocracy. . . . Democracy is not an end; it is a method of aristocracy.

Someday I will show you all that we said and planned" (225). Yet despite this promise, the novel ends before this information is disclosed to Matthew —and to the reader. As readers, we have followed Matthew's quest for three hundred or so pages, and yet, like Matthew, we are also denied any concrete political program. Why are the details of this revolutionary global movement deferred in *Dark Princess*? Why is the articulation of a vision or a program of racial democracy postponed at the novel's end?[16]

The romantic union is realized, but the political program remains deferred, democracy remains "to come." As Derrida explains, the notion of a democracy to come suggests that it is "not something that is certain to happen tomorrow, not the democracy (national or international, state or trans-state) of the *future*, but a democracy that must have the structure of a promise—*and thus the memory of that which carries the future, the to-come, here, now*" (2005, 85–86). The promise of *Dark Princess* lies in Kautilya's articulation of "someday," in the newborn Madhu's potential as a global leader, and in the possibility of a narrative that extends beyond the pages of the novel itself. In its meditations on the possibilities of internationalism and democracy, *Dark Princess* also gestures obliquely to the long reach of American democracy. If we recall that Matthew initially flees the United States in search of racial justice because America is "impossible—unthinkable," perhaps what he discovers upon returning to the fold of Virginia is that for an African American, America has become utterly inescapable— impossible to shake.

Notes

I would like to thank audiences at the University of Padua, Italy; L'Université Sorbonne Nouvelle, Paris 3, France; and UCLA for questions and comments that sharpened my thinking; Diana Paulin for countless inspiring insights while co-teaching *Dark Princess* together; and Victor Bascara, Grace Hong, Farhad Karim, Shirley Lim, Susette Min, and Cynthia Tolentino for indispensable engagements with earlier versions of this essay.

1 For a fascinating account of the shifting meanings of the color line across Du Bois's writings, see Coopan 2007, 36.

2 Here Lowe powerfully examines "the global *intimacies* out of which emerged not only modern humanism but a modern racialized division of labor," by examining interactions between whites and colonized peoples of color, as well as between and among colonized peoples of color themselves (192–93).

3   Also, as Amy Kaplan (2002, 176–77) has noted, few scholars have commented on
    the fact that Du Bois articulated his powerful prophecy in two different public
    speeches that year, in slightly different versions, and from two imperial centers,
    London and Washington, mapping the connection between European and Amer-
    ican imperialism through his words as well as his own geographic location.

4   Letter to Harcourt, Brace, 1927, quoted in Aptheker 1974, 19.

5   In April 1955, leaders from twenty-nine African and Asian nations gathered in
    Bandung, Indonesia, for the first ever Asia-Africa conference to discuss peace,
    condemn colonialism, and strategize the role of what would come to be known as
    the Third World in the Cold War. The nonaligned movement and Third World
    emerged from these discussions. See Richard Wright's powerful chronicle of the
    conference (Wright 1995).

6   Weinbaum 2007, 97. Weinbaum argues that "Duboisean obsession with interra-
    cial romance became constitutive to the substance and success of his antiracist,
    anti-imperialist, internationalist politics in the 1920s."

7   This intrigue would grow into a fuller political engagement with socialism, Marx-
    ism, and internationalism; indeed, Du Bois eventually became so disaffected with
    America that he expatriated to Ghana, where, as a still-prolific nonagenarian, he
    lived out his remaining days. Lewis 2000, 202–3.

8   For Derrida, the expression "democracy to come" is a call for an implicit political
    critique. As he explains, "The 'to-come' not only points to the promise but
    suggests that democracy will never exist, in the sense of a present existence: not
    because it will be deferred but because it will always remain aporetic in its
    structure (force *without* force, incalculable singularity *and* calculable equality,
    commensurability *and* incommensurability, heteronomy *and* autonomy, individ-
    ual sovereignty *and* divisible or shared sovereignty, an empty name, a despairing
    messianicity or a messianicity in despair, and so on)."

9   Many scholars, including Eric Sundquist (1993) and Amy Kaplan (2002), have
    examined Du Bois's interest in linking global struggles against racism and colo-
    nialism.

10 For discussion of the connections between Du Bois's political agenda and his
    fictional endeavors, see Rampersad 1997, 162; Tate 1995, xix; Weinbaum 2007, 97.

11 "Race Discrimination," *New York Times*, May 13, 1928, http://www.nytimes.com/
    books/00/11/05/specials/dubois-dark.html.

12 Elsewhere I explore the complicated ways in which "other nonwhites" have had to
    navigate a color line in the United States that had been drawn emphatically in
    black and white. In particular, I examine the figure of the "Chinaman" who
    appears in Justice Harlan's dissent to *Plessy v. Ferguson* (1896), the landmark
    Supreme Court case that upheld the constitutionality of Jim Crow segregation. I
    argue that rather than confounding the rigid categories of the two races that make
    up the color line, the existence of Chinese Americans in the fin de siècle American
    racial landscape disrupted the notion that there are *only* two races by occupying

simultaneously a position of nonblack *and* nonwhite, as well as noncitizen. See Lwin 2006.

13 Though it is not the focus of my argument here, I would like to raise a question for future consideration: What happens if we think of *Dark Princess* as an Asian American narrative? Or at least a proto–Asian American narrative? Baby Madhu is, after all, a first-generation Asian American as well as African American.

14 General William T. Sherman issued Special Field Order No. 15 "setting aside [a] portion of the low country rice coast South of Charleston, extending thirty miles inland, for the exclusive settlement of blacks. Each family would receive forty acres of land, and Sherman later provided that the army could assist them with the loan of mules." Later, under Andrew Johnson, the same homesteads that had been allotted to freedmen were revoked and restored to the former white plantation owners. See Foner 1988, 70.

15 See Tate 1995, x; Weinbaum 2004, 213–14. Brent Edwards (2007, 219) notes that Du Bois tried to find a black doctor to treat his two-year-old son for diphtheria, as white physicians and hospitals refused to treat black patients. We can see the influence of this experience in Matthew's expulsion from medical school, as well as in the birth of the golden child, Madhu.

16 One answer may lie in Princess Kautilya's claim that "democracy is not an end; it is a method of aristocracy." "Aristocracy" connotes nobility by birth or by talent— here the nobility of the royal princess merges with the exceptional man of science. The other understanding of aristocracy—evocative of the Du Boisian notion of the "Talented Tenth"—is that of a government by a small privileged class believed to be superior.

3 Unincorporated Territories, Interrupted Times

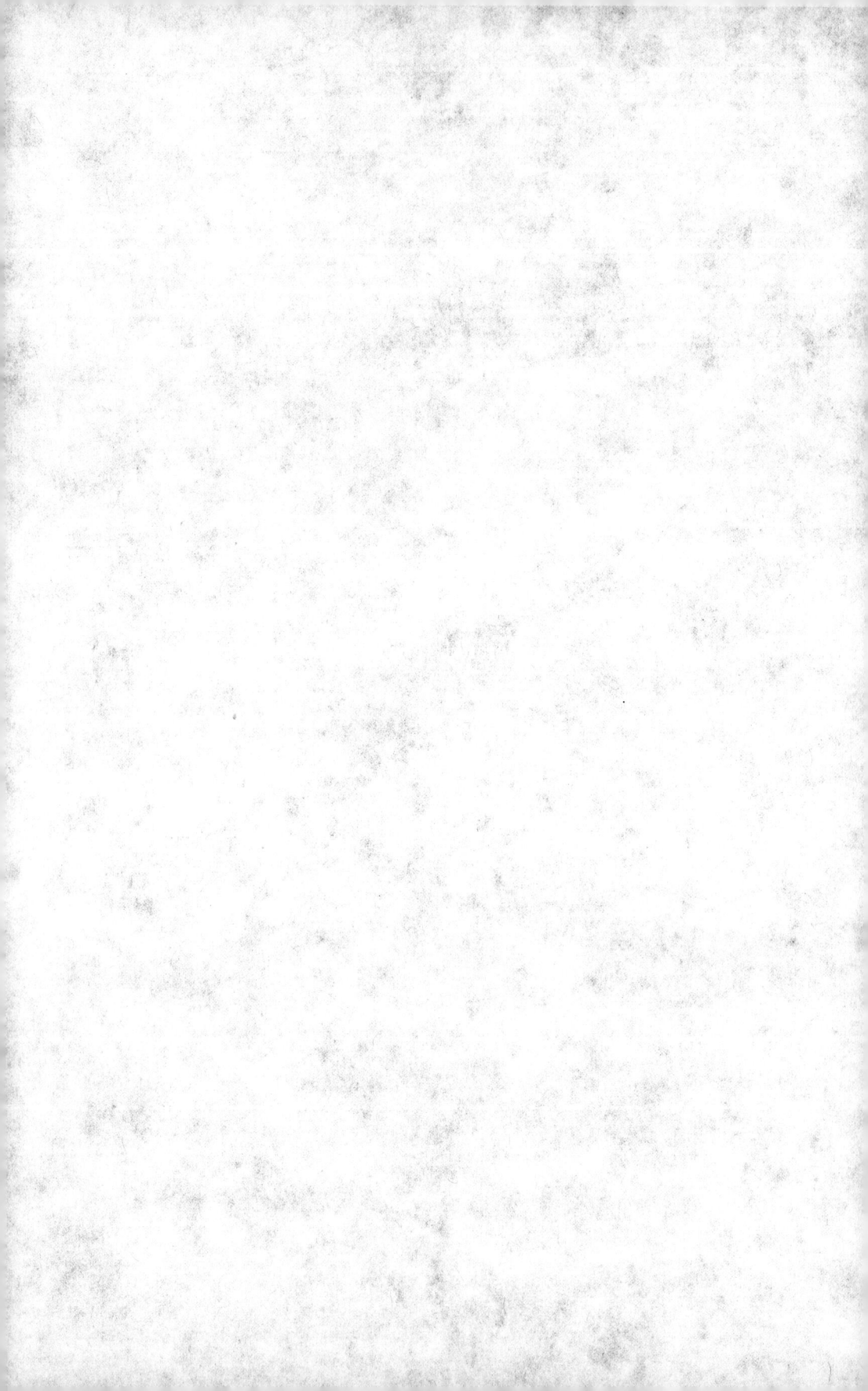

3 Unincorporated Territories, Interrupted Times

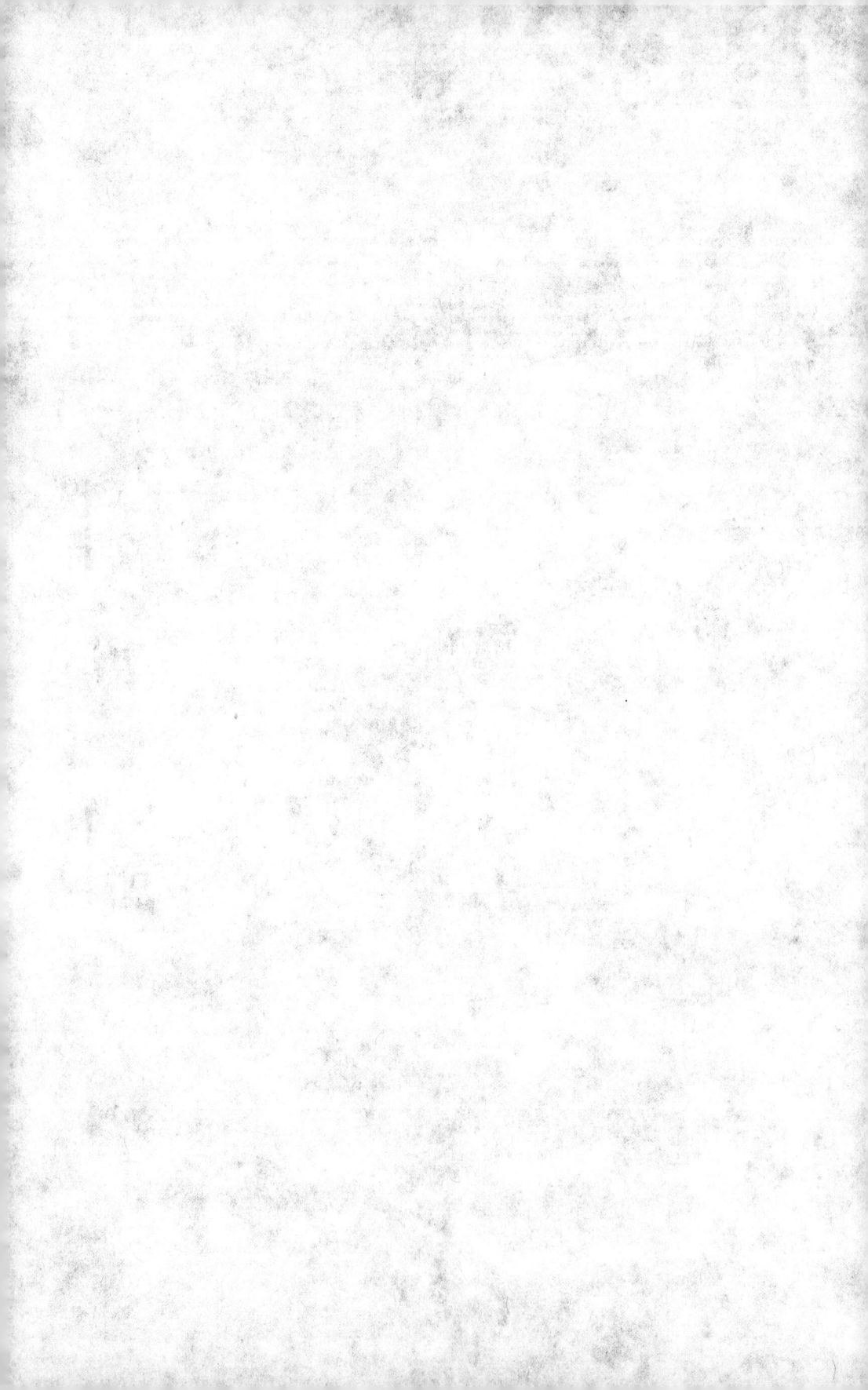

"In the Middle"

The Miseducation of a Refugee

Refugees are an anomaly in a nation-state system.
—Louise Holborn, *Refugees: A Problem of Our Time*

In *The Coupling Convention*, Ann duCille remarks that "black men and women in love and trouble just may be the story contemporary audiences most want to read" (1993, 143). Such stories of courtship and marriage, duCille argues, rather than being a genteel subcategory of a body of literature, occupy a crucial site for invention and intervention in African American literature, for these narratives make "unconventional use of conventional literary forms." DuCille describes how "early black writers appropriated for their own emancipatory purposes both the genre of the novel and the structure of the marriage plot" (3). In this chapter, I examine how a politicized appreciation of a marriage plot draws into sharp focus first how the dynamics of race, class, gender, and empire profoundly shape the terms and conditions of love and kinship, and second how the marriage plot is a uniquely privileged genre for making critical sense of dynamics of race, class, gender, and empire.

The marriage plot in question emerges in *Kelly Loves Tony* (1998), an autobiographical documentary about a young Laotian American (ethnically Mien) refugee couple and their child who live in Richmond, California. Of the three important documentaries Spenser Nakasako produced about Southeast Asian youths in the San Francisco Bay Area, *Kelly Loves Tony* stands apart from the other two, *AKA Don Bonus* (1994) and *Refugee* (2003). These other two documentaries paint compelling portraits of young men trying to understand themselves primarily as sons of their parents and brothers to their siblings. The stories of these documentaries fit most aptly the narrative of development associated with a Bildungsroman. *Kelly Loves Tony*, on the other hand, concerns the transition from child to parent. We see not only a depiction of a complicated and struggling young Asian American woman facing adulthood and a complicated and struggling young Asian American man facing adulthood, but a depiction of both of them as the two halves of a coupling convention. That is, the dynamics of gender play out in the documentary not at the level of a picaresque individual moving through a terrain of gender politics, but rather gender is understood in the context of a nuclear family's tortured genesis. It becomes difficult to treat Kelly's racialization as an Asian American woman and Tony's racialization as an Asian American man in isolation from the stakes that such gendered racializations have for each other. And these are gender roles that do not operate independently of notions of affiliation, desire, and sexuality, as in the by now familiar shorthand way of describing gender politics within racial groups: for example, Alice Walker versus Ishmael Reed, or Maxine Hong Kingston versus Frank Chin. Such gendered dyads have been thought of as existing not in a relationship of private erotic attraction but rather in one of public revulsion and disdain. Further, Orientalism here does not operate at the level of the gendered individual chafing at misperception in the public sphere or a culture-society plotted low on a scale of civilization. Instead we watch, and sometimes cringe at, the ineluctable sustenance and unreasonable demands that make coupling and family a persistent structure of both tradition and modernity. The category of the individual—as well as concomitant processes of individuation—then becomes less central and sovereign and more contingent and dialectically understood.

Besides, for Tony and especially for Kelly, any process of existential individuation is displaced by the onset of parenthood before reaching an educational level that would facilitate middle-class attainment. At odds with the transition from child to parent is another transition the film documents: Kelly's efforts to ascend through an educational system to reap the presumed benefits of completing such a process. She is, in a way, trying to juggle career and family. Such juggling is predictably difficult. Near the end of *Kelly Loves Tony*, Tony is talking with Dave Kakishiba, his boss at the East Bay Asian Youth Center, about Kelly's recently disclosed pregnancy with their second child. "When she found out she was pregnant, she wanted it taken out," Tony says to Dave as they drive around Oakland in an EBAYC van. Tony, on the other hand, is happy at the news that another child is on the way. Dave tries to explain to Tony why Kelly might not be as excited about her pregnancy by saying that there are "school people" and "not school people." Kelly, Dave says, is the former, while Tony is the latter, and another child will make more challenging Kelly's ability to "come up" through her education. In the long run, Dave somewhat harshly says, that contrast may doom their marriage. Tony then responds that Kelly's place on the school-people/not-school-people spectrum is "in the middle."

TONY SAELIO: I mean, it's important to her, but she gotta know now, she gotta a baby. And it's like, college is important, but it's not gonna pay for the baby or the food. She ain't got all that she want, but at least she finish high school and getting' her education already.

DAVE: Yeah, but you know, man, it's like some people, okay, right, and I told you this before. To me, you're not a school person, you know what I mean?

TS: Yeah.

DK: You're not a school person. It don't matter even if you was in Laos, you ain't gonna be a school person.

TS: Yeah.

DK: You know? So that ain't you. But there are other people, and Kelly might be one of them, there's some people that are school people, you know?

TS: I think Kelly is like in the middle, man.

DK: In the middle, huh?[1]

After a slight pause, the scene cuts to one of Kelly's self-reflective, diary-like monologues to the camera. While the documentary may seem to encourage us to see Tony's conversation with Dave as yet another instance of Tony's obtuseness in the face of his gendered privilege—which it is—Tony may also be more right than wrong in his assessment of Kelly's uneasy situation.

Even an honor student like Kelly Saeturn may find herself an anomaly to the main competing institutions that drive and validate her, namely, the family and the school. This moment may also provoke the salvational impulse of modern colonialism that Gayatri Spivak succinctly articulated as "white men saving brown women from brown men" (1988, 296). Kelly's history as a post-1975 refugee from Southeast Asia, for both obvious and subtle reasons, pervades her predicament. Her life with Tony resonates with Louise Holborn's characterization of refugees as an "anomaly in a nation-state system." As such, the civilizing mission that seems to be activated at Kelly's lack of liberation demands that we scrutinize more closely the terms by which Kelly and Tony, as a social unit, embody a revealing convergence of histories and conditions of race, class, gender, empire, and sexuality.

Grasping the abjection and anomaly of refugees helps us to appreciate the critical possibilities that Kelly and Tony articulate and perform. One of the key insights of critical work on race, class, and gender is the explication of institutions invested in categories of abjection, from the heteropatriarchy of family to the disciplinary nationalism of schools to the exploitations of capitalist accumulation. Through a consideration of *Kelly Loves Tony*, this essay examines the category of the refugee and the ways in which the apprehending of the refugee is the apprehending of the anomalies of a multiplicity of structures of social and cultural organization.

To grasp these anomalies, *Kelly Loves Tony* reveals the investment viewers may have in the narratives that legitimate those institutions. Indeed, the refugee has meaning only insofar as he or she can be emplotted into a narrative of innocence, victimization, rescue, and recovery. By the time viewers meet Kelly and Tony, they are presumably in the final stages of a much longer narrative that displaced them from decolonizing Southeast Asia and replaced them in postindustrial Richmond. The narrative drama of the documentary is not whether endangered individuals and groups will survive; they have since passed that stage. Rather, the drama is whether they will thrive in an economy and reproduce institutions and individuals who will outlast the persecutions visited on their forebears.

To speak of the drama of a documentary may seem inappropriate, but drama may be unavoidable. Indeed, the viewing satisfactions of fiction and nonfiction film (a distinction once referred to as documentary versus narrative cinema) depend on similar methods of creating character, situation, tension, and resolution. Containing eighteen months (roughly June 1995 to

December 1996) in two people's lives in fifty-six minutes of footage demands a certain amount of projection and construction of narrative coherence to be intelligible at all. What I argue is that *Kelly Loves Tony* shows us how the category of the refugee powerfully invokes and ultimately explodes narrative expectations in which viewers may have an unexpected investment. The refugee is a figure at the perilous edge of intelligibility, a figure at a site where the fabric of civilization has unraveled to make possible if not also permissible mass persecutions. To follow a refugee's successful return from that edge is to retrace the ontology of modernity and to affirm a belief in fundamental principles, values, and practices. To witness a failed return is therefore devastating, so much so that alternative explanations for failure are entertained. For example, to explain Kelly's transition from honor student in high school to struggling junior-college student, unplanned pregnancies are the result of individuated rather than structural failures. *Kelly Loves Tony* would then have to be considered, to borrow the terms of Deleuze and Guattari, a part of a depoliticized major tradition rather than a fundamentally politicized minor one. To distinguish between major and minor, Deleuze and Guattari write:

> Everything in [minor literatures] is political. In major literatures, in contrast, the individual concern (familial, marital, and so on) joins with other no less individual concerns, the social milieu serving as a mere environment or a background; this is so much the case that none of these Oedipal intrigues are specifically indispensable or absolutely necessary but all become as one in a large space. Minor literature is completely different; its cramped space forces each individual intrigue to connect immediately to politics. The individual concern thus becomes all the more necessary, indispensable, magnified, because a whole other story is vibrating within it. (1984, 17)

Ironically, perhaps, the plausibility of such alternative and individuated explanations for Kelly and Tony is the mark of the refugee's recovery and, by implication, the end of civilization's burden to do anything for or about them. They become, in other words, subjects of (neo)liberalism: responsible for themselves.

Don't Have to Live like a Refugee

The idea of the refugee then tempts viewers with the rewards of affirmation and liberation while also dramatizing the risk of seeing the fundamental failures and contradictions of social formations in the making of the modern world. As Mary Layoun has observed:

> The refugee experience of the community or nation in crisis as it is represented in cultural and oral narratives potentially challenges established boundaries of community or nation. For it is precisely those inviolable boundaries that the refugee knows only too well to be violable. Thus the telling of refugee stories is sometimes also a radical reconceptualization of the very definitions and ground rules of community or nation and of the roles of those who claim to speak for and from them. Refugee stories reconstitute—with a difference that is often ignored in official political discourse—boundaries and official and unofficial rules for crossing over them that are only arguably unimaginable or impossible. (1995, 84)

Kelly Loves Tony conveys just such a crisis of nation and community, of rules and representation. In other words, the terms and conditions of war erupt in the documentary. To the American imagination, these refugees are the so-called collateral damage of a conflict to which they have the misfortune of being adjacent. In such a conception of war, these people are an exception to the rules of war. Yet the exception has, especially since World War II, tragically become the rule as the assault on the putatively innocent came to be a part of military strategy. As Linda Robertson notes in *The Dream of Civilized Warfare*, such "terror or morale bombing" had once been the vilified means of fascist Teutons, but "public morality was changed to accept strategic bombing of cities as worthy of American military power" (2003, 406, 407). What makes these eruptions of contained and strategic war particularly telling is that we see the lives of refugees from military conflicts ostensibly lost by the United States and military conflicts that were seen as "hot" exceptions to the larger conflicts of the Cold War. Indeed, various violent confrontations of the Cold War era were the product of the dismantling of a territorial empire in wars of decolonization after the declarations of peace in 1945. These limited restorations of imperial powers in Southeast Asia would set the stage for such hot spots. In other words, we can now see how these struggles over the Third World were part of a larger war for what we recognize as today's globalization. As an ostensible deterritorialization of the world, globalization is fought not over hills and hamlets but over proverbial hearts and minds. *Kelly Loves Tony* shows us the convergence of both conflicts in a newly developing family in the Oakland area. The inescapable fact of Kelly and Tony as products of such a military past turns out to be, with the exception of a sobering textual prologue to the documentary, quite escapable after all. Militarism is at once pervasive and invisible, even for refugee youths in their day-to-day lives.

The documentary was shot over the course of a year and a half, a project supervised by the filmmaker Spencer Nakasako and funded by the National Asian American Telecommunications Association. The documentary chronicles the East Bay pair as they slouch toward marriage and deal with the challenges of balancing unplanned parenthood, community college, and the criminal justice system, as well as wedding preparations. Two main narratives thread and intersect through the otherwise arbitrarily determined period that the documentary covers: Kelly's efforts to balance career and family as she begins college and motherhood simultaneously, and Tony's efforts to avoid deportation as a consequence of the "moral turpitude" evidenced by his criminal past. Amid these specific and concrete conditions, we can discern and appreciate the changing meaning of the refugee across the transition from the waning of the Cold War to the waxing of the new world order of globalization. *Kelly Loves Tony* helps us to see how the refugee is perhaps the most privileged concept that makes visible the complex disciplinary structures that legitimate the logic of globalization.

With the ascendance of globalization, as well as forms of resistance to it, the refugee has become for the contemporary period a critical site for analyzing the limits of modernity, particularly nation-states and supranational regulatory bodies. That is, the very existence of refugees can be seen as a manifest failure of the current incarnation of modernity. Refugees emerge at locations where stability and order are experiencing violent crisis, where a population becomes a target of persecutions that a nation-state cannot manage. Indeed, nation-states are frequently the very perpetrators of that persecution, thereby demanding the intervention of multinational organizations to police nations and their fragments.

At the same time, due to this provocation of extranational instruments, refugees also function as the fodder for a morphology of what was once called "the civilizing mission." As Edward Said has written, "Refugees . . . are a creation of the twentieth-century state. The word 'refugee' has become a political one, suggesting large herds of innocent and bewildered people requiring urgent international assistance" (2002, 144). In their capacity as those in dire need of "urgent international assistance," refugees approximate what the colonized were to an earlier historical moment: the before to a before-and-after narrative of uplift. This is not, of course, to say that refugees should be ignored, but rather to emphasize that we must critically understand why they cannot be ignored, conceptually and historically. We must ask: what ideological and material functions are served by the creation and salvation of refugee populations? And if refugees, as is both implicit and explicit in discourse on contemporary refugees, are an intolerable creation, why are the numbers of refugees continuing to increase in the current world order?[2]

The ideological function of refugees is neither new nor difficult to grasp. To the extent to which they escape persecution and find new self-sufficiency, refugees dramatize the rehabilitative power of incorporation into modernity. They travel the full distance of "the lengthy and difficult road toward full self-sufficiency" (Gallagher 1998, 247). And in the case of refugees from Southeast Asia after 1975, we see how the collateral damage of an unpopular and nonvictorious military conflict for the United States can almost miraculously be transformed into an argument for the ultimate triumph of the values that a military struggle initially failed to uphold, both on the battlefields and in the hearts and minds of a nation grown weary with war and ready to repress it from memory.

Two crucial differences emerged with the creation of refugee populations in the post-1975 era. First, refugees were increasingly viewed as a category describing large groups. As Philip Marfleet notes, "For two decades after the Second World War refugees occupied a special status. They were viewed in the West as individuals whose specific experiences of persecution under repressive regimes made them deserving of sanctuary. . . . Large groups were rarely accepted" (2006, 147). Rather than undergo case-by-case consideration, class actions grew more acceptable, not unlike the momentary legitimacy of social justice legislation under affirmative action.

Second, the post-1975 refugee populations from Southeast Asia were coming to be understood as products of United States involvements overseas, rather than directly the result of other despotic regimes. In other words, the so-called Pottery Barn theory of geopolitics came to fruition. "You break it, Mr. President, you bought it," quipped Secretary of State Colin Powell to President George W. Bush in the months leading up to Operation Iraqi Freedom in 2003. Secretary Powell memorably articulated the wages of engaging in a foreign war of liberation: like a clumsy consumer in a breakables shop, the United States had to entertain the likely possibility of causing damage to another's property and therefore the need to, in effect, pay for and own those damaged goods. By implication, the breaker also bears the burden of repairing the damaged goods to make them once again salable.

A range of "durable solutions" then emerges as the goals of refugee policy. As Susan Forbes Martin notes: "A major goal of the refugee system is to find durable solutions for those who have been forced to flee their homes. There are three such solutions—voluntary return to one's country of origin, settlement in a country of first asylum, and resettlement in a third country. The most desired is voluntary return to one's country of origin, hopefully after conditions have changed sufficiently to permit safe and dignified rein-tegration" (2004, 101). In these terms, which are emblematic of much of the discourse on the refugee system, there is an implicit narrative of a dream return to a pre-refugee condition. For many a return is unlikely and, in many cases, not really desired (Criddle 1992). More common, particularly for refugees who resettle in the United States, is effectively permanent resettlement.

Arguably new was the gendered racialization of refugees. In tables with titles such as "Current Occupations of Those Who Were Housewives in Southeast Asia and Now Working in the U.S. Labor Force," analyses of refugee resettlement remark on the presumed disruption of gender roles due to aspects of resettlement such as women entering the workforce (Office of Refugee Settlement 1985, 131). The newness is arguable because war refugees are traditionally noncombatants: women, the very young, and the very old. Marfleet observes that "women and children who were in general non-combatants, accounted for most of the dead and injured; they also featured prominently in associated mass displacements. Meanwhile women had become a particular target. During periods of social crisis, civil conflict and war, gender relations become increasingly important. Women are in-variably central to the definition of cultural authenticity, being viewed as a repository of key communal values which maintain the integrity of the group. Subordinated in formal economic and political life, they are exalted in the context of community and of national culture, often appearing as maternal figures representing collective identity and honour" (Marfleet 2006, 116).

As noted earlier, a refugee, in legal terms, is defined as a person having "a well-founded fear of persecution" in his or her home nation-state (see, e.g., Carliner et al. 1990). Presumed alignment with the losing side in a civil war is often at the root of such persecution, which can tragically lead to disappearance and killing fields. To prevent this fate, refugees invoke the *right* of egress and appeal for the *privilege* of ingress to locations with either (1) a reputation for sheltering the embattled or (2) a direct responsibility for that embattlement or (3) both. In *Globalization and Its Discontents*, Saskia Sassen describes how this disparity between what is widely recognized as a human right (the right of a person to exit a nation-state) and what is protected by the terms of nation-state sovereignty (the right to regulate who may enter) remains an impasse in the mobility of persons in the global village. Sassen suggests that the conditions of globalization may make the refugee the paradigmatic migrant, as receiving countries are profoundly implicated in the conditions that make migration a life-and-death situation for the new huddled masses that, were it not for those conditions, might rather remain where they are (Sassen 1998).

Since the Fall of Saigon in 1975, the United States and other Western powers (mainly France) have recognized the refugee status of Southeast Asian populations that aligned themselves with the losing cause in what is broadly referred to as the Vietnam War. Most notably among these persecuted groups are the Hmong and Mien of Laos and Cambodia who have since established communities in the United States, as well as settlements in locations that are part of France, such as French Guiana.

Documenting the Afterlife of the Refugee

Kelly Loves Tony is the second video of Spencer Nakasako's groundbreaking series of documentaries on Southeast Asian refugee youths in the San Francisco Bay Area. As with the other subjects of this series, Kelly and Tony had been given video cameras and access to editing equipment to capture their day-to-day lives. Their one-hour video was aired on PBS and was screened at film festivals. It documents a year and a half in the lives of the eponymous Laotian American pair, a Mien teenage couple who are preparing for marriage after the birth of their son Andrew.

We might broadly pose the question: to what extent does the *form* of apprehending refugees influence our understanding of them? After all, there is no transparency in representation allowing neutral access to experience. The more pertinent question may be: to what extent do refugee narratives engage with the limitations of cultural representation as refugees themselves engage with political unrepresentability? Nakasako's award-winning documentaries blend auto-ethnography and outsider art. Central to the project is the fact that these are first-time filmmakers. The project calls to mind something Greg Toland said after photographing *Citizen Kane* (1941). By 1941, Toland was perhaps the leading cinematographer in Hollywood, yet he sought out the opportunity to work with twenty-five-year-old Orson Welles, a newcomer to moviemaking. Toland felt that it was best to work with talented first-timers because they didn't know what they couldn't do. Nakasako is the Toland to Don Bonus's and Tony and Kelly's Welles. Not only is Nakasako allowing these young people to document their own lives, but he is putting cameras into the hands of those who have not been overly influenced by the techniques and conventions of canonical filmmaking.

For the first two of the three videos in Nakasako's series, the format is fairly straightforward. Over an extended period, teenage filmmakers film their lives, including monologues to a camera on a tripod. Then that mass of material is edited down to approximately one hour of footage, in chronological order. It may be useful to consider some of the stock features of documentary film, as well as the ways in which Kelly and Tony render themselves observable. *Kelly Loves Tony* would most closely approximate the form of documentary called *direct-cinema*, which presents its material with little to no overt narrative. Also called *cinéma-vérité*, this form of documentary, which emerged and flourished in the 1950s and 1960s, is premised on minimal imposition of the filmmaking itself into the events depicted. The autobiographical nature of *Kelly Loves Tony* makes the camera inescapable and ever present as an almost anatomical feature of the subjects, particularly Tony.

Two related issues impose narratives—and narrative satisfactions—onto *Kelly Loves Tony*; we might categorize these along the lines of editing and distribution. Editing in documentaries is perhaps even more important than editing for fictional films (see Bordwell 2001, 288). Since documentary footage is ostensibly "raw," its transformation by editing may dramatically produce meanings that become discernible only when juxtaposed to moments that, for example, produce a series of incidents that argue for a pattern of behavior rather than as seemingly isolated moments. Editing produces Kelly as a long-suffering partner to a boorish fiancé. This is not to say that editing produces deceptions but rather to indicate that editing constructs and encourages certain truths. Film scholars have long pondered the "I" of the camera in both fiction and nonfiction film. For autobiographical documentaries in particular, the ways in which the subject of the film is constructed through camerawork, voice-over, and editing cuts comprise what Michael Renov describes as the "diversity of autographical practices that engage with and perform subjectivity . . . perhaps a poetics of audio-visual autobiography" (2004, 11; see also Rothman 1988).

Distribution matters also encourage meanings in and interpretation of footage that might be ambiguous. Distribution imagines the market and context for a narrative of those truths. While such concerns seem most glaring for big-budget Hollywood films angling for huge opening weekends, independent media are no less concerned with the apparatus for reaching an audience, whether conscious or not. Certainly in the case of *Kelly Loves Tony*, there are important matters of Asian American media outlets, public broadcasting, curricula of educational institutions. These videos may be relatively inexpensive, but the funding structures that make such films possible may exert influence and encourage a horizon of meanings, even progressive, minoritarian ones.

These, then, are the representational rules and priorities that we might actually mistrust in refugee narratives. Layoun argues regarding refugee self-representations: "To postulate past mistrust of dominant narratives in a present in which those narratives have been brutally exposed as inadequate is scarcely surprising or inexplicable. The retrospective skeptical qualification of past 'trust' is, instead, a way of ameliorating the grimness of the narrative present. To tell the story of becoming refugees is to attempt to reconcile the teller of the story with the seemingly unresolvable conflicts that cast her or him in the role of refugee narrator in the first place" (1995, 77–78).

Ostensibly *Kelly Loves Tony* shows to mainstream America the everyday struggles in the lives of a poor, young immigrant couple trying to raise a child in a medium-sized, deindustrializing metropolitan area (greater Oakland). In particular, viewers can readily sympathize with the difficulties that Kelly faces in trying to get a college education while raising an infant. The documentary even opens with an image of Kelly graduating from high school with honors. Tony shakily operates the camera.

Meanwhile Tony, a former juvenile delinquent and gang member, is struggling to hold a steady job to keep from getting deported as a result of the combined efforts of the INS and the Department of Corrections. Tony repeatedly comes across as less sympathetic and even incomprehensibly boorish as Kelly dutifully suffers his routine insensitivities. Eventually Tony does demonstrate his capacity to resist "moral turpitude" and to become a productive member of society.

DAVE: Tony is, uh, cleanin' up right now. You know, he's doin' his work. He's doin' the drivin,' doin' all the kind of office support. He's not fightin.' He's not stealin.' And that's all good. But, Ton's gotta a real big challenge ahead of him right now. The biggest challenge as far is courts are concerned, the INS wants to deport him because of his criminal record, and he has this case comin' up. So, we're basically tryin' to help him out. We've been, we helped him get a lawyer. And we're really tryin' hard tryin' to explain all this legal stuff to him so that he can understand what's goin' on.
[Cut to shot of DK in front of a chalkboard.]

DK: Why are you being deported? The federal law, the law says that if an individual, if an alien, if a non-citizen commit, is convicted of two or more crimes, what they call, of moral turpitude. . . . 'Kay, I don't know what the fuck that means, really. But, basically, some significant crimes, then you are eligible to be deported.

TS: Mm-hmm.

DK: Okay, you got busted on the auto burglary. Then, you got caught for possession of a firearm. And then, I don't know, maybe about a month later, you and some of your buddies robbed a young couple, a couple of young people of their gold chains or necklaces, right?

TS: Uh-huh.

DK: Okay.
[Cut to shot of TS filming while he's driving.]

TS: I spend most my life right here in East Oakland. That's two of my friends. He's saying there might be a fight today. When you live in

Oakland right here, who you hang out with is who you gotta stick with 'cause there's always some other kids mess with you.

TS: This is the hood where I'm from and shit. OJC.

TS: [Inaudible words]

TS: [Voice-over] When I'm not fighting, I'm always out there stealin,' makin' money. That's the kinda thing I would do all my life. And when I think about it, I spend most of my time in jail, you know. And now, it's all catchin' up to me. And if I get sent back, I could lose everything.

[Cut to shot of KS and A sleeping.]

TS: I just got home, and now my lady, she's sleepin.' Turn off the light. [Turns off the light.] You know my lady, Kelly, one thing I haven't really talk about, she doesn't know about my deportation hearing. I haven't told her yet, 'cause it's like, I don't wanna worry her too much.

The judge determines that Tony is permitted to remain in the United States, and this may constitute the resolution of the central drama of the film. This documentary is an instance of the power and the limits of what we now call reality television. By using this genre to document the simultaneously extraordinary and mundane lives of post-1975 refugees from Southeast Asia, we can appreciate the persistent presence of the subaltern. That is, by grasping Kelly's life and failing to grasp Tony's, the video reminds us of the investments in rewarding the sympathetic with procrustean incorporation to modernity and punishing the deviant with near invisibility.

Early in the documentary, but after the graduation scene and Kelly's narrative of her courtship with Tony, Kelly tells us that she became pregnant. So the film is quite eventful. Kelly gives birth to a son, is engaged to be married to Tony, moves in with his family, begins college, and, before the film is over, becomes pregnant again. Needless to say, her life is not easy. The documentary critically recounts Kelly's story of a not-yet-fulfilled American dream of possessive individualism. The film, even from its very title, produces Kelly as its subject who loves and Tony as its object who is—or, more likely, is not—loved by the audience and perhaps even Kelly as well. Kelly is understandably sainted, and Tony is a baffling, boorish man who expects his gender to make his life easier. Kelly, on the other hand, struggles to fulfill her dreams—education, good job, happy family. Her ostensible failure to become what her education taught her to desire makes three things visible: educational failure, filmic failure, and Tony's subaltern status.

At the film's New York premiere at New York University in 1998, Kelly and Tony were in attendance. Upon hearing that Kelly is enrolled in college, the audience spontaneously and predictably applauded. Kelly's desire and ability to continue her education is something that most audiences, especially one at a university, would indeed encourage and applaud. The documentary serves the dramatic function showing an ordinary person, that is, someone with whom an audience can identify, surviving extraordinary circumstances: war, forced migration, loss of family members, resettlement, and acculturation, all the way to educational achievement.

The two central narratives—Kelly's dreams and Tony's trial—that structure the arc of the documentary are both at cross purposes with the couple's ability to be, as Kelly says in voice-over, "a real family." The phrase actually comes up as Kelly describes how, after the birth of their son Andrew, she moved in with Tony's family so that she and Tony and Andrew can be "*like* a real family." In other words, Kelly registers that she and Tony are engaged in a performance of a conception of family. Kelly's thwarted efforts to realize her dreams come across as, to borrow the terms from episodic television, the A-story, while Tony's "happy" outcome in his trial is the B-story. Our first image is that of Kelly's graduation, and Kelly's is the first voice-over. In the rules of both documentary and fictional film, these establish her as our protagonist. Even her tone in the voice-overs is more conventionally inflected, and was added after the footage. Kelly also shoots her own "talking-head" moments to reflect on her situation directly to the camera. She does so often with impressive articulateness, making her situation all the more tragic and sympathetic. That is, she is quite self-aware of the disparity between her aspirations and her powerlessness to realize them. In the one instance when Tony provides narration of the audience, he whispers over images of a sleeping Kelly and Tony, revealing a secret to the audience that he is keeping from Kelly: his unresolved legal problems. The next shot is a rageful and enlightened Kelly, glaring at Tony, who is holding the camera, as he often is.

From the opening shot, Tony is established as the presumed operator of the camera, shooting Kelly. But sometimes he shoots his own life without Kelly. Curiously, the result is that we are granted considerable access into Tony's daily life without Kelly. By contrast, scenes of Kelly's life without

Tony come only in the form of her monologues that have a "Dear Diary" feel. We do not see her study. We do not see her provide child care. In public or in private, the camera does not track her with groups of people that do not include Tony. We never see her confide in anyone else. Yet like the title of the documentary itself, Kelly comes across as the subject. Even at points where Tony's story is clearly the focus of the action, he is not the subject of the camera's gaze. For example, at the conclusion of his hearing, the documentary chronicles the event through Kelly's reactions to it.

In terms of content as well, the reasons for Kelly's centrality may not be difficult to see. Her story is a familiar and inspirational one, that of a person struggling to keep to the straight and narrow path of socioeconomic survival and possible prosperity. She is squarely situated in a narrative of sacrifice for academic success followed by the just rewards for that success. She looks to be, as Dave understandably assesses her to be, "school people."

Tony, on the other hand, is not a sympathetic character; indeed, he is the villain of the piece, a millstone around the neck of the blameless Kelly, the Homer Simpson to her Marge. Tony comes across as an outside agent deferring Kelly's dreams. It is difficult not to conclude that Kelly's path to prosperity would be easier without Tony. She would not have the demanding and avoidable responsibilities of motherhood and of being a new member of his chaotic family. She owns that motherhood and family life are desires that she has, but that the problem is "timing." She prefaces one of her attempts to make her situation clearer to Tony with "It's not that I hate your family." At that point in her life, she would have had only the challenges of thriving at Laney College, perhaps toward transferring to a four-year university and eventual professional life with all its comforts. "You have a lady who wants to come up," Dave tries to tell Tony in language he can understand. "She doesn't want to be no secretary."

What keeps their story from being a stereotypical domestic drama of a cycle of inner-city poverty is their history of being refugees. The problems of these two people, to borrow the phrase from *Casablanca*, amounts to more than a hill of beans. That is, conditions of war intrude on domestic drama, and vice versa. Tony's problems seem ostensibly to be rooted in his activity in gangs. His verbal and sartorial presentation is clearly marked as urban, in other words, commonly coded as African American. Kelly, on the other hand, has been more mainstreamed. Tony uses their war refugee past in a particularly egregious way as he seeks to discipline Kelly by criticizing her inability to conform to his conception of Mien culture. In perhaps the single most tense scene of the documentary, Kelly and Tony are seated side by side on a bed, heatedly discussing their difficulties as the camera rolls. As Kelly tries desperately to convey how difficult it has been for her to be a mother, a student, and an incoming daughter-in-law, Tony shields himself from responsibility for her by accusing her of not being able to abide by "Mien culture," meaning that he thinks she is supposed to take care of him, his family, and their baby, in addition to her own life. Tony sees her education as a disposable distraction. Mien culture, the very thing that served as a basis for their "well-founded fear of persecution," the conditions of their existence that shattered their families, is redeployed by Tony as a cruel basis for criticizing Kelly. They are at an impasse. Here is the exchange:

KS: I think everyone is making excuses for the wedding. First, it's about this. And then it's about your parents. And then it's about them trusting us, not being together and everything. You know . . .

TS: It's just that, you know, right now, it's just the problems that I have kind of hold it off a little bit. And it's not that I don't wanna get married, but you gotta do good to prove to both parents that you have a good relationship goin' on. That's what most Mien people, right, bring their wife to their house.

KS: [Slight scoff]

TS: That's what the women have to do. Saying take care of the house, cook. Not just cookin' for my family, but cooking for the family, you know, like my son and me and my parents.

KS: So that's why they're postponing the wedding? Because I'm not helping them out in every meal?

TS: No, no. It's not . . .

KS: I'm not cleaning every little speck of the room?

TS: For the Mien people way, they gonna think . . . Even everybody gonna say that . . .

KS: Say what?

TS: . . . 'Aww, man. Certain son, he's hella bad in his past. Now he's doing good, he's working . . .'

KS: But his wife is not cooking?

TS: '. . . He gotta wife. And now his wife, she helping out the family, doing this and doing that.' That's what being culture is all about.

KS: Well, I'm not . . .

TS: Being part of the . . .

KS: . . . so much in Mien culture.

TS: . . . marriage and family relationship. Okay then, even though we move, be livin' by ourselves, what make it so different?

KS: You know, you don't have to have any conflict between the both of you because of family. I mean, we're having problems because of the family.

TS: Okay, then what? My parent, your parent don't got nothin' to do with our marriage. We could just go and get married.

KS: Yup. We don't need to marry them! I'm not asking you to marry my family. I'm not gonna marry your family.

TS: You have attitude, man. Then you can never get it through your—

KS: I mean, how would you feel if you were at my house, and I have all these brothers and sisters, and then, I have my mom and I have my father? And then you gonna have to cook for me, you gonna have to clean for me?

TS: If I was your wife.

KS: I mean . . .

TS: If I was a lady, if I was a girl . . .

KS: Yeah, right. [Wipes away tears from her eyes.]

TS: If I was in your position, I would at least help out cook.

KS: And I don't help out at all?! I mean, you don't know how uncomfortable I am.

TS: You not tryin', you not really tryin' get along with them.

KS: I don't know what to do! I mean, especially when it's not my house. And not my family. [Continues crying.] Stop expecting so much from me.

Clarification comes in the form of an education that Tony's mother gives him, displacing his comfortable sense of what Mien culture is. She explains to him that it is his job to help Kelly, to do the work of easing Kelly into their family life. She tells him that the difficulties that Kelly has faced are basically his fault. In effect, Tony's conception of Mien culture is his way of asserting masculine privilege that looks an awful lot like the shiftlessness of a particularly damnable configuration of gendered racialization. Kelly may indeed be ripe for saving, but not from Mien culture.

Soon after this lecture, there is a gap of more than a month in the narrative. When next we see their lives videotaped, we see Kelly on her bed speaking to the camera on a tripod, telling us that she and Tony have somehow reconciled. At this point, she divulges that she is pregnant again and that, like her first pregnancy, it was unplanned. And, initially, it was unwanted. That is, she tells us a narrative that Tony later tells to Dave, leading to the assessment that Kelly is "in the middle." The final scene of the documentary is of a pregnant Kelly and her son Andrew on a stoop, playing with an old tennis ball.

To conclude, I suggest that we strategically invert the film's A-story and B-story to further appreciate the complexities of the lives of resettling refugees. The easy visibility of Kelly's perspective is evidence of her narrative's ready insertion into existing narratives of the salvation, education, and uplift of refugees. By contrast, Tony's behavior, as depicted in the documentary and as evidenced in his criminal record, make him a viable candidate for removal both from Kelly's life and from the United States. The documentary may actually thus make a case against Tony. He would in effect have his rights as a refugee revoked, just as any sympathy from audiences who recognize the legitimacy of Kelly's grievances.

After the trial, when the court does not issue a deportation order for Tony, Kelly's response is telling. She says to Tony, who is holding the camera, "I'm happy for you." She does not simply say that she is happy. In this moment we can discern another narrative that unfolds over the course of the film: that of Kelly's acquisition of an ability to separate her life from Tony's. Tony, on the other hand, seemed to have that ability already, much to the audience's dismay. For Kelly, however, such detachment is a virtue. This may be the epiphany of the documentary, when there is a moment of clarity that does not recuperate family or education or national culture or other institutions of possessive individualism. Kelly manifests a relationship with each of these institutions that positions her in a space to which hot war refugees of the Cold War era know quite intimately: "in the middle." That is to say, for Kelly "I'm happy for you" equals "in the middle."

What does this mean for Tony as their nuptials loom? Tony does not fit his mother's conception of their family's traditional practices, nor does he fit the dream of modernity that Kelly has. Tony is, in his way, in the middle, too; it's just not the middle that Kelly occupies. Instead Kelly and Tony are anomalies to the models of social order that seek to recruit or reject them.

Who knows but that this commonality, this strange affinity, might in practice be a viable basis for a plausible conception of wedded bliss, or at least survival.

Notes

1 Transcription by Lindsay Gervacio (unpublished, 2008).
2 Such figures would include both transnational refugees (i.e., refugees "proper") and so-called internally displaced people (IDPs). Some statistics track a decline in proper refugees in the same period that saw increases in IDPs. Marfleet 2006, 14–17.

Deconstructing the Rhetoric of Mestizaje through the Chinese Presence in Mexico

Before the rebellion in Chiapas, the key word in Mexico was "modernization," the illusion that Mexico's economic stability was around the corner with the signing of NAFTA (Monsiváis 1996). The powerful Zapatista movement that erupted in January 1994 destroyed the mirage of modernity and, more importantly, provided evidence that the cultural, social, and political cohesiveness of Mexico is a myth. Since then, the Zapatista movement has denounced interlocking oppressions at the global scale so as to account for the multiplicity of those in the margins. In this conjuncture, it is pertinent to reveal the lack of closure in the construction of mestizaje.

One of the aims of this work is to problematize the concept of mestizaje in the Mexican and Chicano discourse of cultural kinship, authenticity, and ethnic difference based on the idea that most Mexicans are mestizos—half Spanish and half Indian. In particular, I want to participate in a dialogue in which the concept of mestizaje gives an account of the multiplicities of histories that are part of Mexico and El Mexico de Afuera.[1] Although other racialized diasporic communities have been excluded from the national and ethnic consciousness of Mexicans and Chicanos, I focus on making visible the presence of Chinese in Mexico through the analysis of a poem of a diasporic subject ("Chio Sam") and of a national gendered icon (La China Poblana).

Mestizaje

The rhetoric of mestizaje is similar to the rhetoric of the melting pot in that it attempts to conceal histories and practices of displacement and forced transition. The political discourse of mestizaje was consolidated after the Mexican Revolution and is part of a Pan-American project, a common feature of Latin American politics of community making. According to Bonfil Batalla, the Mexican Revolution tried to redeem the Indians by incorporating them to the "universal" civilization.[2] The redemption plan for the Indians was via their disappearance and conversion to mestizo. Mestizaje is based on the idea that Mexicans and Chicanos are the result of a facile and homogeneous equation made of the syncretic fusion of Spanish-plus-Indian components and that no other ethnic groups are part of such mixing.[3]

According to Frantz Fanon (1963), one of the main challenges of nationalist projects after experiencing colonialism is to create a system that does not reproduce the practices of cultural domination of colonialism, such as uncritical nativism or the consolidation of old colonial racial structures. In postcolonial Mexico, the task of constructing a nation under universal political and cultural principles seemed difficult in view of the diversity of race, religion, language, and culture, in addition to geographic isolation. Nevertheless the project became urgent in the face of Mexico's struggle to repel the threat of European invasions after Mexico's independence.[4]

Analyzing the discourse of Mexican political elites regarding "indigenous people," Van Dijk (2003) states that despite the official discourse of Mexico being a mestizo country and the use of mestizaje as a source of collective national pride in the national and international arenas, the collective millenary experience of indigenous groups has not been part of national projects, from Mexico's independence to the present. Clear binaries maintain the privilege and authority of the political and economic elite along racial lines.

In Mexico, European values are still associated with positive qualities such as intelligence, education, beauty, honesty, kindness, and the like. Contrasting qualities depict non-European subjects as ugly, lazy, delinquent, irresponsible, stubborn, and uneducated.

The political public and official discourse in Mexico constructs the elite in extremely positive terms so that they are not perceived as explicitly racist (Van Dijk 2003). In fact, the official ideology is constructed as a "racial democracy" that values the cultural legacy of the indigenous people, the richness of their languages, and the necessity of preserving it. On the other hand, the same elites use a political discourse that is quite Eurocentric, paternalistic, and rarely incorporates the voices of indigenous people into decision-making processes directly affecting them (i.e., educational, health, and community development projects). This discourse tends to focus on the elite's duty to "improve" the situation of the indigenous groups, perceiving them as lagging behind and needing to be fully integrated with the rest of the nation.[5] Nevertheless the official positive political discourse is not translated into, nor is it a guarantee to, equal access to resources or equal treatment.

Although the Mexican elite political discourse tends to be politically correct, it is based on European supremacist assumptions that have barely evolved since the early Spanish colonization over the past five centuries. The dominant discourse does not need to be openly racist as long as the racial hierarchies remain intact. Some of the main stereotypes of the indigenous persons in the political discourse are based on the idea that they are a problem: they are poor, they are malnourished, and although they speak their own language (which nobody is really interested in learning), for all purposes they are considered illiterate because they do not speak the dominant language, or they speak it with a "nonstandard" accent.[6] Programs that incorporate the study of indigenous languages do not necessarily stimulate literature and other forms of expression; on the contrary, they facilitate literacy into the Spanish language (Bonfil Batalla 1987). To confirm the social space that indigenous persons occupy in Mexico, there is an ample repertoire of insults and jokes about them, and few white politicians would feel honored to be called *indigena* or even *mestizo* as a compliment (Van Dijk 2003). There is a contrast between the public, political discourse and the private, individual, informal discourse: one is quite tolerant and even inclusive, and the other, the private one, loaded with racial supremacist remarks.[7] The strong numerical presence of indigenous people is not translated into economic or political power.[8]

Extending beyond the geopolitical Mexican border, the mestizo identity among Chicano nationalists has been articulated as a political statement against racial oppression. In opposition to racial purity and white supremacism in the United States, the Chicano community tends to embrace the identity of the mestizo as constructed by the Mexican state. Nevertheless Chicano nationalism has excluded in its synthesis of mestizaje other indigenous groups that are not Aztec or Mayan,[9] and in accordance with the Mexican state idea of mestizaje, it has also omitted other racialized minorities, such as the Chinese.

Reproducing oppressive and exclusionary schemes, particularly those based on racial purity, delays or nullifies our efforts to face modern racism. Perhaps it is time to reimagine Chicano and Chicana artistic and political representations to generate productive debates about the fixed ideas of race that have limited our social spaces as racialized individuals. As Cherríe Moraga, a feminist Chicana lesbian writer, has stated, "What was right about Chicano nationalism was its commitment to preserving the integrity of the Chicano people"; what was wrong about it "was its institutionalized heterosexism, its inbred machismo, and its lack of a cohesive national political strategy" (1993, 148). Moraga admits that nationalism's "tendency toward separatism can run dangerously close to biological determinism and a kind of fascism" (149). The significance of the Chinese, African, Japanese, and Arab historical experiences in the global economic circuits of colonialism has consistently been unacknowledged from national projects of mestizaje, leaving only biological determinism as part of the criteria to be a mestizo/a.[10]

In Mexico, the dominant discourse has produced representations of Chinese that make illegitimate their presence in the national imaginary. The discovery of hidden histories within this marginalized community is essential to the articulation of a countermemory, as well as to the production of an identity that validates its existence and finds its coherence in the margins of the national discourse of mestizaje. As Stuart Hall (1997a) warns us, hidden histories play a crucial role in the most important social movements of our time. Among those hidden stories, the texts of Selfa Chew represent a fissure in several racial myths promoted by the state.

Selfa Chew's volume of poems, *Azogue en la Raiz*, focuses on her life as a borderland Chinese Mexican. Her texts explore quotidian, intimate spaces where the search for personal and communal affirmation of identity takes place: giant theaters showing kung fu movies, plazas, and grocery stores fuse the Mexican and the Chinese cultural elements that shape the life of Chew. From this collection, "Chio Sam" (Chew 2005, 77) deals more directly with the recovery of personal memory in an attempt to challenge the official history that has omitted any representation of Chinese communities:

Chio Sam
Dice mi madre que no es posible
que yo recuerde el olor a pan
ni el bambú sosteniendo el vapor que se escapaba
de la cocina de mi abuelo.
No es posible que recuerde su canto en cantonés
en su mirada delgada y orgullosa
en su bastón y sus zapatos quietos.
Veo todavía el olor a cigarro y sus dientes amarillos
la vitrina, el nombre rojo del lugar
en que mi abuelo cocinaba
y los trajes, los inmóviles sombreros
contemplando el pan blanco
almohada tenue que envolvía
el sabor definitivo del almuerzo.
Veo la penumbra y sus palabras cortas
como las galletas adivinas
que ahora dan en restaurantes chinos
y que mi abuelo no supo ganarían algunos clientes
y una expectativa más
de lo que debemos ser o dar los orientales.
Crecerás
Construirás murallas
Olvidarás la marcha detenida
en el café de mesas rojas
y la cascada de cubiertos a lavar
interminable detergente al fondo
el vapor del pan blanco

suave
tibio.
Pero mi madre dice es imposible
que yo entendiera los avisos del abuelo:
yo no hablaba aún y él
sólo cantaba cantonés.

My mother says it is not possible
that I remember the smell of the bread
nor the bamboo sustaining the steam that was escaping
from my grandfather's kitchen.
She says it is not possible that I remember his song in Cantonese
in his slip and proud glance
in his cane and quiet shoes
I still see the smell of a cigarette and his yellow teeth
the display cabinet, the red name of the place
where my grandfather used to cook
and the suits and the unshaken hats
gazing at the white bread
faint pillow that wrapped
the definite breakfast flavor.
I see the penumbra and its short words
like those in the fortune cookies
that nowadays give in Chinese restaurants
and my grandfather did not know they would bring some clients
and one more expectation
of what we, the Orientals, should be or give.
You shall grow
build great walls
you will forget the long march nested
in the coffee shop of red tables
and the fall of chinaware to be washed
endless detergent in the backroom
the steam of white bread
soft
warm.
But my mother says it is impossible

that I understood the warning of my grandfather:
I did not speak then and he
could only sing in Cantonese.

The space revisited by Chew is an intimate yet public site due to the
working and social conditions of her Chinese Mexican family. She sees and
describes in detail what has often been ignored by the daily restaurant
patrons. The day-after-day work, as well as the little pleasures and gestures
of love exchanged among the members of the Chinese Mexican family, take
place in front of a clientele who can smell the bread and feel the warmth that
stems from the family's kitchen. The life of our family has always been the
domain of the customers who own a fixed set of expectations from the
Chinese. Nevertheless the perception of the same objects, events, and persons has been different for all parties involved in the history of Asian
migration, for which Chew's narrative unearths a hidden, alternative story
and recovers the small pieces to articulate a different account, a dignified
representation of Mexican Chinese that is individual and public at the same
time. Hidden histories are opened by the personal within the space that
Homi Bhabha describes as the "unhomely," where "the home does not
remain the domain of domestic life, nor does the world simply become its
social or historical counterpart. . . . [The unhomely, then] is the shock of
recognition of the world-in-the-home, the home-in-the-world" (1997, 445).
Chew registers a frozen instant of astonishment before the unhomely, in
what Benjamin (1999) calls a moment of awakening, a reconstellation of the
lost objects of the everyday.

The "moment of awakening" is a moment of rupture where the past and
present can recognize each other, not in a linear way, but in a sudden
moment of almost involuntary memories that are part of the experiences of
being Chinese Mexican. In "Chio Sam," two generations are brought together by shared histories and experiences of community vulnerability and
isolation, histories of exploitation and racial expulsion. Chew's attempt to
restore forgotten connections reconfigures existing social relations in our
cultural landscape, transcending as a form of activism that reshapes our
collective memory and, therefore, our consciousness of the presence of the
Chinese in Mexican history. Recovering the debris of history becomes an
ongoing process of contestation and resistance (Hall 1997b). Chio Sam, the
author's grandfather, *cantaba en cantonés*. He cannot speak the official lan-

guage, and his granddaughter does not speak Cantonese, yet the poem is about oral history, about making an epistemology out of the fragments. While the poet refuses to accept her mother's erasure of the memory that represents her Chinese heritage, she articulates her own sense of history with the fragments she can recollect. In the process of picking up pieces of history, some could argue that the erasure of the memory is not warranted and that literary evidence is not evidence at all, or that there is no necessary connection between the author's experience (or pretended experience) and reality. It could also be argued that the mother of the poet was not necessarily erasing anything; she could simply have been pointing out the inconsistency between facts (evidence) and constructed memories. However, it is important to realize that under Eurocentrism, the experiences and interpretation of history of those in the margin are dismissed or at best erased from the national consciousness. In this context, minority writers become political writers, and as Homi Bhabha states, "The intimate recesses of the domestic space become sites for history's most intricate invasions. The private and the public become part of each other, the home does not remain the domain of domestic life, nor does the world simply become its social or historical counterpart" (1997, 445). Minority writers have to take a political stand about the unique tensions they face between their experiences and the overall hegemonic or, in this case, the Mexican experience. In this sense, the lives and the art of minority writers are political because their work challenges official constructions of national histories. The poet makes the presence of Chinese in Mexico not only real and legitimate but also important in the national landscape. And in tracing her past, she engages with all her senses the process of resistance in a trance that is gratifying and dignifying. By confronting her hidden history, the writer sets new patterns and forms of presentation, representation and association, transforming cultural practices that are of interest in exploring pluralisms. She does not stand as an ahistorical, abstract, Oriental entity, but she simultaneously sees herself as a child, a woman, a Chinese, a granddaughter, a daughter, and a Mexican, embracing many identities in a viscous social process of individual recognition.

By reconstructing individual, fragmented pieces of our colonized past, we engage in a form of remembrance that can illuminate radical possibilities for altering the material conditions and social relations of the world in which we live. Chew looks at the past to fortify her future. Her recognition of stereotypes and expectations through the metaphoric "fortune cookies" is only a step to continue her life beyond the constrictions of stereotypes, to value her own grandfather's expectations: "You shall grow . . ." Recovery, in this sense, is a critical practice that takes place in our everyday experience, because it is in "the closest, tritest, most obvious" (1999, 156) situations that the promise of the past is to be found, as Benjamin states when formulating his view on history. When Chew rejects the commodification of Chinese people and their cultural artifacts, she uncovers at the same time the social agency of Chinese migrants and their daily negotiations with the clients of Chinese coffee shops: "like those in the fortune cookies / that nowadays give in Chinese restaurants / and my grandfather did not know they would bring some clients / and one more expectation / of what we, the Orientals, should be or give."

In noticing the presence of the "other Mexicans," Selfa Chew acknowledges that the relationship between her family and the ideal Mexicans is an everyday occurrence that determines the way in which she regards the family's cultural productions. At the same time, she addresses the manner in which the Mexicans consume those same cultural artifacts (i.e., foods). Mexican parents admonish their children that they must be suspicious of Chinese cooks, who kidnap and eat little kids. When Chew writes that Mexican men "gaz[ed] at the white bread / . . . that wrapped / the definite breakfast flavor," she reconfigures the role of each participant at the table. In "Chio Sam" it is the middle-class Mexican men who desire to eat, who look forward to consuming the Chinese Mexican foods in an act that emblematizes the social contradiction generated by a racial ideology that allows Mexicans to literally devour Chinese artifacts and lives of hard work while accusing Chinese immigrants of practicing cannibalism (a common urban myth in Mexico). The Chinese restaurant becomes a space of racial and ethnic commodification. Consequently Chew does not construct the dominant Mexicanness as an enviable social identity but challenges its construction on the basis of exclusion. She reminds us of the continuous play of history and power in the identity of Chinese Mexicans and the nation, about the unstable and complicated generational levels of identification with the homeland and levels of assimilation with Mexican culture. To Chew, "the display cabinet, the red name of the place / . . . the coffee shop of red tables" are visible traces of the Chinese presence in Mexico and also tools of negotiation, the items with which, within the constraints of racism,

La China Poblana. Courtesy
Pedro Manuel Chew-Barraza.

her family has chosen to set the stage in which they live their social and intimate lives. Chew opens these changing cultural spaces as a strategy to destabilize the construction of sameness and the exclusion of difference.

Perhaps because any presentation of the everyday, when aspiring to challenge social restrictions, must begin with awakening, Chew deals with specific historic and political moments that affect her day-to-day life as a woman of Chinese descent. The fragmentation and interruption implicit in her text have been central to the identity of those who experience enforced diaspora, slavery, and forced migration. These experiences begin to heal when hidden and intertwined histories are exposed, connected, opened, clarified, and embraced as part of people's identities. Chew describes the kitchen of the Chinese restaurant, a soft, warm place, as an important location of her childhood, a determining factor in the shaping of her identity. Yet the intimate place is the site of a historical displacement, since being a cook or washing dishes was (and still is) one of the few options available to Chinese migrants such as her grandfather.[11] The invocation of the kitchen, the chinaware waiting to be washed, the display cabinet, and the red tables of the coffee shop tells us all those small and yet significant details about the boundaries of a racialized society: what spaces Chinese people could occupy, what they could eat, have, aspire, and dream of. Essentially "Chio Sam" deals with the fragmentation of Chinese everyday life, yet these fragments are being reclaimed and placed back in the national history to construct a different notion of mestizaje that challenges the national ideal.

La China Poblana

Textbooks and other official narratives of national history have failed to account for the Asian diaspora as an integral part of Mexican society. It is therefore noteworthy that La China Poblana, one of the main symbols of Mexican national folklore, has its origins in China. In spite of her title, reminiscent of the presence of Chinese in Mexico, the image of the Pueblan Chinese Woman remains a signifier of cultural unity among Mexicans. The relationship between Mexicans and Chinese so boldly inscribed in this image evokes important social psychological aspects of the various communities that have accepted La China Poblana as a Mexican symbol. Undoubtedly La China Poblana is the most significant cultural legacy of the earliest intercultural relations between Mexico and China.[12]

In 1941 La China Poblana was officially adopted as a national archetype for Mexican women, together with El Charro Mexicano as her male counterpart.[13] Her geographic origins within Mexico made her image suitable to represent the notion of national unity. Puebla is situated in the Oriental section of Mexico, while Jalisco (the place of origin of El Charro) is located within the Occidental zone. Whereas Jalisco's cultural representations are often associated with European heritage (particularly the art, technique, and celebration of cattle management, and horsemanship), the presence of indigenous peoples in Puebla is stronger than in Jalisco, in spite of the large concentration of white people in this small state. Consequently the fusion of El Charro and La China Poblana has entered the national consciousness as a representation of mestizaje that both incorporates and submerges the presence of Asia in America.

La China Poblana incorporates various aspects of the lives of Asian women in Mexico. The representation of La China Poblana has changed over time from a virtuous person very near the state of sainthood to a fiercely independent and patriotic woman. During World War II, the Mexican cultural industries were active in strengthening Mexican nationalism. It is not a coincidence that during that time, El Jarabe Tapatio, or the "hat dance," was constructed as the national dance, and La China Poblana and El Charro were articulated as archetypes of Mexican women and men. As La China Poblana became a spokesperson for regional and national tourism, her features were whitened. Although several representations of this icon resemble indigenous women, she is frequently portrayed as a European woman. This act of ethnic transvestism is similar to the way in which Frida Kahlo, the German Mexican painter (and more recently Salma Hayek and Lila Downs) transformed the "ethnic suit of la Tehuana." Ethnic transvestism is a condescending way of attempting to embody and "eat the other," as bell hooks states (2001)—a way to embody exotic women to be in closer contact with nature and to rejuvenate and innovate oneself. The fascination with the ethnic transvestism of Frida by some privileged white woman is based on fantasy and denial of the historical, economic, ethnic, and social connections between them and those whom they commodify, exoticize, consume, and fix. Ethnic transvestites are happy to wear the clothes of the other as a performance of progress and understanding of other cultures as long as the racial, ethnic, national, and economic boundaries and hierarchies remain intact and their status quo is not challenged. The transformation of La China Poblana into a white person who dresses in an outfit culturally associated with a woman of color represents the complex process of dealing with the Chinese in Mexico. Desire, cultural cannibalism, and economic exploitation are some of the elements that shape our present consumption of La China Poblana.

During national festivities during the Day of Independence, the day of the Mexican Revolution, and (in the United States) El Cinco de Mayo, many Mexican men wear El Charro suits,[14] while women who can afford to buy or sew the expensive outfit proudly dress in La China Poblana attire. The legend says that when La China Poblana arrived at the port of Acapulco, she wore beautiful clothes consisting of a richly embroidered shirt, a colorful petticoat, a pair of silk sandals, and long braids (Monteón González and Trueba Lara 1988). Nowadays women who dress as La China Poblana use a luxurious costume that includes a cloth skirt, or *zagalejo*, usually red and covered in sequins with geometric designs and the Mexican eagle in the center at the front. Chinas Poblanas normally carry earrings and coral necklaces. The blouse, short-sleeved and finely embroidered around the neck with a bead or *chaquira*,[15] displays flowers, birds, and butterfly patterns with lively colors. La China Poblana's hairstyle consists of two braids with both ends tied with ribbon bows of the same hue as the waistband and the lower part of the skirt.

There are different versions of the legend of La China Poblana. However, most of them state that she was born in a pagan royal family as Princess Minah, or Mirrah, the daughter of the great Humayu, the king of the Mongol empire; and that she was kidnapped by different Portuguese slave traders who resold her at various times and places linked to the Portuguese and Spanish colonial powers in the Pacific and the Americas.[16] From the Philippines, she was sent on a Spanish trading galleon to New Spain. The Portuguese took Mirrah to Acapulco, where her name was changed to Catarina de San Juan.[17] She was sold in Acapulco to a prominent childless couple and made into a privileged domestic servant. After the couple died, Catarina took a position as a domestic servant to a noted priest, who ordered her to marry another *chino* slave, Domingo. The legend states that she maintained a chaste marriage with an abusive husband and that after his death she was left with her husband's debts and his mistress's child. More importantly, she was at last free. Although she took no formal religious vows, according to the legend, she lived a life of reclusion and became a lay holy woman, following a charitable, contemplative, visionary path for the last four decades of her life.

Because the Mexican state has actively participated as an administrator of a racial project that regulates geopolitics and nationality, the analysis of La China Poblana in the Mexican cultural landscape becomes pertinent for the deconstruction of Mexican nationalism. The presence of Chinese migrants is intrinsically linked to the provision of the labor needed to sustain the economy of the Spanish colonies. The story of Catarina de San Juan, La China Poblana, is a remarkable exception to the account of Chinese presence in Mexico for at least two reasons: most Chinese migrants were men, and the few Chinese female migrants were virtually invisible (Hu-DeHart 1991). La China Poblana's account became unique when she was made an icon of national identity, an icon that exposes and at the same time hides the importance of the Asian community in the history of Mexico.

La China Poblana represents the denial and the oppression of the Asian presence in Mexico.[18] Her placement, both in the popular memory and in the official imagery, generates a series of contradictions that calls for the study of colonial and modern societies from the perspective of a racialized, foreign woman. Catarina de San Juan, the "real" person, managed not only to survive but to associate herself with the ecclesiastic and social elite of Puebla, the criollo center with the largest white population of New Spain, and therefore one of the most religious and conservative cities that enforced strict racial segregation. From all the accounts that trace her trajectory in Mexico, it is possible to infer that Catarina de San Juan developed a self-empowered subjectivity that grew remarkably when she was free from marriages and servitude. As a member of her community, she identified with the sick and the poor; she assisted them and fulfilled her subjectivity. Her process of self-liberation was carried out through her engagement with other racialized and oppressed colonial subjects. Catarina's self-actualization is a resistive process against objectifying colonial definitions of Asian women. Her decision to live within a dominant institution that refused to grant nonwhite women the status and responsibilities conferred to nuns appears to be the product of her assessment of the possibilities available to her. Her status as a Catholic holy woman offered her a degree of protection as well as the freedom to openly take care of marginalized individuals.

Through her position in the Catholic Church and in a number of diverse social spheres, La China Poblana altered the local and national identity of colonial Puebla and of the Mexico that was white, Spanish, and male. The colonial economy, based on the exploitation of racialized subjects and of women, found in Catarina de San Juan a level of resistance and a number of strategies that she used to assert her agency. She embodied the economy of pleasure and desire, the economy of domination of power, but she also embodied the difference inscribed in the colonial discourse that was created to justify colonial domination and rationalize colonial force. By acting and living as a nun, Catarina avoided hypersexualization and attempted to retire her public body from sexual advances on religious grounds. While decolonizing herself in a communal context, she built mutual trust between her and the Poblanos[19] who have insisted on remembering her as part of their collective oppressive colonial experience by celebrating La China Poblana's image. This migrant female, who was enslaved, raped, sold, and resold, finally emancipated herself and developed her own subjectivity. Her continuous experience of engagement with her surroundings, and her evident constant learning from those experiences, empowered her within a community with which she established a highly synergetic relationship.

Despite the absence of Asian communities within the official narrative, the presence of Catarina de San Juan in the religious community of Puebla acquired a large importance after her death. Catarina de San Juan's association with the Jesuit community in Puebla, as well as her opposition to the *encomienda*,[20] became emblematic in a time of genocide and contempt toward the indigenous population. Puebla's merchants and landholders of Spanish descent were eager to establish the importance of their city within the Spanish empire and Christian history by promoting local religious heroes, among other tactics. La China Poblana was a valuable local religious example to both the New World and the Old. At various points in time, Catarina de San Juan was postulated for an official recognition of her sainthood. Her sainthood was never granted, perhaps because she was a slave, because she was not a virgin, or because she did not have a Spanish ancestry.

Catarina's popularity survived more than a century of censorship.[21] She lives on today in the collective memory as La China Poblana, a commemoration of the life and work of Catarina San Juan. Nevertheless this celebration does not consciously address the presence of Asian persons in Mexico.

In a patriarchal, racially constrained world, La China Poblana's legacy took a different shape from that of Sor Juana Inés de La Cruz, another woman who entered a religious order to escape sexism and who died in 1695, seven years after Catarina de San Juan died. In particular, Sor Juana was a wealthy criolla who could write her own life story and had many privileges that Catarina did not enjoy. While Sor Juana Inés de La Cruz is celebrated in popular culture as a notable feminist, the erotic content of her poems was diluted to maintain her intellectual and religious image. On the other hand, Catarina San Juan was transformed as a sensual object while her religious and social work was overlooked and eventually forgotten.

The presence of an Asian element in a national symbol within an anti-Chinese context may be explained if we look at El Charro Mexicano and La China Poblana from a gender-race perspective. Although most Chinese migrants have been men, male immigrants have frequently been perceived as a threat to the nation, and intermarriage with Mexicans was never fully accepted (Schiavone Camacho 2006). As a docile, sexualized, and commodified woman, Catarina San Juan was transformed into a desirable object for the consumption of Mexican men. Only a feminine, submissive version of Asian immigration could become an icon and the celebrated counterpart of El Charro Mexicano. To understand the presence of Chinese people in Mexico, it is important to analyze the global colonial chains of production, first as part of Mexico's colonial link with Spain, then within the context of the expansion and colonialism of the United States.

Chinese Presence in Mexico

Spaniards and white Mexicans in New Spain made laws that segregated Chinese in the outskirts of the various towns in which they attempted to reside, restricting their activities, revoking their licenses, and limiting their numbers in New Spain.[22] As stated by Ngai (2005, 7), "Race is always historically specific. At any time, a confluence of economic, social, cultural and political factors has impelled major shifts in society's understanding (and construction) of race and its constitutive roles in national identity formation."

After Mexico's independence, the Chinese presence became more strongly linked to the expansion and colonialism of the United States. Before the 1870s, U.S. immigration laws were designed to encourage foreign immigration, particularly in the newly conquered territories of the Southwest. In 1882, however, the Chinese Exclusion Act made illegal migration a criminal offence for the first time in U.S. history (E. Lee 2002). The Chinese Exclusion Act was instrumental in equating and defining full U.S. citizenship to whiteness. This act secured European descendants and European immigrants their privilege to have legal access to, and opportunities of, full participation in the larger U.S. social, economic, and political arena. When Chinese responded to this exclusion by taking advantage of cracks in the government's enforcement practices, they became the country's first illegal immigrants, both in legal terms and in the context of popular and political representations (E. Lee 2002). During the Exclusion Acts, Chinese people would still cross to the United States from Mexico. According to Erika Lee (2002), the Chinese were the first community explicitly excluded from entering the country. U.S. immigration laws and control were central to the country's imperial expansion and racial protectionism, in which the Chinese were perceived as a threat to the control and sovereignty of the population of European descent.

The imperialism of the United States greatly affected Mexican immigration laws. The U.S. imperialist and nativist project of the late nineteenth century not only created a tight system of control along the Mexican and Canadian borders but also put pressure on the Mexican and Canadian governments to change their immigration laws so that those countries would not be a point of entrance to the United States. The treatment of European and Chinese immigrants was quite different. The Chinese Exclusion Act remained in effect until 1943. At the same time, the United States did little to discourage the large numbers of European immigrants who arrived in the late nineteenth century. There were no immigration quotas for European immigrants until 1921. The perils experienced by Chinese individuals when attempting to cross the border uninspected were similar to the danger and humiliation experienced lately by the most recent illegal aliens who cross the border at the same point: El Paso.[23]

At the same time, Mexico experienced the Porfiriato, the thirty-five-year dictatorship of General Porfirio Díaz, which lasted from 1876 to 1911. During that time, British, U.S., and French interests arrived in the country, bringing more roads, mining interests, and land colonization companies (Puig Llano 1992). Just as in the United States, Mexican officials believed that foreign immigration was essential to the modernization of the country. The government of Porfirio Díaz first attempted to attract European colonizers as the most desirable migrants, but the demand for labor pushed the government to sign the Treaty of Amity and Commerce with Japan and China in 1893.[24]

The northern Mexican states became closely linked to the economy of the United States because of their geographic proximity as well as the demand for minerals and other economic resources. During the Porfiriato, northern Mexico was strategic for Chinese migrants because it was a frontier region in the process of rapid social and economic development, and because it was the main crossing point to the United States. To many Chinese, migration to Mexico left open the possibility of eventual migration to the United States. Mexico in itself was a less attractive destination than the United States. By the time the treaty was signed, Chinese colonies were already established in several northern states: Baja California (then a territory), Sinaloa, Chihuahua, Tamaulipas, Coahuila, and Sonora (Puig Llano 1992).[25]

Chinese immigrants in Mexico filled the commercial and service demands created by the opening of mines, the construction of railroads, the growth of towns, and the expansion of internal markets. The economy of northwestern Mexico has been closely linked to that of the United States, so it is not surprising that the presence of Chinese in northern Mexico happened during the development of the U.S. western and Mexican northwestern economies. The Chinese immigrants who settled in Mexicali, Baja California, were attracted to the region when the inter-California railroad was contracted by the Colorado River Land Company in 1904. Mexicali is a border city in the northwest of Mexico that today has the largest population of Chinese in Mexico.

When the Porfiriato ended with the Mexican Revolution of 1911, Mexico had experienced a decade of constant civil war. During the revolution and the subsequent years of solidification, the Chinese became a target of violence and xenophobia mainly because they were felt to be opposed to the interests of the working class and their revolutionary ideas. China also had a weak international position that did not allow it to protect its nationals, and the U.S. Exclusion Acts (along with the denial of citizenship to Chinese and other racialized groups from Asia) seemed to have formed a canon under which the Mexican elite worked. Meanwhile the Chinese labored in the most important sectors of the economy. They were not only denied full political participation and the rights of most citizens but were the target of personal injuries and looting.

The Mexican state emulated the U.S. racial and national hierarchies and ideologies that were crystallized in immigration policies that drew the lines of inclusion and exclusion. Such policies and ideologies of white supremacy articulated the desired composition of the nation, where Asians and particularly Chinese were unassimilable and undesirable subjects. The Mexican elite was also quite active in organizing and enforcing a domestic racial nativism, particularly in the northern states of Mexico.

After the Mexican Revolution, *ligas-antichinas* (anti-Chinese societies) were created in the northern states, the strongest one being in Sonora. This new wave of anti-Chinese campaigns was in part a response to the Great Depression of 1929, when American investment in Sonora's key economic sectors, such as mining, the cattle industry, and commercial agriculture, dropped sharply.[26]

The racialization of the Chinese in Mexico was similar to the racialization they experienced in the United States, especially with regard to masculinity as a requisite for citizenship and for membership in the racial ranks of the elite. As Stuart Hall (1997b) states, all the attributes of patriarchy are denied to the subordinate group: property, citizenship rights, and familial authority. When the Sonoran government implemented the Código Sanitario (sanitary code) and a ban on Chinese-Mexican marriages, the Chinese were denied access to the same privileges of patriarchy that the social elite of northern Mexico enjoyed.

Mexico made Chinese women particularly inadmissible. This, in turn, affected the decisions of many Chinese to avoid the immigration of their wives, daughters, and sisters. The possibilities of forming a Chinese community made up of monogenic patriarchal families (the dominant ideal) was curtailed not only by the obstacles of bringing Chinese women to the American continent but also by the social restrictions imposed on possible marriages between Chinese men and Mexican women (Schiavone Camacho 2006). Thus several generations of Chinese Mexicans were born illegitimate, since their parents did not have state-sanctioned marriages. This type of mestizo, a socially unacceptable racial composite, born of the instability and transient status of Chinese workers in Mexico, was rejected on the grounds of legal status and immorality. In the same vein, the Exclusion Acts operating in the United States shaped the ways in which Chinese individuals were perceived in the borderlands. Their mere presence in the border area made them suspects of attempting to commit a crime: entering the United States illegally (Schiavone Camacho 2006). While Mexicans were not precluded from entering the United States at this time, they witnessed the mistreatment that immigration officials inflicted on the Chinese, regardless of their class or legal status, when attempting to "cross the line" toward the United States. The Chinese, as well as many other racialized minorities, became the symbol of unassimilability in both Mexico and the United States.

The experience of the Chinese in Mexico is distinctive because Chinese men and Chinese Mexican families faced mass expulsion from Mexico between 1931 and 1933, at the peak of racial hostility and discriminatory laws against the Chinese. Although most of the Chinese and their families were expelled, some stayed with the permission of the authorities or by hiding. These Mexican Chinese families were allowed official repatriation in the 1960s.[27] The perception and construction of the Chinese in Mexico by the national ideology of the Mexican state throughout history seems to be linked to that of the United States, often as a result of political and economic pressure from the United States. La China Poblana was adopted by the Mexican government in 1941 as the national female emblem, at about the same time the Exclusion Act was repealed in the United States. Nowadays the myth of Chinese and other Asian groups as "model minorities" (but also perpetual foreigners) that persists in the United States is also followed in Mexico.

As stated before, the concept of the modern Mexican state, built on an ideology of racial mixing or mestizaje and ethnic tolerance, materialized in Mexico in the 1930s. However, the same revolutionary state enforced and perpetuated an anti-Chinese sentiment, particularly in the northern part of Mexico, that prevented the official recognition of the Chinese community as part of the diversity that characterized the Mexican population. Ironically, the concept of mestizaje, or hybrid culture, has been fixed, essentialized, and is now substantially unchanging. It continues to deny the participation of Chinese individuals in the making of mestizos.

The Chinese Mexican population in the border states of Mexico is still significant. For example, Mexicali claims to have the highest per capita concentration of Chinese residents in Mexico. During the late nineteenth century and the early twentieth, the U.S.-Mexico border became a refuge for Chinese fleeing the violence in both countries (Books 1983; Farrar 1972). This diasporic community has provided a complex dynamics of identity that calls for the formulation of new national identities. The presence of Mexican Chinese in the border region demonstrates how a national issue can only be understood in a wider, transnational context. Chinese immigration and exclusion in Mexico are intertwined with the border expansion and maintenance of its northern neighbor, the United States.

In this chapter, I have deconstructed the historical significance of the Mexican nation in politics and culture through the reinscription of the Chinese presence in Mexico as a countervailing form of national identity. The 1910 revolutionary project of the economic and social elite sacrificed pluralism for the sake of nationalism that benefited mainly the national elite. The Chinese in Mexico have been both welcome and unwelcome; they are part of the economic and cultural fabric but are located outside the cultural and racial boundaries of Mexico. Mexican national identity has been forged on an abstract mestizaje that is defined by whiteness—that is, by the Spanish blood that Mexicans have. Chinese and other groups from

Asia have been defined as permanently foreign and therefore racially ineligible to be part of Mexican history and Mexican identity.

The construction of mestizaje as a static and overritualized formula where Indians and Spanish come together and form supposedly traditional Mexican culture is problematic, particularly when it forms the base of Mexican symbols as represented in the stereotyped art of some Mexicans and Mexican Americans. The construction of mestizaje leaves out the presence of other ethnic and racial groups that is part of fully understanding the diversity that can be found within the Mexican population.

Conclusion

The Zapatista movement demonstrated that despite the inclusive political discourse of mestizaje, the reality is that indigenous people have been living for centuries in oppressive social structures. In 2005, a year after the Zapatista uprising, Vicente Fox, the presidential candidate of the opposition conservative party (PAN), promised to solve the "problem in Chiapas in fifteen minutes" (Ramírez Cuevas 2009). Once in power, the elected president made the Zapatista call for cultural pluralism into an illegitimate and unviable national project. The political elite resorted to a self-congratulatory discourse of all the efforts they have made to integrate indigenous people into the homogeneous mestizo nation.

While the celebration of the China Poblana hides in full light the contributions of the Asian communities to the economy and culture of Mexico, the study of this cultural icon reveals aspects of the Asian diaspora in terms of gender, class, religion, and sexuality that have previously been overlooked. On the other hand, the poem "Chio Sam" creates a point of aperture that is congruent with the Zapatista movement and its call for cultural pluralism with the commitment to acknowledge the rights of historical collectivities. Selfa Chew invites us to think of mestizaje in Mexico in ways that have liberatory and healing dimensions because those hidden experiences and histories of non-European communities are told and connected while opened to revision. It takes us away from the "happy middle" of mestizaje and tells us about multiple social perspectives and positions with concrete material forms of oppression or privilege based on race that exist in Mexico.

Notes

1 Mexico outside its political boundaries, or the Mexican diaspora. The term was coined by Américo Paredes, a pioneer scholar of Chicano studies, to refer to the social spaces where there are Mexicans and their cultural and economic practices are evident. The term is in contrast to geopolitical borders.

2 According to Bonfil Batalla (1987), during the Mexican Revolution, the elite selectively appropriated indigenous elements to construct the image of Mexico as a mestizo country. Indigenous cultures were assumed to be inferior; the objective of the educational programs targeted at indigenous people was therefore not to create conditions to nurture their literature and culture but to integrate them into the nation and teach them Western educational canons.

3 Clara Lida (1997) states that although the Spanish presence in Mexico has been continuous since the conquest, their numbers in Mexico have been quite limited in comparison to Argentina, Chile, Uruguay, Venezuela, Cuba, and Puerto Rico. However, it is fascinating that although such migration has been limited, it has had extremely powerful influences in Mexican culture and has been quite rich in cultural terms. It is also worth noting that in the construction of mestizaje, there was little talk about African migration to Mexico, which was the largest migration during the Spanish colonial times. Recently, Miriam Jiménez and Juan Flores (2010) have problematized the lack of acknowledgment of the African presence in Latin America through their studies on Afro-Latinos in the United States.

4 During much of the nineteenth century, Mexico suffered civil wars and was invaded three times by foreign powers: the United States, Spain, and France. Furthermore, Mexico was conceived as a reaction against over three hundred years of Western domination and bore its painful emergence through three national movements: the independence of 1810, the reform of 1857, and the revolution of 1910. Although each war in Mexico was driven by its own sociopolitical objectives, the struggle against foreign domination—political, military, or economic—remained central to all three movements. However, the main concern of the national elite during most of the nineteenth century was to promote unity among the country's diverse regions and peoples: to forge *patria* (nation), as Manuel Gamio (1960) put it. However, most nativist leaders reproduced and replaced the racial hierarchies of the colonizers (Batalla 1987, 17).

5 Such official discourse often mentions indigenous people in ambiguous terms such as "indigenous populations or communities." Rarely are they mentioned by specific names and locations.

6 In this regard, it is ironic that Spanish is the only official language in Mexico, although about 11 percent of the population, around thirteen million people, speak different indigenous languages, such as Nahuatl, Mayan, Mixteco, Zapoteco, Tetzal, Toztil, Otomí, Totonaca, Mazateco, Huasteco, Chinanteco, Mixe, Tarahumara, Mayo, and others (Comisión Nacional para los Pueblos Indígenas 2009).

7   In Mexico it is still common to insult people in both public and private discourse with the phrase "pareces Indio" (You look or behave as an Indian), meaning that you are backward, not intelligent, lacking education or sophistication, primitive, lazy, or even picturesque.

8   Although the indigenous population of Mexico is about 12 percent, most of the states in southern and central Mexico have a strong indigenous presence: in Yucatán, 60 percent of the population is Mayan; in Oaxaca over 50 percent of the population is indigenous; and in Quintana Roo and Chiapas, 40 percent of the population is indigenous (Comisión Nacional para los Pueblos Indígenas 2009).

9   According to La Comisión Nacional para los Pueblos Indígenas (2009), there are sixty indigenous groups in Mexico, each with a unique language, although certain languages have multiple dialects that may be mutually unintelligible. The majority of the indigenous population is concentrated in the central and southeastern states. There are fifteen groups that have a population larger than 100,000, lead by the Nahuatl with 2.5 million, followed by Mayan with about the same population, and by Zapotecas and Mixtecos. However, Bonfil Batalla (1987) warns us that the census categories are insufficient and defective. Every group establishes its limits, ways of belonging and being accepted, and ways of losing membership. The problem is not linguistic in nature. It is important to account for the social and cultural elements that they share, their vision of the world, philosophy, and nonverbal codes. It is not about external factors that are obvious to outsiders but about their organized collectivities. The real problem is not the linguistic or external profile to categorize people as indigenous but colonial domination of cultures that were in Mexico and experienced genocide and are still experiencing systematic exclusion.

10   Tiya Miles and Sharon Holland (2006) discuss the problems raised by Native Americans' refusal to accept African Native Americans as tribal members of several communities. The blood quantum and racial purity arguments may reduce the number of tribal members in the near future, along with the political presence of Native Americans.

11   According to Monteón González and Trueba Lara (1988), around twenty thousand Chinese lived in Mexico by the end of the seventeenth century, for the most part cooks, barbers, *médicos herbolarios* (doctors who practice herbal medicine), and a few merchants. Spaniards and white Mexicans in New Spain made laws that segregated Chinese in the outskirts of town, restricting their activities, revoking their licenses, and limiting their numbers in New Spain. Monteón González and Trueba Lara (1988) state that although the Chinese never ceased to be part of the Mexican landscape, their presence was of greater importance in other Latin American countries, especially in the Caribbean, because Mexico prohibited slave traffic after independence. In 1815 La Nao de China (large sailing ships from China) ceased to have commerce between New Spain and the Spanish colonies in the Pacific during the turbulent times of the war of independence (1810–21).

12　The global expansion of capitalism and modernity projects brought up unprecedented transatlantic and transpacific mobility of people from the sixteenth century onward. In Mexico the Chinese presence has been influenced by labor
market incorporation, capital accumulation, trade relations, and the development
of global commodity chains and is the product of economic, colonial, political,
and military interventions of the West in both China and Mexico. It is especially
noteworthy that the Spanish empire made the first transpacific commercial circuit, which connected Asia with New Spain and New Spain with Europe. In the
1640s, New Spain became the commercial bridge between Europe and Asia
(Monteón González and Trueba Lara 1988; Puig Llano 1992; Chen 1980).

13　Charro comes from the Vasque *Txarro*, and literally it means *jinete* (horseman).
In Spain, it is the adjective for those born in the Salamanca province in Spain
(mainly Alba, Vitigudino, Ciudad Rodrigo, and Ledesma villages). In Mexico, the
charro is the horseman or cowboy, a tradition that came from Spanish horsemen
who settled in western Mexico. During the Spanish colonial period, indigenous
people were prohibited from owning or riding horses. Therefore, jinetes became
a symbol of whiteness, wealth, and heteronormativity. After the Mexican independence from the Spaniards, there was a proliferation of small landlords who
were jinetes and were called *chinacos*, because they were normally mestizos or
mulattos. Their jinete suit was totally different from the charros,' who liked
to dress ostentatiously to display their social and economic power. Interesting
enough, initially, the partner of the China Poblana was a chinaco, a racialized
horseman and landlord, and over time he changed to a charro, a wealthy horseman and landlord of European descent.

14　*El traje de charro* is often associated with wealthy landlords, with Spanish ethnic
and cultural heritage, and patriarchal rural values. El traje de charro should not be
confused with a mariachi suit. A typical charro suit is made of a short jacket, tight
pants, a hat, and a white shirt. This garb is usually very expensive because it is
made of wool or suede with delicately embroidered designs in silver or gold. The
shirt has ornamental buttons, which may also be made of gold or silver. A charro
wears a soft tie called *moño* (bow), which can be plain or embroidered with a
variety of designs or letters, depending on his economic status. The handmade
belt is engraved and it is called *cinto piteado*. Charros wear ankle-high boots called
botines.

15　A plastic or glass decorative material.

16　Most accounts of La China Poblana plot a story that has elements of baroque
narrative, including captives' tales, picaresque novels, hagiographies, and biographies.

17　La Nao de China was the most important commercial link between Europe and
Asia. *Las naos* used to set sail from Veracruz, Mexico, to Europe with Asian
merchandise that arrived on the coast of Acapulco from Manila. The *naos* set sail
from Acapulco and used the equatorial currents to arrive in the Marianas Islands
and continue their trip to the Philippines. On the way back to Acapulco from the

Philippines, las naos would go north to Japan to find the currents that would take them to California and from there go south to Acapulco. These "global commodity chains" are central to transnational production systems as well as in the understanding of the social links and embeddedness of production networks. Migrants play a key role in the social making of global commodity chains. In colonial Mexico, the two main points of this transpacific commercial circuit were Manila and Acapulco. For a long time the Philippines was administered through New Spain (currently Mexico), through which a vigorous transpacific exchange occurred under the rule of the Spanish colony. Ships traveling from Acapulco to Manila carried a variety of goods: silver, seeds, sweet potato, tobacco, chocolate, watermelon, wine, olive oil, chili, chickpeas, and figs. In turn, las naos would bring silk textiles, Persian rugs, cotton from India, fans, lacquered jewelry cases, chests, bells, china, folding screens, jade, wood, pearls, gunpowder, ivory, fruits, spices, and other goods to Mexico. Once this merchandise arrived in Acapulco on the Pacific coast, it would be transported by land to Veracruz on the Atlantic coast, then shipped to Spain (Monteón González and Trueba Lara 1988).

18 It is common in Latin America to call all people from Asia *chinos*, and *poblana* refers to people living in Puebla.

19 Puebla has been a point of resistance to all the foreign invasions that Mexico has endured. Because of its strategic location, Puebla was not only a rich center for trading, grain production, and the textile industry during the colonial period but also a zone of conflict and contact of cultures. Art crafts and cuisine are a testimony of the area's cultural diversity. The city is known for its fine Talavera pottery, which has a strong Arabic and Chinese influence, and also for its exquisite gastronomy, incorporating strong Arabic, Spanish, and Chinese influences.

20 An institutionalized system of slavery by Spanish colonial government where they were given property rights and Indian labor by the crown.

21 The politics of the Catholic Church resulted in the Inquisition's intervention to diminish the presence of Catarina de San Juan in the colonial cultural practices. The portraits of Catarina de San Juan were prohibited from being published or owned. This decision left a void in the visual records of Catarina. Furthermore, that Catarina de San Juan apparently never learned to write helped to develop her legend and mystery.

22 Monteón González and Trueba Lara (1988) state that although the Chinese never ceased to be part of the Mexican landscape, their presence was of greater importance in other Latin American countries, especially in the Caribbean, because Mexico prohibited slave traffic after independence.

23 According to Erika Lee (2002), a highly organized industry exists to find ways to help Chinese cross from Mexico to the United States, mainly via El Paso. It was a common practice to produce fraudulent Mexican citizenship documentation and to do racial crossing so as to appear "Mexican." The banding together of the Chinese of El Paso with the Chinese coming from the border city of Ciudad Juárez, Mexico, reflects not only the transnational connections between and

among Chinese immigrant communities in the United States and Mexico but also the fluidity of the border region of Chinese illegal immigrants.

24 Historians such as Hu-DeHart (1991) and Chang-Rodríguez (2007) report that during the first decades of the twentieth century, most Chinese had an irregular status and were undocumented when the northern states of Mexico went through a new process of colonization. Most of the indigenous populations that resisted occupation during the Porfiriato were killed or sent to prison camps; consequently there was a need to populate the North.

25 According to Monteón González and Trueba Lara (1988), Chinese were second only to the North Americans and well ahead of the Germans, English, and Spanish in the state of Sonora.

26 A particular strategy to harass the Chinese consisted in the creation of the General Public Health Agency in 1930 (Puig Llano 1992). The agency was supposed to watch vigilantly over the health practices of Chinese establishments. Among other things, the agency restricted what any particular establishment could sell— either groceries, meats, drugs, or bread, for example, but not a combination of these. On the other hand, Mexicans—U.S. citizens or not—were repatriated, and many of them stayed in the northern states of Mexico to look for jobs.

27 By October 1931, with most of the Chinese out of the state, the new governor Rodolfo Calles triumphantly declared the campaign successfully concluded. The Chinese announced their plans to abandon the state once they sold their goods, lands, and properties. However, in many instances, Chinese were not even given the chance to do so and had to go into hiding, crossing the border to the United States or going back to China. Most Chinese in the state of Chihuahua were forced to run and hide in small towns, waiting for the anti-Chinese movement to calm down (Hu-DeHart 1991). The expulsion of Chinese workers in Sonora was a serious setback to many local economies. To this day, border cities such as Nogales have not regained the economic prosperity they once enjoyed as a result of Chinese commerce and a taxpaying Chinese labor force. Nevertheless Mexicans gradually moved into the vacuum and nationalized the petit bourgeois class of local society (Hu-DeHart 1991).

Fun with Death and Dismemberment

Irony, Farce, and the Limits of Nationalism in
Oscar Zeta Acosta's *The Revolt of the Cockroach
People* and Ana Castillo's *So Far from God*

A na Castillo's novel *So Far from God* (1993, 19) begins:
"La Loca was only three years old when she died."
While the death of a child is not usually the stuff of comedy,
the first chapter recounts, with the novel's characteristic dry
wit, the miraculous resurrection of La Loca at her own
funeral and the ensuing panicked argument among the
parishioners about whether the event is an act of God or the
devil. This, we find out, is but the first of many deaths that
occur throughout Castillo's book, along with assorted dis-
memberments, diseases, ritual self-mutilations, and other
embodied distresses. Oscar Zeta Acosta's loosely autobiographical novel *The Revolt of the Cockroach People*,
which documents his involvement in the Chicano movement in the late 1960s and early 1970s, is likewise fascinated
with death, albeit in a different affective register (1989).

In this chapter, I argue that these texts' engagement with
death become the modality through which they critically
remember Chicano nationalist movements, in particular
the possibilities and limitations of these nationalist movements' deployment of death and mourning. As befitting

someone who, in legal terms, was the first to argue for "Mexican American" as a distinct racial category different from "white" because of the relationship to what Ian Haney López (2001, 4) calls "legal violence, encompassing both judicial mistreatment and police brutality," Acosta writes about death in *The Revolt of the Cockroach People* in a properly mournful, nationalist fashion. However, this text simultaneously laments the ways in which nationalism becomes the only available language for making sense of death. *So Far from God* approaches this question in a different way but ends up with a similar response to death. Castillo's novel undermines metanarratives, one of the most important of which is the metanarrative of nationalism. As such, *So Far from God* has been read as a postmodern text that undermines all sense of certainty through the deployment of irony. Yet the novel at moments defends the fixity of meaning and the sanctity of death and, in so doing, insists on the necessity, at particular moments, for a kind of earnest mourning attributable to nationalist sentiment. In so doing, both texts enact a complex and ambivalent rereading of oppositional nationalist ideologies of the social movements of the 1960s and 1970s.

These ambivalent rereadings operate not only in *what* they remember but *how* they remember. These texts must refuse the traditional genres of heroism or elegy, which are themselves deeply nationalist formal strategies, and mobilize new, hybrid, or debased formal strategies that remember social movements differently. In Castillo and Acosta, these formal strategies might be called irony. Yet, as I will elaborate, their form of irony cannot be encapsulated either by the bourgeois literary notion of irony as constitutive of a knowing subject or by the postmodern variant that shatters that knowing subject. Rather, Castillo's and Acosta's ironic representations of nationalist culture, both oppositional nationalism and official state nationalism, emerge from the racialized and gendered contradictions of nationalism itself. In particular, Castillo's and Acosta's disidentificatory relationship to nationalism emerges through an ironic relationship to its primary idiom: death.

The notion that nationalisms are able to inspire surprisingly passionate attachments and identifications through the deployment of death and mourning is fundamental to our understanding of the term itself. In *Imagined Communities*, Benedict Anderson notes that nationalism's power lies in its ability to mobilize structures of feeling more commonly associated with religions than with political ideologies. In particular, religion gives meaning to human mortality and vulnerability by "transforming fatality into continuity (karma, original sin, etc.)" (1991, 11). While Marxism and liberalism approach questions of human mortality with "impatient silence" (10), nationalism provided a "secular transformation of fatality into continuity, contingency into meaning" (11), by inventing an immemorial past for the nation and narrating this nation into the future.

Anderson uses the ubiquity of various national incarnations of the Tomb of the Unknown Soldier, a form of mourning that he observes is unique to nationalism, to illustrate how the nation-state interpellates citizens into its narrative history (11). The Tomb of the Unknown Soldier commemorates not a specific death but a generalizable death that interpellates the citizen, rather than the individual, as mourner. The connection to the dead that allows the living to mourn is not familial or individual but national. The interpellated mourner is not the friend, parent, spouse, or child of an individual, particular soldier but is the citizen of a nation for whom the soldier ostensibly gave his life. But even that is too facile: shared grief binds the citizenry, not by *transcending* the claims of friendship or family but by harnessing them to the nation-state. The Unknown Soldier's sacrifice sutures the individual and known soldier's sacrifice for a particular family, spouse, children, or parents with the protection of the nation's families, indeed, for the protection of a nation's ability and right to have families at all. This is, at base, a struggle over meaning and truth: nationalism claims a community, by providing one irrefutable meaning for, and one possible affect—earnestness, mournfulness, grief—toward, death. The death of the Unknown Soldier has only one possible interpretation, one that mobilizes his sacrifice in defense of the nation, and incorporates individual soldiers' deaths into that narrative. Any difference or excess between that particular soldier, that particular family, and the Unknown Soldier and the national family is exactly what must be repressed. Any other meanings that the particular soldier's death—and, by extension, life—might have had beyond or in contradiction to the nationalist narrative of heroic sacrifice are rendered illegible.

Yet this difference and excess are never perfectly repressed, and we might see oppositional nationalist movements as one way of expressing these differences. The Chicano antiwar movement—and the Chicano Moratorium in particular—was organized precisely around the difference between the racialized specificity of the Chicano soldier and the supposedly universal soldier as the ultimate citizen of the U.S. nation-state. In so doing, the Chicano Moratorium was the "return of the repressed" of the nationalist sentiment inspired by the Unknown Soldier. Initiated by concerns over the disproportionately high rates of Chicano enlistment and fatality in the Vietnam War, the Chicano Moratorium movement eventually grew to encompass a transnational connection to, and identification with, the deaths of the Vietnamese as fellow anti-U.S. imperialist fighters. Cofounded by UCLA student body president Rosalío Muñoz and UCLA graduate student Ramsés Noriega, the National Chicano Moratorium Committee, in concert with the Brown Berets and other movement groups, organized a series of demonstrations and marches, most infamously the march of August 20, 1970, at which the LA County Sheriff's officers murdered the *Los Angeles Times* journalist and KMEX-TV general manager Ruben Salazar. As the historian Lorena Oropeza recounts in her history of the Chicano antiwar movement, the Chicano Moratorium brought together Chicanos/as with a diversity of political viewpoints and made antiwar protest central to the Chicano movement at that moment (2006, 114–15).

From its inception, the Chicano Moratorium's critiques of the Vietnam War were based on the hypocrisy of the United States' universalist narratives of death. This movement ultimately associated the United States with the dispersal of death rather than with the protection of life. Revealing the hypocrisy of a nation-state that claimed to protect life universally but actually operated as the very agent of death for some, the Chicano antiwar movement revealed race to be exactly that process by which people were rendered differentially vulnerable to death. In noting that Chicanos were recruited to serve as soldiers at greater rates and died in battle in greater rates as well, the Chicano antiwar movement undermined the claim implicit in the Tomb of the Unknown Soldier. If the Tomb of the Unknown Soldier claimed that citizens were all interpellated similarly and that the Unknown Soldier could represent any or all of the war dead, the Chicano Moratorium attested that this was not the case. Rather than suturing Chicanos to the U.S. nation-state, the deaths of Chicano soldiers instead revealed the incommensurabilities between Chicanos and the U.S. citizen-subject. Such incommensurabilities, Chicano/a activists claimed, stemmed from material histories of labor exploitation, disenfranchisement, and dispossession.

Rosalío Muñoz's speech refusing to enlist at his September 16, 1969, induction explicitly connected the military projects of the United States with the greater exploitation of Chicanos. In a speech later widely reprinted in Chicano movement newspapers, Muñoz said, "Specifically, I accuse the draft, the entire social, political, economic system of the United States of America of creating a funnel which shoots Mexican youth into Viet Nam to be killed and to kill innocent men, women, and children."[1] Targeting the "educational system," "welfare system," and "law enforcement agencies" as working in concert to give Chicano youth no better alternative than the military, Muñoz's speech renarrated Chicano soldiers' deaths, wresting them away from any narrative that might represent them as heroes of the U.S. nation-state and recasting them as martyrs for the nation of Aztlán. One group, Las Adelitas de Aztlán, marched in the Moratorium demonstration in black mourning clothes, carrying crosses emblazoned with the names of male family members who had died in Vietnam, symbolically mobilizing mourning as a means of producing nationalist identification (Espinoza 2001, 37).[2]

The events of the Chicano Moratorium march and demonstration of August 29, 1970, underscored even further the hypocrisy of the U.S. state toward Chicano lives and deaths. Initially a peaceful march of between twenty and thirty thousand people through East Los Angeles, culminating in a demonstration and speeches at Hollenbeck Park, the march ended with rampant police brutality, including the LAPD in full riot gear assaulting unarmed protesters, ultimately killing four. Most infamously, a sheriff's deputy fired a high-velocity tear gas projectile without warning into the open doorway of a local bar, striking the journalist Ruben Salazar and killing him instantly.

A special issue of *La Raza* published in the aftermath of the demonstration is replete with images of the state's contradictions in the face of Chicano death.[3] In contrast to official state accounts of police behavior, the journal printed dozens of photographs, many taken by editor Raúl Ruiz himself, of complete disregard for Chicano life on the part of the LAPD and the Los Angeles County sheriff. Ruiz happened to be across the street from the Silver Dollar as the episode leading to Salazar's death was occurring, and he took a particularly chilling series of photographs documenting the entire police action that belie official accounts.

Yet in the face of this documentary evidence, as well as eyewitness accounts by other Chicanos who consistently contradicted the sheriff's office's account of the incident, the sheriff's deputy who fired the tear gas projectile, Thomas Wilson, was exonerated when the district attorney declined to prosecute the case after the inquest. Various articles in the volume point out that Wilson's and other sheriff's representatives' testimony clearly contradicts the physical evidence and that the hearing officer Norman Pittluck continually turned the questioning toward unruly behavior on the part of Chicano/a demonstrators, not only at the Moratorium but in other contexts, in an effort to represent the use of deadly force by the police as necessary and appropriate. In *La Raza*'s reportage, the inquest is repeatedly called a "farce."[4] In deploying the trope of farce, the authors of *La Raza* reveal the contradiction within U.S. national culture: while claiming to mourn death equally, the state deploys and values death differentially along the lines of race. Naming the inquest a farce highlights the ways in which the state itself does not take seriously its own claims to universally value and protect life for all citizens regardless of race. The U.S. state does not truly mourn or grieve Chicano death; instead, *La Raza* claims, the state uses the genre of farce—a broadly comic, performative theatrical form that entertains by presenting, in straight-faced fashion, improbable, credulity-straining scenarios—to legitimate violence against Chicanos. By using the term *farce*, which implies multiple levels of meaning—straight-faced presentation, on the one hand, combined with a winking acknowledgment of the absurdity of the scenario presented, on the other—to describe the U.S. state, the authors of the articles in *La Raza* demonstrate that the mobilization of mourning on the part of U.S. national culture produces racialized difference at the very moment it claims to transcend that difference.

In response to the state's hypocrisy, Chicano/a movement activists created an alternative system of valuation in which Chicano deaths mattered, were mourned, and were not dismissed or subject to derision. If the U.S. nation-state would not take Chicano deaths seriously, Chicanos/as would instead. Chicano/a nationalists' mourning of Chicano death made visible the difference between the state's claims to earnestness around death and its farcical representation of Chicano death. By truly insisting on the fixity of the meaning of death—that is, that death should be mourned and earnestly grieved—Chicano/a nationalists demonstrated that U.S. national culture in truth deployed dual meanings for death: mourning and grief as a privilege of whiteness, farce as a sign of Chicano racialization.

In so doing, these movements highlighted the conditions of extreme exploitation and racialized violence operating for Chicano communities.

Norma Alarcón notes that Mexican nationalism and Chicano nationalism (like European bourgeois nationalisms) emerged against "feudal mode[s] of power," both "the Hispanic New World 'feudal mode of power' (which in Mexico gave way to the construction of mestizo nationalism)" and "an Anglo-American 'feudal mode of power' in the isolation of migrant worker camps and exchange labor (which in the United States gave rise to Chicano nationalism of the 1960s)" (1999, 69). If, as Alarcón notes, Chicano nationalism is a mode of "defeudalization" and the feudal modes of power over Chicano/a communities not only continue to exist but are exacerbated by global processes of hyperexploitation and concomitant state violence, then we must conclude that this process of defeudalization is still ongoing (69).

Chicano/a movement discourses engaged in a process of defeudalization by revealing the *farce* and *falsity* of official nationalist deployments of mourning. That is, they highlighted the hypocrisy inherent in the state's use of a feudal mode of power—brute force and violence—against Chicano/a communities while at the same time maintaining the fiction of universal citizenship. Yet movement discourses did so by figuring Chicano/a nationalists as the real bearers of a singular truth—that is, of the value of Chicano life—erased by official nationalism. Mourning mobilized different meanings, some that mask the limits of nationalism, others that trace its fissures and contradictions. Yet oppositional nationalist mourning is indebted to the same dialectic of power and abjection that marks official state nationalism, with all its attendant reinscriptions of belonging and expulsion. In other words, the continuing existence and allure of minority or oppositional nationalisms signal the ways in which the feudal mode of power still operates as a mode of racialization. However, this feudal mode of power exists *alongside* liberal modes of power, which are supported, rather than undermined, by minority nationalisms. As such, Alarcón notes, Mexican and Chicano nationalisms, which we can understand as a " 'communal form of power' under the sign of the cultural nationalist family" while importantly deployed against the feudal mode of power, "may be bankrupt, especially for [the] female wage-worker" (1999, 69).

Alarcón's observations have been borne out historically, as this enforcement of community boundaries happened most violently against Chicana feminists. The historic first national conference of Chicana movement activists in Houston, Texas, in May 1971 is exemplary of the disciplining uses of Chicano nationalist definitions of death. Organized by Elma Barrera, the conference drew over six hundred Chicanas from twenty-five states. While largely succeeding in bringing Chicanas together to outline issues of importance for Chicanas in the movement, including reproductive rights, sexual agency, and critiques of the Catholic Church, as well as immigration laws, political prisoners, police brutality, and the welfare system, the conference is largely remembered for the divisive walkout staged by a number of participants on the last day. As Maylei Blackwell (2003) has documented, the leaders of the walkout accused the YWCA, who had helped to organize the conference, of racism and maintained that organizing around women's issues was misguided. The feminist critiques generated at the conference were, they claimed, trivial when compared to the plight of marchers on César Chávez's pilgrimage from Delano who were getting shot at and of Chicanos dying in the Vietnam War in increasing numbers, and worse, they were deflecting attention and energy away from these more important issues. In other words, because Chicano nationalism constituted itself so resolutely around a critique of official state nationalism's hypocrisy about Chicano death, the sanctity of Chicano death came to be the delimiting boundary for Chicano/a identity and community, which had to be defined in a singular way, brought together around shared mourning and grief around Chicano death. Chicana feminism's interrogation of community boundaries was then figured as a betrayal and as insufficiently respectful of Chicano death.

One of the earliest Chicana feminist theorists, Ana Nieto Gomez, for example, is precise about the ways in which Chicano nationalism delineated gendered and sexualized boundaries for what constituted the Chicano/a community: "I am a Chicana feminist. I make that statement very proudly, although there is a lot of intimidation in our community and in the society in general against people who define themselves as Chicana feminists. It sounds like a contradictory statement, a *Malinche* statement—if you're a Chicana you're on one side, if you're a feminist, you must be on the other side. . . . In fact, the statement is not contradictory at all, it is a very unified statement" (1997, 52–53). As Blackwell (forthcoming) has documented, Nieto Gomez's defiance of the gender and sexual norms of Chicano nationalism did not go unpunished, resulting in reprisals by Chicano nationalist men, from her being buried in effigy on the Cal State Long Beach campus as an undergraduate student leader to being denied tenure in Chicano studies at Cal State Northridge years later.

Because Chicano/a nationalism had its most brutal and normativizing effects on women and queer subjects, Chicana feminist and queer critiques provide the most cogent and nuanced engagement with Chicano nationalism and so offer us a critique of both feudal and liberal modes of power.[5] Oppositional nationalisms had to take a cultural turn. As Wahneema Lubiano has observed, while this recourse to a common culture is central to nationalism as a general epistemological formation, it is particularly useful for minority nationalisms, as severe political and economic alienation produces culture as the only consistently productive site of contestation.[6] Chicana feminists as a part of a tradition of women of color feminism have long noted the ways in which oppositional nationalisms deploy the idea of culture as a means of naturalizing masculinism and patriarchy. In so doing, Chicana feminists disidentify with the dialectic of power and abjection that inheres in patriarchal nationalism. Nationalism interpellates subjects by assuming the subject's injury insofar as subjects approach the state to regain a power to which it presumes it is entitled but has lost.[7] This loss permeates nationalism, producing mourning as its primary affect.[8] In the context of Chicano oppositional nationalism, the ultimate symbol of this loss is the very real deaths of Chicanos from economic exploitation as the agricultural peonage class of the United States, brutal police violence, and war, to name just a few examples. Under this rubric, compensation for this loss, or, in Rosalind Morris's (2002, 30) words, "the fantasy of return," comes with the reassertion of one's "rightful" place as patriarch of a family, narrated as the regaining of "traditional" culture.

Under such a regime, as Norma Alarcón (1989, 69, 70) observes, there are two roles for women: the "unquestioning transmitter of tradition" and the " 'betrayer' of tradition, of family, of what is ethically viewed as 'pure and authentic.' " In the Chicano/a context, Alarcón writes, these roles are figured as the Virgen de Guadalupe, the "silent mediator," and her "monstrous double" (69, 68), La Malinche, who subjects the community and culture to the indignities of the process of translation, which by definition can never be faithful or accurate. La Malinche, who as a historical personage was the literal translator (and consort) of Hernan Cortés, becomes the figure for the speaking subject that rejects "ritualized repetition" of tradition for "interpretive language" (70).[9] In a context in which "traditional culture," organized around the citizen's entitlement to his patriarchal power, acts as the compensatory mechanism for that citizen's losses, undermining this sense of tradition constitutes betrayal, an implicit complicity with the forces of colonialism and neocolonialism, state violence, and labor exploitation that produced such losses.

Chicana feminists negotiated such disciplinary regimes with subtlety and complexity, crafting an alternative political imaginary that took seriously the injuries attendant to racialization (via the feudal mode of power) but did not depend on a static and desubjectivizing position for women as the compensation for these losses (a compensation the very existence of which implied internalization of a liberal mode of power). Chicana feminism did so through renegotiating the dialectic of power and abjection. In the face of the losses of race, Chicana feminism, rather than attempting to resolve or compensate for loss and in this way overcome the state of abjection, instead mobilized abjection. Many found themselves doing so through a critical recuperation of La Malinche, as we see in the passage above from Nieto Gomez.

Chicana feminism cannot be organized around a quest for a lost wholeness and authority if it is to undermine the epistemes of nationalism, either oppositional nationalism or state nationalism. As Sandra Soto has observed, perhaps no other Chicana feminist has so centrally engaged in articulating a different relationship to the dialectic of power and abjection as Cherríe Moraga. Moraga's most famous essay, "A Long Line of Vendidas," from *Loving in the War Years*, activates the process of embracing betrayal by taking on La Malinche as the figure through which to speak. Yet as Alarcón and Soto both note, Moraga's entire body of work, and indeed, the motivating impulse behind her creative process, can be seen as what Alarcón calls "spiritual kinship with the 'lost'" (1999, 66). As Soto notes, Moraga "place[s] a high premium on the public elaboration of private feelings of anxiety, guilt, and fear" (2005, 254). Yet the purpose of this writing is not, as in nationalist mobilizations of such affects, to overcome the losses that produced such feelings: "Moraga's lesson to her students is no self-help healing regimen, nor is it a call to put forth universal truths about the shared pain of being human. Rather . . . Moraga means to intertwine meaningful personal revelation with ethnonationalist desire. . . . The more affective and visceral the experience or desire recounted, the more meaningful and tangible the political result" (Soto 2005, 255). In other words, rather than use loss as a way of justifying a compensatory formation, whether that formation is the patriarchal family or the ethnonationalist community, Moraga finds her politics in the very location of loss and its attendant affects.[10]

Alarcón reads Chicana feminism's recuperation of La Malinche as part of a larger relationship to the figure of the "native" woman, which she understands as quite different from the way in which this figure operates within Mexican mestizo nationalism or Chicano nationalism. These nationalisms use the native woman as the figure for barbarity, savagery, and backwardness to forge a "consensus for most others, men and women," over and against her (68). Alarcón writes, "It is worthwhile to remember that the historical founding moment of the construction of mestizo(a) subjectivity entails the rejection and denial of the dark Indian Mother as Indian, which has compelled women to collude in silence against themselves" (68). In the nationalist ideology of "actually deny[ing] the Indian position even as that position is visually stylized and represented in the making of the fatherland," Alarcón identifies the ways in which nationalism must sanitize the Indian woman, evacuating her of her "noncivilized" nature and "*barbarie* [savagery]" to situate her as the foundation of a mestizo civilization (1999, 68). In this perverse fashion, the figure of the Indian woman is used to reproduce the very ideologies that situate her as backward; for her to represent the mestizo nation, she must be rescued from her own abjection. In contrast, Chicana feminism identifies with the native woman as excluded and abject. Unlike mestizo nationalism, Chicana feminism's use of the figure of the native woman is not a project of representation or visibility but one that critiques and undermines such projects.

As I have noted, the ultimate sign of loss under nationalism is death, which is why Acosta and Castillo might refuse a relationship with death that is simply about resolution and rejects the abjection of death as loss. In so doing, these texts cast the social movements of the 1960s and 1970s as not simply about the redress of injury but about exploring the limits of such a politics of injury and attempting to craft a new vision of the political. Yet in so doing, there are moments when each text insists on the importance of nationalist modes of mourning because the conditions of state-sponsored violence, agricultural and industrial peonage, and ideological demonization that make Chicanos and Chicanas particularly vulnerable to death are still painfully present. The process of defeudalization that inspired anticolonial nationalisms has not concluded.

As such, while nationalism was an important and dominant epistemological formation for Chicano movement politics in the 1960s and 1970s, it was neither monolithic nor unchallenged. The most forceful critique of oppositional nationalism came from women of color feminists, and we see that this is the case within the Chicano/a movement as well. Yet other subjects also tested the limits of nationalist thought. While no one would accuse Acosta of feminism—quite the opposite, actually—his text indexes the inherent contradictions within nationalism, contradictions that inhere in Chicano versions of the form, by simultaneously validating and lamenting the limits of nationalist mourning.[11]

Not only a now-canonical text within Chicano studies, Acosta's follow-up to his *Autobiography of the Brown Buffalo* is also explicitly a narrative of his politicization through radical Chicano movements in the late 1960s and early 1970s. In the same "gonzo journalism" style of *Brown Buffalo*, Acosta resurrects the masculinist, hedonistic, hypersexualized persona first introduced in the earlier text, describing himself as a "dope addict, a bum like me with all my vices, with my love of wild women and song" (1989, 25) in a depiction that has now become a cliché of early Chicano movement machismo. A fictionalized rendering of Acosta's experiences as a somewhat reluctant lawyer for the Brown Berets and the Catolicos por la Raza (CPLR) during the late 1960s and early 1970s, the narrative represents Acosta as a simultaneously central and peripheral figure to the movement. The novel follows Acosta's literary alter ego, Buffalo Zeta Brown, as he defends movement participants in the 1968 blowouts, in which thousands of Chicano/a high school students walked off their campuses in protest of racist teachers and curricula and poor conditions, the 1969 St. Basil protest against racism in Los Angeles Catholic diocese, and the Chicano Moratorium. (Hereafter I refer to the author as Acosta and to the narrator-character in the novel as Zeta.)

Staged as a narrative of politicization or even conversion, the novel opens with a description of Zeta's role in the St. Basil's demonstration, when members of the Catolicos por la Raza stage a protest at the church during midnight mass on Christmas Eve of 1969. The novel then flashes back two years, with Zeta returning to Los Angeles after sobering up from the drug- and drink-fueled excesses that comprised the narrative elements of this novel's predecessor, *Autobiography of a Brown Buffalo*. On a purely self-motivated mission to "find 'THE STORY' and write 'THE BOOK' so that I could split to the lands of peace and quiet where people played volleyball, sucked smoke, and chased after cool blondes," Zeta hears about the Chicano militants and is drawn to them, more in the hopes that they will provide the meat of his narrative than because he has any political investment (Acosta 1989, 22). Indeed, he writes, "Politically I believe in absolutely nothing. I wouldn't lift a finger to fight anyone" (28). As he gets increasingly drawn into the ranks of Chicano militants, however, he struggles with movement politics and his own cynicism. Practically stumbling into participation in the school blowouts, Zeta asks, "All around me is a new breed of savages, brown-eyed devils who shout defiantly to the heavens. And what am I to do? Is this all to write some story? Do up-and-coming great men march at the command of a wretched voice over a bullhorn? Is this the place for a lone buffalo? Will they bust me for passing out Camels? I am divided against myself, torn in two" (42).

This state of being "torn in two" characterizes Zeta throughout the book. As in this passage, in which Zeta's interrogation of the integrity of his political commitments is interrupted by a flippant aside about a much more prosaic and petty concern regarding being caught giving cigarettes to teenagers, the tone of the book as a whole oscillates between the mournfully earnest affect of radical nationalist politics and the caricaturing of that affect. Zeta is unable and unwilling to take lightly the all-too-real deaths, at the hands of the LAPD, of Robert Fernandez and Roland Zanzibar (a thinly veiled version of the Chicano journalist Ruben Salazar, killed by police during the Chicano Moratorium march). Yet neither can he remain completely within the idioms of nationalist belonging that would turn these men into martyrs for *la raza*. The entire narrative explores both the seductions and limits of nationalist modes of belonging.

The Revolt of the Cockroach People certainly plays its part in turning such men into martyrs. In his own life, Acosta did indeed represent the family of a young man who died under suspicious circumstances while in police custody. In the narrative, the same happens to Robert Fernandez, and his family attempts to contest the initial autopsy that rules it suicide. In his role as lawyer for the family, Zeta is forced to direct the second autopsy, which brutally dismembers and violates Fernandez's body, an experience Acosta describes as "death as a world of art" (89). At the end of the description of the autopsy, he addresses a moving prayer to the dead Robert Fernandez. This prayer lifts Fernandez to the status of a martyr, a Christ figure whose suffering saves the race or, in Acosta's language, the "living brown":

I, Mr. Buffalo Z. Brown. Me, I ordered those white men to cut up the brown body of that Chicano boy, just another expendable Cockroach. . . . Forgive me, Robert, for the sake of the living brown. Forgive me and forgive me. I am no worse off than you. For the rest of my born days, I will suffer the knowledge of your death and your second death and your ashes to my ashes, your dust to my dust . . . Goodbye, *ese*. Viva la Raza! (104)

Robert functions in this text as the focal point of mourning that knits together the imagined community of "la Raza." In this context, mourning Robert's death is a way of protesting the violence of the state toward racialized bodies, as represented by police violence (Robert's first death) and again by the autopsy (his "second death"). We might see this prayerlike address as figuratively creating a Tomb of the Chicano (Street) Soldier. This portrayal of Fernandez's sacrificial death operates to call a Chicano into being, as the Tomb of the Unknown Soldier calls a citizen into being. These examples demonstrate the ways in which a common oppositional nationalist narrative that bases the notion of a universal racialized experience through the violence of the nation-state does so through interpellative mechanisms. In other words, what it means to be racialized is to experience the state as not the institution that guarantees the universal protection of life but one that is the very agent of death.

Chicano nationalism challenges this notion of protection of life for all as equal by exposing the ways in which the state is the agent of death for racialized people. In this vein, Acosta mobilizes the rhetoric of Third World solidarity that narrates a connection between Chicano racialization and U.S. imperialist war: "We are the Viet Cong of America. Tooner Flats is Mylai. . . . The Poverty Program of Johnson, the Welfare of Roosevelt, Truman, Eisenhower and Kennedy, the New Deal and the Old Deal, the New Frontier as well as Nixon's American Revolution . . . these are further embellishments of the government's pacification program" (201).

Yet while Acosta's narrative is certainly articulated through an oppositional nationalist idiom, it is not consistently so. It often strays from the dictates of nationalist affect. As such, although Acosta articulates Fernandez's death in this moment within a nationalist frame, his death produces an excess that expresses nationalism's limits, as conveyed in the dialogic and increasingly hysterical description of the autopsy. The autopsy is represented as a kind of dialogue between the doctors doing the autopsy and Zeta, whose permission is needed to guide the doctor's knives as they cut into Fernandez's body:

> Uh oh! Now we get really serious. If he died of strangulation . . . We'll have to pull out the . . . uh, neck bone.
>   Go right ahead, *sir*! Pull out that goddamn gizzard.
>   Uh, we have to . . . take the face off first.
>   Well, Jesus Christ, go ahead!
>   Slit. One slice. Slit. Up goes the chin. Lift it right up over the face . . . the face? The face goes up over the head. The head? The head is the face. Huh? *There is no face!*
>   What do you mean?
>   The face is hanging down the back of the head. The face is a mask. The mouth is where the brain . . . The nose is at the back of the neck. The hair is the ears. The brown nose is hanging where the neck. . . . Get your goddamn hand out of there.
>   My hand?
>   That is the doctor's hand. It is inside the fucking face.
>   I mean the head. (102–3)

Acosta's text certainly mourns the racialized violence by the state that forecloses access to a universal version of life for racialized Chicano subjects. Yet as we can see by the foregoing passage, it also mourns the fact that *there is no language* through which to understand death and dismemberment in any way but as loss. As he narrates the event, his ability to convey the dismemberment through language starts to break down, signaling the failure of language to represent the horrific and surreal nature of state violence against radicalized bodies. Yet this very failure is exactly what conveys the tone of horror and despair. This passage is marked by the slippage of meaning of head and face, of hair and ears, the nose and neck, mouth and brain. Dismemberment disorganizes language, making it impossible to describe a dismembered body precisely and accurately, because the very words one might use to describe it—head, face, hair, ears—imply a whole body, with one universal order and relationship between the various parts. At one moment, Zeta is confused about what to even call the corpse: "This ain't Robert no more. It's just a . . . no, not a body . . . body is a whole" (102). When the wholeness and order of the body are disrupted, language fails in its descriptive duty—it is impossible to call a head without a face a head, or a body that is dismembered a body. In other words, this passage does not merely mourn the inability to ascribe to a definition of subjectivity dependent on a universal sense of life; rather, it mourns the fact that there is no alternative language for subjectivity but this language of life.

This failure of language pervades the entire scene, affecting not only Fernandez but Zeta himself. The violation of the sanctity of the body describes both Fernandez and Zeta at this moment. By being forced to direct this autopsy, he becomes the state's surrogate, which begins to blur his sense of the divide between self and other. Although cast as a dialogue, the passage lacks quotation marks and identifying language, making the coroner's words and Zeta's responses seem more like an internal debate taking place within one subjectivity. At a particular moment, Zeta loses any sense of there being a difference between himself and the coroner: "Get your goddamn hand out of there. My hand? That is the doctor's hand." Here is perhaps the clearest illustration of the contradiction inherent in the term "Chicano lawyer" and, by extension, "Chicano nationalist." The antagonism toward the state that impelled his involvement in this case and constituted his desire to try the state for violence against Chicano bodies is the very thing that puts him in this situation where he becomes a surrogate for the state, demanding and directing the autopsy that enacts the further gruesome violations of Fernandez's body that constitute his "second death." The prayer that Zeta directs toward Fernandez at the end of the passage, then, must be read as mourning the fact that Chicano nationalism, born out of a critique of the U.S. state for Fernandez's "first death," is the cause of Fernandez's "second death." This prayer thus does not merely interpellate the Chicano but also mourns the *limits* of such an interpellation, a response to the violence of the state that replicates that violence. The passage decries the ways in which there is no other language besides that of oppositional nationalism to address the violence of state nationalism.

Similarly, *The Revolt of the Cockroach People* describes the compelling nature of nationalist affect but also simultaneously and consistently highlights Zeta's failure to fully inhabit this affect. In so doing, the novel underscores the process of abjection that is necessary to the construction of a heroic narrative. That is, if figures such as Fernandez are to be mourned as the sacrificial and "good" dead, there must be by implication the morally flawed, the selfish, those unwilling to sacrifice all for the common good.

That morally flawed being is Zeta himself, whose commitment to the radical struggle of Chicano nationalist politics is always tinged with doubt, failure, uncertainty, and resentment.

The Revolt of the Cockroach People effectively conveys the ways in which the interpellative power of nationalist affect is organized around death and mourning. Staged as a narrative of conversion, Acosta suggests a number of "savior" figures, men whose sacrifice and martyrdom give meaning to Chicano identity and around whom an ostensibly unified Chicano collectivity may be constituted. One figure is, predictably, César Chávez, who is depicted as saintly and Christlike. Arriving in Delano in the middle of one of Chávez's fasts, Zeta must pass through a chapel to arrive at the room where Chávez is on his twenty-fifth day of a fast. From an author known for his vivid and earthy descriptions of embodiment, both his and others, this passage is remarkable for how absolutely it refrains from describing Chávez's embodied form, especially given the implication that Chávez was suffering from the effects of a long hunger strike. Rather, the narrative's representation of Chávez is almost as a disembodied voice who, being halfway between life and death, is a kind of ghost. In this text, Chávez is a frail, gentle figure whose pacifist politics are represented as a form of martyrdom: "The height of manhood, César believes, is to give of one's self" (44). Acosta's recounting of a poem that hangs at the door of the chapel heightens the comparison between Chávez and Christ. The poem reads, in an echo of the familiar story of Christ dying for mankind's sins: "Life is not as it seems, / Life is pride and personal history, / Thus it is better that one die / and that the people should live, / rather than one live and the people die" (47). A tearful and heartfelt conversation with Chávez seals Zeta's conversion and inspires his commitment to the struggle.

But the conversion never really sticks. Despite the interpellative power of nationalist affect, this power always creates an unrealizable ideal. Zeta is never outside the realm of suspicion, either by himself or by others. Acosta throughout the book underscores Zeta's inability to fully belong, his consistently questionable and questioned motivations and commitments. In an allegory of guilt and commitment, dying for the cause is the ultimate sign of radicalism, and an unimpeachable proof of belonging. Those unwilling to sacrifice become suspect, and as a hedonist, Zeta falls firmly into this category. Early in the narrative, Zeta asks resentfully, "Who in the shit ever said that revolution has to be a drag? Why can't one be serious and have fun at the same time?" (85). His conflicted state of interpellation by saintly and martyred figures such as Chávez and his unwillingness to fetishize self-sacrifice structure the ambivalent moral edifice of Zeta's subjectivity.

Another such moment of ambivalence emerges exactly around Zeta's involvement with the East Los Angeles Chicano Moratorium rally of 1970. After a series of victories, including successfully defending the East L.A. Thirteen for their involvement in the blowouts of 1968, in which thousands of Chicano/a students walked out of their schools in protest of substandard conditions and lack of relevant education, Zeta retires to Acapulco to enjoy a lascivious, drug-fueled lifestyle in the company of his twin brother, Jesus. Zeta is brought back to Los Angeles only by the news of the death of Roland Zanzibar during the Chicano Moratorium rally. Snapped out of his period of self-gratifying hedonism by yet another sacrificial hero, Zeta muses, "Our first martyr, Roland Zanzibar is dead" (197).

Yet his return to Los Angeles is far from triumphant, and he finds his former radical Chicano compatriots dismissive and suspicious about his absence from the movement. The rhetoric they use situates death as the ultimate form of commitment to the cause, next to which all else pales in significance. Death becomes the basis for moral outrage. In response, Zeta must articulate another relationship to death that defies such moral absolutes:

> "Acapulco!" snorts Waterbuffalo. "Vatos are dying and you're off gettin' a tan."
>
>   This is it. With more energy than I have ever used at one time, I shout: SHUT UP!
>
>   There is a surprising silence. I calm down, just a little.
>
>   "Listen, you guys. I'm no kamakazi! Are you? Do you *want* to die? I'm a writer, yeah, and a singer of songs. I just happen to be a lawyer and a fighter. If I'm not all that, I'm dead! What the fuck are we fighting for? For land and to live just like we want." (207)

He finds that his differently articulated relationship to death alienates him from others in the movement. In the days that follow his declaration, he finds that "some of the men look at me strangely. They know I'm no wimp, but here I am, running around the world, talking of writing and revolution and women and death. Everyone in the room is committed to death. But my commitment to death is different, larger than theirs. It is a night for inter-rogation and I catch them wondering in the corners of their eyes. I'm different" (211). Zeta's "different," "larger" relationship to death manifests in the undermining of moral absolutes, in the impossibility of a quest for moral purity that the sanctifying of death demands.

While the irony of Acosta's text emerges from the uneasy fit between Zeta's hedonism and the morally earnest affect of nationalism, *So Far from God*'s critique of Chicano nationalism is of a piece with its general ironic undermining of a number of sacred metanarratives. The by-turns funny, grotesque, and wrenching tale of the trials and tribulations of a Chicano family in New Mexico, Ana Castillo's *So Far from God* juxtaposes a variety of tones: the fantastical and the sacred exist side by side with the banal and the cynical. The reference to Latin American magical realism in this text has been widely discussed, most specifically by Frederick Luis Aldama (2003). It's not hard to see why: each of the four sisters in this family, as well as all their various friends and relations, lives the most mundane and fantastical of lives and exists similarly in death. Yet these startling juxtapositions, when coupled with a wry, gossipy, and sometimes exasperated narrative voice, combine to produce a formal strategy that is its own significant stylistic mode: an ironic and blackly humorous tone.

B. J. Manriquez situates this use of irony and humor as an instance of postmodernist absurdism (2002). Manriquez understands absurdism as having had its heyday in the 1960s as an epiphenomenon of the postmodern collapse of master narratives.[12] She notes, "The novel of the absurd ignores the ideological, and like *So Far from God*, rebels against essentialist beliefs of both traditional culture and literature. . . . Because for [Castillo] and for other absurdists, human beings exist in a silent, alien universe that possesses no inherent truth or meaning. Human actions seem senseless and absurd" (39). Manriquez importantly situates parody as a formal strategy that produces this absurdism, or, in her definition, a postmodern critique of a sense of totality. She notes that parody ridicules "any construction that tries to impose direction, order, or meaning upon existence.... any pretension that life is understandable—literature, history, philosophy, religion" (44). Manriquez lists a series of "cultural beliefs that Castillo ridicules and rejects," highlighting primarily those that decree the sanctity of church and family (44).

Manriquez's characterization of irony and absurdism as forms that emerge from the collapse of totalizing narratives must be contextualized. This breakdown in totalizing narratives emerged from the challenge that social movements posed to universalizing Enlightenment narratives that

were based on colonial political, economic, and epistemological formations. We must understand that the context for the emergence of postmodern irony and critique of metanarratives is the radical social movements of
the 1960s and 1970s that, as Roderick A. Ferguson (forthcoming) argues,
challenged the universality of Man in Enlightenment thought. One manifestation of this challenge, as I have noted, was oppositional nationalist
critique of the hypocrisy of U.S. national culture's claims to universality, in
particular the farce of U.S. national culture. Yet oppositional nationalist
mourning of racialized death itself began to act as a metanarrative, a metanarrative about the sanctity of death.

As such, I would add another set of "holy" beliefs to this list of totalizing
narratives mocked and deflated by Castillo's text: the race-based social
movements of the 1970s. To wit, the following passage introduces the family's eldest daughter:

> Esperanza had been the only one to get through college. She had gotten
> her B.A. in Chicano Studies. During that time, she had lived with her
> boyfriend Rubén (who, during the height of his Chicano cosmic con-
> sciousness, had renamed himself Cuauhtemoc). This despite her moth-
> er's opposition, who said of her eldest daughter's unsanctified union:
> "Why should a man buy the cow when he can have the milk for free?" "I
> am not a cow," Esperanza responded, but despite this, right after gradua-
> tion, Cuauhtemoc dumped her for a middle-class gabacha with a Cor-
> vette; they bought a house in the Northeast Heights in Albuquerque
> right after their wedding. (1993, 26)

Rather than represent the moment of 1960s and 1970s social movements
with the usual earnest and reverent canonization, the text subjects them to
the same gently mocking tone, representing them through situations difficult to take seriously, such as Rubén's somewhat self-important (and ultimately hypocritical) politicization via Chicano studies. Indeed, we can see
Castillo's Rubén as very much a caricature of the 1970s Chicano machismo
figure at the center of Acosta's text, particularly in the ways in which Rubén
seems to regard Esperanza as simply an object for casual sex and self-
gratification and is characterized by a sometimes comical, sometimes exas-
perating, mix of genuine political conviction and self-indulgent narcissism.
The passage is striking for the way in which it presumes the reader's familiarity with Chicano studies, as well as with what it presents as a clichéd

trajectory of students who are temporarily radicalized by Chicano studies but ultimately end up being absorbed, without much resistance, into the ranks of the bourgeoisie after graduation.

Further, the text also wryly (though a bit more sympathetically) comments on a kind of Chicana feminism that emerges primarily as a critique of Chicano masculinity. The text ironically presents a Chicana critique of machismo through an efficient and perfunctory treatment that makes this kind of feminism come across as clichéd and not particularly revelatory. When Esperanza, years later, takes back up with the divorced Rubén, now engrossed in Native American spirituality, he teaches her "the do's and don'ts of his interpretation of lodge 'etiquette' and the role of women and the role of men and how they were not to be questioned. And she concluded as she had during their early days, why not?" (36). Given that the novel sets up this relationship as so patently unreasonable, it is hardly surprising when Esperanza finally puts Rubén in his place by unceremoniously dumping him (though, all things considered, it is not an unsatisfying scene). Yet if the convention in "women's" literature is that feminist moments like this produce a similarly feminist epiphany in the reader, Castillo's text interrupts that function by making Esperanza's version of feminism seem a bit clichéd.

So Far from God certainly puts the sanctimoniousness of cultural nationalist (and liberal feminist) affect in its place. We can see the text's diverse representations of death, through a number of different affects, as a marked contrast to the fixity of death under nationalist imaginaries. Like *The Revolt of the Cockroach People*, Castillo's text creates a language for talking about death as a differentiated condition. Rather than death and dismemberment signifying a universal condition of abjection and alienation, they are inhabited heterogeneously. Various characters die or are horribly mutilated, but this does not seem to impede their ability to have complex existences, through miraculous resurrections, restorations, or ectoplasmic visitations of one form or another. The eldest, Esperanza, dies while taken as a hostage during the first Iraq war, but comes back to Tome in ghostly form. Unlike most ghosts, Esperanza returns not to silently and mysteriously haunt the living but only to launch into long-winded, opinionated political discussions with her sister Caridad. Caridad, once a promiscuous beauty prone to "making it in a pickup off a dark road with some guy," is brutally mutilated to the point of near death but is miraculously perfectly restored. Caridad's "death" occurs when she leaps off the edge of a mesa, hand in hand with a woman with whom she has fallen in love (27). Yet neither of their bodies is anywhere to be seen and is never found. The youngest sister, La Loca, dies of an epileptic fit in childhood, only to be resurrected at her own funeral. La Loca dies again in adulthood of AIDS but makes "occasional ectoplasmic appearances" at the national and international conventions of M.O.M.A.S., or Mothers of Martyrs and Saints, an organization founded by her mother, Sofi. Castillo may be using the conventions of magical realism, but she does so to free herself from the constraints of a nationalist definition of Chicano racialization that mourns death as a universalizing abjection.

Yet while *So Far from God* resists the totalizing narrative of nationalist mourning, it is not true that it does so categorically. Thus the text does not dismiss the materiality of death as a process to which racialized bodies are rendered particularly vulnerable. One of the four sisters, Fe, dies of cancer caused by the chemicals she is forced to use in her job cleaning weapons parts for a military contractor. Fe's death is recounted thus:

> The rest of this story is hard to relate.
>
> Because after Fe died, she did not resurrect as La Loca did at age three. She also did not return ectoplasmically like her tenacious earth-bound sister Esperanza. Very shortly after her first prognosis, Fe just died. And when someone dies that plain dead, it is hard to talk about. (186)

There are two ways that "hard to talk about" can be read, of course, and I think this passage means them both. There is the idiomatic meaning, in which it is difficult to talk about an event because it is too painful, too emotionally taxing, to talk about something that can only be narrated as tragic. But we can also understand this statement literally; something might be hard to talk about because there is simply no vocabulary, no language, that describes such a thing. The phrase "it is hard to talk about" in this case describes an epistemological crisis, which, like the autopsy passage from Acosta's text, marks a moment when Chicano death must rightly be mourned. This is an acknowledgment, in other words, that the process of defeudalization has not been completed and, indeed, has been exacerbated by globalization; and as such, oppositional nationalisms' protestations of death must be honored, even as alternative relationships to death must be invented. In that instance, there are no alternative modes of narrating subjectivity except through narratives of wholeness and life, no way to have fun with death and dismemberment. Castillo thus switches between creating a new language for subjectivity and lamenting the lack of such a language. In truth, this is the irony of this text. Insofar as Acosta's text does the same, as demonstrated in the discussion of Robert Fernandez's death, *The Revolt of the Cockroach People* also deploys a kind of irony.

Conclusion

This chapter has situated Castillo and Acosta as remembering Chicano movements of the 1960s and 1970s to intervene in the ways in which these movements, as part of the new social movements of those decades, have been recognized and incorporated, at least nominally, by neoliberal multiculturalism. In other words, creating a narrative of worth about these movements becomes another incarnation of power, or, in Michel Foucault's language, a governmentality of attention and care that incorporates these movements (1991). In the contemporary moment, certain aspects of 1960s and 1970s social movements have been mobilized for the aims of power and rendered legitimate, albeit in contingent and constantly vulnerable ways.[13]

This is not to argue that Chicano/a communities are protected from state violence. As James Kyung-Jin Lee (2004) has persuasively noted, state multiculturalism operates to legitimate the brutal punishment and violation of actual communities of color, including Chicano/a communities. Further, any nostalgia for movement culture comes at the expense of rampant anti-immigrant mobilizing that particularly targets Mexican immigrant communities. The anti-immigrant sentiment overlaps with notions of U.S. vulnerability to terrorism as white nativist hysteria associates the permeability of the U.S.-Mexico border with both migration and terrorist infiltration. Yet these attacks exist side by side with the valuation, however facile, of Chicano movements and movement culture.

The example of Chicano nationalist movements illuminates how contemporary neoliberal governmentality seizes on and deploys nationalist idioms to legitimate racialized exploitation. This governmentality is global but can easily use nationalism as a mode of neoliberalism. Globalization means the different deployment and manifestation, rather than the disappearance, of nationalisms. Yet social movements were complex, and neoliberal governmentality seizes on and remembers some elements within them and forgets others. In this chapter, I have traced the complexities of racialized minority nationalism or, to use David Lloyd's appellation, "nationalisms against the state," which both replicates and articulates the limits of the idioms of official state nationalism. As such, I engage with Lloyd's observation that dismissive accounts of nationalism are "able neither to do historical justice to the complex articulation of nationalist struggles with other social movements or, consequently, to envisage the radical moment in nationalisms that, globally, are not resurgent but continuous, not fixated, but in transformation" (1997, 14). This chapter, then, looks to early Chicano movements to identify how they articulated the complexity of nationalist idioms as deployed by movements, and also to identify strains of thought that evade or are in excess of nationalist articulation. Literary texts like the novels of Acosta and Castillo are after-the-fact "revisions" that perform exactly this work of producing countermemories of nationalist movements to ensure that they are not entirely seized by neoliberal governmentalities. I attend to these later literary acts of memory to find a usable tradition that emerges from them that can animate contemporary social movements and political and epistemological projects.

One alternative political and epistemological project, and an important one, is a new form of comparative analytic. The Chicano Moratorium had a transnational comparative analytic, though one that merely extended nationalist modes of comparison. Rather than acceding to U.S. national culture's deployment of death as a means of interpellating an American citizenry, the Chicano antiwar movement narrated another form of solidarity, finding common cause between Chicano soldiers and the Viet Cong who were ostensibly their enemy. Oropeza recounts:

> By 1970 the Chicano Movement's opposition to the Vietnam War, including the nascent moratorium effort, broadened beyond a strict emphasis on who was serving and dying to disputing the war's aims and the value of military service. A telling example was a bilingual pamphlet called *La batalla está aqui* (The battle is here) that Ybarra and Genera coauthored in 1970. . . . Featuring several horrific photographs of dead and wounded Vietnamese children, all victims of American bombs, the booklet aimed to compel Mexican Americans to consider the suffering of

the Vietnamese as much as the danger faced by their relatives in combat. . . . Most important, by drawing parallels between the American conquest of Mexico's northern territories in 1848 to the U.S. military efforts in Southeast Asia, Chicano antiwar activism embraced and promoted the radical thesis that Chicanos and Vietnamese *were together a "Third World" people facing a common enemy.* (2005, 211, 212–13; italics mine)

Thus Chicano/a antiwar activists interrupted the seemingly coherent U.S. national narratives of martyred soldiers by redeploying death in the service of a Chicano movement and Third World imaginary. The deployment of transnational identifications countered U.S. nationalist and imperialist interests advanced through the performance of national mourning. These discourses created a sense of Chicano solidarity and Third World commonality in opposition to U.S. nationalist identification.

The notion of commonality between Chicanos and Vietnamese that animated Chicano/a opposition to the war is yet another example of the nationalist mode of comparison that Roderick A. Ferguson and I detail in the introduction to this volume. While we note the ways in which the notion of internal colonialism produced a minority nationalist mode of comparison that situated racialized groups *within* the United States as analogously exploited by the U.S. imperialist state, this concept also implied a larger Third World connection. The very notion of internal colonialism implies comparison and commonality with those under the yoke of external colonialisms.[14] In the 1960s and 1970s, the most obvious, immediate, and egregious manifestation of U.S. imperialism abroad was the war in Southeast Asia. One of the stakes of examining alternative imaginaries of death beyond nationalist mourning, either deployed by official state nationalism or deployed by oppositional nationalism, then, is to suggest the possibility of different modes of solidarity and comparison that might emerge from those imaginaries.

Notes

I am indebted to the other contributors to this volume for their insightful comments on an earlier draft of this essay in our workshop process. The members of LOUD Collective, in particular Erica Edwards, Arlene Keizer, Aisha Finch, and Jodi Kim, provided generous and supportive readings. I must single out one particular member of LOUD, Maylei Blackwell, whose rigorous readings and suggestions were invaluable. I am also grateful to Helen Jun and Randall Williams for suggestions regarding scholarship on nationalism. I also thank the anonymous reviewers of the volume. All errors, of course, are my own.

1   Rosalío Muñoz, "Speech Refusing Induction," *La Raza*, December 10, 1969, 6.

2   Espinoza 2001, 37. The East Los Angeles–based Las Adelitas de Aztlán was composed of women who were formerly members of the Brown Berets but left the organization in protest of masculinism and male supremacism. As we can see by their mobilization of a nationalist affect of mourning in the Chicano Moratorium march, they still adhered to nationalist ideologies and principles even after their departure from the Brown Berets. However, as Espinoza argues, within the context of cultural nationalist rubrics both during their participation in the Brown Berets and after their departure, these women invented their own agendas and analytics, took on leadership positions and maintained autonomy, and resignified discourses of family away from heteropatriarchal models toward women-identified ones. Espinoza calls this form of negotiation "feminist nationalism" (2001, 42).

3   *La Raza* 1 (3) (n.d.).

4   "The Murder of Ruben Salazar," *La Raza* 1.3 (n.d.): 38. Sanchez, n.d., 53.

5   Many Chicana feminist critiques of cultural nationalism can be said, following José Muñoz, to *disidentify* with cultural nationalism to different degrees. That is, Chicana feminist critiques are not complete rejections of Chicano movement politics and of the nationalism that was a founding ideology of the movement, nor are they a complete dismissal of so-called identity politics. Instead they tend to articulate nationalism and feminism as sometimes contestatory, sometimes overlapping ideologies that address similar sets of historical circumstances, albeit in different ways. In their earliest writings, Chicana feminists such as Marta Cotera spoke *from within* and *to* the Chicano movement. When these authors, in their early writings, traced an alternative genealogy of Chicana feminism, which they imagined as something that is organic to Chicana and Mexicana participation in Mexican and Chicano/a anticolonial and antiracist struggles, they were doing so within a conversation within the Chicano movement, to refute detractors who narrated feminism as a corrupting outside ideology created by white women. In her essay "Our Feminist Heritage," Cotera traces Mexican feminist activities beginning with the participation of women in the Mexican Revolution and articulates a parallel with, rather than causal relationship between, white women's movements and Chicana feminism, explaining that "a [white] women's movement *happened to come on the scene* when Chicanas were ready to take the step toward stronger development and realistic approaches to family problems" (1997, 44; italics mine). In reference to Las Hijas de Cuauhtémoc, an influential Chicana feminist organization founded by Ana Nieto Gomez, Maylei Blackwell coins the term "retrofitted memory" to describe a similar reappropriation of Mexican and Chicano history to invent a Chicana feminist tradition. In the context of the Yucatan's El Partido Liberal Mexicano during the Mexican Revolution, Emma Perez's "feminism-in-nationalism" describes the ways in which Mexicana working

women used the terms of an incipient Mexican nationalism to articulate their specific concerns. In so doing, Perez argues, they created a "third space," which, even or perhaps especially in the moments when they attempted to faithfully reiterate Mexican nationalist sentiments, created a dissonance or contradiction. Dionne Espinoza distinguishes between "feminism-in-nationalism," which operates within the terms of nationalism, and feminist nationalism, which creates a new narrative that borrows from nationalism but is not entirely of it. See also note 11. In her essay about the twin figures of Guadalupe and Malinche, Alarcón notes that La Malinche has been an important figure for Chicana feminists to speak through, and notes that "in order to break with tradition, Chicanas, as writers and political activists, simultaneously legitimate their discourse by grounding it in the Mexican/Chicano community and by creating a 'speaking subject' in their reappropriation of Malintzin" (1981, 71). In other words, Alarcón argues, although Malinche allows Chicana feminists to undermine the bounds of "tradition," she does so from *within* Mexican and Chicano cultural reference. Sandra Soto's analysis posits a slightly different kind of disidentification with Chicano nationalism. Soto sees Moraga as thoroughly undermining the stable subject of ethnonationalism, but notes that Moraga does so *by reproducing ethnonationalist and essentialist idioms and affects*, albeit through shame and alienation in a way that does not allow for resolution. In this way, Soto's argument is aligned with Perez's, insofar as they both argue that even seemingly faithful reproductions of nationalist sentiments necessarily exacerbate nationalism's inherent contradictions. Yet the others also *implicitly* characterize Chicana feminism as undermining any sense of coherent subjectivity or "voice" by underscoring the fundamentally invented nature of Chicana feminism, which subverts any stable sense of origins or a heroic narrative of historical progress (Blackwell), or a faith in language as reflective of meaning (Alarcón), as in Chicano nationalism. In a number of ways, then, these queer and feminist Chicana scholars and activists simultaneously refute cultural nationalist claims that Chicana feminism colludes with racist modes of power, but they also undermine white feminist or postmodernist analyses that would dismiss all antiracist nationalisms as only reactionary, and social movement actors as dupes of nationalist articulations of power. See Muñoz 1999; Cotera 1997; Blackwell (forthcoming); Perez 1999; Espinoza 2001; Alarcón 1989; Soto 2005. See also in the body of my essay further readings of Soto and Alarcón.

6   In an essay that rigorously critiques minority nationalism for its maintenance of heteropatriarchy, Wahneema Lubiano (1997) first observes, in the African American context, that "black nationalism is of inestimable ideological—commonsensical—importance given the reality that U.S. blacks, in their 'being-as-a-group,' control no means of production, no land mass, and until about thirty years ago, were excluded from meaningful participation in formal, political politics. Necessarily, culture has been our terrain of struggle."

7   Brown (1995) tends to see antiracist mobilizations and critiques by people of color as a reductive sense of identity politics entirely motivated by a *ressentiment*

that simply reinvests the state with power. My argument in this essay, which sees Chicano/a cultural production as *both* reinscribing nationalist mourning *and* articulating its limits and contradictions, is partly an attempt to contest arguments like Brown's.

8 Rosalind Morris notes, in the context of contemporary Thai nationalism, the commonness of news stories about the resolution of deaths through proper burial, whether it be "the processes by which a body is recovered, a death reconciled with its corpse, or burial accomplished long after the fact of mortality" (2002, 29). Morris argues that such stories are allegories of the process by which nationalism gives meaning and existence to the present, but only in retrospect, in the same way that deaths are rendered meaningful by their after-the-fact proper treatment. Morris observes: "This suggests to us that nationalism is itself a formation produced in the space of loss or at least in the space of anticipated loss" (30).

9 Ibid., 70. Guadalupe herself, as the figure that must represent "ritualized repetition," or, in other words, the woman who faithfully reproduces Mexican/Chicano communities and traditions without her own subjectivity, is a sacrosanct figure, which sheds light on why queer and feminist Chicanas have found it useful to take up, in complicated and critical ways, the Virgen, as well as why such controversy ensues. For a thoughtful analysis of how such refigurations of the Virgen, in particular by the queer Chicana artist Alma Lopez, enable the articulation of queer Chicana desire in the face of Chicano nationalist attempts to discipline desire, see Calvo 2004.

10 This is not to claim, of course, that Moraga does not herself desire these compensatory mechanisms, as Soto notes. Soto notes that "there is a nagging sense that in relation to the poststructuralist orientation of queer theory, Moraga's occasional objectification of race, reification of binary oppositions, refusal to critique models of authenticity, and modernist-inflected conceptions of power and resistance can seem misguided, if not flat footed" (2005, 238). Yet Soto insightfully argues that because these tendencies in Moraga's work occur in the context of Moraga's constant sense of shame over her inadequacy as a racialized subject because of her ability to pass as white, her half-white parentage, her lack of Spanish linguistic ability, and her queerness, Moraga's writing can never produce a sense of belonging within an ethnonationalist community or of attainment of a nuclear family ideal.

11 Acosta's masculinism has been critiqued by many scholars. Carl Gutiérrez-Jones (1995) offers a particularly insightful reading of *Revolt of the Cockroach People* in which he convincingly recounts the homosocial bonding that forms the basis of Acosta's nationalism, a relationship organized between men and through heterosexism, misogyny, and homosexual panic. That is, Gutiérrez-Jones notes that Acosta's definition of Chicano identity is organized around a "conflation, which joins the desire for partners and the quest of revolutionary righteousness. . . . Thus, in the logic of this narrative, to be a Chicano (male) means to sleep with Chicanas" (130). Ultimately, for this nationalist masculine formation, women are

mere units of exchange between men. The instrumentalist view of women found in Chicano nationalism results from its organization around homosocial bonding, which, as Gutiérrez-Jones observes, "is not the same as to argue that such a group is latently homosexual. . . . In fact, as Sedgwick argues, how a man succeeds in the patriarchal environment, in the world of men granting entitlements to men, depends fundamentally on how well he manipulates this gray area" (133). Arguing that we must pay attention to not only "overt examples of sexism, but also . . . the sharing of that sexism among Chicano males" as the necessary bond that organizes Chicano nationalism, Gutiérrez-Jones insightfully points out this text's "disturbing vision in which the law promulgates homosocial bonds in such a way as to limit revolutionary actions by setting marginalized groups into patterns of self-inflicted violence" (133). In other words, Gutiérrez-Jones argues that the homosocial organization of Chicano nationalism is its limit, the point at which its radical politics are reined in by its nationalism.

12 For the most-cited articulation of this definition of postmodernism as the critique of metanarratives, see Lyotard 1984.

13 For a discussion of the ways in which state racial projects work to incorporate and dissipate radical challenges, see Omi and Winant 1994, esp. chap. 6, "The Great Transformation."

14 For an insightful analysis of the ways in which Third World anticolonial struggles inspired U.S.-based antiracist social movements, see Young 2006.

Becoming Chingón/a

A Gendered and Racialized Critique of the Global Economy

In the mid-1960s, the Mexican government conceived of tourism as a solution to its economic crises. Tourism would modernize the countryside and transform indigenous peasants into urban workers, thus dampening political unrest among indigenous communities. This vision culminated a few years later in the construction of Cancún, the international tourist center built along Mexico's Caribbean coastline that served as the model for tourist centers in the Mexican states of Baja California, Oaxaca, and Guerrero. With its promise of jobs, Cancún attracted thousands of indigenous people from Mexico's southern states, the bulk of whom came from Maya communities in Yucatán. Cancún's transformation from fishing village to Mexico's most popular tourist destination was framed within an evolutionary narrative of progress. Funded by the Mexican government and the Inter-American Development Bank, this project came to represent a model for capitalist development and indigenous integration.

For Maya migrants from Kuchmil (a fictitious name), Yucatán, this move has forced them to engage with capital-

ism's homogenizing tendencies and with narratives of progress and enlightenment. To participate and succeed in a global tourist economy, Maya
migrants are asked to physically leave their communities and to transform
themselves from Indian (conceived as backward and primitive) to mestizo
(conceived as modern and urban and thus envisaged as non-Indian) by
shedding many of the social markers that index their indigeneity (e.g.,
clothing and language). Faced with limited social mobility and job opportunities, Maya migrants have not uniformly experienced the salvation inherent in Cancún's tale of development. Not surprisingly, the new locations—
social, economic, and political—that Maya communities find themselves in
can be disorienting and depressing. The cultural critics Lisa Lowe and
David Lloyd (1995, 5) suggest that placing these (dis)locations within the
frame of the "progressive narrative of Western developmentalism" results in
the perpetuation of assimilation models that cannot explain or contain the
social formations actually produced. Rather, it is more productive to examine the "contradictions [that] emerge between capitalist formations and the
social and cultural practices they presume but cannot dictate" (25).

To interrogate the progressive narratives embedded in projects like Cancún (where an international development logic is converted into a nationalist one), I analyze the contradictions that Maya migrants face as they participate in a global tourist economy. Until recently, the emphasis on structural
explanations in migration studies ignored migrants' self-awareness and
worldviews (Napolitano 2002). Works by Douglass Massey, Alejandro
Portes, Saskia Sassen, and Eric Wolf, among others, stress macrostructural
forces (e.g., economics, class, and history) in determining migration patterns, even as they acknowledge that individual agency and social ties also
matter (see, e.g., Durand and Massey 2004; Massey and Espinosa 1997;
Portes and Rumbaut 1996; Sassen 1988; Wolf 1959). To explain the rise in
female migration and the growing diversity among migrant communities,
migration experiences, and settlement practices within a global market-
place, feminist scholars like Lourdes Arizpe, Pierrette Hondagneu-Sotelo,
and Patricia Pessar seek alternative explanations, beyond structural models,
to account for how gendered practices, social networks, and conflicts of
interest within households shape migration processes (see Arizpe 1981;
Grasmuck and Pessar 1991; Hondagneu-Sotelo 1994; Rouse 1989). Indeed,
considering that migrants' responses to economic transitions are also visceral and embodied, new forms of subjectivity arise in reaction and in

contestation to the homogenizing processes of global capitalism. For indigenous communities, becoming modern citizens entailed a shift in self-perception and the acquisition of new attitudes and behaviors, many of which clashed with previous models for self-actualization and collective engagement. Under these circumstances, Maya migrants from Kuchmil appropriated the Mexican discourse of being *chingón* (to be an aggressive, astute person) as a way to survive in the new economy with a sense of dignity and agency. Thus when Maya migrants speak of being chingón, they offer a gendered and racialized critique of the global economy.

Unpacking Progressive Narratives

Development as an applied approach for understanding and organizing social change in impoverished countries gained currency after World War II. But its roots run deep to anthropological models of social evolution based on stages of development in which "savage" and "civilized" peoples fell at opposite ends of a linear continuum. As a result, development theories are premised on the idea of discrete societies made up of autonomous rational individuals whose social development follows a universal path, albeit not always at the same pace (J. Ferguson 1997). Critics point out that the discourse of development is ahistorical and reinforces an uneven system of value in which certain cultures, people, and economic systems are unfairly valued over others (see Escobar 1995; Cooper and Packard 1997). Nonetheless, bounded, static, and racialized conceptions of peoples (as primitive or civilized, childlike or adult, Indian or non-Indian), of societies (traditional or modern), of space (rural or urban, core or periphery), and of time (ahistorical or historical) popularized by nineteenth- and early twentieth-century models of social evolution have persisted over time (see Fabian 1983; Gupta and Ferguson 1992). This ahistorical, racialized discourse can also be found in development projects like Cancún that target for social improvement "untouched" spaces and the "traditional and authentic" Indians who reside there.

Since social transformation is central to ideas of development, it is not surprising that development discourse has impregnated theories of migration. Structural explanations invoking evolutionary models have dominated academic discussions of why people move. Robert Redfield's (1941) folk-urban continuum model of social change provided a framework for early understandings of Maya migration. As Maya peasants migrated between rural communities and urban centers, they adopted modern cultural traits (e.g., individualism and rationalism), which, once infused into rural communities, provided the catalyst for their eventual metamorphosis from "folk" to "urban." Like the folk-urban continuum, the neoclassical migration model of "push-pull" was predicated on assumptions of a universal linear progression and assimilation. Beginning in the 1960s, social scientists challenged depictions of isolated communities by historicizing them within colonial projects and capitalist systems, and questioned portrayals of migrants as rational male actors guided by cost-benefit analyses by focusing on female migrants and by highlighting the significance of households and social networks in determining migration patterns.[1] Migration, however, continued to be envisaged as linear. To displace this deep-seated paradigm, recent studies conceptualize migration as a circuit (see Levitt 2001; Rouse 1991).

Considering that human transformation and agency are central to development theories, it is not surprising that scholars have begun studying migration as a subjective and embodied experience (see Malkin 2004; Rouse 1995). In a study of migrants who moved from rural communities to Guadalajara, one of Mexico's largest cities, the anthropologist Valentina Napolitano (2002) calls our attention to how migrants narrate this movement. Her subjects frame these experiences (subconsciously, possibly) within an evolutionary discourse of the rural as backward, primitive, and lacking consciousness. For many migrants, Napolitano argues, migration was viewed as a process of enlightenment because "the transition from rural to an urban environment is perceived as a step from an unconscious to a conscious life, and is represented in terms of both self-empowerment and the loss of that power" (53).[2] This move from conscious to consciousness echoes development models of subjectivity that privilege the autonomous, conscious individual as the archetype for all members of premodern societies (Saldaña-Portillo 2003).

However, this teleological view of human agency does not account for subjectivities and social formations that aim to disrupt these narratives. What does it mean, then, when migrants narrate their migrations as a process of enlightenment? Scholars of migration suggest that the movement from *pueblo* (village) to *ciudad* (city) has become a "rite of passage" for young men and women.[3] Yet this metaphor reinforces a linear progression, conceptualizing migration as moving from one state of being to another. What behaviors and ideas, what kind of consciousness, does this process reinforce, establish, undermine? We cannot assume that this rite of passage is experienced homogeneously across ethnic, racial, gender, and class lines. Therefore, understanding the subjective and embodied experiences of migrants requires us to pay critical attention to the historical, economic, cultural, and racial roots of the moral and theoretical frameworks that structure these experiences.

Maya Subjectivity in a Global Economy

Kuchmil migrants who moved to Cancún experienced migration as a learning process that "awakened" their senses, their knowledge, their understanding of the world. However, among the Maya, this developing consciousness was not something particular to an urban experience but formed part of the process of becoming a person. Experiencing migration became a life stage added to the life stages of marriage and parenthood, among others, by which Kuchmil residents acquired the knowledge and experience that would allow them to achieve full maturity or personhood. But becoming a full person was not contingent on migration. Kuchmil residents who did not migrate acquired this knowledge by passing through the life course stages of rural life (e.g., *quinceañeras*, marriage, parenthood, cultivating one's cornfield, holding public office).[4] Kuchmil residents spoke of these stages as part of the learning process of becoming a person. The Maya phrase *Má' t'in ná'atik* (I am not learning it) was commonly used to refer to one's lack of experience and knowledge and to the initial stage of exposure to a new practice, activity, or knowledge. At first, I considered this assertion to be a sign of humility but soon recognized it to be a proclamation of the learning process involved in becoming a person. The Maya noun *ná'at* refers to intelligence, reason, and knowledge (see Bricker, Po'ot Yah, and Dzul de Po'ot 1998). To exclaim *má' t'in ná'atik* registers one's awareness of life as a continuous journey toward maturity, knowledge, and full consciousness that can only be obtained over time through practice and observation.

In Cancún, Kuchmil migrants took advantage of get-togethers to build on and impart the knowledge and experience that defined adulthood. During ritual celebrations and casual get-togethers, they constantly compared wages and work experiences and shared information on medical care, child rearing, and employment opportunities. Through these discussions, mi-grants acquired and shared knowledge that would help each other become more socially and politically conscious of the systems of power in which they were enmeshed. Eventually, through such exchanges and the practice of everyday life, one becomes more *despierto* (awake) and adept at maneu-vering these systems of power.[5]

To acknowledge the new experiences migrants faced, the community of Kuchmil incorporated these activities and practices into the recognized life stages commonly experienced by men and women. Some of these practices replaced traditional markers of personhood rooted in an agricultural-based economy. For example, the practice of spending summer vacations in Can-cún as early as the age of eleven and working in Cancún during these vacations became a marker of adolescence and part of the transition to full personhood. This insertion into the Cancún labor market exposed youths to the demands of this market, which increasingly required more schooling. In addition, children's interest in school and their households' economic needs prompted parents to educate all their children. As children began to spend more years in school, the age of marriage was expanded, creating a longer period of adolescence than had existed before.

For youths who attended boarding schools and migrated to Cancún and other neighboring cities, space, place, and community—and how to be a person within such temporal and moral frameworks—were imagined dif-ferently as they established connections within and across this expanded space (cf. Anderson 1991). This imagining, however, cannot be explained simply as a linear process of enlightenment, as a form of acculturation, but must be understood as part of a long history in which " 'indigenous cultures' have been historically produced in a dialectical relation of resistance and domination with the Mexican nation-state" and capitalist structures (Her-nández Castillo 2001, 233). Unlike the consciousness promoted by develop-ment models of the rational actor unencumbered by social ties, this type of awareness was grounded in a collective and racialized experience.

As we construct histories of these embodied processes, we cannot ignore the interconnectedness and interdependence of the city and the country-side. Migration in Mexico has become part of the rural experience, making the ciudad central to the rural imaginary, not only as a foil to the rural but as an expanded sense of place. Considering that place is a mediated experi-ence, forged out of the social relations through which it is understood, claims to geographic distinctions, particularly between the rural and the urban, need to be reevaluated (see Hastrup and Olwig 1997; Massey 1994; Olwig 1997). Yet binaries (core-periphery, tradition-modernity, rural-urban, Indian–non-Indian) serve as central tropes in theories of migration. Indeed, Robert Redfield's folk-urban continuum was premised on a sharp division between rural and urban traits and between traditional and modern societies. Works by Saskia Sassen and Alicia Re Cruz offer more recent examples of this continued reliance on binaries to explain migration processes. The sociologist Saskia Sassen's assertion that "international migrations are conditioned, patterned and bounded processes" is predicated on a core-periphery model, in which rich, industrialized cores attract or seek out labor from underdeveloped and impoverished regions (1999, xxi). In her study of the Maya community of Chan Kom, the anthropologist Alicia Re Cruz (1996) also relies on the dichotomies of peasant-capitalist, rural-urban, and tradition-modernity to explain the conflict engendered by Maya migration. She argues that these dualisms not only reflect the political divisions within this community but also are deployed strategically by Maya political factions in their attempts to take control of community resources. Yet the anthropologist Michael Kearney (1996) contends that the continued use of these dualisms simplify peasant identities and affirm typologies that disconnect rural societies from global processes. Instead Kearney suggests we disrupt these typologies by studying their internal differentiation. Likewise, anthropologists such as Roger Rouse and Nina Glick Schiller suggest we dismantle these binaries through a transnational approach that emphasizes the social ties migrants develop across communities and geographic spaces (Basch, Glick Schiller, and Szanton Blanc 1994; Rouse 1991). Consequently these categories (rural-urban, tradition-modernity, Indian–non-Indian) are fraught terms because they reinforce a racialized discourse that presumes that these categories are natural and spatial (Gupta and Ferguson 1992), and that one can become more or less Indian based on distance traveled. Being Maya, however, is not based on living in a particular place or location but grounded in the social and historical relations and collective experiences of a particular community. As indigenous people move to urban spaces, social scientists should be less concerned with processes of acculturation and more concerned with how these new articulations disrupt naturalized categories and create new categories of difference.

Even as migration and displacement blur the edges of concepts previously considered to be bounded categories such as the pueblo, the city, and the nation, Akhil Gupta and James Ferguson suggest that we pay attention to the hierarchical relations between these concepts and spaces, particularly as they become "*re*territorialized" and reconceptualized over time and as a result of changing practices (1992, 20). These spaces are also deeply gendered places that are not always gendered in the same way across different sites (Massey 1994). Through a description of a Maya migrant circuit situated within local, regional, and international spaces, I map out the complex ways that Maya migrants negotiate the power hierarchies of these interconnected spaces.

Becoming Chingón/a

The anthropologists John and Jean Comaroff (2001) remind us of the importance of understanding the historical and cultural specificity of personhood within economic labor systems. In the Yucatán Peninsula, changes in the political economy resulted in the interruption of previous acts that modeled gender, race, class, and ethnicity. New acts and discourses initiated by local communities, government institutions, and economic systems intended to teach rural and indigenous communities how to become modern citizens. These acts and discourses did not always complement each other, nor did they change many of the class, gender, and racial parameters within which indigenous communities were located. Not surprisingly, at times the process of nation building boils down to how to produce liberal citizens without destroying local cultural practices and without rupturing the social ties that bind communities together (see B. Williams 1991). This tension is evident in the performance of Maya personhood.

For Kuchmil parents, teaching their children to be despierto (literally, to be awake, but in this context it refers to astuteness) in this age of global capitalism becomes central to guiding their children's mental, physical, and religious development.[6] Parents hope that with such guidance their children will learn to handle government bureaucracy, to cope with the oppressive aspects of wage labor, and to fulfill their social and economic obligations to their community. The anthropologist Paul Sullivan shows that in contrast to the earlier years (1920s to 1940s) in which "notions of justice, fair exchange, divine will, and political alliance in terms of 'goodness, love, and propriety' " marked Maya interactions with foreigners, "nowadays in-justice, unequal exchange, and political subordination seem to them [the Maya of Quintana Roo] like nothing so much as 'getting fucked' in the social intercourse of daily life" (1989, 175–76). Sullivan suggests that like the Spanish word *chingar*, whose usage predominates in Mexican society, the Maya word *top* (to fuck, to screw, but also to harm, to bother) "sums up contemporary assessments of the results of those dealings" with foreigners, including Mexican officials (176).[7]

Indeed, scatological references provide Maya migrants in Cancún with a way to critique their subordinate positions and oppressive conditions with-in the tourist economy. Instead of using the Maya word *top*, they adopt the Spanish term *chingar* but imbue it with the multiple meanings of *top*: to fuck, to be brave, to be beautiful. Likewise, José Limón (1994, 131) suggests the usage of the term *chingar* among working-class Mexican Americans in South Texas constitutes "symbolic expressions of an essentially political and economic concern with social domination, not from below ... but from above —from the upper levels of the structure of power." Similarly, for Maya mi-grants, the verb *chingar* offers a way to critique the global economy, but it also provides a way for migrants to reposition themselves within this economy.

The word *chingar* is a raw, brutal word with multiple meanings. Octavio Paz (1985) suggests that its origins lie in the Nahuatl language spoken by the Aztecs. Paz characterizes this word as an "aggressive" word that "we utter ... in a loud voice only when we are not in control of ourselves" (74). Paz also recognizes its magical and lyrical nature in Mexican usage. "It is a magical word: a change in tone, a change of inflection, is enough to change its meaning" (76). Use it with a flirtatious tone, and *chingar* means to tease, to make merry, to be great, to be manly, to defy. Use it soberly, and it implies failure, neglect, and frustration. Use it aggressively, and it has a deadly and violent ring: to be deceptive, to contradict, to sexually penetrate, to rape, to destroy.

Chingar is also a gendered and sexualized word. *La Chingada*—the fucked one—the noun form of *chingar*, refers to Malinche, *Malintzin*, or doña Marina, the Indian woman who served as translator and mistress to the Spanish conquistadors and is historically recognized as the mother of the mestizo (a Mexican of mixed race). Gloria Anzaldúa (1987, 22) suggests that among Mexicans and Chicanos, the term *chingar* cannot escape its gendered and sexualized origin: "She has become the bad word that passes a dozen times a day from the lips of Chicanos." For Anzaldúa, this contempt is indicative of the resentment Mexicans and Chicanos feel toward their indigenous selves, and toward women in general: "The worst kind of betrayal lies in making us believe that the Indian woman in us is the betrayer. We, *indias y mestizas*, police the Indian in us, brutalize and condemn her. Male culture has done a good job on us" (22). Likewise, Paz (1985, 86) reflects that La Chingada is the "cruel incarnation of the feminine condition."[8] In many ways, this racialized metaphor includes all Indians, not just women.

In contrast, to be chingón—to commit the sexual act, violence, deception—represents an "active, aggressive and closed person," the *macho* in opposition to the inert female body of La Chingada (Paz 1985, 77). According to Paz, power "sums up the aggressiveness, insensitivity, invulnerability and other attributes of the macho" or chingón (81). Matthew Gutmann (1996, 241) suggests that being a working-class macho has been "a male Mexican project," a project central to defining Mexico as a nation. In spite of this national reification of the working-class macho as representative of *lo mexicano* (authentic Mexican traits and culture), Gutmann reminds us that the meanings of macho are multiple, shift with time, and thus cannot be "justifiably called exclusively national in character" (241). Gutmann's critique is useful in deconstructing what it means to be chingón among Maya men and women who use this term to refer to themselves. I suggest that adopting a national discourse, rather than a regional one through the use of *top*, allows Maya migrants to participate in a shared sense of oppression. In my analysis of its usage among Kuchmil migrants, I rely on Mexican, American, and Chicano authors' analyses of this word as a way to think through how the term and its meanings relate to people's lives. However, I do not assume that the meanings Chicanos and working-class Mexicans attach to the word are automatically applicable to Kuchmil migrants.

According to Octavio Paz, humor serves as a weapon by which to display the macho's power:

> The *macho* commits *chingaderas*, that is, unforeseen acts that produce confusion, horror and destruction. He opens the world; in doing so, he rips and tears it, and this violence provokes a great, sinister laugh. And in its own way, it is just: it re-establishes the equilibrium and puts things in their places, by reducing them to dust, to misery, to nothingness. The humor of the *macho* is an act of revenge. (1985, 81)

In his ethnography of working-class Mexican American men in South Texas, José Limón (1994, 125) examines these chingaderas as a "discourse of the dominated." The homoerotic meanings inherent in the term are obvious and frequently used by Mexican American men to assert power through humor. Limón claims that humor in the form of "doing or saying *chingaderas* (fuck ups)" creates a "powerful yet contradictory sexual and scatological discourse" rooted in a Mexican working-class folk tradition (127, 129). Additionally, Limón suggests that the word *chingar* is used in "speech body play" that constitutes "dynamic forums that interactionally produce meaning, mastering anxiety by inverting passive destiny through active play" (125, 133). Regardless, the gendered and sexual nature of the term imbues it with contradictory meanings that resonate with the contradictions that working-class machos face in an industrialized postmodern South Texas. Limón suggests:

> Here humor becomes not existential angst and cultural ambivalence but carnivalesque critical difference, though never without its own internal contradiction, for the fact that here . . . I deal with a world of men from which women are excluded qualifies the "positive" and "resistance" character of this humor. (125–26)

While Limón cautions that the male carnivalesque reproduces female subjugation, I suggest that the internal contradictory nature of the term *chingar* allows it be used as a critical space for expressions of power by other subjugated groups, in particular indigenous people and women. More than just play, this speech becomes part of an active refashioning of people's subjectivities in actual life. Indeed, the desire for their children to not be screwed or harmed in life constitutes one of the main reasons why Maya parents constantly push their children to be alert. Néstor Canul Canche explained, "Era medio tonto. Me costó trabajo aprender" ([Growing up] I was somewhat dumb. I had to work hard to learn). By teaching his son Raúl to be more despierto, more self-aware, Néstor expected this awareness not only to help Raúl with his schoolwork but also to help him to avoid being *tó'op* (the passive of *top*; that is, to be fucked, to be harmed) in life. Self-awareness leads to a greater awareness and sensitivity to the social condition of the world in which one lives. More importantly, being despierto transforms the Maya from victims to agents. Being despierto makes one chingón, which describes an aggressive, assertive person, capable of under-standing how power works and using it to one's advantage.

The term *chingón* was employed by both Maya men and women in everyday talk. While *chingón* traditionally and in many places refers to a "masculine actor" (Alarcón 1989, 61), among Maya communities, this actor need not be male. Instead men and women can both be chingón because the term is used as the Spanish equivalent of the gender-neutral Maya word *top*. For Kuchmil residents, the meaning of the word *top* depends on its usage. Use it pejoratively, and it implies to be fucked or harmed. Use it positively, and it implies to be intelligent, beautiful, and brave. By infusing *chingar* with the multiple meanings of *top*, Kuchmil migrants expand its meaning to reflect their particular racialized experiences. In addition, be-coming or being chingón has become flexibly gendered in its daily use and reference. Yet the word *chingón* retains a masculine sense of power because it is a reference to power, a concept that continues to be rooted in mas-culinity because for many Mexicans, reality represents power as such. This reference to power is what makes being chingón an attractive positionality for Kuchmil migrants. Becoming chingón, then, allows Maya men and women to position themselves within national identity discourses.

When children are taught to be despiertos, they are being taught to be *chingones* in the aggressive sense of the term. Violeta May Chen described her one-year-old daughter Yasmín as *chingona* because she used her obser-vation skills to quickly solve problems. Violeta's proclamation occurred after Yasmín outsmarted me, the anthropologist. On a hot September after-noon, Violeta was busy preparing the midday meal of pork with beans while I sat in a hammock that traversed her tiny kitchen. Yasmín sat on a nearby chair and watched me intently as I pulled out my writing materials from my shoulder bag. As Violeta talked about her experiences as a young mother in Cancún, I jotted down a few notes in my wire-bound notebook. Yasmín was fascinated by my notebook and kept trying to get a hold of it. With each attempt, I moved slightly out of reach. I soon became engrossed in the conversation and stopped paying attention to Yasmín, who took advantage of my absorption to snatch the notebook from my lap. Once I noticed the missing notebook, I reached out to recover it, but Yasmín smiled mis-chievously, slid off her chair, taking the notebook with her, and scampered behind the chair. Violeta and I burst out laughing at Yasmín's antics. Violeta applauded and cheered her daughter's fearlessness, inventiveness, and problem-solving skills. "Mi hija es chingona!" (My daughter has got balls), she exclaimed. On other occasions, when Yasmín failed to solve a problem and cried in frustration, her family jokingly teased her, "¡Ya te chingaste!" (You've been screwed). Yasmín was being taught at a very young age to use her intellect and spunk to solve life's dilemmas.

Kuchmil migrants also used the term *abusado* (from the verb *abusar*)—a less vulgar term than *chingón*, but one that also has its roots in violence and aggression, meaning to abuse, mistreat, take advantage of, or impose on—as another way to describe being despierto, being astute. This term was used because it offered a less vulgar way of describing women who were chingonas. Mariela Can Tun described her sister Jovana as being *abusada* because she learned how to do things swiftly. For example, Jovana easily learned to get around Cancún by bus and lobbied successfully for her land plot. These examples demonstrate that the meanings of being chingón and abusado were not always tied to a particular gender but were linked to gendered behavior in which aggressiveness, but not aggression, and creative problem solving were considered attributes necessary for both men and women to live with dignity within changing fields of productive relations.

Being despierto, abusada, and chingón indicates a strong sense of self, but these attributes are also gendered depictions of a powerful self located within a masculine world. Octavio Paz (1985) points out that the aggressive, masculine nature of the verb *chingar* hints at an underlying violence (physical, sexual, and psychological). Ruth Behar (1990, 242, 249) suggests that this desire to take on a "male role" and the "desire to be *macha*" represent for women, particularly indigenous women, a desire to be "a woman who won't be beaten, won't forgive, won't give up her rage, a *macha*, too, in the sense of wanting to harness a certain male fearlessness to meet evil and danger head-on." Behar identifies *coraje* (rage)—a state of emotion and illness generated by strife between kin or other inequities—as a "culturally forceful state of consciousness, whether it refers to feminist rage or the diffuse anger that oppressed people feel in colonial settings" (241). The concepts of being despierto, abusada, chingón, or a person full of coraje are rooted in masculinity because power is usually depicted as masculine and legitimated through a masculine discourse. However, the awareness generated by such emotional and intellectual states gives people knowledge to resist and claim power for themselves (see Behar 1983).

The term *chingón* also encompasses the "logic of the absurd" because the underlying violence present in the word is accompanied by humor (Paz 1985, 81; Gutmann 1996). Indeed, Renato Rosaldo (1989, 150) notes that "culturally distinctive jokes and banter play a significant role in constituting Chicano culture, both as a form of resistance and as a source of positive identity." Through such humor, Paz (1985, 81) suggests that the use of the verb *chingar* "re-establishes the equilibrium and puts things in their places, by reducing them to dust, to misery, to nothingness." When the Maya point out how chingón they are, there always exists a tongue-in-cheek effect to this assertion, particularly among women, because they are conscious of the limitations to their "contestative discourse," limitations that are rooted in the gender, class, and racial hierarchies in which indigenous people are situated (Limón 1994, 139). This discourse and positionality contain excesses too—one can be seen as too chingón/a.

Becoming Too Chingón/a

When Kuchmil parents teach their children to be chingón/a, they nurture their children's sense of individuality. However, the Maya concept of the person or individual is not equivalent to the Western concept of the autonomous individual who seeks to advance the self as a way to achieve modernity (see Comaroff and Comaroff 2001). In contrast, Maya persons are taught that self-awareness is rooted in a collective identity. This sense of the collective creates the framework through which personhood is enacted. Most important, this moral framework keeps people from becoming too chingón/a. Individuals who attempted to become successful by abusing their relationships with their neighbors and relatives were quickly sanctioned by the community. For example, in 1996, don Teo May Balam was asked to leave Kuchmil because he failed to meet the mandatory work requirements imposed by the *ejido* system and because he overcharged the residents for the use of his mill. He lost his house, his mill, and his land. Becoming rich at the expense of the needs of the community was considered a shortsighted act that demonstrated a lack of a social and political conscience.[9] Don Teo was accused of being too chingón.

Migration can also lead to excess. In Cancún, Kuchmil migrants are taught by multinational corporations to become the autonomous individual who is "now conceivable as a subject, independently of social context," pulls himself up by his bootstraps, and is alienated from his labor (Sayer 1991, 58). Here I purposely mark this individual as male because more men than women work for the corporations. Migrants are taught that to succeed economically and socially, they need to become modern individuals. When migrants follow this dictum, however, they run the risk of becoming too chingón.

Take the case of twenty-five-year-old Javier Can Po'ot. Javier purchased a car because, due to his busy work schedule, he needed a secure form of transportation in the evenings. The car also made it possible for him to secure employment in managerial and supervisory positions that required extensive travel to visit corporate franchises. After buying a car, Javier was criticized for being too chingón by Kuchmil residents. Each time he drove into town, his neighbors (many of whom were kin) treated him hostilely. They were upset because Javier no longer spent time in the community. During his visits, Javier spent a few hours with his immediate family and left for Cancún soon afterward. Before he purchased a car, Javier arrived by bus. The public transportation schedule was organized in such a way that one was required to spend the night in Kuchmil; even the bus driver slept in the village located at the end of his route. In the past, Javier spent this time hanging out in the park, playing basketball or visiting friends. The hostility directed toward him and his new car motivated Javier to keep his visits brief, but he missed the social gatherings among his peers in Kuchmil. Although Javier's family appreciated the comfort, convenience, and social capital that came with access to an automobile, they also considered Javier's visits to be too brief. Access to a car allowed Javier to make more frequent trips but spend less time in Kuchmil. Additionally, his family was upset by the purchase because to save for the car, Javier stopped sending remittances. This struggle over remittances hints at the problems that result from the clash between community and familial expectations and the demands of the labor market.

Assertive, independent women also faced the risk of being sanctioned for being too abusadas. Fernanda Can Hernández's experience with migration illustrates this process. Fernanda migrated to Cancún in 1996 when she was sixteen. She worked as a store clerk six days a week, which made it difficult for her to travel to Kuchmil. Fernanda's parents were not concerned because she was living with her mother's uncle and his family. She periodically sent money home through her mother's relatives. On the few occasions that she traveled to Kuchmil, she was stylishly dressed and brought presents and money. However, since the residents of Kuchmil and the migrants living in Cancún rarely saw Fernanda (she was absent from community events for several years) and did not know the uncle with whom she was living, they became suspicious of how she was earning her money. "No one knows about her. She hardly ever returns to the village," Kuchmil residents and migrants exclaimed. The community's concern with Fernanda's absence from community activities reflected their anxieties about women's new economic roles. As a result, gossip questioning Fernanda's morality began to circulate between Kuchmil and Cancún. According to this gossip, due to a family feud, Fernanda no longer lived with her aunt and uncle. I was told that her *padrino* (godfather), a local schoolteacher, went to Cancún to search for her. "He began to cry" when he discovered that she worked as a waitress in a bar, which the residents of Kuchmil equated with prostitution. Her padrino could not believe that she had fallen "tan bajo" (so low). Stories like these circulate quickly within the regional network in which Kuchmil is embedded. To counter this narrative, Fernanda began spending more time with her family in Kuchmil. Fernanda invited me to visit her at work because she knew that as a frequent traveler between Kuchmil and Cancún, I could witness and testify to her virtue and her housing accommodations.

Through these visits to Kuchmil, Fernanda contradicted the narrative of her downfall and demonstrated that she was a good daughter and a morally upstanding woman. It was during one of these visits that she agreed to be a *madrina* (godmother). She also asked to accompany me when I visited the homes of Kuchmil migrants in Cancún. During these visits, she was treated warmly by the migrants, many of whom were kin, and made arrangements to visit again. Fernanda never hinted that she knew about the gossip, but her socializing began soon after the gossip commenced. A few months afterward, people stopped telling this story.

In April 2001, Fernanda returned to serve as madrina of *héetz-méek'* for friends of the family who lived in a *ranchería* (hamlet) near Kuchmil. She brought the child diapers, a set of clothes, a plastic baby bottle, a pair of shoes, baby wipes, and moisturizing lotion. The godparents' responsibility is to guide the child's religious education and intellectual development. As such, the role is traditionally filled by a married couple. Fernanda's unmarried state was overlooked because of her "wealth"—as an unmarried migrant, she earned a healthy income. Her younger brother Matías played her counterpart in this ritual. This display of goods reinforced Fernanda's success in Cancún. Migrant women's purchasing power has elevated their social status within the community. Regardless of their marital status, female migrants are now viewed as attractive choices for *comadres* (ritual co-motherhood). In this instance, her success was not perceived as being too chingóna because Fernanda was redistributing resources through culturally appropriate channels. Money from migration was frequently channeled into making rituals more elaborate in size and complexity, which increased the prestige of families in the community.[10]

Paula Cime Yah was also considered *muy abusada*. She met Macario while they both studied at a boarding school near Valladolid. After she left the school, Paula took a seamstress course to improve the basic sewing skills that she learned in boarding school. She was talented and soon established an informal sewing business within her home in Cancún. Her talent, her prices (she charged less than a tailor, about five dollars per tailored piece of clothing), and her gregarious personality kept her constantly busy with *pedidos* (requests). Kuchmil women were impressed with Paula because she earned her own money and was not afraid to attend fiestas without her husband and dance all evening with her young son. Paula allocated the money she earned to her elderly mother, who cared full-time for Paula's epileptic sister.

However, Macario, Paula's husband, took advantage of Paula's extra income to reduce his own contributions to their nuclear family. He accused Paula of being too chingona, too independent, of being too vocal about how much money she earned. "If you earn so much money, then you can take care of your children!" he accused Paula when she requested money for the children's school uniforms and supplies. Yet he never complained about Paula's trips to the village fiestas because she was accompanied by her children and Macario's relatives. Although he was proud of his wife for being a modern, independent woman (this was how he imagined himself), Macario had a difficult time accepting the behaviors that came with this type of persona.

Being too chingón also created problems in the workplace. Many of the hotel and nightclub employers appreciated the energy, hard work, and strong educational backgrounds of Kuchmil migrants. As a result, these migrants were promoted quickly, in many cases before employees who had more seniority. However, since most migrants acquired jobs via their social networks, these promotions caused friction among acquaintances. Néstor's experience provides a clear example of the struggle between collectivism and individualism in the workplace. Before getting married, Néstor spent time working as a steward (busboy) alongside his friends in a nightclub in Cancún. The manager really liked Néstor because he had *estudios* (an education), so he promoted him to chief steward. Since many of his friends and colleagues had more seniority, they were upset that he was promoted before them and that he accepted the position. To put Néstor in his place, they accused Néstor of stealing an American guest's purse and convinced the American woman that Néstor was the perpetrator. The manager fired Néstor on the spot. Néstor's brothers and a neighbor who was a policeman suggested that he file a complaint against his accusers, but Néstor refused because they were his *paisanos* (countrymen from the southeastern peninsula) who came from "la misma ruta" (literally, the "same road," but refers to being from the same place or on the same path). In spite of the incident, both Néstor and these young men remained on friendly terms because they needed each other for future job references and soon would become kin by marriage. A year later, when Néstor returned with his wife Ramona to Cancún after spending a year in Kuchmil, these relations helped him obtain a job in a hotel.

Challenging Capitalism's Inequities

The person who is despierto and challenges the structural relations of power in which he or she is embedded also faces the risk of being sanctioned by employers and corporations. Ramona May Pat's narrative reflects this process. Ramona quit her job in a luxury hotel in the Zona Hotelera (Hotel Zone) in part because she discovered a Help Wanted sign while shopping in the *crucero*, the busiest commercial area downtown. Many businesses were hiring temporary staff for the winter holiday season. Ramona applied to be a sales clerk at a popular national clothing store chain that I will call Santiago (a fictitious name) because she would earn commission for every item she sold. She could also use her discount to stock up on clothes for herself and her family. The schedule was more demanding than hotel work, but the pay was supposed to be much better than a chambermaid's salary. Ramona worked seven days a week from 8 a.m. to 11 p.m. with a lunch break at 2 p.m. The store was extremely busy, which meant that the temporary staff were the first to arrive, the last to leave, and the last to eat, if they were given a break at all. To accommodate this schedule, Ramona sent her son to Kuchmil, where her mother cared for him.

Ramona quickly made friends with the staff. She hoped that they would like her enough to keep her on after the season ended. In spite of the long hours, which kept her from spending much time with her family and young son, she enjoyed the liberty of working independently and talking to the customers (the majority of whom were working-class Mexicans, many of whom were Maya). Her colleagues were primarily women from the states of Veracruz and Tabasco, while the supervisors were all male. However, when Ramona received her first paycheck, she was devastated. "$195! Wasn't it a paycheck?" she exclaimed. "I couldn't made heads or tails of it." She showed it to her brother Francisco, who declared, "What's this? This isn't a check." Her husband made a similar comment. Both Néstor and Francisco had spent the past fifteen days helping with the cooking and cleaning so that Ramona could work. When I visited Ramona that afternoon, she complained to me about the check. She was upset that her employer had not paid her the commissions she earned, and that the other employees earned an extra $100 for the same time period. She was also concerned about not getting paid for ten working days that fell within the pay schedule. Finally, since the manager did not give her the check until after the banks closed their check-cashing counters, Ramona was not be able to send money home to her mother with the *combi* driver who was traveling to Kuchmil.

Ramona decided that she would not keep working for such low wages and immediately asked the assistant manager for the wages from the ten days she had worked. She had expenses to pay: she owed her brother $50 for money he lent her to pay for a doctor's visit, and she owed her mother $30 for her son's *gastos* (expenses), his diapers, food, and clothes. The assistant manager refused to pay her and even attempted to take her check away from her. He demanded that she pay back the $30 loan she took out when she first started the job, money she used to send her son to Kuchmil. Ramona was furious that they would withhold ten days' salary and still demand that she pay them the loan. "You can sue me but I won't pay you. I don't plan to come back to work!" she exclaimed, and walked out of the store.

Ramona acknowledged that she was being punished for refusing the assistant manager's sexual advances. After he made repeated attempts to touch her, Ramona told him that "she would never fail to respect her husband." Her coworkers, on the other hand, did not resist his flirtations because they needed the job. According to Ramona, these women had few work options because they did not have the proper paperwork needed to work for a hotel corporation or a more discriminating business. The employee who earned the highest commission, close to $300 (not including the daily minimum-wage salary), was married, but she spent afternoons with the assistant manager away from work. She explained to Ramona that this was the best way for her to improve her child's life.

I suggested to Ramona that she speak to the manager about the deductions in her paycheck. She asked me if I would accompany her, and that afternoon we visited the clothing store. Ramona greeted the secretary warmly and introduced me as a friend. She then asked if she could speak to the manager. Her request immediately stifled the secretary's lighthearted attitude. After stonewalling us for fifteen minutes or so, the second assistant manager, accompanied by one of the security guards, offered to answer Ramona's questions. His answers frustrated us even more. Commissions, according to this manager, were up to the discretion of each assistant manager and not based on personal feelings. Regardless, he claimed that since Ramona had missed several days of work when she was sick, she did not merit commission for the entire pay period. Santiago employees' paychecks were also automatically deducted $5 per pay period, money that was transferred into a savings account offered by the company. Since she quit her job, Ramona would not be able to access this money. We left the store feeling frustrated at the injustice and exploitation. Ramona never recuperated the money she was owed. She was also blacklisted from working in Santiago franchises.

In spite of her negative experiences in Cancún's labor market, Ramona made another attempt to enter the workforce a few months later. She submitted an application to work in her profession, accounting, for a private hospital in town. One of the secretaries was out sick that day. The hospital needed someone to answer the phones. "Can you handle the switchboard?" the manager asked. "If you show me how, I can," replied Ramona. Since they were short-staffed, Ramona was hired as a receptionist. The manager agreed to let her spend part of her workday working in accounting. Ramona enjoyed her work immensely, especially now that she was actually working in her profession, but was not pleased with the limited benefits the job provided or the lack of job security. "After my experience with Santiago," she reminded me, "I know that I have to keep fighting for my rights." According to Ramona, in spite of the problems she encountered in the workforce, becoming chingona made her aware of her rights.

Conclusion

A few months after his inauguration, President Felipe Calderón (2006–12) applauded tourism for capitalizing on Mexico's natural and cultural resources and for creating jobs for its most marginalized people.[11] Tourist jobs offered Maya farmers a wage, which subsistence farmwork did not provide. Not surprisingly, Maya farmers encouraged their children to find work in the tourism industry. Maya migrants moved to Cancún expecting to benefit from the national rhetoric of progress and modernization. But for those with minimal education (most migrants had a high school diploma), tourist jobs were poorly paid and failed to provide more economic stability than agricultural work. To advance the tourist economy (and for workers to advance in it), corporations trained workers to adopt a new attitude and work ethic based on the dedicated, self-reliant, and flexible worker.

However, Maya migrants like Ramona, Javier, and Fernanda did not fully embrace this mind-set because doing so would devastate familial, social, and cultural ties that nurtured their sense of self and well-being. Instead Maya migrants relied on a nationalist and masculine discourse of chingaderas (bullshit, acts of mischief and treason) to resist development's alienating discourse of liberal individualism. Becoming chingón/a—being astute, aware, and assertive—made it possible for Maya migrants to withstand the racial and economic discrimination directed toward indigenous people within a tourist economy and to maintain a sense of agency without shedding the collective orientation promoted in rural life. Indeed, to avoid being fucked by the global economy, Maya migrants imagined new spaces that permitted a continual and palatable engagement with the modern nation, even if these terms were not equal to, or even simply better than, previous circumstances.

Notes

This chapter was much improved by the editorial suggestions of Grace Hong and Roderick Ferguson and by the insightful comments of Irene Lara, David Karjanen, and two anonymous reviewers. I also thank Kelsey Weber for providing research assistance.

1   For studies that challenged ahistorical depictions of migrants, see Cardoso and Faletto 1979; Frank 1967. For studies that focused on households and social networks, see Arizpe 1981; Lomnitz 1977; Rouse 1989.

2   Napolitano acknowledges that migration is not always experienced as a process of enlightenment and empowerment. For many migrants, it can be a harrowing, violent experience that serves to reinforce their vulnerability and marginality and ruptures native understandings of the self, of the other, and of their conception of progress. See, e.g., Conover 1987; Hernández Castillo 2001; Ibarra 2003; Urrea 1993.

3   Arnold van Gennep coined this term in his classic book *The Rites of Passage* (1960). Victor Turner's use of the concept in his essay "Betwixt and Between: The Liminal Period in *Rites de Passage*" (1989) made its usage popular in anthropology. For a discussion of migration as a rite of passage, see Chavez 1992; Kearney 1991.

4   This quinceañera ritual marks a girl's fifteenth birthday party. In 2001 I attended a quinceañera to celebrate the birthdays of a girl and a boy. In this case, to save money, the family took advantage of their daughter's birthday to celebrate her male cousin's birthday, as well.

5   In her analysis of Maya subjectivity in K'anxoc, Yucatán, Ana Rosa Duarte Duarte (2006) refers to this sense of exploration and experimentation as an *espíritu de lucha* (an internal desire to know and seek knowledge).

6   For a discussion of the role religion plays in rural Maya communities, see Redfield and Villa Rojas [1934] 1990. For a discussion of the role religion plays in migration, see Castellanos 2007.

7   For a critique of Paul Sullivan's interpretation of the Cruzob Maya as victims of the Caste War, see Martos Sosa 1994. Martos Sosa suggests that contemporary Cruzob Maya continue to oppose the Mexican government through their oral histories, which recall the government's misdeeds and offer millenarian prophecies of the government's demise.

8   The depiction of Malintzin as "evil goddess," "mother-whore," and traitor has been contested by Chicana feminists. See Alarcón 1989, 1999; Anzaldúa 1987; Candelaria 1980; Gonzáles 1980; Moraga 1983; Villanueva 1985.

9   For an extended analysis of this case, see Castellanos 2010.

10 Presently, rituals such as baptisms, héetz-méek' ceremonies, *novenas*, and weddings are elaborate affairs. In the past, the absence of cash kept rituals modest because people could not afford to purchase many goods. Migration, however,

has increased rural residents' access to cash. To pay for these rituals, people borrow money from migrants and ask them to be padrinos of these events. Some rituals now take place in Cancún because the facilities are grander and the location makes it easier for migrants to attend.

11 "El turismo como prioridad nacional," message by President Felipe Calderón Hinojosa, posted on the Ministry of Tourism's (Secretaría de Turismo) website in 2007, http://www.sectur.gob.mx/wb2/sectur/sect_Mensaje_del_Presidente_ _El_Turismo_como_Prior.

Black Orientalism

Nineteenth-Century Narratives of Race
and U.S. Citizenship

> But now observe the practical superiority of slavery over Chinese
> immigration, as an impelling force for good. Slavery compelled
> the heathen to give up idolatry, and they did it. The Chinese have
> no such compulsion and they do not do it. . . . Slavery compelled
> the adoption of Christian forms of worship, resulting in universal
> Christianization. The Chinese have no such influence tending to
> their conversion, and rarely—one or two in a thousand—become
> Christian. . . . Slavery took the heathens and by force made them
> Americans in feeling, tastes, habits, language, sympathy, religion
> and spirit; *first* fitting them for citizenship, and then giving them
> the vote. The Chinese feel no such force, but remaining in charac-
> ter and life the same as they were in Old China, unprepared for
> citizenship and adverse in spirit to our institutions.
> —Reverend Blakeslee, Special Report to the Senate on Chinese
> Immigration (1877)

In his testimony before the senate in 1877, a white minister
makes an argument for Chinese exclusion in which his
Orientalist construction of the Chinese alien generates its
contrasting other in the figure of the properly developed,
black, Christianized former slave. Reverend Blakeslee's
rather predictable and ubiquitous discourse of the unassimilable Oriental is particularly disturbing in that chattel
slavery is figured as a necessary civilizing institution that
"successfully" transforms African heathens into modern
American citizens. Twenty years later, Supreme Court Justice Harlan also deploys this black-Chinese racial tandem in
the case of *Plessy v. Ferguson* (1896), when he challenges the

Court's majority ruling by constructing the Chinese immigrant as the negative instance of national belonging:

> There is a race so different from our own that we do not permit those
> belonging to it to become citizens of the United States. . . . But by the
> statute in question, a Chinaman can ride in the same passenger coach
> with white citizens of the United States, while citizens of the black race in
> Louisiana, many of whom perhaps risked their lives for the preservation
> of the Union, who are entitled by law, to participate in the political
> control of the state and nation, who are not excluded, by law or by reason
> of their race, from public stations of any kind, and who have all the legal
> rights that belong to white citizens, are yet to be declared criminals,
> liable to imprisonment, if they ride in a public coach occupied by cit-
> izens of the white race. (Thomas 1997, 36–37)

Harlan's attempt to dramatize the injustice of Jim Crow segregation works
by imagining privileges unfairly enjoyed by Chinese aliens to powerfully
illustrate what was being wrongfully denied to black citizens.[1] In other
words, Harlan's rhetoric deploys Orientalist difference to assimilate U.S.
blacks into a universalized American national identity.

   Both Blakeslee's and Harlan's statements surprisingly suggest that in the
late nineteenth century, the juxtaposition of Chinese immigrants and the
black community could somehow generate a naturalized, commonsensical
recognition of the deeply American character of black domestic subjects.[2]
This discourse of provisional black inclusion in relation to Chinese exclusion is initially counterintuitive given the manner in which today we often
observe how in the nineteenth century, blacks and Chinese were represented as *similarly* loathsome or degraded in terms of the "other," that is, the
"Negroization of the Chinese" or the "Asianization of blacks." Of course,
Harlan's and Blakeslee's public statements about race and citizenship spoke
to radically different questions and motivations—one endorsing Chinese
exclusion, the other arguing against the legality of black-white racial segregation. The differences, however, behind such similar Orientalist figurations within these narratives of black domestication are all the more sugges-
tive of the significance of Chinese exclusion and American Orientalism
within nineteenth-century discourses of black citizenship.

   This chapter examines how the nineteenth-century black press waged
struggles for political inclusion within this dominant discursive context of

racialized citizenship, as the anti-Chinese movement critically defined the racial, cultural, and political boundaries of the United States. An analysis of black newspapers across the country reveals how Orientalist discourses of Asian cultural difference ambiguously facilitated the assimilation of black Americans to ideologies of political modernity and consolidated black identification as U.S. national subjects. Nineteenth-century discourses of "black Orientalism" can be best understood as a specific formation of racial uplift, generating narratives of black moral, political, and cultural development, which in turn reified the Orientalist logic of the anti-Chinese movement. This argument de-emphasizes notions of black intentions, perceptions, or attitudes to foreground the narrative demands on U.S. black subjects to constitute their humanity and citizenship through racialized and gendered Enlightenment discourses of morality, ethicality, and rationality. In other words, this essay foregrounds how the institution of citizenship produces an imperative for racialized subjects to tell particular stories about themselves and others in the struggle for inclusion. Such a focus suggests that racist or antiracist principles are not the most relevant terms for interpreting nineteenth-century black press representations of the Chinese; rather, the institution of citizenship constitutes a narrow discursive field within which differentially racialized groups are forced to negotiate their exclusion in relation to others.

Differential Racializations

Although Orientalism has been discussed primarily within the historical context of European colonialism, the discursive production of an utterly foreign, premodern, alien Oriental in opposition to a rational, modern Western subject has also been operative within the United States, albeit in different ways.[3] In the context of mid-nineteenth-century America, Orientalism constitutes an Oriental other through exclusionary U.S. state policies on Asian immigration and regulates racialized Asian labor through the institution of citizenship (Lowe 1996, 19). The historian John Tchen (1999) also points out that before the 1850s, there was another Orientalist formation not organized solely around immigration. Tchen observes that during this earlier period, increased trade with China and a growing port culture situated the Chinese as an exotic, curious spectacle for consumption within an emergent industry of urban popular entertainment.[4] Broadly, then, we can understand nineteenth-century American Orientalism as discursive formations that are determined by and determining of U.S. economic and political engagements with East Asia and the Pacific, and that provide the ideological structure for domestic processes that produce and manage Asian racial difference within the United States. These processes, which involve instances of Asian incorporation (as circus exhibits, as coolie labor, as U.S. colony) and instances of Asian exclusion (from immigration, citizenship, and U.S. national culture), define an American genealogy of Asian racialization that variously produces the Oriental as alien to the United States (Lowe 1996). My objective is not to produce an overview of the various forms through which American Orientalism has manifested itself throughout U.S. history but to isolate particular instances of how Orientalism has been engaged to negotiate black racialization. I refer to this contradictory process of negotiation as "black Orientalism" in an attempt to name the critical dilemma that the struggle for black citizenship (or black political modernity) embodies. We see the contours of this dilemma, for instance, in Blakeslee's observation that slavery "did wonderfully elevate the slave and prepare him for citizenship" with the "one exception" that "it legally denied human rights to the slave" (*Chinese Immigration*, 247). This paradox, in which the systematic dehumanization of racialized populations is the condition of their entry into the civilized world to become modern subjects of democratic freedom, is the contradiction endemic to the project of modernity itself (see Goldberg 1993; Gilroy 1992). Racialized subjects, therefore, in their struggle to challenge their conditions of exploitation and oppression, must negotiate these epistemological contradictions that structure modern institutions and liberal narratives of freedom and liberation. Put another way, racially excluded populations must somehow manage to reconcile the liberatory promises of enlightenment and civilization with processes of brutalization that are deemed historically necessary.[5]

It should thus be clear that black Orientalism is *not* employed as an accusatory and reductive condemnation that functions to chastise black individuals or institutions for being imperialist, racist, or Orientalist. Black Orientalism is a heterogeneous and historically variable discourse in which the contradictions of black citizenship engage with the logic of American Orientalism. In other words, black Orientalism has no singular meaning or manifestation but encompasses an entire range of black imaginings of Asia that are in fact negotiations with the limits and disappointments of black citizenship.[6] This would include, for example, W. E. B. Du Bois's fascination with China as a utopic site of revolutionary possibility, black admiration for Japanese empire in the World War II period, or even signifiers of the "Orient" within hip-hop culture.[7] In these instances, one can see how the dichotomous otherness of the Orient is precisely what makes it so appealing to disidentified black subjects who are attempting to imagine liberatory possibilities, identifications, and historical futures in spaces that have been defined as *not* the United States or defined in opposition to the West.

In the nineteenth century, black Orientalism emerges out of the historical conditions of black racialization and the Chinese exclusion movement as a heterogeneous discourse of black citizenship and national identity. In the interest of pursuing a broader critique of citizenship, this chapter analyzes what might be deemed liberal discourses of black national identity rather than oft-cited oppositional positions taken by figures such as Frederick Douglass, a well-known, highly vocal opponent to the anti-Chinese movement since the 1850s. However, liberal black discourses on citizenship and immigration are in themselves highly complex negotiations and cannot simplistically be regarded as unfortunate and "prejudicial" black attitudes toward the Chinese. Comparative race scholarship may miss important opportunities to critically discuss liberal discourses of racialized citizenship due to a teleological investment in "interracial solidarity"—a notion that relies heavily on the premise of identification. The following analysis of the nineteenth-century black press considers black Orientalism to be a form of cultural politics that does not illuminate the ideological limits or shortcomings of those who engaged it, but rather reveals the various contradictions of citizenship and modern subjecthood that it ultimately failed to resolve for black national identity.

The Heathen Chinese

Black press representations of Chinese alterity engaged with a discursive field of American Orientalist ideologies that found expression as the anti-Chinese movement in the mid-nineteenth century. Anti-Chinese political agitation emerged in the mid-1850s along the West Coast, fueled by competing white immigrant workers who racially defined free labor in antagonism to blacks and the Chinese (see Saxton 1995). Initially a regional and class-based formation, anti-Chinese legislation became part of the national political platform that ultimately culminated in the Chinese Exclusion Act of 1882, the first and only time a specific ethnic group was legally barred from immigrating to the United States. White labor, clergymen, and nativists generally constructed Chinese immigrants as an invasive yellow peril that posed a grave moral and economic threat to the survival of the white working man and the American family: "Can we compete with a barbarous race, devoid of energy and careless of the State's weal? Sunk in their own debasement, having no voice in government, how long would it be ere ruin would swamp the capitalist and poor man together?" (Saxton 1995, 59, quoting "an address to the working men of Nevada," reprinted in the *Daily Alta*, June 17, 1869). Anti-Chinese sentiments were not merely racialized expressions of a white working-class ideology, however, but were tied to a larger discourse of American Orientalism that cut across class lines.[8]

In his study of disease and racial classification in San Francisco's China-town, Nayan Shah points to how journalists, politicians, and health officials worked in tandem to produce "a way of knowing" Chinatown as an alien space of filth, disease, and contamination. As Shah argues, "The cartography of Chinatown that was developed in government investigations, newspaper reports, and travelogues, both established 'knowledge' of the Chinese race and aided in the making and remaking of Chinatown" (2001, 19). Thus white public-health officials "scientifically" corroborated the dominant press's sensational descriptions of Chinatown as "ankle-deep in loathsome slush, with ceilings dripping with percolations of other nastiness above, [and] with walls slimy with the clamminess of Asiatic diseases" (17). The overwhelmingly male composition of the Chinese immigrant community, secured through exclusionary legislation prohibiting the immigration of Chinese women, was central to the discourse of moral panic in areas surrounding Chinatown ghettos. Dominant images of Chinese men as depraved opium addicts and lascivious sexual predators of innocent young white girls dominated an American Orientalist discourse that constituted Chinatown and its residents as alien contaminations of the white national body.

Black press representations of Chinatown ghettos and their inhabitants also consistently constructed these spaces and persons as embodiments of premodern, alien difference.[9] The number and frequency of articles about the Chinese are noteworthy, in that the vast majority of U.S. blacks never directly encountered the Chinese, who began immigrating in significant numbers in the 1850s and were geographically concentrated in the West.[10] Much of the coverage in the black press before 1882 concerned legislative and political matters, although most stories were sensationalist, such as those in the *New Orleans Tribune*, which described an exotic Chinatown temple where priests "shout, yell, groan, spin around amid the racket of gongs, orums, and fiddlers, and smoke opium until they are quite drunk."[11] The *Topeka Tribune* reprinted an article that described the immoral depravity of an opium den in Chicago's Chinese quarter, "where some were sprawling on a filthy floor, and others had rolled into dirty bunks, and all were contemplating a glorious orgie,"[12] and the *Washington Bee* ran a front-page headline that read "The Chinese in New York: Peculiarities of the Orientals Described."[13] In his study of the black press, the historian Arnold Shankman (1978, 10) observes that "from 1880–1935 almost every time the Chinese were mentioned in the black press, it was in connection with intrigue, prostitution, murder, the sale of opium or children for money . . . superstitious practices, shootings or tong wars."[14]

Stories on Chinese cultural difference even predated the arrival of Chinese immigrants to the United States. As early as 1827, the first issue of *Freedom's Journal* printed an article titled "Chinese Fashions" that described Chinese foot binding as a "well-known" and "ridiculous" custom in China.[15] The description includes a good amount of empirical detail, as in the following: "The length was only two inches and three-fourths; the breadth of the base of the heel seven-eighths of an inch; the breadth of the broadest part of the foot, one and one-fourth of an inch; and the diameter of the ankle three inches above the heel, one and seven-eighths of an inch." The highly empiricist, scientific language of ethnographic observation sharply contrasts with the incomprehensible, primitive Oriental practice that the article describes. *Freedom's Journal*, the first black newspaper to be published in the United States, was a relatively short-lived but historically significant press that was dedicated to the defense of free blacks and to the abolition of slavery by disseminating "useful knowledge among our brethren, and to their moral and religious improvement . . . and to vindicate our brethren, when oppressed." Other stories in this inaugural issue are more clearly related to the paper's stated commitments. For instance, "Memoirs of Capt. Paul Cuffe," "People of Colour," "Cure for Drunkenness," and "Advantages of Choosing a Wife by Proxy" work to emphasize male leadership, racial solidarity, temperance, and family—crucial elements in narrating black aptitude for citizenship. Thus the seemingly random, peripheral article on a backward Oriental practice works to underscore the story of black modern development in which "useful knowledge" and "moral and religious improvement" are indelibly tied to the paper's commitment to the rights of free blacks and the abolition of slavery.

Producing Black Citizens

As a cultural institution, the black press played a highly significant role in defining black national identity, and nineteenth-century black newspapers were particularly invested in narratives of racial uplift and development. Benedict Anderson has linked the emergence of print capitalism to the production of nationalist consciousness, arguing that the newspaper produced an experience of simultaneity that enabled imagined "horizontal" identification among strangers across broad geographic areas (see Anderson 1991).[16] Larger, national black presses regularly received news from correspondents across the country and reprinted articles from black and dominant white media considered relevant to a black national population. This production and consumption of print media not only created an arena for black public discourse but also was constitutive of the very experience of identifying as a subject of a black national community.

The discourses of development, progress, and self-improvement that are so central in *Freedom's Journal* are crucial throughout the nineteenth-century black press, which was a particularly effective institution for the production and dissemination of ideologies of racial uplift.[17] Most black newspapers and periodicals aspired to produce narratives of black racial progress while attacking racist legislation and policies that threatened to impede the development of the race. If we understand the black press as the technical means for representing the *kind* of imagined community that defines black racial identity, then the process by which that identity is defined is always a contestation among competing and heterogeneous interests that are homogenized under the unifying rubric of race. The nineteenth-century black press cannot be understood as a monolithic institution possessing a cohesive racial or class ideology; however, the material reality that the majority of editors were educated black men with sufficient financial resources critically informs how black national identity was narrated through print media. As African Americanist historians such as Kevin

Gaines and Jane Rhodes have noted, these editors by and large "promoted the virtues of education, individual progress, and racial uplift as the means for African Americans to transcend the debilitating legacy of slavery and racial oppression" (see Rhodes 1998, 100; Gaines 1996). Therefore, while the institutional formation of the nineteenth-century black press is characterized by competing interests and conflicts, ideologies of racial uplift were constitutive of the discursive terrain where such differences were articulated and debated.[18]

Kevin Gaines has discussed how educated blacks engaged in a cultural politics of citizenship that promoted a developmental ideology of racial progress that emphasized black moral and cultural propriety. Negotiating the political, cultural, and social violence of white supremacy, ideologies of racial uplift encouraged the emulation of what Gaines tentatively calls "middle-class" values and ideals, which were the authoritative signifiers of respectability and humanity.[19] While racist discourses constructed blacks as immoral, irrational, and violent savages incapable of self-regulation, the educated black community responded by embracing values of temperance, thrift, chastity, and patriarchal domesticity as a means of proving their worthiness and entitlement to citizenship. Embracing Victorian morality or performing heteronormativity enabled black communities to move as far away from the stereotypes as they could, to provide their tormentors with no evidence for their charges, and to strategically claim a moral superiority.[20] What is most useful about Gaines's analysis is the theorization of how the violent denial of black political and economic enfranchisement facilitates the formation of a *cultural* politics that symbolically embodies citizenship. While Gaines's study begins at the end of Radical Reconstruction, his theorization of racial uplift provides insight into understanding black Orientalism as a related form of nineteenth-century cultural politics. Tropes of Chinese underdevelopment enabled the discursive production of black modern subjects who were capable of incorporation into a narrative of Western historical progress, even in the face of brutal material contradictions that countered the very notion of "Western civilization."

The material history of white supremacist violence that saturated the political, economic, and social spheres of nineteenth-century America constitutes the contradictions of black citizenship to which I continually refer. The abolition of slavery did not resolve these contradictions, nor did the institution of citizenship, which was formally granted to black persons with the passage of the Fourteenth Amendment in 1866. Immediately after the ratification of the Fourteenth and Fifteenth Amendments, almost all the former Confederate states quickly instituted black codes that criminalized blacks in ways that served as substitutes for slavery.[21] Thus various state laws required that these recently freed subjects sign work contracts with plantations (often the same ones they worked as slaves) and to carry these papers with them at all times. Black persons could be stopped and questioned at any time, and the absence of a work contract was criminalized as "vagrancy," at which point the person was arrested and put to work through the convict lease system. Numerous studies have shown how systematic economic and political disenfranchisement left many of the freedmen as vulnerable to exploitation and violence as they were during slavery (Du Bois 1995d; Hartman 1997). These postbellum political, economic, and social relations were enforced through campaigns of racial terror that maintained the privilege of whiteness through the brutal regulation of black bodies. The well-known work of Ida B. Wells, for instance, has demonstrated how the widespread practice of lynching in the South was a crucial means of maintaining the economic, political, and social authority of white supremacist patriarchy (Wells-Barnett 1969; see also A. Davis 1983). The African American feminist critic Hazel Carby (1978, 18) notes that, in addition to the practice of lynching, the institutionalized rape of black women was also "an instrument of political terror . . . in the South." From the end of the Civil War to the turn of the century, whites committed countless acts of violence against black persons, in addition to the hundreds of documented lynchings that were enacted as public rituals of torture that used the imagined violations of white women to reconstitute the patriarchal and capitalist authority of white men (see also Davis 1983, 172–201). It is within this context of racial terrorism that ideologies of racial uplift emerged as strategies of survival against intense dehumanization.

Religious ideologies of Christian morality were absolutely central to discourses of racial uplift that sought to contest the historical violence that denied U.S. blacks their humanity and citizen status. As Reverend Blakeslee's statements implied, Christianity was critically linked to nineteenth-century discourses of black citizenship, in that the Christian conversion of the African heathen was understood as the foundation of moral development and ethical citizenship.[22] Subsequently, ideologies of racial uplift seeking to produce a civilized black subject emphatically promoted Christian

propriety and moral self-improvement in an effort to refute dominant characterizations of blacks as depraved and immoral savages.[23] Racial uplift
constituted black Christian subjects, therefore, as part of a larger effort to
represent the modern development of blacks under Western civilization.[24]
The developmental ideologies of American modernity demanded Christian
morality as the precondition for transforming the primitive slave into the
modern political subject. This imperative would subsequently have profound implications for black understandings of Chinese racial difference.

The heathenism that the Chinese came to signify in nineteenth-century
America was a powerful Orientalist trope for black Americans, whose assertions of humanity and claims to citizenship had largely been predicated on
negotiating discourses of Christian morality. Appeals to Christian ideologies have been crucial to black critiques of white supremacy since the
eighteenth century, becoming an important means of refuting their object
status in black struggles for recognition as legal subjects of the state. Abolitionist discourse relied predominantly on religious ideology, arguing that
slavery violated fundamental principles of Christianity and engendered
sinful and immoral relations among both slaves and their masters. Additionally, the American school of ethnology created damaging, hierarchical
classifications of racial groups, which they claimed had emerged from various and unequal origins, subsequently undermining the theological basis of
a universal humanity, which had provided U.S. blacks with a fragile but
important legitimating discourse in their struggle against racialized exploitation. After the formal abolition of U.S. slavery, Christian doctrine and
monogenesis posed the greatest theoretical challenges to scientific racism
as various disciplines sought to provide a scientific basis for white supremacy and manifest destiny (Saxton 1990; Fredrickson 1971).[25] Religious
discourses therefore continued to be relevant for U.S. blacks in relation to
citizenship and to modern institutions such as the university.

The following news story delineates fundamental connections between
black Christian morality and political aptitude in the nineteenth century
and underscores how racialized groups have been differentially located in
relation to religious and other cultural institutions of the U.S. state. This
article on May 17, 1962, from the *Pacific Appeal*, a black newspaper in San
Francisco, makes an explicit argument for black rights of testimony and
deploys an antiracist critique that distances black development from the
heathen Chinese and Indian:

In the same oppressive spirit they deprived the Indian and Mongolian of their right of oath. . . . They oppressed them and reduced them to the same social and political level of the Negro. This was inhumane, barbarous, and unjust, but a more plausible excuse might be offered for depriving the Indian and the Chinese of their oaths than the Colored American: they being heathens and not comprehending the nature and obligation of our oath or affirmation. . . . The Negro is a Christian: there is a strong religious sentiment in his nature, a feeling of awe and reverence for the sanctity of an oath which renders his judicial testimony sacred to him. . . . Perjury is abhorrent to his soul;—he looks upon it as the unforgiven sin.

The Indian and Chinese immigrant are represented as atavistic yet wrongfully oppressed subjects of discrimination and are empathetically characterized as underdeveloped heathens who are nonetheless entitled to recognition by the courts. While the article harshly condemns the "inhumane" treatment of "uncomprehending" Native Americans and the Chinese, it consolidates the legitimacy of black male rights to citizenship by describing, in contrast, the proper ethical formation of the black subject who *has* developed the modern capacity to appropriately engage state institutions. This discursive disidentification must not be interpreted as some kind of hypocritical inconsistency that contradicts the article's critique of racist exclusion. Emphasizing the Christian formation of the black national subject is an ideological imperative in narrating black aptitude for citizenship, which, by consequence, Orientalizes or discursively disciplines the Chinese and Indian as inadequate to political modernity.

Recalling Gaines's analysis, black Orientalism is operative as a cultural politics of citizenship even in the absence of an explicitly "political" discourse, such as the case of *Freedom's Journal* and its seemingly apolitical article on Chinese foot binding. This next article, from *Frederick Douglass' Paper*, is submitted by a San Francisco correspondent and chronicles the "progress made by the colored people in this city," describing the three black churches, school, and literary association, which have "given tone and character to Society."[26] The article's emphasis on black religious, educational, and cultural institutions reflects their crucial ideological significance in the ethical formation of proper subjectivities that the article attempts to demonstrate. The narrator shifts abruptly from the black community's "large number of respectable ladies and their influence" to conclude with an ethnographic description of Chinese immigrants:

> San Francisco presents many features that no city in the Union presents. Its population is composed of almost every nation under heaven. Here is to be seen at a single glance every nation in minature.—The Chinese form about one-eighth of the population. They exhibit a most grotesque appearance. Their "unmentionables" are either exceedingly roomy or very close fitting. The heads of the males are shaved, with the exception of the top, the hair from which is formed into a plaited tail, resembling "pig tail tobacco." Their habits are filthy, and their features totally devoid of expression. The whites are greatly alarmed at their rapid increase. They are very badly treated here. Every boy considers them lawful prey for his boyish pranks. They have no friends, unless it is the colored people, who treat everybody well, even their enemies. But I must close this already too long letter.[27]

The representation of the Chinese immigrant's "grotesque" and "filthy" appearance, undergarments, and habits are sharply juxtaposed to the proper formation of the black community's "intelligent audiences," "handsome" churches, "respectable ladies," and "eminently qualified . . . gentlemen," who speak with "chaste and elegant" language. Once again, these polarized representations cannot be interpreted reductively as an instance of racism or anti-Chinese sentiments, which the article strongly criticizes and disavows, even asserting that the Chinese are befriended by only "the colored people."[28] As in the *Pacific Appeal*, this article expresses clear empathy toward the "persecuted" Chinese, even as it objectifies Chinese immigrants through an anthropological gaze that methodically recounts their foreign signs of bodily and cultural difference.[29] This Orientalist account generates neither a negative nor a positive representation but narrates the alien cultural formation of the Chinese immigrant to negotiate black exclusion, which the article previously addresses in an otherwise celebratory testimonial: "We suffer many deprivations, however. We have no oath against any white man or Chinaman. We are debarred from the polls. The Legislature refused to accept our petition for the right to testify in courts of justice against the whites; but not withstanding all these drawbacks, we are steadily progressing in all that pertains to our welfare."[30] In response to the degradation of black disenfranchisement, the article's Orientalist gaze is constitutive of a modern black subject of the West just as the refined churches, schools, and literary association stand in as markers of black development and civilization.

While papers such as the *Pacific Appeal* and *Frederick Douglass' Paper* had expressed earlier sympathetic positions regarding the Chinese, by 1873 the black press in California emphasized the derogatory impact of Chinese immigrants on the black community and the nation as a whole. These papers consistently narrated the cultural and moral underdevelopment of the Chinese in an effort to distance blacks from the dangerous implications of anti-Chinese legislation that occupied the political discourse of California.[31] One telling article published in 1867 denied any link between the black and Chinese situations, arguing that "there is no analogy between the cases," since "the negro is a native American, loyal to the Government . . . American in all his ideas . . . and a believer of the truths of Christianity," who "ask[s] for the rights of citizenship as [his] just due."[32] Discourses of the Chinese as a racial problem were not confined only to California, as evidenced by the *New Orleans Louisianian*, which stated that "the Negro question was being replaced by that of the Chinese" (quoted in Hellwig 1974, 105). As the anti-Chinese movement gained political momentum throughout the nation, it became increasingly necessary and commonplace that black claims to citizenship articulate Orientalist disidentification with Chinese immigrants.[33] The formulaic narration of black military service, Christian morality, and nationalist identification that constructed blacks as American subjects would become a repetitive and frequent articulation with respect to discourses of Chinese exclusion.

Black Orientalist discourses of disidentification were not merely nativist ideologies, since they were deployed to demonstrate the assimilability of black immigrants. One article rhetorically dismissed the notion of Chinese immigration as a problem in the context of discussing the modification of naturalization laws that would allow immigrants of African descent to become naturalized citizens. Arguing that such legislative changes had little relevance to the Chinese, the article characterized West Indian immigrants as "already Americans; their habits, customs, and associations are identical with ours. . . . They have practically renounced their allegiance to their original government and are truly Americanized. . . . The same advantages should be extended to the colored alien as are enjoyed by white foreigners."[34] The article contrasts the Chinese as foreigner with black immigrants from the West Indies, whose formation under European colonialism has made their "habits, customs, and associations . . . identical with ours" and therefore easily assimilable into the U.S. national body. It is particularly striking that the allegiance of West Indies black immigrants "to their *original* government" is linked to a colonial state whose importation of African slave labor has produced a Western black colonial subject, who is "known for . . . adherence to our customs and institutions." The suppressed ambiguity surrounding the black immigrant's national identification is an index of how the history of the African slave trade and Euro-American colonialism positioned blacks in the Americas in a radically different relationship to the institution of citizenship from the Chinese, who were not similarly incorporated as cultural or political subjects of the West during the nineteenth century.

Although black Orientalism was a means of narrating the development of black subjects into American modernity, the passage of the Chinese Exclusion Act in 1882 did not consolidate black national identity but rather exposed the tenuous status of black citizenship itself. Thus when the anti-Chinese movement garnered national support for federal legislation to prohibit Chinese immigration, the black press voiced almost unanimous national opposition to this unprecedented form of race-based immigration exclusion.[35] As the *Christian Observer* stated, "One of the most hopeful signs of the times is the unanimity of the press, especially the religious, in opposition to the Chinese bill."[36] While the *San Francisco Elevator* was one of the few exceptions and was chastised in the black press for having "failed to stand up for equal rights," other black presses on the West Coast condemned Chinese exclusion.[37] Historians who have studied black press representations of Chinese immigrants have found this pervasive opposition either surprisingly anomalous or a commendable sign of the black community's alliance with another racially oppressed group.[38] If we understand the ideological relationship of black Orientalism to discourses of black modernity and citizenship, black press opposition to the Chinese Exclusion Act is neither a "curious" aberration nor transparent evidence of the black community's "dedication to the image of America as a composite nation of diverse peoples" (Hellwig 1974, 99). The discursive limits of black Orientalism as a means of narrating the modern development of the black American subject were exceeded when the Chinese Exclusion Act unequivocally signified the racial reification of U.S. citizenship that undermined aspirations of black national incorporation. In other words, while an Orientalist discourse on Chinese alien difference was a form of cultural politics that could underscore the Americanness of black citizens, the Chinese Exclusion Act was itself a clear threat to the circumscribed legal rights already undermining black citizenship. Thus black Americans rightly felt threatened by the notion that federal legislation employing racially exclusionary language with respect to Chinese immigration could be aimed at them next.

Frederick Douglass waged the most prominent and vocal critiques of the anti-Chinese movement, recognizing the dangerous consequences of race-based exclusion for liberal principles of American democracy (Hellwig 1974, 102). Douglass's *New Era* criticized both Republican and Democratic politicians for supporting the anti-Chinese movement in an effort to garner the political support of trade unions.[39] Douglass was hardly alone, however, and the religious and secular black press alike strongly condemned the Chinese Exclusion Act and recognized its racist implications for blacks, whose recent political gains had been violently contested by white ethnics:

> Only a few years ago the cry was not, "The Chinese must go," but "The niggers must go"; and it comes from the same strata of society. There is not a man to-day who rails out against the yellow man from China but would equally rail out against the black man if opportunity only afforded. Nor have they given up all hope of that opportunity coming in the near future.[40]

The "same strata of society" is a clear reference to the white working class and its political institutions, which not only exercised considerable power within the Democratic Party but also practiced racist union policies that culminated in violent hate-strikes and riots that targeted black laborers (Hellwig 1974, 115–16; see also Hill 1985, 13–21). Black Americans were particularly antagonized by Irish immigrants, whose political, economic, and cultural incorporation often came at the expense of black displacement (Hellwig 1974, 79–98; see also Ignatiev 1995). Therefore the proponents of Chinese exclusion—the white ethnic working class—were largely regarded as enemies of black workers throughout the country. Black critiques of the Chinese Exclusion Act did not necessarily oppose the general idea of immigration restrictions, which were often advocated within the black press, but rather criticized the political power of white labor to mobilize federal legislation that was racially exclusive. Several papers urged creative solutions to slowing Chinese immigration, such as prohibiting the common practice of sending the deceased back to China, which would not require federal legis-lation that employed exclusionary race-based language and yet might achieve the same desired results.[41]

It would therefore be imprecise to understand opposition in the black press to the Chinese Exclusion Act as evidence of black subjective *identifica-tion* with the Chinese, whose alien and immigrant formations stood in cultural, linguistic, and religious contradiction to black national identity. Many articles opposing Chinese exclusion were careful to simultaneously narrate black Orientalist disidentification, stating, "We honestly confess that we have no sympathy for the Chinese. Their habits, customs, modes of living, manner of worship . . . [are] an abhorrence to us."[42] Despite the overwhelming evidence of black opposition to Chinese exclusionary legisla-tion, black press fascination with Chinese immigrants and Chinatown ghettos as grotesque sites of immorality, filth, and alien difference was a discourse that consistently shaped black ways of knowing Chinese racial difference from the 1850s well into the twentieth century. The Chinese Exclusion Act's interrup-tion of black Orientalism suggests that while the possibilities for black and Asian *identification* are often highly constrained (or even formed in mutual exclusion) due to specific historical processes of racialization, such identifica-tion was not a necessary condition for nineteenth-century black opposition to the Chinese Exclusion Act. Race emerged as the contradiction to the promise of equality as universal citizens, underscoring the utter vulnerability of the status of black Americans as subjects of the state.

Thus it should be neither surprising nor disappointing that after the ratifi-cation of the Chinese Exclusion Act in 1882, black press Orientalism persisted and even intensified, with a particularly strong emphasis on Chinatowns as depraved sites of criminality and sexual vice.[43] While nineteenth-century black Orientalism might have been an effective means of provisionally under-scoring the deeply "American" character of blacks in the United States, this discourse of inclusion had stark limitations. Black press concerns that the Chinese Exclusion Act would be followed by more race-based legislation were dramatically substantiated less than a decade later by the Supreme Court's decision that racial segregation was an entitlement of white citizen-ship. If the Chinese Exclusion Act defined the U.S. citizen against the Oriental alien, the constitutionality of *Plessy v. Ferguson* suggested that although U.S. blacks were not Orientalized immigrants, the reification of black racial differ-ence would remain at the very core of American national identity.

Notes

My deep appreciation goes out to advisors, colleagues, and friends in Los Angeles, Santa Barbara, San Diego, Taipei, and Chicago. Additional thanks to the editors of this volume and the comments of anonymous reviewers, as well as to Barry Masuda for last-minute editing assistance.

1   *Yick Wo v. Hopkins* determined that the Chinese were Mongolian, not white, and thus subject to racial segregation (McClain 1994, 115–19).

2   The particular racial tandem that I isolate and track in this essay is clearly not representative or exhaustive of the meanings generated when blacks and Chinese immigrants were juxtaposed in nineteenth-century America. See Aarim-Heriot's (2003) outstanding study of the relationship between the so-called Negro question and the Chinese question, in which she examines the similar degrading traits and characteristics attributed to both groups.

3   On the specificity of U.S. Orientalism, see Lowe 1996, 178n7; Tchen 1999.

4   Tchen terms this "commercial orientalism" (1999, 63–124).

5   For example, we can see this negotiation in Booker T. Washington's statement that "notwithstanding the cruelty and moral wrong of slavery, the ten million Negroes inhabiting this country who themselves or whose ancestors went through the school of American slavery are in a stronger and more hopeful condition, materially, intellectually, morally, and religiously, than is true of an equal number of black people in any other portion of the globe" (1965, 37). Washington's striking image of U.S. slavery as a "school" that produced the moral, intellectual, and economic development of blacks in America constructs slavery not as a contradiction to modern ideologies of civilization or democracy but as an institution that enabled black historical progress. Washington's liberal narrative, in which black emancipation is achieved through hard work, humility, and the American ethos of self-help, produces a developmental resolution of this constitutive paradox between enslavement and enlightenment.

6   The heterogeneity of black Orientalism is underscored by numerous excellent, widely circulated projects such as Mullen 2004. Mullen builds on works such as Okihiro 1994 and Prashad 2001, 2000. All these authors delineate a long-standing and global history of black and Asian peoples in "mutual struggle against Western empires" (Mullen 2004, xviii). See also Jones and Singh 2003.

7   See Mullen 2004; Prashad 2000. For specific articles focusing on black discourses around Japanese imperialism and empire, see Lipsitz 1997. See also Allen 1995; Widener 2003.

8   Aarim-Heriot's study does an excellent job of showing how Republicans in the 1870s consistently attempted to disarticulate the Chinese from legislation that enfranchised black Americans (2003, 140–55).

9   In my analysis, the black press refers primarily to newspapers and does not include periodicals or the many newsletters that were circulated by black churches in the

nineteenth century. My secondary sources regarding black press representations of Chinese immigrants also examine almost exclusively black newspapers in their studies. See Hellwig 1974; Shankman 1978. I regard any press material that was directed at a black readership and edited and managed by black workers as a "black newspaper."

10   Southern planters expressed considerable interest in importing Chinese labor to replace black sharecroppers during Reconstruction; however, their efforts resulted in only a "trickle of migrants," and by 1880, the Mississippi census reported only fifty-one Chinese. See Loewen 1988, 22–26. The few cases in which Chinese immigrants were used in an attempt to displace black workers in the postbellum South ultimately failed owing to a number of factors, including unanticipated transportation costs, poor productivity, and decreased political necessity (26).

11   New Orleans Tribune, November 12, 1864, quoted in Hellwig 1974, 112. For an account of the paper's history, see Wolseley 1971, 111.

12   "Opium Eating in Chicago," Topeka Tribune, October 23, 1880.

13   "The Chinese in New York: Peculiarities of the Orientals Described," Washington Bee, November 22, 1884.

14   Shankman concludes that these pervasive representations were produced by economic competition, Chinese racism, and negative perceptions of China. However, his discussion of California becomes more nuanced: "But there were other more subtle reasons for blacks to dislike the Chinese and to seek to disassociate themselves from them. California Negroes were insecure, unsure about their proper place in society. . . . Realizing that sentiment against Chinese voting was widespread, blacks sought to show that they were different from the Asians" (5–6).

15   "Chinese Fashions," Freedom's Journal, March 16, 1827. I thank Dr. Francis Foster for referring me to this source.

16   During and after the Civil War, hundreds of local black newspapers not only emerged in the larger cities of the North and South but were also moving westward, where they were produced and consumed by small black communities in Kansas, California, and throughout the Northwest. See Bullock 1981.

17   Hence this study's focus on the nineteenth-century black press as a site of textual evidence in no way regards these discourses of black citizenship as representative of black imaginings of freedom and justice in the nineteenth century. In my attempt to critically interrogate the limits of citizenship, I look to a cultural institution that has a disproportionately significant role in producing discourses of black national identity.

18   Difficult conditions of production and the minimal possibility of garnering significant, if any, profits indicate that the black press at this time was either an organ of black institutions or the determined endeavor of a few committed men and women who sought to provide blacks in their community with what they regarded as relevant local and national news. The types of articles that these papers and magazines offered ranged from religious teachings to reports of local community events, sensationalism and gossip, black success stories, politics, and ac-

counts of racial violence, depending more or less on the interests of the press itself. However, quite often a combination of all these elements appeared within many local black newspapers, while periodical magazines tended to be more specialized by topic, especially toward the end of the nineteenth century. See Bullock 1981, 3.

19 As Gaines (1996) notes, it is difficult to categorize the educated black community during this period as "middle-class" given that their economic status was not often considerably different from that of less-privileged blacks. It is precisely this lack of a concrete material distinction between the educated black community and blacks who lacked such "cultural capital," Gaines argues, that made uplift ideology so appealing.

20 The relationship between heteronormative performance and the rehabilitation or development of racialized citizenship has been well theorized by Shah (2001).

21 See Hartman 1997, 125–63, for an extensive discussion of black codes and range of postemancipation practices that produced an "indebted" black subject. Also, for discussion of black codes and the convict lease system, see A. Davis 2003, 22–39.

22 Slave narratives of the eighteenth and nineteenth centuries, as well as the religious discourse of the abolitionist movement, clearly reveal how the enslaved and free black community relied heavily on the discursive terms and narratives of Christianity as a means of repudiating their relegation to property and of critiquing systematic exploitation. Abolitionist discourse relied predominantly on religious ideology, arguing that slavery violated fundamental principles of Christianity and engendered sinful and immoral relations among both slaves and their masters. See Saxton 1995, 227–41. Slave narratives also demonstrate the extent to which the free and enslaved black community deployed Christianity as the moral basis from which to condemn their dehumanization under chattel slavery. The literary historian and critic Francis Foster notes that the protagonists of eighteenth-century slave narratives were generally represented as "exemplary Christians whose sufferings and deliverances are proofs of God's power and mercy" (1979, 42). This strong emphasis on the religious formation of the enslaved was crucial to asserting their humanity as "children of God" but also demonstrated their superior fitness as Christian subjects who survived and escaped the barbarism of slavery through divine intervention and salvation.

23 Pointing to the structural significance of Christianity within developmental narratives of Western modernity is in no way intended to render the importance of religious ideologies within African American history as a sign of "colonized consciousness" or black capitulation to Euro-American hegemony. See Wilmore 1998; Lincoln 1974. See also Baker-Fletcher 1994.

24 See Wilmore 1998, chap. 3, "Black Religion and Black Nationalism" (125–62), for a provocative and thoughtful account of the profound missionary ideologies that underscored the discourses of prominent black nationalist leaders and organizations.

25 Baker-Fletcher (1994) also discusses the use of religious discourse to negotiate scientific racism in the work of Anna Julia Cooper.

26 Nubia, "Progress of the Colored People of San Francisco," *Frederick Douglass' Paper*, September 22, 1854.

27 Ibid.

28 During this period, anti-Chinese sentiment in California was primarily associated with the white working class, and mainstream publications directed at a middle-class or "not-working-class" readership generally condemned anti-Chinese racism and even constructed Chinese immigrants favorably compared to the Irish and other white ethnic immigrants. See Hong 2004. An educated black community seeking to emulate the values promoted by racial uplift, therefore, could disavow racist attacks on the Chinese and constitute themselves as more civilized than the ignorant and vulgar white working class, whose racist class interests also threatened the black community. At the same time, however, Orientalist discourse functioned simultaneously to consolidate a modern black national subject through the logic of cultural disidentification with Chinese, alien difference.

29 In a later issue of *Frederick Douglass' Paper*, the same author reports: "The Chinese have taken the places of the colored people, as victims of oppression.—The poor Chinese are, indeed, a wretched looking set; that they are filthy, immoral, and licentious—according to our notion of things—is unquestionable. But these vices do not justify the whites in oppressing them" (April 16, 1855). Again, the author condemns anti-Chinese racism as she simultaneously recites the "vices" or cultural underdevelopment of the Chinese as "filthy, immoral, and licentious," and implicitly constructs black identification with the culture of Western civilization, which she articulates as "*our* notion of things."

30 Nubia, "Progress of the Colored People."

31 See the *San Francisco Elevator*, May 24, 1873; December 17, 1869; March 29, 1873; November 19, 1869. Numerous articles attempted to contrast the "Negro [who] seeks to be an integral part of the nation" with the Chinese, who were "unlikely to become converted to the tenets of our religion, incapable to understand the system of our government, to appreciate our civilization, morals and manners, and persistently adhere to the doctrine of the inferiority of the races." Another typical characterization described Chinese immigrants as "people who use no common dictates of reason while among us, who are pagans in religion, inhuman in their traits, most scurrilous when their feelings are irritated, illiterate in intellectual education and of the doctrines of morality, and lastly wholly incompetent to become true citizens" (*San Francisco Elevator*, March 29, 1873). While this mode of black disidentification is clearly linked to the discourse analyzed earlier in "Letters from Nubia," the relationship between black citizenship and Oriental alterity is explicitly articulated in response to the growing significance of the anti-Chinese movement in defining the national citizenry.

32 "Democratic Logic," *San Francisco Elevator*, August 30, 1867. See Aarim-Heriot's

analysis of congressional reconstruction debates in which proposed legislation was continually engaged in relation to its consequences for the Chinese question, as Republicans successfully delinked black enfranchisement from the political costs of Chinese inclusion (2003, 85–155).

33   However, it is clear that anti-Chinese legislation in California was also regarded as an attack on the rights of free and unfree blacks before the Civil War. See *Frederick Douglass' Paper*, in which one writer stated, "Mr Flint's bill to prevent the Chinese and all others not eligible to citizenship from holding mining claims, has been published. The Chinese cannot be effected half so much by the passage of the bill, as the colored people. The most of the Chinese . . . are satisfied to make from one to two dollars per day, as it costs them little or nothing to live. The same objections cannot be urged against the colored people as are urged against the Chinese, viz.: that their habits and customs entirely prevent their amalgamation with Americans; that they degrade labor, because their wants are so few, that they can afford to work for a third of what is necessary to support an American. I am apprehensive that the real object of this bill is to enable owners of slaves to work them in the mines for it must be recollected that California is not altogether a free State" (April 13, 1855).

34   *San Francisco Elevator*, July 8, 1970.

35   See Hellwig 1974, 101–18, for over twenty-five citations from a range of black newspapers that spoke out from the 1870s to the 1880s in opposition to Chinese exclusion.

36   *Christian Recorder*, March 30, April 6, 1882.

37   Other black presses on the West Coast, including the *Pacific Appeal* and the *Washington Bee*, also perceived Chinese immigration as a major problem but did not condone race-based legislation as the solution, in part because of their opposition to the white nativist Workingman's Party, which black leaders often described as a group of radical, racist communists, primarily composed of immigrant or first-generation Irish workers. See Lortie 1970; Beasley 1919.

38   Because Shankman interprets black-press Orientalism as black hostility toward the Chinese (which his study seeks to account for), he states that "curiously enough, there is little evidence of black newspapers being willing to support the various exclusion acts. . . . Negro sentiment on Chinese exclusion was atypical; in general blacks of the late nineteenth and early twentieth century found the 'moon-eyed Celestials' to be 'absurd, unwholesome, and unacceptable [for] Americanization'" (Shankman 1978, 8–9). On the other hand, Hellwig's analysis begins on the basis of black press opposition to Chinese exclusion, arguing that black Americans were largely supportive of Chinese immigrants, despite their admitted "revulsion at the appearance of the alien," which Hellwig tends to naturalize and mitigate in his argument. Therefore, after discussing the large body of Orientalist disidentification in the black press, he states: "The importance of the black reaction to the Chinese, however, is not that Afro-Americans shared some of the broader American prejudices and fears. As native Americans, one

would expect them to be somewhat alarmed at the exotic looking stranger. . . . One might also anticipate blacks to have been even more hostile toward the Chinese than white Americans since they stood to suffer most from an influx of unskilled workers. But this was not the case. With rare unity, and consistency, Afro-Americans spoke out against discriminatory action" (Hellwig 1974, 118). While Hellwig's and Shankman's analyses emphasize different aspects of the same body of evidence and emerge with opposite conclusions, their studies in tandem are not contradictory.

39 *New Era*, July 14, 1870.

40 *Christian Recorder*, April 6, 1882.

41 *San Francisco Elevator*, April 26, 1873; *Savannah Tribune*, May 20, 1893.

42 "Have Chinese Any Rights Which Americans Are Bound to Respect," *San Francisco Elevator*, May 24, 1873.

43 "Opium Eating in Chicago," *Topeka Tribune*, October 22, 1880; "The Chinese in New York: Peculiarities of the Orientals Described," *Washington Bee*, November 22, 1884; "The Murderous Mafia," *New York Age*, November 1, 1890; "Chinese Girls Are Sold for Sixty Dollars," *Baltimore Afro-American*, December 24, 1920; "Color Line Is Chop Suey," *New York Age*, January 26, 1905; "The Chinese in the United States," *New York Age*, April 12, 1906; "One Blessing of the San Francisco Quake," *Alexander's Magazine* (Boston), May 1906. See also Shankman 1978, 10–12, for numerous other articles of similar content.

"A Deep Sense of No Longer Belonging"

Ambiguous Sites of Empire in Ana Lydia Vega's
Miss Florence's Trunk

In 1856, an English governess sees the Union Jack flying at the home of the British vice consul in Puerto Rico in Ana Lydia Vega's novella *Miss Florence's Trunk*. More precisely, she relates that this spectacle evokes neither pride in her national origins nor a nostalgic longing for home: "The years I have lived away from England have somehow blurred my pleasant memories of Oxfordshire, and I find that I recall only my father's long illness, his slow decay, and upon the finality of his death, a deep sense of no longer belonging" (1994, 174).[1] To depict the relationship between two national symbols, the British flag and the English governess, as one of disidentification, she points to a patriarchal culture that underwrites the gradual process of a daughter's economic dispossession, entry into domestic service, and emigration. Her memory of home registers the gaps between the nation-state, the governess's interior landscape, and emblematic representations of the pastoral English countryside and in so doing, critiques a nationalist epistemology that privileges a subject formed through a singular identification with national culture. But even as she links the nation to her economically subordinate governess status, she overhears her Anglo-American employer remark on the British tendency to import "their tea and their butlers" to the colonies, and she takes pleasure in identifying with such representations of the British as culturally select (182). As both critic and interpellated subject of British nationalism in the context of mid-nineteenth-century Puerto Rico, the British governess evokes the blur between disaffection and affiliation. Through her production of this overlapping space, she clarifies understandings of colonial projects at the same time that she complicates them, invoking the entrenchedness of a narrative that centers on the production of citizen-subjects in metropoles and colonies and the need for analyses that can attend to the multidimensional social actors and nonterritorial forms of imperialism that transcend both the colonial state and the populations under its rule (see Cooper and Stoler 1997, 20).[2]

Identity-driven readings make it difficult to treat the figure of the British governess as an allegory for Puerto Rico, which is frequently conceptualized in terms of a shift from Spanish colony to U.S. possession. The notion of successive forms of colonial rule, specifically the passage of island territories from Spanish tyranny to democratic rule by the United States, combined with conceptions of the islands as inhabited by alien peoples that were different from and inferior to a Euro-American majority in the continental United States, form the basis for the U.S. legal doctrine of Incorporation of 1901, which deemed Puerto Rico and the Philippines ineligible for "immediate incorporation" and stated that they could become part of the U.S. nation only through separate congressional initiatives. To circumvent the problem of absorbing alien races and taking action outside the Constitution, the U.S. Supreme Court positioned Puerto Rico and the Philippines in a new legal category of the "unincorporated territory" and defined them as belonging to, yet also being separate from, the United States (Kaplan 2002, 7). As unincorporated territories, Puerto Rico and the Philippines were conceptualized as exceptions, as they did not follow the model of European colonies or U.S. territories that would eventually become states and were considered to be neither foreign countries nor domestic to the United States (Thompson 2002).

Yet the concept of an unincorporated territory was envisaged not only as a legal quandary but also as a haunting, domestic problem. Emphasizing the anxiety that the Supreme Court's deliberations generated about Puerto

Rico's boundaries as well as United States national identity, Amy Kaplan (2002, 5) observes that the Supreme Court justices frequently depicted Puerto Rico as a ghost, or "disembodied shade," that lay outside any sanctioned trajectory or temporal order, haunting the borders of the embodied U.S. nation. The ambiguous space of Puerto Rico "unsettled the American nation's domestic sense of itself as a home and threatened to turn it into a haunted house" (6). How might this allow us to consider Puerto Rico's ambiguous status with an eye to its various "domestic" incorporations of "foreign" bodies? Put another way, how might we use the lingering "problem" of Puerto Rico's status to understand the gaps and standard narratives that such understandings have produced?[3] Rethinking the unincorporated territory as an epistemological object can open up other lines of inquiry and enable us to develop new methodologies for understanding the structural effects and legacies of nation-based narratives in the study of U.S. empire.

My reading of Vega's novella suggests that the work of imagining notions of the domestic and the foreign does not originate with the formation of the legal category of the unincorporated territory but takes shape through discourses of gender and sexuality. The figure of the British governess, whose status as both foreign and domestic serves as a metaphor for figurations of Puerto Rico as an ambiguous space, offers a unique lens through which to view the notion of the unincorporated territory. Published in Spanish in 1991, *Miss Florence's Trunk* does not suggest itself as a lens into historical relationships characteristic of mid-nineteenth-century Puerto Rico so much as it offers a meditation on the persistent category of the unincorporated territory. As my reading suggests, Vega's text thematizes the governess's cultural and sexual ambiguity to reflect on Puerto Rico's geopolitical ambiguity. The novel opens in 1885, with Florence's discovery of an article about the mysterious disappearance of Susan Morse Lind, her "dear benefactress, friend, and employer," on the front page of the newspaper that has just been delivered to Florence's New York City apartment (165). Most of the novel is drawn from Florence's journal from her three years in Puerto Rico (1856–59) and is narrated in the first person as an episodic series of her encounters with difficult situations. In the first half, she travels from Britain to Puerto Rico to tutor the grandson of Samuel Morse, the American inventor of the Morse code and a vocal defender of the institution of slavery. The second part takes the form of Florence's later journal to tell the story of her return to Puerto Rico after her twenty-seven-year absence.

If the widespread public interest in the English governess's "plight" in the mid-nineteenth century is part of a larger discourse about notions of gender, class, and labor, then *Miss Florence's Trunk* might be seen as relating the "governess problem," which carried the underlying assumption that the economic independence of women would lead to sexual independence, to anxieties over informal labor in Puerto Rico. I begin by examining how the novella links the cultural and sexual ambiguity of the governess to other transgressive, racialized, sexual formations, particularly African slaves, and in so doing illuminates the social contradictions operating in and reinforced by the geopolitical ambiguity of Puerto Rico. Second, I treat the British governess as an interstitial figure, a civilizing agent charged with instructing North Americans on elite whiteness and imperial governmentality. By way of a conclusion, I consider the implications of the novella's foregrounding of the British governess as the protagonist for a story that is ostensibly "about" Puerto Rico for understandings of transnational processes of formal and informal empire.

This essay situates the story of the English governess within other stories—the narrative of U.S. global ascendancy, nationalist histories of U.S. colonial and neocolonial formations, and representations of racial and sexual ambiguity. In turn, it tries to present another story—one in which the governess's migration brings into focus the specific colonial migrations of people, services, ideas, and goods to and from the island. Following the figure of the governess allows us to view Puerto Rico through connections with places that include the state of Louisiana, the coastal region of Guayama, the French colony of Guadeloupe, and Paris. Through a cast that includes African slaves, a French abolitionist, Anglo-American aristocrats, creole elites, and sugar capitalists, Puerto Rico emerges as a transnational and multiracial meeting ground for slaveholding interests, rather than strictly a Spanish colony.

My interest in using cultural and sexual ambiguity as a lens through which to view geopolitical ambiguity builds on recent studies that frame Puerto Rico within discourses of sexuality. More specifically, these studies show that production of Puerto Rico's difference as the exemplar of cultural and sexual pathologies allows us to challenge the absence of empire in U.S. historiography and question its emphasis on formal imperialism. Approaching Puerto Rico through the lens of sexuality can, as Eileen Findlay (1999, 4) demonstrates, decenter binary analyses that dichotomize nationalism and colonialism, while attending to Puerto Rico's material, cultural, and political specificity. While taking into account the profound impact of Spanish and U.S. imperialism in shaping Puerto Rican history, along with other attempts to create a coherent national identity, Findlay invokes the significance of Puerto Rico's internal divisions and self-representation—the ways that Puerto Ricans have historically defined themselves along class, gender, racial, and regional lines—to point out that national identity is not the only analytical coordinate for the island. As Laura Briggs shows, examining the overlap between notions of Puerto Rican "difference" and discourses of sexuality and reproduction highlights the linkages between knowledge production, domestic policies, and foreign policy and shows how empire is invested in managing the development of gender and sexuality. For Briggs, the movement and reproduction of British colonial norms for the management of women and domestic policies in mid-nineteenth-century Puerto Rico are a case in point. If women, disease, and armies moved, then they were accompanied by the methods of managing them. Such policies were then adapted for the United States and its overseas ventures (Briggs 2002).

The Governess Novel

If the nineteenth-century governess novel has been valued by many critics for the multiple ways in which it uses the social ambiguity of the governess to expose the contradictions in Victorian domestic and class relations, Vega's appropriation of the genre rejects assumptions about the transparency of this writing and instead insists on its historic engagement with a racialized climate of anxiety concerning unregulated female sexuality, which was closely tied to issues over the employment of middle-class white women and the nature of governess labor. Indeed, much of the debate about governesses revolved around what was seen as their ambiguous and shifting "intermediate" position. Victorianists such as A. James Hammerton and Mary Poovey have explained the historical (and arguably enduring) fascination with British governesses in terms of their introduction of sexual and class instabilities, particularly through the question of whether governesses should be considered the gatekeepers of sexual and class structures or were themselves the weakest links in the middle-class household.[4] As Mary Maurice writes in her pamphlet of 1849, "There is a strong prejudice against governesses": "Frightful instances have been discovered in which she, to whom the care of the young has been entrusted, instead of guarding their minds in innocence and purity, has become their corrupter—she has been the first to lead and to initiate into sin, to suggest and carry on intrigues, and finally to be the instrument of destroying the peace of families" (Maurice 2004, 135). Following this logic, the emigration of governesses was seen as one solution to the problem of unregulated white female sexuality in over-crowded Britain, as well as to the moral crisis in the colonies. Not only could governesses help to strengthen and stabilize the middle classes in the colonies to ensure that their interests continued to support their counter-parts "at home," but they could also escape what was seen as an "unnatural state of celibacy" (Hammerton 1979, 45). Though they were regarded as a social problem in Britain, governesses could be constructed abroad as re-formers and agents of British civilization and, even more specifically, as sexual and gender missionaries.

Generally conceptualized through narratives that detail the condition of English middle-class women, the figure of the governess has become syn-onymous with narratives that formulate universal forms of subjectivity and nationalist notions of culture. Victorian governess novels typically feature a governess as a central protagonist and explore themes of marginalization, exclusion, dependency, and reversed fortunes through a narrative of female development. By focusing on the governess's intermediate position be-tween her pupils and employers, governess novels could use this angle as a formal literary device that emphasized the governess's ambiguous social position and economic vulnerability.[5] At the same time, these novels also figured the governess as a convenient tool for social observation, particu-larly of the lives of her middle- and upper-middle-class employers.

Miss Florence's Trunk parodies elements of the governess narrative me-morialized in texts that include *Jane Eyre* and *The Turn of the Screw*. *Miss Florence's Trunk* narrates Florence's life as one of hardship, textured by a series of humiliations, highlighting, in the tradition of Brontë's novel, the dismissal of governess labor as nonlabor and inscribing an economic narra-tive into a narrative of courtship. For Vega, however, the governess novel is an ideal genre for exploring the discursive silences around slavery, the gaps in historical memory, and the unwritten historical record.[6] The novella locates the ambiguous and shifting position of the governess within a dis-course of civilization and, more specifically, situates Florence's understand-ing of her ambiguous position as governess within the racialized hierarchies engendered by slavery. Recalling Jane's relationship to the temperamental Rochester, Florence's encounters with the mercurial sugar mill owner and slave master Lind are narrated through a discourse of seduction that obscures the asymmetries and particularities of their power relation but is also situated within a discourse of slavery. While her account of Lind's brusque dinner table manners helps to narrate the increasing slave rebellions in the region from the perspective of slave owners, she is also figured as the object in such narratives. Lind describes her at one point as having the toughness of an African woman, thus depicting her in relation to the racialized bodies of female slaves.

As Mary Poovey (1988, 145) cogently explains in her analysis of the competing roles of middle-class mother and governess, the governess occupied a contradictory position as the gatekeeper between classes of women at the same time that her sexuality classified her with those from whom she ought to differ. Recounting her employer's insistence on outfitting her for a party that she is also being required to attend, Florence notes that her gown was fitted on the body of the new maid, Selenia, a "tall, well-built mulatto woman," whose measurements are said to "closely approximate" her own. To register the intended humiliation, she brings into focus her employer's delight in positioning her body in proximity to that of a female slave. By undermining the standards of propriety that define her sense of professional integrity, the gown is meant to suggest her sexual susceptibility and destabilize her claim to an elite status and white racial identity. Significantly, Selenia is not figured exclusively as Florence's double in the novella but is framed as a figure that intersects a series of women, including Florence's employer and Bella, the cook, and defines them as part of a racialized gender hierarchy. By mapping the relations among the three women, the scene demonstrates how sexual, gender, and class norms are inscribed within processes of comparative racialization.

The ambiguity of the governess's position is also staged through the structure of the story. Like *The Turn of the Screw*, Vega's novella employs a framing technique to center the governess's first-person written account. But it also seems to expand on James's figuration of the governess as a recorder of ambiguity or, as he put it, the "intense anomalies and obscurities" that she was engaged in, though her explanations of them were often inaccurate.[7] Vega's novella is, in this sense, less concerned with the British governess as a historical figure and more interested in examining her attempts to negotiate her status as both subject and object. By positioning Florence as a tourist who is reviewing her collection of colonial impressions as well as a participant in the story, *Miss Florence's Trunk* also references a domestic literary tradition of white women's writing in the colonies. As Vicente Rafael observes, women's writings often took an epistolary and autobiographical form that seemed particularly well suited for dramatizing their recurring feelings of alienation in the tropics. As he explains, letters and memoirs provided perspective on women's displacement by framing their travels as a series of "episodic, multiply mediated encounters with the otherness of empire" (Rafael 2000, 57). Significantly, these accounts of their encounters with otherness referred not only to the land and peoples of the islands but also to the colonial machinery that structured their own positioning and mobility.

Criticism on the Victorian governess novel has productively attended to the imperialist foundations and preoccupations of governess narratives, particularly by identifying the conditions of colonialism, slavery, and economic imperialism that constitute marriage as a separate and secured space for women. But the same views have also produced dismissive interpretations of the governess's individualism and actions as weak apologies for imperialism or as part of an effort to deny the entangling of colonialism in racism and slavery (Qualls 1994, 370). As my reading attempts to show, Vega's novella takes a different approach in at least two ways. First, it relates the figure of the governess to other racialized sexual formations engendered by slavery and colonialism. In doing so, the novella disrupts the assumption that these figures belong to different spheres and histories and are discursively separate from each other. Second, the novella opens up questions of agency by making available the tense space in which the governess remains both invested in, and dependent on, particular constructions and self-representations of herself as a British subject.

A Civilizing Agent

Upon her arrival in Puerto Rico, Florence, burdened by her encounter with the too "abundant" native dishes, takes in the panoramic expanse of the island from her small servant's room and partakes of the sensation of what it means to possess an empire: "In this small room, then, on the second floor of the main house, its enormous window opening onto a spectacular cloud-filled sunset, I now sit, and perched as I am, I find that I too am mistress of this empire of sugar cane stretching as far as the eye can see toward the dark-blue Caribbean" (Vega 1994, 169). To develop the ways in which Florence's shifting relation to her Anglo-American employer in Puerto Rico offers her—even temporarily—different possibilities than those offered by the narratives associated with the pastoral Oxfordshire landscape, the novel offers a snapshot of Florence's production of a vantage point that allows her to regard her American mistress as an imperial peer, rather than her employer and superior, in the context of Puerto Rico. Rather than treating the British governess as an anomaly in the mid-nineteenth-century Puerto Rico that Vega imagines, I argue that the novella specifically depicts Florence as a civilizing agent charged with the task of instructing the Lind household on imperial governmentality, highlighting various ways in which governess work is intended to instill a comparative logic in the Lind household by simultaneously producing horizontality between the United States and England as imperial custodians and verticality between whites and nonwhites.

As the novella suggests, governess work is both a racial duty that involves the production of elite whiteness and instruction on how to behave like an imperial power.[8] Remarking on how her arrival in the Lind household prompted the adoption of the daily ritual of tea and cake, select customs associated with English culture, Florence reveals the way in which her presence enables the family to assert their claim to a white racial and upper-class identity. Her contradictory position as both instructor and object is further emphasized when she is required to accompany the Lind family at social gatherings where she is displayed as a possession of the family, symbolizing their financial success, class status in Puerto Rico, and racialized ties to Europe and the United States. By bringing into focus the racial dynamics of American appropriations of British cultural superiority, the novel suggests how Anglo-Saxon racial discourse played a defining role in Puerto Rico in a way that politicized the distinction between U.S. and English identity. Framing her employment as "civilization work" and a racial duty historically performed by British governesses, Florence remarks, "I am not the first—though I hope to be the last—to have accepted the challenge of the domestication of this spoiled little wild beast of the Linds" (170). In identifying the crucial role of domesticity in the production of elite whiteness in Puerto Rico, she rejects sole proprietorship over this racial duty while also asserting that she, as an Englishwoman, is better suited than others for the job. Florence sees her governess work as a continuation of her efforts to stake out Puerto Rico's compatibility with English domesticity.

The exportation of British colonial expertise took place through the emigration of British nannies and eventually, through the outpouring of manuals for colonial rule after the Spanish-American War in 1898. As Michael Salman (2001, 29) and others observe, the annexation of Hawaii, Puerto Rico, and the Philippines by the United States spurred intense interest in the subject of how to operate a colony. In addition to the publication of extensive bibliographies of works on colonialism and also on the new U.S. territories by the Library of Congress, many studies also took the form of manuals, focusing specifically on the issues of colonial rule. Several major studies were published that could best be called "how-to" manuals for colonial rule. Alleyne Ireland, in his highly influential book *Tropical Colonization* (1899), remarks on his good fortune at having arrived at the beginning of the Spanish-American War, a moment in which the demand for literature about the colonial experience helped to authorize British writers as experts on issues of colonialism. As Vega's novel suggests, the form of gendered expertise that emerges through the exportation of British nannies can be juxtaposed to these manuals of empire in ways that explicitly foreground questions of racialized gendered agency.[9]

I argue that Vega uses the governess narrative to consider how domesticity was not only directed at natives in Puerto Rico but also intended to domesticate a creole elite, toward the goal of strengthening the bond between Euro-American elites and the colonies. Acquiring a British governess enabled Euro-American elites to produce a hierarchy of whiteness that could strengthen and expand their claim to white racial identity and its association with European civilization while also distancing themselves from Spanish and African influences. Florence's narrative also enables her to turn her gaze on to her employer in a way that masks her subordinate position as their servant. By pointing out her employer's lack of propriety in declining to be addressed by her married title and also in embracing her favored black female servant, Florence registers her disapproval of the way in which her American mistress groups Florence with "all the servants" and also asserts her superior cultural authority. Her narrative brings into focus her efforts in counteracting the anarchic potential and damaging effects of her employers' American laxness by reinscribing the racial and class hierarchy. In depicting the creole son's physical characteristics, she insists that he is like "any young European gentleman" and reveals "no sign whatever of that underlying yellowish sort of tint which so blemishes the appearance of white persons born in this part of the world" (168). Her employer explains that the impact of the tropics has been lessened by their extended summer visits to her father's house in New York State, which allows them "to repair the harm done the lungs and the blood by the rigors of the tropics" (169), thus figuring the United States as separate from, and a corrective antidote to, Puerto Rico. This scene engages a narrative of domesticity to pursue an English-oriented Anglo-Saxonism and suggest that Americans are the weak link.

To further explore the instability and unevenness of the imagined racial bond between British and Americans, Vega's text develops the idea that what matters are not Florence's relationships with "natives" but her relationships with "peers."[10] As Paul Kramer notes, the relationship between the United States and Britain was not only about inspiration but also about rivalry that involved economic and military competition as well as various struggles over spheres of influence. When the United States took up similar tasks as British empire, it was seen as merely fulfilling the Anglo-Saxon responsibilities necessitated by its racial character. In seeking British guidance and models of colonial rule, U.S. imperialism responded in what might have been perceived as a colonial manner (Kramer 2006, 11).

Florence's narrative reinforces the notion that the British intervention is necessary—but not always successful—in maintaining racial categories when she records her discomfort at the physical familiarity with which Miss Susan embraces Bella, the black cook, as she emphasizes her long service with the family ("She has been with me since the day I married" [Vega 1994, 169]). Rather than noting how the language of family affection is also used to mask and disavow Bella's status as a slave, Florence does not see the racist logic that is employed to define Bella's existence as coterminous with the events of Susan Morse's life, and instead interprets the moment as evidence of her employer's American impropriety. She then employs racist imagery to assert the racial hierarchy that her employer's laxness has compromised, dehumanizing Bella by describing her "sweetly canine eyes." Florence emphasizes her professionalism to assert her superior cultural authority over her wealthy Anglo-American employer, but she also calls attention to her precarious social position and economic vulnerability as a servant: "Still, in order not to mar that first impression which is so important to the career of any governess, I kept to myself as best I could my reservations" (168).

In his travelogue *Greater Britain: A Record of Travel in English-Speaking Countries*, Charles Wentworth Dilke (1890) offered an extended demonstration of the transformative potential of Anglo-Saxon racial discourse, defining Englishness in terms of a mobile form of expertise, or "the ability to project Anglo-Saxons, their institutions, and their culture even beyond the formal reaches of British colonial power." In imagining a English global hegemony in terms of the spread of English language and institutions, Dilke writes: "America is becoming, not English merely, but world-embracing in the variety of its type; and, as the English element has given language and history to that land, America offers the English race the moral directorship of the globe, by ruling mankind through Saxon institutions and the English tongue. Through America, England is speaking to the world" (1890, 224; see also Kramer and Plotz 2001, 8). For Dilke, America could be viewed as a place where people from all over the world are being fused together, but "run through an English mould."

Interpreting the way that Charlie speaks Spanish to her during their lessons as a sign of impertinence, Florence remarks that his accent not only is inappropriate for a member of an elite class but also "betrays the African origins of his school" (Vega 1994, 170). Though she also describes his knowledge of Spanish as prodigious, she perceives it as a threat to the racial and class boundaries that her civilizing work is meant to secure. By framing her governess work as a means of redeeming Charlie from "inappropriate" Spanish and African influences, she also puts askew the unique claim the United States makes to an educational mission in Puerto Rico. Education figured centrally in the story of the development of an "inclusionary" American colonial state in the Caribbean and the Pacific, informing the discourse about the self-proclaimed mission of the United States to build modern, efficient colonies within an atmosphere of international competition. As Julian Go (2003, 183) ironically explains, the colonized populations under U.S. leadership would receive a "course of tuition" that would enable them to acquire the character, mentality, and sentiment necessary for self-government.

An Interstitial Figure

To show how discourses of gender and sexuality are inscribed into racial exclusion, the novella highlights the way that racial segregation is given the task of protecting gender and sexual norms within a discourse of civilized domesticity. Though René Fouchard, a French doctor with abolitionist sympathies, is figured as a potential suitor for Florence, the scene in which he would conventionally attempt to seduce her is rescripted as the moment in which he initiates her to the institution of slavery that structures her daily life at the Lind estate. Urging her to look at the "men and women who bring sweetness to our coffee," he produces a spectacle of black humanity to instruct her in the link between slave labor and civilized domesticity. Remarking that the blindness that she exhibits toward the existence of slavery is not hers alone but part of a wider practice of concealing the presence and continuation of slavery on the island, Fouchard points out how an ideology of separate spheres, exemplified by her employer's insistence that she remain within the "magic circle of the gardens," conspires with the unrecognizability of slavery and ensures its continuation: "It's curious that they are not called by their true name—slaves. It is as though we insisted upon denying their real condition, as though if we can but avoid naming it we may allow ourselves to be blind to the true horror of their state" (Vega 1994, 199). However, Florence's reaction—to instruct the black cook to turn Fouchard away the next time that he calls—indicates that she has not internalized the lesson but also questions its universalist assumptions.

Conceptions of Puerto Rico's exceptional status in relation to slave trade networks had political and economic consequences but also impacted knowledge production about Puerto Rico. Of the impact of nation-based frameworks in narrowing understandings of Puerto Rico, Joseph Dorsey (2003, xiii) writes, "African, Asian, and European immigration played a variety of roles in Spanish American history during and after the colonial period. Puerto Rico is no exception." Researchers of slavery in Puerto Rico, according to Seymour Drescher (2004, 727), are challenged by the fact that the island's archives do not offer a counterpart to the import registers found in other Caribbean islands, particularly Cuba, and must thus rely on "scattered data that only tangentially offer evidence about the flow of Africans." Existing documents, Drescher contends, need to be analyzed with an eye to the ideological hegemony of anti-abolitionism and the numerous motivations that officials, merchants, and planters had for systematically encoding and concealing information pertaining to illegal slave transactions (727).[11] Focusing on this period as a story that is not about formal colonialism enables us to consider more broadly the shift in slave importation in Puerto Rico from the re-exportation of slaves from the non-Hispanic Caribbean to direct transport from the West African Coast to Puerto Rico and the moves by France, Denmark, and the Netherlands to honor their abolitionist contracts with Great Britain that dated back to its internationalization of abolitionist campaigns in the early nineteenth century.

Miss Florence's Trunk spans the years from the 1850s to 1885 and can be said to take place during the Spanish colonial period and the U.S. Civil War and before the Spanish-American War of 1898. By connecting the ambiguous position of the British governess to African slaves, Vega's novella situates conceptions of Puerto Rico's ambiguous status in U.S. historiography in relation to Puerto Rico's marginal status in metropolitan understandings of empire and in the regionality of the Caribbean. The novella takes the form of an archive of interactions, one that registers the existence of normative readings and their contributions to exceptionalist representations of Puerto Rico. In this way, the story stages nationalist renderings of Puerto Rico and holds them out for further examination.

Ricardo Gutiérrez Mouat (2001, 120) offers an enlightening analysis of *Falsas crónicas del sur*, the book in which Vega's novella appears, claiming that it is concerned not with examining issues of national or Caribbean identity but with reproducing historical episodes drawn from the regional archives of the southern part of Puerto Rico, as well as recovering narrative traditions from towns connected to Vega's family's history. For Mouat, Vega's emphasis on local and regional archival traditions disrupts the deterritorialization of the nation as a standard feature of globalization and so might be seen as bypassing the nation. The novella, following his formulation, might thus be said to present a "foreshadowing [of] the deterritorialized identities of the contemporary global order" (122). Noting Vega's engagement with a local and regional archive, Mouat sees it not as lending itself to transparent or reflective ethnographic readings but as reconceptualizing the figure of the archive as a "deposit of literary forms" (127). Employing the insights of Mouat's framing of the novella as a "prenational

past in a postnational work," I consider its epistemological critique of
Puerto Rico in conjunction with its appropriation of a specifically gendered
form of the governess novel.

Unincorporating 1898

As an unincorporated territory of the United States, or a colonial possession
with commonwealth status, Puerto Rico's relation to the United States resonates with important contemporary debates about Guantánamo as an ambiguous legal space of unclear sovereignty and deepened interest in defining
the physical areas of the United States and the analytical frameworks used to
map the boundaries of U.S. and Puerto Rican political, legal, and economic
power.[12] Defined by U.S. legal discourse as "foreign to the United States in
the domestic sense," Puerto Rico puts the international boundaries of the
United States into question. At the same time, the political status of Puerto
Rico has become a critical flashpoint for scholars seeking to place U.S.
national development in a global frame and, in so doing, to highlight narratives of U.S. territorial and political expansionism and empire.

The question of the unincorporated territory has been revived through
the substantial contributions of recent revisionist historical accounts and
legal scholarship that engage the centennial of the Spanish-American War of
1898. These studies have been important in challenging official accounts of
the Spanish-American War that foreground the United States role as libera-
tor of the islands.[13] They have shown how neglecting to account for Cuban
resistance to Spanish colonial rule and reductively framing the Philippine-
American War and Hawaiian resistance as nonevents and minor insurrec-
tions in what was otherwise a universally desired and logical progression
from a despotic Spanish regime to enlightened, modern U.S. colonialism
have assisted the invisibility of U.S. empire and also opened up new archives
and interpretations. But even as these approaches render resistance to
colonization visible, they also reinscribe U.S. nationalist narratives through
their centering of the relationship of colonizer and colonized.

Cultural studies and legal scholarship have focused on U.S. constitutional law to investigate the contemporary legacies of late-nineteenth-
century territorial expansion by the United States.[14] Though such revisionist histories and legal scholarship have been critical in figuring the territories
as a pivotal but neglected chapter in the longer narrative of U.S. national

development, they tend to identify constitutional jurisprudence as the source and origin of the ambiguous colonial status of territories while also establishing their formal annexation as the departure point for the study of U.S. empire. In theorizing Puerto Rico through the overlap between its foreign and domestic figurations, Amy Kaplan notes that the Supreme Court regarded Puerto Rico as a foreign object that had to be incorporated into the U.S. nation and was thus imagined through the metaphors of a household and embodied human form. On the other hand, she explains, from Puerto Rico's perspective the United States was the "foreign object casting its shadow across every aspect of political, economic, and social life of the island; it was the foreign body that Puerto Rico had to incorporate" (Burnett and Marshall 2001, xi). In their analysis of the series of legal decisions that resulted from the Insular Cases of 1901, Christina Duffy Burnett and Burke Marshall (2001, xi) point to the articulation of new forms of limited sovereignty and dependency that positioned the inhabitants of Puerto Rico and the Philippines in a liminal space and time, where they were neither citizens "at home" nor foreigners from a different nation. But by assigning originary authorship to the U.S. Supreme Court for the "ambig-uous space of Puerto Rico," their analyses retain the legal framing that reinforces understandings of the United States as "new" to Puerto Rico and advances the definition of Puerto Rico as principally a Spanish colony.

The critical emphasis on the shift from Spanish to U.S. rule in legal scholarship and revisionist historical accounts that deal with the unincor-porated territory and the Spanish-American War produces some troubling effects. I characterize these effects as troubling because the grounding of U.S. authorship also recenters territorial forms of imperialism and formal empire.[15] This emphasis, in turn, obscures the complicated roles of tempo-rary, multiple, and incomplete migrations, as well as the formations that Rhacel Salazar Parreñas (2001) calls "informal streams" that are not moni-tored by the state. Attention to these processes of migrations and migrant formations allows us to consider different, if systematically linked, forms of dominance and dislocation, specific colonial migrations, while also alluding to what the historic privileging of citizenship and national subjectivity has not allowed us to see.

The view I have presented of Vega's novella also suggests that the inter-section between geopolitical ambiguity and cultural-sexual ambiguity of-fers a unique lens for viewing the unincorporated territory as an epistemological object. As an example of what epistemological critique offers for the study of U.S. empire, Teemu Ruskola argues that there is a largely neglected story of American extraterritoriality and U.S. legal imperialism that works through nonterritorial forms. Its invisibility is secured by the focus on territorial forms of imperialism and formal colonialism that focuses inquiry on the British; the invisibility of this story within U.S. histories is largely due to a similar logic that focuses inquiry on formal U.S. territorial possessions. Moreover, the notion of American power overseas is largely analyzed in military and economic terms. In contrast, Ruskola (2005, 861) treats law as an "important currency in its own right in American overseas imperialism," with an eye toward its subject-making capacities ("how law dynamically both constitutes and deconstitutes sovereigns at both national and international levels").

Rather than treating ambiguity as a superficial description, I have tried to think about how its overlapping configurations open up another path of inquiry about the unincorporated territory. In contrast, nation-state celebrations of citizenship and national subjectivity and treatments of subjectivity as justice, as Kandice Chuh (2006, 9–10) contends, have obscured the processes by which subjects emerge through epistemological objectification. Writing from Paris to his former governess, Charlie relates his disdain at being seen as Puerto Rican: "A French friend took me a few days ago to the studio of an artist whose specialty is the fruits and vegetables of the tropics (in paint, I mean). 'I understand he is Puerto Rican like you,' my enthusiastic cicerone told me, and only my fear of offending him restrained me from laughing in his face. Puerto Rican? What does this new epithet mean, whose syllables never once assailed my ears in all the time I lived in Arroyo? Geographic proximity is surely not sufficient reason for bestowing adjectives of birth and antecedence so cavalierly, much less when one's parents have always behaved as though La Enriqueta were the displaced center of an eternally foreign universe" (Vega 1994, 236). By characterizing the notion of a Puerto Rican identity as a "new epithet," Charlie rejects being classified with the tropical artist. He locates himself in the island town of Arroyo, but also describes his sense of estrangement in Puerto Rico as a type of inheritance from his parents. As a globalized individual who also identifies locally, Charlie embodies a fragmented subject: at once the privileged interloper as well as a figure for the exotic, primitive culture implied by the artist. This scene asks us to take into account multiple interpellations as they are articulated in tension with the inclusionary and homogenizing effects of nation-based conceptions of Puerto Rico. But it also points to the possibilities that situating the unincorporated territory of Puerto Rico in relation to other ambiguous imperial formations might generate for the study of U.S. empire.

Notes

I thank Grace Hong, Rod Ferguson, Kara Keeling, and the *Strange Affinities* participants, as well as Adria Imada, Aisha Khan, Sanda Lwin, Eric Reyes, and Lok Siu for their valuable comments and suggestions on earlier drafts. Irmary Reyes-Santos generously gave me the benefit of her insights, advice on sources, and encouragement. Dalia Kandiyoti pointed me to Ana Lydia Vega's governess novel for my comparative colonialisms course for the Comparative Literature Program at the University of Oregon. My thanks to her and to the students in the course for stimulating discussions.

1 The novella was originally published as *El baúl de Miss Florence: Fragmentos para un novelón romántico; Falsas crónicas del sur* (Rio Piedras: University of Puerto Rico, 1991).

2 I draw on Julian Go's argument that colonial rule was "a matter of an extensive series of connections that joined the fate of colonial populations on the ground to a diverse set of metropolitan actors on the home front—a matter, in sum, of imperial chains in which all were entangled" (Go 2003, 208).

3 As Avery Gordon poignantly asks, "How do we reckon with what modern history has rendered ghostly? How do we develop a critical language to describe and analyze the affective, historical, and mnemonic structures of such hauntings?" (1997, 18). Gordon also proposes that we use hauntings as a way of seeing differently, or otherwise: "Paying attention to the disjuncture between identifying a social structure (or declaring its determinate existence) and its articulation in everyday life and thought, I have hoped that working at understanding these gaps, the kinds of visions they produce, and the afflictions they harbor would enable us not to eradicate the gap—it is inevitable—but to fill in the content differently" (19).

4 To name just a few contemporary examples: the best-selling novel *The Nanny Diaries* and the upcoming film adaptation; the Broadway musical version of *Mary Poppins* (2006); the film *Nanny McPhee* (2005), with Emma Thompson in the title role; and the ongoing ABC television show *SuperNanny*, featuring Jo Frost as the nanny.

5 For an account of the Victorian governess novel as a literary form that reveals contradictions in Victorian domestic and class relations, see Peterson 1973; Poovey 1988; K. Hughes 2003; Lecaros 2001. Lecaros notes that "the peak of the

genre . . . coincided with the intense debate about governess work in the 1840s to the 1860s" (30).

6   When asked about the impact of her formal education on her writing, Vega responded that she attended a Catholic parochial school in which instruction was given in English, so that English was her first literary context. "My favorites were those nineteenth century English novels—especially those written by women—in which you immerse yourself completely. When I wrote *Miss Florence's Trunk*, the novella that appears in *Falsas crónicas del Sur*, I reread those novels, especially the ones with a governess in them. My writing often parodies different literary genres, and in that text, I wanted to re-create those writers' reticence, their ability to keep something secret, to say very little about a central element in a story. They give out a very small clue, and the reader has to do the rest" (Hernández 2000, 54).

7   In response to complaints that the figure of the governess was not fully drawn, James writes: "It was 'déjà très-joli,' in *The Turn of the Screw*, please believe, the general proposition of our young woman's keeping crystalline her record of so many intense anomalies and obscurities—by which I don't of course mean her explanation of them, a different matter; and I saw no way, I feebly grant (fighting at the best too, periodically, for ever grudged inch of my space) to exhibit her in relations other than those; one of which, precisely, would have been her relation to her own nature" (H. James 2004, 183).

8   As Joseph Dorsey observes, "The quiet alliance between government-protected Spanish, Danish, Dutch, and French subjects—be they independent nationals or corrupt public officials—was neither facile nor uniform. . . . But throughout the period of transition, from the 1820s to the 1830s, cross-national threads of illegal cooperation remained strong enough to carry the Puerto Rican slave trade into the 1840s" (2003, 117).

9   If, as Jane Tompkins argues, domestic manuals written by United States women served as a "prerequisite" for territorial conquest, then Vega's novel both expands on and complicates this notion by using domesticity to decenter the masculine relationship of colonizer and colonized (quoted in Kaplan 2002, 184).

10   For more discussion of the logic of imperial "peers," see Kramer and Plotz's (2001) discussion of Kipling's famous poem "The White Man's Burden" (1899). As they argue, "It is not natives here but peers who matter, Britons whose dear-bought wisdom allows them both to pave an imperial way and to judge America's success in following it. Joseph Conrad's exactly contemporaneous *Lord Jim* proposes a similar kind of evaluation in its prolonged debates about whether the central character possesses the internal fortitude to be 'one of us.' "

11   In his review essay, Drescher comments on the challenges that confront researchers of slavery in Puerto Rico and questions Dorsey's critical approach: "Faced with this combination of blank spaces and doctored discourse, Dorsey focuses as much upon the discursive tactics, as well as silences, of his subjects as on the collective outcome of their actions."

12   I am thinking here of Dudziak and Volpp 2005 and Stoler 2006.

13   Examples of this important body of scholarship include Ileto 2002; and Silva 2005. Ada Ferrer (1999) points out how slavery and an "ascendant racism" provided the context for an anticolonial and antiracist revolution in Cuba against Spanish rule from 1868 to 1878, as creole (Cuban-born) elites opted to maintain the colonial bond with Spain in part so that they could preserve a prosperous and expanding sugar industry that depended on the labor of African slaves. Silva argues for the significance of a Hawaiian language archive, undervalued sources such as songs and poetry, and also attending to the ways in which women's political activity and contributions were often kept out of colonial and postcolonial histories (2005, 7). In his essay "The Philippine American War: Friendship and Forgetting," Reynaldo Ileto considers the politics of Filipino "forgettings" of the 1899 Philippine-American War: "Why is it so difficult to speak of the [Philippine-American] relationship in terms such as invasion, resistance (so readily applied to the Japanese in World War II), war, combat, colonialism, exploitation, discrimination? There are a number of explanations for this attitude, but from a historian's perspective the 'problem' persists mainly because a special relationship with America has become an intrinsic part of the history of the Filipino nation-state's emergence and development" (2002, 3), speaking of war as betrayal of Filipino nation's emancipatory progress from "colonialism to independence, tradition to modernity."

14   Burnett and Marshall observe: "U.S. constitutional jurisprudence—most notably the Insular Cases of 1901—is the source of the colonial status in which the territories are still trapped" (2001, xi).

15   Ruskola (2005, 860) remarks that studies of colonialism in China tend to focus on British actions and not those of the United States and that legal accounts of American imperialism tend to emphasize legal shifts in the territories rather than nonterritorial forms of imperialism.

I thank Sanda Lwin for bringing this essay to my attention. On the little known history of United States imperialism in China, see also Kim (2010), "The El Dorado of Commerce: China's Billion Bellies," 63–93.

References

Aarim-Heriot, Najia. 2003. *Chinese Immigrants, African Americans, and Racial Anxiety in the United States, 1848–82*. Urbana: University of Illinois Press.

Acosta, Oscar Zeta. 1989. *The Revolt of the Cockroach People*. New York: Vintage Books.

Agamben, Giorgio. 1993. *The Coming Community*. Trans. Michael Hardt. Minneapolis: University of Minnesota Press.

Alarcón, Norma. 1981. "Chicana's Feminist Literature: A Re-vision through Malintzin/or Malintzin: Putting Flesh Back on the Object." In *This Bridge Called My Back*, ed. Cherríe Moraga and Gloria Anzaldúa, 182–90. New York: Kitchen Table Press.

———. 1989. "Traddutora, Traditora: A Paradigmatic Figure of Chicana Feminism." *Cultural Critique* 13:57–87.

———. 1999. "Chicana Feminism: In the Tracks of the 'Native' Woman." In *Between Woman and Nation: Nationalisms, Transnational Feminisms, and the State*, ed. Caren Kaplan, Norma Alarcón, and Minoo Moallem. Durham: Duke University Press.

Aldama, Frederick Luis. 2003. *Postethnic Narrative Criticism: Magicorealism in Oscar "Zeta" Acosta, Ana Castillo, Hanif Kureshi, and Salman Rushdie*. Austin: University of Texas Press.

Alexander, M. Jacqui. 1994. "Not Just (Any)Body Can Be a Citizen: The Politics of Law, Sexuality, and Postcoloniality in Trinidad and Tobago and the Bahamas." *Feminist Review* 48:1–23.

Allen, Ernest. 1995. "When Japan Was 'Champion of the Darker Races': Satokata Takahashi and the Flowering of Black Messianic Nationalism." *Black Scholar* 24 (1).

Anderson, Benedict. 1991. *Imagined Communities: Reflections on the Origin and Spread of Nationalism.* London: Verso.

Ansen, David. 1994. "Pulp Friction." *Newsweek,* October 10.

Anzaldúa, Gloria. 1987. *Borderlands/La Frontera: The New Mestiza.* San Francisco: Aunt Lute Books.

Appadurai, Arjun. 1996. *Modernity at Large: Cultural Dimensions of Globalization.* Minneapolis: University of Minnesota Press.

Aptheker, Herbert. 1974. Introduction to *Dark Princess: A Romance,* by W. E. B. Du Bois. Millwood, N.Y.: Kraus-Thomson.

Arendt, Hannah. 1958. *The Origins of Totalitarianism.* 2nd ed. Cleveland: Meridian.

Arizpe, Lourdes. 1981. "Relay Migration and the Survival of the Peasant Household." In *Why People Move: Comparative Perspectives on the Dynamics of Internal Migration,* ed. Jorge Balan, 187–210. Paris: UNESCO.

Baker, Michael K. 1985. "Memory and Practice: Politics and the Representation of the Past in Eighteenth-Century France." *Representations* 11:134–64.

Baker-Fletcher, Karen. 1994. *A Singing Something: Womanist Reflections on Anna Julia Cooper.* New York: Crossroad.

Barrett, Lindon. 1999. *Blackness and Value: Seeing Double.* Cambridge: Cambridge University Press.

Bascara, Victor. 2006. *Model-Minority Imperialism.* Minneapolis: University of Minnesota Press.

Basch, Linda, Nina Glick Schiller, and Cristina Szanton Blanc, eds. 1994. *Nations Unbound: Transnational Projects, Postcolonial Predicaments, and Deterritorialized Nation-States.* Basel, England: Gordon and Breach.

Baugh, Bruce. 2000. "Death and Temporality in Deleuze and Derrida." *Angelaki: Journal of Theoretical Humanities* 5 (2): 73–83.

Beal, Frances. 1995. "Double Jeopardy: To Be Black and Female." In *Words of Fire: An Anthology of African American Feminist Thought,* ed. Beverly Guy-Sheftall. New York: New Press. (Orig. pub. in *The Black Woman,* ed. Toni Cade Bambara. New York: New American Library, 1970.)

Beasley, Delilah L. 1919. *The Negro Trail Blazers of California.* San Francisco: R and E Research Associates.

Behar, Ruth. 1990. "Rage and Redemption: Reading the Life Story of a Mexican Marketing Woman." *Feminist Studies* 16 (2): 223–58.

———. 1993. *Translated Woman: Crossing the Border with Esperanza's Story.* Boston: Beacon.

Bello, Walden. 1994. *Dark Victory.* Oakland: Pluto.

Benjamin, Walter. 1968. "Theses on the Philosophy of History." In *Illuminations,* ed. Hannah Arendt. New York: Schocken Books.

———. 1999. *The Arcades Project.* Cambridge: Belknap Press.

Bhabha, Homi K. 1997. "The World and the Home." In *Dangerous Liaisons: Gender, Nation, and Postcolonial Perspectives,* ed. Anne McClintock, Aamir Mufti, and Ella Shohat. Minneapolis: University of Minnesota Press.

———. 2004. *The Location of Culture.* New York: Routledge.

Blackwell, Maylei. 2003. "Contested Histories: *Las Hijas de Cuautemoc,* Chicana Feminism, and Print Culture in the Chicano Movement, 1968–1973." In *Chicana Feminisms: A Critical Reader,* ed. Gabriela F. Arredondo, Aída Hurtado, Norma Klahn, Olga Nájera-Ramírez, and Patricia Zavella. Durham: Duke University Press.

———. Forthcoming. *Retrofitted Memory: Contested Histories of Gender and Feminism in the Chicano Movement.* Austin: University of Texas Press.

Bonfil Batalla, Guillermo. 1987. *México profundo: Una civilización negada.* México, D.F.: CIESAS/SEP.

Books, W. 1983. "East Meets West: El Pasoans of Chinese Descent." *Password* 28 (2).

Bordwell, David, and Kristin Thompson. 2001. *Film Art: An Introduction.* New York: McGraw-Hill.

Boyle, Elizabeth Heger, and Fortunata Ghati Songora. 2004. "Formal Legality and East African Immigrant Perceptions of the 'War on Terror.'" *Law and Inequality* 22:301–36.

Bricker, Victoria, Eleuterio Po'ot Yah, and Ofelia Dzul de Po'ot. 1998. *A Dictionary of the Maya Language as Spoken in Hocabá, Yucatán.* Salt Lake City: University of Utah Press.

Briggs, Laura. 2002. *Reproducing Empire: Race, Sex, Science, and U.S. Imperialism in Puerto Rico.* Berkeley: University of California Press.

Brown, Wendy. 1995. *States of Injury.* Durham: Duke University Press.

Buff, Rachel Ida. 2008. "The Undergraduate Railroad: Undocumented Immigrant Students and Public Universities." In *Immigrant Rights in the Shadows of Citizenship,* ed. Rachel Buff. New York: New York University Press.

Bullock, Penelope. 1981. *The Afro-Americans Periodical Press, 1838–1909.* Baton Rouge: Louisiana State University Press.

Burgos, Adrian. 2002. "Learning America's Other Game: Baseball, Race, and the Study of Latinos." In *Latino/a Popular Culture,* ed. Michelle Habell-Pallán and Mary Romero, 225–39. New York: New York University Press.

Burgos-Debray, Elisabeth, ed. 1998. *I, Rigoberta Menchú: An Indian Woman in Guatemala.* London: Verso.

Burnett, Christina Duffy, and Burke Marshall. 2001. *Foreign in a Domestic Sense: Puerto Rico, American Expansion, and the Constitution.* Durham: Duke University Press.

Calhoun, Craig. 1995. *Critical Social Theory: Culture, History, and the Challenge of Difference.* London: Wiley-Blackwell.

California Department of Corrections and Rehabilitation. 2008. Adult Operations and Adult Programs. Facts and Figures, Fourth Quarter. http://www.cdcr.ca.gov/Divisions_Boards/Adult_Operations/Facts_and_Figures html.

Calvo, Luz. 2004. "Art Comes to the Archbishop: The Semiotics of Contemporary Chicana Feminism and the Art of Alma Lopez." *Meridians* 5 (1): 201–24.

Candelaria, Cordelia. 1980. "La Malinche, Feminist Prototype." *Frontiers* 5 (2): 1–6.

Cannick, Jasmyne. 2006. "Gays First, Then Illegals." *Advocate*, April 4, http://www .advocate.com/exclusive_detail_ektid28908.asp.

Carby, Hazel. 1978. *Reconstructing Womanhood: The Emergence of the Afro-American Woman Novelist*. New York: Oxford University Press.

Cardoso, Fernando Henrique, and Enzo Faletto. 1979. *Dependency and Development in Latin America*. Trans. Marjory Mattingly Urquidi. Berkeley: University of California Press.

Carliner, David, et al. 1990. *The Rights of Aliens and Refugees: The Basic ACLU Guide to Alien and Refugee Rights*. 2nd ed. Carbondale: Southern Illinois University Press.

Castellanos, M. Bianet. 2007. "Adolescent Migration to Cancún: Reconfiguring Maya Households and Gender Relations in Mexico's Yucatán Peninsula." *Frontiers* 28 (3): 1–27.

———. 2010. "Don Teo's Expulsion: Property Regimes, Moral Economies, and Ejido Reform." *Journal of Latin American and Caribbean Anthropology* 15 (1): 144–69.

Castells, Manuel. 1991. *The Informational City*. Cambridge: Blackwell.

Castillo, Ana. 1993. *So Far from God*. New York: Penguin.

Chang-Rodríguez, Eugenio. 2007. *Latinoamérica: su civilización y su cultura*. Florence, Ken.: Heinle and Heinle Publishers.

Chauncey, George. 2004. *Why Marriage? The History Shaping Today's Debate over Gay Equality*. Cambridge: Basic Books.

Chavez, Leo R. 1992. *Shadowed Lives: Undocumented Immigrants in American Society*. Fort Worth: Harcourt Brace College Publishers.

Chen, Jack. 1980. *The Chinese of America*. San Francisco: Harper and Row.

Chew, Selfa. 2005. *Azogue en la raíz*. México, D.F.: Ediciones Gráficas Eón.

Chinese Immigration: Its Social, Moral, and Political Effect. 1978. Report to the California Senate of Its Special Committee on Chinese Immigration. Sacramento: State Printing Office.

Chuh, Kandice. 2006. *Imagine Otherwise: On Asian Americanist Critique*. Durham: Duke University Press.

Cohen, Cathy. 1999. *The Boundaries of Blackness: AIDS and the Breakdown of Black Politics*. Chicago: University of Chicago Press.

———. 2004. "Deviance as Resistance: A New Research Agenda for the Study of Black Politics." *Du Bois Review: Social Science Research on Race* 1 (1): 27–45.

Cole, C. L., and Alex Mobley. 2005. "American Steroids: Using Race and Gender." *Journal of Sport and Social Issues* 29:3–8.

Comaroff, John L., and Jean Comaroff. 2001. "On Personhood: An Anthropological Perspective from Africa." *Social Identities* 7 (2): 267–83.

Combahee River Collective. 1979. "Why Did They Die?" *Radical America* 13 (6).

———. 1981. "Black Feminist Statement." In *This Bridge Called My Back: Writings by Radical Women of Color*, ed. Gloria Anzaldúa and Cherríe Moraga. Boston: Persephone Press.

Comisión Nacional para los Pueblos Indígenas. 2009. *Los pueblos indígenas en México*. March 11. http://www.cdi.gob.mx/index.php?option=com_docman& Itemid=24.

Conover, Ted. 1987. *Coyotes*. New York: Vintage Books.

Coopan, Vilashini. 2007. "Move On down the Line: Domestic Science, Transnational Politics, and Gendered Allegory in Du Bois." In *Next to the Color Line: Gender, Sexuality, and W. E. B. Du Bois*, ed. Susan Gillman and Alys Eve Weinbaum. Minneapolis: University of Minnesota Press.

Cooper, Frederick, and Randall Packard, eds. 1997. *International Development in the Social Sciences: Essays on the History and Politics of Knowledge*. Berkeley: University of California Press.

Cooper, Frederick, and Ann Laura Stoler. 1997. "Between Metropole and Colony." In *Tensions of Empire: Colonial Cultures in a Bourgeois World*, ed. Frederick Cooper and Ann Laura Stoler. Berkeley: University of California Press.

Cotera, Marta. 1997. "Our Feminist Heritage." In *Chicana Feminist Thought: The Basic Historical Writings*, ed. Alma M. Garcia. New York: Routledge. (Orig. pub. in *The Chicana Feminist*, ed. Marta Cotera. Austin: Information System Development, 1977.)

Coultard, Lisa. 2007. "Killing Bill: Rethinking Feminism and Film Violence." In *Interrogating Postfeminism: Gender and the Politics of Popular Culture*, ed. Yvonne Tasker and Diane Negra, 153–75. Durham: Duke University Press.

Crenshaw, Kimberlé. 1995. "Race, Reform, and Retrenchment: Transformation and Legitimation in Anti-discrimination Law." In *Critical Race Theory: The Key Writings that Formed the Movement*, ed. Kimberlé Crenshaw et al. New York: W. W. Norton and Co.

Criddle, Joan. 1992. *Bamboo and Butterflies: From Refugee to Citizen*. Dixon, Calif.: East/West Bridge.

Cvetkovich, Ann. 2003. *An Archive of Feelings: Trauma, Sexuality, and Lesbian Public Cultures*. Durham: Duke University Press.

Davis, Angela. 1983. *Women, Race, and Class*. New York: Vintage Books.

———. 2003. *Are Prisons Obsolete?* New York: Open Media.

Davis, Mike. 1990. *Prisoners of the American Dream*. New York: Verso.

Deleuze, Gilles. 1989. *Cinema 2: The Time-Image*. London: Alone.

———. 1994. *Difference and Repetition*. New York: Columbia University Press.

Deleuze, Gilles, and Félix Guattari. 1984. *Kafka: Towards a Minor Literature*. Trans. Dana Polan. Minneapolis: University of Minnesota Press.

Derrida, Jacques. 2005. *Rogues: Two Essays on Reason*. Stanford: Stanford University Press.

Dilke, Charles Wentworth. 1890. *Greater Britain: A Record of Travel in English Speaking Countries*. London: Macmillan.

Doane, Mary Ann. 2007. "Indexicality: Trace and Sign Introduction." *Differences* 18 (1): 1–6.

Dorsey, Joseph C. 2003. *Slave Traffic in the Age of Abolition: Puerto Rico, West Africa, and the Non-Hispanic Caribbean, 1815–1859*. Gainesville: University of Florida Press.

Drescher, Seymour. 2004. Review of *Slave Traffic in the Age of Abolition: Puerto Rico, West Africa, and the Non-Hispanic Caribbean, 1815–1859*, by Joseph C. Dorsey. *Hispanic American Historical Review* 84 (4): 726–28.

Duarte Duarte, Ana Rosa. 2006. "Espíritu de lucha: Cuerpo, poder y cambio sociocultural." Ph.D. diss., Universidad Autónoma Metropolitana, Unidad Iztapalapa.

Du Bois, W. E. B. 1920. *Dusk of Dawn: An Essay toward and Autobiography of a Race Concept*. Reprint. New York: Schocken Books.

——. 1924. *The Gift of Black Folk: The Negroes in the Making of America*. Boston: Stratford.

——. 1995a [1906]. "The Color Line Belts the World." *Collier's Weekly*, October 29. Collected in *W. E. B. Du Bois: A Reader*, ed. David Levering Lewis. New York: Henry Holt.

——. 1995b. "To the Nations of the World." In *W. E. B. Du Bois: A Reader*, ed. David Levering Lewis. New York: Henry Holt.

——. 1995c. [1928]. *Dark Princess: A Romance*. Jackson, Miss.: Banner Books.

——. 1995d. *Black Reconstruction in America, 1860–1880*. New York: Simon and Schuster.

——. 2007 [1903]. *The Souls of Black Folk*. Ed. Brent Edwards. New York: Oxford University Press.

duCille, Ann. 1993. *The Coupling Convention: Sex, Text, and Tradition in Black Women's Fiction*. New York: Oxford University Press.

Dudziak, Mary, and Leti Volpp. 2005. "Legal Borderlands: Law and the Construction of American Borders." Special issue, *American Quarterly* 57 (3).

Duggan, Lisa. 2003. *The Twilight of Equality? Neoliberalism, Cultural Politics, and the Attack on Democracy*. Boston: Beacon Press.

Durand, Jorge, and Douglas S. Massey, eds. 2004. *Crossing the Border: Research from the Mexican Migration Project*. New York: Russell Sage Foundations.

Eaton, Mary. 1995. "Homosexual Unmodified: Speculation on Law's Discourse, Race, and the Construction of Sexual Identity." In *Legal Inversions: Lesbians, Gay Men, and the Politics of the Law*, ed. D. Herman and C. Stychin. Philadelphia: Temple University Press.

Ebadi, Shirin, with Azadeh Moaveni. 2006. *Iran Awakening: A Memoir of Revolution and Hope*. New York: Random House.

Edwards, Brent Hayes. 2001. "The Uses of Diaspora." *Social Text* 19 (1): 45–73.

——. 2003. *The Practice of Diaspora*. Cambridge: Harvard University Press.

——. 2007. "Late Romance." In *Next to the Color Line: Gender, Sexuality, and W. E. B. Du Bois*, ed. Susan Gillman and Alys Eve Weinbaum. Minneapolis: University of Minnesota Press.

Escalante, Gonzalbo P., B. García Martínez, L. Jáuregui, J. Vázquez, E. Speckman, J. Garcíadiego Dantan, and L. Aboites Aguilar. 1981. *Nueva historia mínima de México*. Centro de Estudios Históricos. México, D.F.: El Colegio de México.

Escobar, Arturo. 1995. *Encountering Development: The Making and Unmaking of the Third World*. Princeton: Princeton University Press.

Escobar, Edward. 1999. *Race, Police, and the Making of a Political Identity*. Berkeley: University of California Press.

Eskridge, William N., Jr. 2001. "Equality Practice: Liberal Reflections on the Jurisprudence of Civil Unions." *Albany Law Review* 64:853.

Espinoza, Dionne. 2001. " 'Revolutionary Sisters': Women's Solidarity and Collective Identification among Chicana Brown Berets in East Los Angeles, 1967–1970." *Aztlán* 26 (1).

Ethnic Studies Committee of the Department of Ethnic Studies, University of California, Berkeley. 1974. "A Proposal for the Establishment of the College of Third World Studies." Unpublished manuscript, dated September 18.

Fabian, Johannes. 1983. *Time and the Other: How Anthropology Makes Its Object*. New York: Columbia University Press.

Fanon, Frantz. 1963. *The Wretched of the Earth*. New York: Grove Weidenfeld.

Farrar, Nancy. 1972. *The Chinese in El Paso*. El Paso: Texas Western Press.

Ferguson, James. 1997. "Anthropology and Its Evil Twin: 'Development' in the Constitution of a Discipline." In *International Development in the Social Sciences: Essays on the History and Politics of Knowledge*, ed. Frederick Cooper and Randall Packard, 150–75. Berkeley: University of California.

Ferguson, Roderick A. 2004. *Aberrations in Black: Toward a Queer of Color Critique*. Minneapolis: University of Minnesota Press.

Ferguson, Roderick A. 2007. " 'W. E. B. Du Bois': Biography of a Discourse." In *Next to the Color Line: Gender, Sexuality, and W. E. B. Du Bois*, ed. Susan Gillman and Alys Eve Weinbaum, 269–88. Minneapolis: University of Minnesota Press.

———. Forthcoming. *The Reorder of Things: The Birth of the Interdisciplines*. Minneapolis: University of Minnesota Press.

Ferrer, Ada. 1999. *Insurgent Cuba: Race, Nation, and Revolution, 1868–1898*. Chapel Hill: University of North Carolina Press.

Findlay, Eileen J. Suarez. 1999. *Imposing Decency: The Politics of Sexuality and Race in Puerto Rico, 1870–1920*. Durham: Duke University Press.

Foner, Eric. 1988. *Reconstruction: America's Unfinished Revolution, 1863–1877*. New York: Harper and Row.

Foster, Francis Smith. 1979. *Witnessing Slavery: The Development of Ante-bellum Slave Narratives*. Westport: Greenwood.

Foucault, Michel. [1970] 1994. *The Order of Things: An Archeology of the Human Sciences*. New York: Vintage Books.

———. 1972. *The Archaeology of Knowledge and the Discourse on Language*. New York: Pantheon.

———. 1977. "Nietzsche, Genealogy, History." In *Language, Counter-memory, Practice*, ed. Donald F. Bouchard. Ithaca: Cornell University Press.

———. 1980. *Power/Knowledge: Selected Interviews and Other Writings, 1972–1977*. Ed. Colin Gordon. New York: Pantheon.

——. 1991. "Governmentality." In *The Foucault Effect: Essays on Governmentality*, ed. Graham Burchell, Colin Gordon, and Peter Miller. Chicago: University of Chicago Press.

——. 2008. *The Birth of Biopolitics: Lectures at the College de France, 1978–1979*. New York: Palgrave Macmillan.

Frank, Andre Gunder. 1967. *Capitalism and Underdevelopment in Latin America: Historical Studies of Chile and Brazil*. New York: Monthly Review Press.

Franke, Katherine. 1999. "Becoming a Citizen: Post-bellum Regulation of African American Marriage." *Yale Journal of Law and Humanities* 11.

Fredrickson, George. 1971. *The Black Image in the White Mind: The Debate on Afro-American Character and Destiny, 1817–1914*. New York: Harper and Row.

Fregoso, Rosa Linda. 2003. *MeXicana Encounters: The Making of Social Identities on the Borderlands*. Berkeley: University of California Press.

Gaines, Kevin. 1996. *Uplifting the Race: Black Leadership, Politics, and Culture in the Twentieth Century*. Chapel Hill: University of North Carolina Press.

Gallagher, Dennis. 1998. "United States and the Indochinese Refugees." In *Indochinese Refugees: Asylum and Resettlement*, ed. Supang Chantavanich and E. Bruce Reynolds. Bangkok: Chulalongkorn University.

Gamio, Manuel. 1960. *Forjando Patria*. 1916; reprint, México, D.F.: Editorial Porrúa.

Gilmore, Ruth Wilson. 1998–99. "Globalisation and U.S. Prison Growth: From Military Keynesianism to Post-Keynesian Militarism." *Race and Class* 40 (2–3): 171–87.

——. 2007. *Golden Gulag: Prisons, Surplus, Crisis, and Opposition in Globalizing California*. Berkeley: University of California Press.

Gilroy, Paul. 1992. *The Black Atlantic: Modernity and Double Consciousness*. Cambridge: Harvard University Press.

Glissant, Édouard. 2001. *The Fourth Century: Le Quatrieme Siecle*. Lincoln: University of Nebraska Press.

Go, Julian. 2003. "The Chains of Empire: State Building and 'Political Education' in Puerto Rico and the Philippines." In *The American Colonial State in the Philippines: Global Perspectives*, ed. Julian Go and Anne L. Foster. Durham: Duke University Press.

Goldberg, David Theo. 1993. *Racist Culture: Philosophy and the Politics of Meaning*. Cambridge: Blackwell.

Gonzáles, Sylvia. 1980. "Chicana Evolution." In *The Third Woman: Minority Women Writers of the United States*, ed. Dexter Fisher, 418–22. Boston: Houghton Mifflin.

Gopinath, Gayatri. 2005. *Impossible Desires: Queer Diasporas and South Asian Public Cultures*. Durham: Duke University Press.

Gordon, Avery F. 1997. *Ghostly Matters: Haunting and the Sociological Imagination*. Minneapolis: University of Minnesota Press, 1997.

Grasmuck, Sherry, and Patricia Pessar. 1991. *Between Two Islands: Dominican International Migration*. Berkeley: University of California Press.

Gray, Herman. 1995. *Watching Race: Television and the Struggle for "Blackness."* Minneapolis: University of Minnesota Press.

Grewal, Inderpal. 2005. *Transnational America: Feminisms, Diasporas, Neoliberalisms.* Durham: Duke University Press.

Gupta, Akhil, and James Ferguson. 1992. "Beyond 'Culture': Space, Identity, and the Politics of Difference." *Cultural Anthropology* 7:16–23.

———. 1997. "Beyond 'Culture': Space, Identity, and the Politics of Difference." In *Culture, Power, Place: Explorations in Critical Anthropology*, ed. Akhil Gupta and James Ferguson. Durham: Duke University Press.

Gutiérrez, Ramon. 1997. "Paradigm Shifts and Shifting Boundaries." Julian Samora Research Institute Research and Publications Occasional Paper Series 15. July. http://www.jsri.msu.edu/RandS/research/ops/oc15.html.

Gutiérrez-Jones, Carl. 1995. *Rethinking the Borderlands: Between Chicano Culture and Legal Discourse.* Berkeley: University of California Press.

Gutmann, Matthew. 1996. *The Meanings of Macho: Being a Man in Mexico City.* Berkeley: University of California Press.

Halberstam, Judith. 1993. "Imagined Violence/Queer Violence: Representation, Rage and Resistance." *Social Text* 37:187–201.

———. 2005. *In a Queer Time and Place: Transgender Bodies, Subcultural Lives, Sexual Cultures.* New York: New York University Press.

Halley, Janet. 2000. "Like Race." In *What's Left of Theory*, ed. Judith Butler et al. New York: Routledge.

Hall, Stuart. 1996. "New Ethnicities." In *Stuart Hall: Critical Dialogues in Cultural Studies*, ed. David Morley and Kuan-Hsing Chen. New York: Routledge.

———. 1997a. "The Local and the Global." In *Dangerous Liaisons: Gender, Nation, and Postcolonial Perspectives*, ed. Anne McClintock, Amir Mufti, and Ella Shohat. Minneapolis: University of Minnesota Press.

———. 1997b. *Representation: Cultural Representation and Signifying Practices.* Milton Keynes, U.K.: Open University Press.

Hammerton, A. James. 1979. *Emigrant Gentlewoman: Genteel Poverty and Female Emigration, 1830–1914.* Totowa, N.J.: Rowman and Littlefield.

Hansen, Mark B. N. 2006. *New Philosophy for New Media.* Cambridge: MIT Press.

Hardt, Michael. 2007. "Jefferson and Democracy." *American Quarterly* 59 (1).

Hartman, Saidiya. 1997. *Scenes of Subjection: Terror, Slavery, and Self-Making in Nineteenth-Century America.* New York: Oxford University Press.

Harvey, David. 2007. *A Brief History of Neoliberalism.* New York: Oxford University Press.

Hastrup, Kirsten, and Karen Fog Olwig. 1997. Introduction to *Siting Culture: The Shifting Anthropological Object*, ed. Karen Fog Olwig and Kirsten Hastrup, 1–16. London: Routledge.

Hellwig, David. 1974. "The Afro-American and the Immigrant, 1880–1930: A Study of Black Social Thought." Ph.D. diss., Syracuse University.

Hernández Castillo, Rosalva Aída. 2001. *Histories and Stories from Chiapas: Border Identities in Southern Mexico.* Austin: University of Texas Press.

Hernández, Carmen Dolores. 2000. "A Sense of Space, a Sense of Speech: A Conversation with Ana Lydia Vega." *Hopscotch: A Cultural Review* 2 (2): 52–59.

Hill, Herbert. 1985. *Black Labor and the American Legal System: Race, Work, and the Law*. Madison: University of Wisconsin Press.

Holborn, Louise. 1975. *Refugees: A Problem of Our Time*. Metuchen: Scarecrow Press.

Holland, Sharon Patricia. 2000. *Raising the Dead: Readings of Death and (Black) Subjectivity*. Durham: Duke University Press.

Holloway, Karla. 2002. *Passed On: African American Mourning Stories: A Memorial*. Durham: Duke University Press.

Hondagneu-Sotelo, Pierrette. 1994. *Gendered Transitions: Mexican Experiences of Immigration*. Berkeley: University of California Press.

Hong, Grace Kyungwon. 2004. "Race, Empire, and the Not Working Class: Bret Harte's Overland Monthly and the Chinatown Photographs of Arnold Genthe." *Journal of the West* 43 (4): 8–14.

———. 2006. *The Ruptures of American Capital: Women of Color Feminism and the Cultures of Immigrant Labor*. Minneapolis: University of Minnesota Press.

hooks, bell. 2001. "Eating the Other: Desire and Resistance." In *Media and Cultural Studies: Keyworks*, ed. Meenaskshi Gigi Durham and Douglas M. Kellner. London: Blackwell.

Hu-DeHart, Evelyn. 1991. "From Area Studies to Ethnic Studies: The Study of the Chinese Diaspora in Latin America." In *Asian Americans: Comparative and Global Perspectives*, ed. Shirley Hune. Pullman: Washington State University Press.

Hughes, Joe. 2000. "Three men killed when speeding car hits trees; a fourth walks away." *San Diego Union-Tribune*, March 25, B2.

Hughes, Kathryn. 2003. *The Victorian Governess*. London: Hambledon and London, 2003.

Hutchinson, Darren Lenard. 1997. "Out Yet Unseen: A Racial Critique of Gay and Lesbian Legal Theory and Political Discourse." *Connecticut Law Review* 29 (2): 562–646.

Ibarra, María de la Luz. 2003. "Buscando La Vida: Mexican Immigrant Women's Memories of Home, Yearning, and Border Crossings." *Frontiers* 24 (2–3): 261–81.

Ida B. Wells. *On Lynchings: Southern Horrors, A Red Record, Mob Rule in New Orleans*. New York: Arno Press, 1969.

Ignatiev, Noel. 1995. *How the Irish Became White*. New York: Routledge.

Ileto, Reynaldo. 2002. "The Philippine American War: Friendship and Forgetting." In *Vestiges of War: The Philippine American War and the Aftermath of an American Dream, 1899–1999*, ed. Luis H. Francia and Angel Velasco Shaw. New York: New York University Press.

James, C. L. R. 1993. "Black Studies and the Contemporary Student." In *The C.L.R. James Reader*, ed. Anna Grimshaw. Oxford: Blackwell.

James, Henry. 2004. "Preface to the 1908 New York Edition of *The Turn of the Screw*." Reprinted in *The Turn of the Screw: Complete, Authoritative Text with Biographical, Historical, and Cultural Contexts, Critical History, and Essays from Contemporary Critical Perspectives*, ed. Peter G. Beidler. Boston: Bedford–St. Martin.

Jiménez, Miriam, and Juan Flores. 2010. *The Afro-Latin@ Reader: History and Culture in the United States*. Durham: Duke University Press.

Jones, Andrew F., and Nikhil Singh. 2003. "The Afro-Asian Century." Special issue, *Positions: East Asia Cultural Critique* 11 (1).

Jordan, June. 1989. "Moving Towards Home." In *Naming Our Destiny: New and Selected Poems.* New York: Thunder's Mouth Press.

Kang, Laura Hyun Yi. 2002. *Compositional Subjects: Enfiguring Asian American Women.* Durham: Duke University Press.

Kaplan, Amy. 1990. "Romancing the Empire: The Embodiment of American Masculinity in the Popular Historical Novel of the 1890s." *American Literary History* 2.

——. 1993. "'Left Alone with America': The Absence of Empire in the Study of American Culture." In *Cultures of United States Imperialism,* ed. Amy Kaplan and Donald Pease, 1–22. Durham: Duke University Press.

——. 2002. *The Anarchy of Empire in the Making of U.S. Culture.* Cambridge: Harvard University Press.

Kearney, Michael. 1991. "Borders and Boundaries of State and Self at the End of Empire." *Journal of Historical Society* 4 (1): 52–74.

——. 1996. *Reconceptualizing the Peasantry: Anthropology in Global Perspective.* Boulder, Colo.: Westview Press.

Keeling, Kara. 2007. *The Witch's Flight: The Cinematic, the Black Femme, and the Image of Common Sense.* Durham: Duke University Press.

Kelley, Robin D. G. 1996. *Race Rebels: Culture, Politics, and the Black Working Class.* New York: Free Press.

Kennedy, Randall. 2005. "Marriage and the Struggle for Gay, Lesbian, and Black Liberation." *Utah Law Review* 781.

Keshavarz, Fatemeh. 2007. *Jasmine and Stars: Reading More than Lolita in Tehran.* Chapel Hill: University of North Carolina Press.

Kim, Jodi. 2010. *Ends of Empire: Asian American Critique and the Cold War.* Minneapolis: University of Minnesota Press.

Kozol, Jonathan. 1992. *Savage Inequalities: Children in America's Schools.* New York: Harper Perennial.

Kramer, Paul. 2006. *The Blood of Government: Race, Empire, the United States, and the Philippines.* Chapel Hill: University of North Carolina Press.

Kramer, Paul, and John Plotz. 2001. "Pairing Empires: Britain and the United States, 1857–1947." *Journal of Colonialism and Colonial History* 2 (1).

Krauss, Rosalind. 1977. "Notes on the Index: Seventies Art in America, Part 2." *October* 4:58–67.

Kusz, Kyle W. 2001. "'I Want to Be the Minority': The Politics of Youthful White Masculinities in Sport and Popular Culture in 1990s America." *Journal of Sport and Social Issues* 25:390–416.

Lapham, Lewis J. 2004. "Tentacles of Rage: The Republican Propaganda Mill, a Brief History." *Harper's Magazine,* September, 31–41.

Layoun, Mary. 1995. "(Mis)trusting Narratives: Refugee Stories of Post-1922 Greece and Post-1974 Cyprus." In *Mistrusting Refugees.* Berkeley: University of California Press.

Lecaros, Cecilia Wadsö. 2001. *The Victorian Governess Novel.* Lund: Lund University Press.

Lee, Erika. 2002. "Enforcing the Borders: Chinese Exclusion along the U.S. Borders with Canada and Mexico, 1882–1924." *Journal of American History* 89 (1): 54–86.

Lee, James Kyung-Jin. 2004. *Urban Triage: Race and the Fictions of Multiculturalism.* Minneapolis: University of Minnesota Press.

Levitt, Peggy. 2001. *The Transnational Villagers.* Berkeley: University of California Press.

Lewis, David Levering. 2000. *W. E. B. Du Bois: The Fight for Equality and the American Century, 1919–1963.* New York: Henry Holt.

Lida, Clara. 1997. *Inmigración y exilio: Reflexiones sobre el caso español.* México, D.F.: Siglo XXI.

Limón, José E. 1994. *Dancing with the Devil: Society and Cultural Poetics in Mexican-American South Texas.* Madison: University of Wisconsin Press.

Lincoln, Eric. 1974. *The Black Experience in Religion.* Garden City: Anchor Books.

Lipsitz, George. 1997. "Frantic to Join . . . the Japanese Army: the Asia Pacific War in the Lives of African American Soldiers and Civilians." In *The Politics of Culture in the Shadow of Capital,* ed. Lisa Lowe and David Lloyd, 324–53. Durham: Duke University Press.

———. 1998. *The Possessive Investment in Whiteness: How White People Profit from Identity Politics.* Philadelphia: Temple University Press.

Lloyd, David. 1997. "Nationalisms against the State." In *The Politics of Culture in the Shadow of Capital,* ed. Lisa Lowe and David Lloyd. Durham: Duke University Press.

Lo, Clarence Y. H. 1995. *Small Property versus Big Government.* Berkeley: University of California Press.

Loewen, James. 1988. *The Mississippi Chinese: Between Black and White.* Prospect Heights, Ill.: Waveland Press.

Lomnitz, Larissa. 1977. *Networks and Marginality: Life in a Mexican Shantytown.* New York: Academic Press.

López, Ian Haney. 2001. "Protest, Repression, and Race: Legal Violence and the Chicano Movement." *University of Pennsylvania Law Review* 140 (1).

Lorde, Audre. 1993. "Age, Race, Class, and Sex: Women Redefining Difference." In *Zami, Sister Outsider, Undersong.* New York: Quality Paperback Book Club.

———. 2007. *Sister Outsider: Essays and Speeches.* Trumansberg, N.Y.: Crossing Press.

Lortie, Francis. 1970. *San Francisco's Black Community, 1870–1890: Dilemmas in the Struggle for Equality.* San Francisco: R and E Research Associates.

Lowe, Lisa. 1996. *Immigrant Acts: On Asian American Cultural Politics.* Durham: Duke University Press.

———. 2001. "Epistemological Shifts: National Ontology and the New Asian Immigrant." In *Orientations: Mapping Studies in the Asian Diaspora,* ed. Kandice Chuh and Karen Shimakawa. Durham: Duke University Press.

———. 2005. "Insufficient Difference." *Ethnicities* 53.

———. 2006. "Intimacies of Four Continents." In *Tense and Tender Ties: Intimacy and the Politics of Comparison in North American Empires,* ed. Ann Laura Stoler. Durham: Duke University Press.

Lowe, Lisa, and David Lloyd. 1997. Introduction to *Politics of Culture in the Shadow of Capital*, ed. Lisa Lowe and David Lloyd. Durham: Duke University Press.

Lubiano, Wahneema. 1997. "Black Nationalism and Black Common Sense." In *The House That Race Built: Black Americans, U.S. Terrain*, ed. Wahneema Lubiano. New York: Pantheon.

Lwin, Sanda Mayzaw. 2006. "A Race So Different from Our Own: Segregation, Exclusion, and the Myth of Mobility." In *AfroAsian Encounters*, ed. Heike Raphael-Hernandez and Shannon Steen, 17–33. New York: New York University Press.

Lyotard, Jean-François. 1984. *The Postmodern Condition: A Report on Knowledge*. Minneapolis: University of Minnesota Press.

Mahmood, Saba. 2005. *Politics of Piety: The Islamic Revival and the Feminist Subject*. Princeton: Princeton University Press.

Malevich, Kasmir. 1968. "Suprematism." In *Theories of Modern Art: A Source Book by Artists and Critics*, ed. Herschel B. Chipp. Berkeley: University of California Press.

Malkin, Victoria. 2004. " 'We Got to Get Ahead': Gender and Status in Two Mexican Migrant Communities." *Latin American Perspectives* 31 (5): 75–99.

Manovich, Lev. 2002. *The Language of New Media*. Cambridge: MIT Press.

Manriquez, B. J. 2002. "Ana Castillo's *So Far from God*: Intimations of the Absurd." *College Literature* 29 (2).

Marfleet, Phillip. 2006. *Refugees in a Global Era*. New York: Palgrave Macmillan.

Mariscal, Jorge. 2003. "They Died Trying to Be Students: The Future for Latinos in an Era of War and Occupation." *CounterPunch*, April 18. http://www.counterpunch.org/mariscal04182003.html.

———. 2009. "Tracked into Combat Jobs: Military Targets Latino Youth." *War Times / Tiempo de Guerras* 13 (2003): 3. http://www.war-times.org/issues/13arts.html.

Martin, Philip L. 1994. "The United States: Benign Neglect toward Immigration." In *Controlling Immigration: A Global Perspective*, ed. Wayne A. Cornelius, Philip L. Martin, and James F. Hollifield, 83–100. Stanford: Stanford University Press.

Martin, Susan Forbes. 2004. *Refugee Women*. 2nd ed. Lanham, Md.: Lexington Books.

Martinez, Brandon. 1997. Paper assignment for Mira Mesa High School, San Diego, Calif.

Martinez, Christine, and Jesse Martinez Jr. 2000. "Death and Funeral Notices: Martinez, Brandon Jesse." *San Diego Union Tribune*, March 29, B5.

Martinez, Ramiro, Jr. 2002. *Latino Homicide: Immigration, Violence, and Community*. New York: Routledge.

Martínez, Rubén. 2001. *Crossing Over: A Mexican Family on the Migrant Trail*. New York: Metropolitan Books.

Martínez, Rubén, and Los Illegals. 2000. Performance at Expresso Mi Cultura, Los Angeles, April 22.

Martinez, Trisha. 2000. "You Just Don't Know." Death and Funeral Notices: Martinez, Brandon Jesse. *San Diego Union Tribune*, March 29, B5.

Martos Sosa, Lorena. 1994. "Projecting the Past to the Present: The Historical Knowledge of a Mayan People." Ph.D. diss., Stanford University.

Massey, Doreen. 1994. *Space, Place, and Gender.* Minneapolis: University of Minnesota Press.

Massey, Douglas S., and Nancy A. Denton. 1993. *American Apartheid: Segregation and the Making of the Underclass.* Cambridge: Harvard University Press.

Massey, Douglas S., and Kristin E. Espinosa. 1997. "What's Driving Mexico-U.S. Migration? A Theoretical, Empirical, and Policy Analysis." *American Journal of Sociology* 102 (4): 939–99.

Maurice, Mary. 2004 [1849]. "There Is a Strong Prejudice against Governesses." Reprinted in *The Turn of the Screw,* by Henry James, ed. Peter G. Beidler. Boston: Bedford–St. Martin's, 2004.

McClain, Charles J. 1994. *In Search of Equality: The Chinese Struggle against Discrimination in Nineteenth-Century America.* Berkeley: University of California Press.

McConnell, Eileen Díaz. 2005. *No Place like Home: The State of Hispanic Housing in Chicago, Los Angeles, and New York City, 2003.* Notre Dame: Institute for Latino Studies, University of Notre Dame. http://www.nd.edu/latino/research.htm.

McMichael, Philip. 2000. *Development and Social Change: A Global Perspective.* 2nd ed. Thousand Oaks, Calif.: Sage.

Melamed, Jodi. 2006. "The Spirit of Neoliberalism: From Racial Liberalism to Neoliberal Multiculturalism." *Social Text* 24 (4): 1–24.

———. 2008. "The Killing Joke of Sympathy: Chester Himes's *End of a Primitive* Sounds the Limits of Mid-century Racial Liberalism." *American Literature* 80 (4): 769–97.

———. Forthcoming. *Represent and Destroy: Antiracism, Global Capitalism, and the Political Cultures of American Literature, 1945–2008.* Minneapolis: University of Minnesota Press.

Miles, Tiya, and Sharon Holland, eds. 2006. *Crossing Waters, Crossing Worlds: The African Diaspora in Indian Country.* Durham: Duke University Press.

Miller, Jerome G. 1997. *Search and Destroy: African American Males in the Criminal Justice System.* Cambridge: Cambridge University Press.

Miyoshi, Masao. 1996. "Globalization and the University." In *The Cultures of Globalization,* ed. Fredric Jameson and Masao Miyoshi, 247–70. Durham: Duke University Press.

Molina Guzmán, Isabel. 2005. "Gendering Latinidad through the Elián News Discourse about Cuban Women." *Latino Studies* 3:179–204.

Monsiváis, Carlos. 1996. "Will Nationalism Be Bilingual?" In *Mass Media and Free Trade: NAFTA and the Cultural Industries,* ed. Emile G. McAnany and Kenton T. Wilkinson. Austin: University of Texas Press.

Monteón González, Humberto, and José Trueba Lara. 1988. *Chinos y Antichinos en México.* Documentos para su estudio. Guadalajara, Jalisco, Mexico: Gobierno de Jalisco. Secretaría General. Unidad Editorial.

Moraga, Cherríe. 1981. Preface to *This Bridge Called My Back: Writings by Radical Women of Color,* by Cherríe Moraga and Gloria Anzaldúa. Watertown, Mass.: Persephone Press.

——. 1983. *Loving in the War Years: Lo Que Nunca Pasó por los Labios*. Cambridge: South End Press.

——. 1993. *The Last Generation: Prose and Poetry*. Cambridge: South End Press.

Moraga, Cherríe, and Gloria Anzaldúa. 1983. *This Bridge Called My Back: Writings by Radical Women of Color*. New York: Kitchen Table, Women of Color Press.

Morris, Rosalind. 2002. "Returning the Body without Haunting: Mourning 'Nai Phi' and the End of Revolution in Thailand." In *Loss: The Politics of Mourning*, ed. David Eng and David Kazanjian. Durham: Duke University Press.

Mouat, Ricardo Gutiérrez. 2001. "Dismembering the Nation: Ana Lydia Vega's *Falsas crónicas del sur*." *Journal of Latin American Cultural Studies* 10 (1): 119–28.

Mullen, Bill. 2004. *Afro-Orientalism*. Minneapolis: University of Minnesota Press.

Muñoz, José Esteban. 1996. "Ephemera as Evidence: Introductory Notes to Queer Acts." In "Queer Acts," special issue, *Women and Performance: A Journal of Feminist Theory* 8 (2): 5–17.

——. 1999. *Disidentifications: Queers of Color and the Performance of Politics*. Minneapolis: University of Minnesota Press.

Murase, Mike. 1976. "Ethnic Studies and Higher Education for Asian Americans." In *Counterpoint: Perspectives on Asian America*, ed. Emma Gee. Los Angeles: Asian American Studies Center, University of California.

Nafisi, Azar. 2003. *Reading Lolita in Tehran: A Memoir in Books*. New York: Random House.

Napolitano, Valentina. 2002. *Migration, Mujercitas, and Medicine Men: Living in Urban Mexico*. Berkeley: University of California Press.

Nelson, Dana. 1998. *National Manhood: Capitalist Citizenship and the Imagined Fraternity of White Men*. Durham: Duke University Press.

Ngai, Mae M. 2005. *Impossible Subjects: Illegal Aliens and the Making of Modern America*. Politics and Society in Twentieth-Century America. Princeton: Princeton University Press.

Nguyen, Viet Thanh. 2002. *Race and Resistance: Literature and Politics in Asian America*. New York: Oxford University Press.

Nieto Gomez, Ana. 1997. "Chicana Feminism." In *Chicana Feminist Thought: The Basic Historical Writings*, ed. Alma Garcia. New York: Routledge. (Orig. pub. *Caracol* 2, no. 5 [1976]: 3–5.)

Norman, Brian. 2007. " 'We' in Redux: The Combahee River Collective's *Black Feminist Statement*." *Differences* 18 (2): 103–34.

Nowatzki, Robert. 2002. "Foul Lines and the Color Line: Baseball and Race at the Turn of the Twentieth Century." *Nine: A Journal of Baseball History and Culture* 11:82–88.

Office of Refugee Settlement. 1985. *Southeast Asian Refugee Self-Sufficiency Study: Final Report*. Office of Refugee Settlement, U.S. Department of Health and Human Services.

Office of the Assistant Secretary of Defense. 2004. *Population Representation in the Military Services, Fiscal Year 2002*. Office of the Assistant Secretary of Defense.

Okihiro, Gary. 1994. *Margins and Mainstreams: Asians in American History and Culture.* Seattle: University of Washington.

Oliver, Melvin, and Thomas Shapiro. 1997. *Black Wealth/White Wealth: A New Perspective on Racial Inequality.* New York: Routledge.

Olwig, Karen Fog. 1997. "Cultural Sites: Sustaining a Home in a Deterritorialized World." In *Siting Culture: The Shifting Anthropological Object,* ed. Karen Fog Olwig and Kirsten Hastrup, 17–38. London: Routledge.

Omi, Michael, and Howard Winant. 1994. *Racial Formation in the United States from the 1960s to the 1990s.* New York: Routledge.

Ong, Aihwa. 2006. *Neoliberalism as Exception: Mutations in Citizenship and Sovereignty.* Durham: Duke University Press.

Orfield, Gary, Susan E. Eaton, and Elaine R. Jones. 1997. *Dismantling Desegregation: The Quiet Reversal of Brown v. Board of Education.* New York: New Press.

Oropeza, Lorena. 2005. *¡Raza Si! ¡Guerra No! Chicano Protest and Patriotism during the Viet Nam War Era.* Berkeley: University of California Press.

Pagán, Eduardo Obregón. 2003. *Murder at the Sleepy Lagoon: Zoot Suits, Race, and Riot in Wartime L.A.* Chapel Hill: University of North Carolina Press, 2003.

Palumbo-Liu, David. 1995. *The Ethnic Canon: Histories, Institutions, and Interventions.* Minneapolis: University of Minnesota Press.

Parreñas, Rhacel Salazar. 2001. *Servants of Globalization: Women, Migration, and Domestic Work.* Palo Alto: Stanford University Press.

Paz, Octavio. 1985. *The Labyrinth of Solitude.* Trans. Yara Milos Lysander Kemp and Rachel Phillips-Belash. New York: Grove Press.

Perez, Emma. 1999. *The Decolonial Imaginary: Writing Chicanas into History.* Bloomington: Indiana University Press.

Perkins, C. A. 1978. *Border Patrol, with the U.S. Immigration Service on the Mexican Boundary, 1910–54.* El Paso: Texas Western Press.

Peterson, M. Jeanne. 1973. "The Victorian Governess: Status Incongruence in Family and Society." In *Suffer and Be Still: Women in the Victorian Age,* ed. Martha Vicinus. Bloomington: Indiana University Press.

Pile, Steve. 1997. "Introduction: Opposition, Political Identities, and Spaces of Resistance." In *Geographies of Resistance,* ed. Steve Pile and Michael Keith, 1–32. New York: Routledge.

Poovey, Mary. 1988. *Uneven Developments: The Ideological Work of Gender in Mid-Victorian England.* Chicago: University of Chicago Press.

Portes, Alejandro, and Rubén G. Rumbaut. 1996. *Immigrant America: A Portrait.* Berkeley: University of California Press.

Posnock, Ross. 2002. *Color and Culture: Black Writers and the Making of the Modern Intellectual.* Cambridge: Harvard University Press.

Prashad, Vijay. 2000. *The Karma of Brown Folk.* Minneapolis: University of Minnesota Press.

———. 2001. *Everyone Was Kung-Fu Fighting: Afro-Asian Connections and the Myth of Cultural Purity.* Boston: Beacon Press.

Pratt, Mary Louise. 2001. "*I, Rigoberta Menchú* and the 'Culture Wars.'" In *The Rigoberta Menchú Controversy*, ed. Arturo Arias, 29–57. Minneapolis: University of Minnesota Press.

Puar, Jasbir. 2007. *Terrorist Assemblages: Homonationalism in Queer Times*. Durham: Duke University Press.

Puig Llano, Juan M. 1992. *Entre el río Perla y el Nazas: La colonia china en Torreón y la matanza de 1911*. México, D.F.: Consejo Nacional para la Cultura y las Artes.

Qualls, Barry V. 1994. "'Speak What We Think': The Brontes and Women Writers." In *The Columbia History of the British Novel*, ed. John Richetti. New York: Columbia University Press.

Rafael, Vicente. 2000. *White Love and Other Events in Filipino History*. Durham: Duke University Press.

Ramírez Cuevas, Jesús. 2009. "Después de la fiesta: Chiapas; El primer pendiente." *La Jornada* (Mexico), December 3, 2000. http://www.jornada.unam.mx/2000/12/03/mas-chiapas.html.

Rampersad, Arnold. 1997. "Du Bois' Passage to India: *Dark Princess*." In *W. E. B. Du Bois on Race and Culture*, ed. Bernard W. Bell. New York: Routledge.

Re Cruz, Alicia. 1996. *The Two Milpas of Chan Kom: A Study of Socioeconomic and Political Transformations in a Maya Community*. Albany: State University of New York Press.

Reagon, Bernice Johnson. 1983. "Coalition Politics: Turning the Century." In *Home Girls: A Black Feminist Anthology*, ed. Barbara Smith. New York: Kitchen Table Press.

Reddy, Chandan. 2005. "Asian Diasporas, Neoliberalism, and Family: Reviewing the Case for Homosexual Asylum in the Context of Family Rights." *Social Text* 23 (3–4): 101–19.

Redfield, Robert. 1941. *The Folk Culture of Yucatan*. Chicago: University of Chicago Press.

Redfield, Robert, and Alfonso Villa Rojas. 1990. *Chan Kom: A Maya Village*. Prospect Heights, Ill.: Waveland Press. (Orig. pub. 1934.)

Regalado, Samuel O. 2002. "Hey Chico! The Latin Identity in Major League Baseball." *Nine: A Journal of Baseball History and Culture* 11:16–24.

Renov, Michael. 2004. *The Subject of Documentary*. Minneapolis: University of Minnesota Press.

Rhodes, Jane. 1998. *Mary Ann Shadd Cary: The Black Press and Protest in the Nineteenth Century*. Bloomington: Indiana University Press.

Rich, B. Ruby. 2004. "Day of the Woman." *Sight and Sound* 14 (6): 24–27.

Richie, Beth E. 1996. *Compelled to Crime: The Gender Entrapment of Battered Black Women*. New York: Routledge.

Robertson, Linda. 2003. *The Dream of Civilized Warfare: World War I Flying Aces and the American Imagination*. Minneapolis: University of Minnesota Press.

Rodríguez, Richard T. 2000. "On the Subject of Gang Photography." *Aztlán* 25:109–43.

——. 2009. *Next of Kin: The Family in Chicano/a Cultural Politics*. Durham: Duke University Press.

Rosaldo, Renato. 1989. *Culture and Truth: A Remaking of Social Analysis*. Boston: Beacon Press.

Rothman, William. 1988. *The "I" of the Camera: Essays in Film Criticism, History, and Aesthetics*. Cambridge: Cambridge University Press.

Rouse, Roger C. 1989. "Mexican Migration to the United States: Family Relations in the Development of a Transnational Migrant Circuit." Ph.D. diss., Stanford University.

——. 1991. "Mexican Migration and the Social Space of Postmodernism." *Diaspora* 1 (1): 8–23.

——. 1995. "Questions of Identity: Personhood and Collectivity in Transnational Migration to the United States." *Critique of Anthropology* 15 (4): 351–80.

Rumbaut, Rubén. 1994. "Origins and Destinies: Immigration to the United States since World War II." *Sociological Forum* 9 (4).

Ruskola, Teemu. 2005. "Canton Is Not Boston: The Invention of American Imperial Sovereignty." In "Legal Borderlands: Law and the Construction of American Borders," ed. Mary Dudziak and Leti Volpp, special issue, *American Quarterly* 57 (3): 859–84.

Said, Edward. 1979. *Orientalism*. New York: Vintage Books.

——. 1998. *Edward Said on Orientalism*. Videotape. Media Education Foundation. 26 Center Street, Northampton, Mass. 01060.

——. 2002. *Reflections on Exile and Other Essays*. New York: Vintage.

Saldaña-Portillo, Maria Josefina. 2003. *The Revolutionary Imagination in the Americas in the Age of Development*. Durham: Duke University Press.

Salman, Michael. 2001. *The Embarrassment of Slavery: Controversies over Bondage and Nationalism in the American Colonial Philippines*. Berkeley: University of California Press.

Sanchez, Arturo. n.d. "La farsa del 'inquest.'" *La Raza* 1 (3).

Sandoval, Chela. 2000. *The Methodology of the Oppressed*. Minneapolis: University of Minnesota Press.

Sassen, Saskia. 1988. *The Mobility of Labor and Capital: A Study in International Investment and Labor Flow*. Cambridge: Cambridge University Press.

——. 1998. *Globalization and Its Discontents: Essays on the New Mobility of People and Money*. New York: New Press.

——. 1999. *Guests and Aliens*. New York: New Press.

Saxton, Alexander. 1990. *The Rise and Fall of the White Republic: Class Politics and Mass Culture in Nineteenth-Century America*. London: Verso.

——. 1995. *The Indispensable Enemy: Labor and the Anti-Chinese Movement in California*. Berkeley: University of California Press.

Sayer, Derek. 1991. *Capitalism and Modernity: An Excursus on Marx and Weber*. London: Routledge.

Schiavone Camacho, Julia María. 2006. "Crossing Boundaries, Claiming a Homeland: The Mexican Chinese Transpacific Journey to Becoming Mexican, 1910s–1960s." Ph.D. diss., University of Texas, El Paso.

Schneider, C., and P. E. Amar. 2003. "The Rise of Crime, Disorder, and Authoritarian Policing: An Introductory Essay." *NACLA Report on the Americas* 37 (2): 12–16.

Shah, Nayan. 2001. *Contagious Divides: Epidemics and Race in San Francisco's Chinatown.* Berkeley: University of California Press.

Shankman, Arnold. 1978. "Black on Yellow: Afro-Americans View Chinese-Americans, 1850–1935." *Phylon* 39 (1): 1–17.

Silva, Noenoe. 2005. *Aloha Betrayed: Native Hawaiian Resistance to American Colonialism.* Durham: Duke University Press.

Singh, Amritjit. 1976. *The Novels of the Harlem Renaissance: Twelve Black Writers, 1923–1933.* University Park: Pennsylvania State University Press.

Singh, Nikhil Pal. 2004. *Black Is a Country: Race and the Unfinished Struggle for Democracy.* Cambridge: Harvard University Press.

Somerville, Siobhan B. 2005. "Queer *Loving.*" *GLQ* 11 (3): 335–70.

Sommer, Doris. 1992. *Founding Fictions: The National Romances of Latin America.* Berkeley: University of California Press.

Soto, Sandra. 2005. "Cherrié Moraga's Going Brown: 'Reading like a Queer.'" *GLQ* 11 (2).

Spivak, Gayatri Chakravorty. 1988. "Can the Subaltern Speak?" In *Marxism and the Interpretation of Culture,* ed. Cary Nelson and Lawrence Grossberg. Urbana: University of Illinois Press.

———. 1993. *Outside in the Teaching Machine.* New York: Routledge.

———. 1994. "Can the Subaltern Speak?" In *Colonial Discourse and Postcolonial Theory: A Reader,* ed. Patrick Williams and Laura Chrisman. New York: Columbia University Press.

———. 1996. "Diasporas Old and New: Women in the Transnational World." *Textual Practice* 10 (2).

———. 1999. *A Critique of Postcolonial Reason: Toward a History of the Vanishing Present.* Cambridge: Harvard University Press, 1999.

———. 2003. *Death of a Discipline.* New York: Columbia University Press.

———. 2004. "Righting Wrongs." *South Atlantic Quarterly* 103 (2–3): 523–81.

Stephens, Chuck. 2004. "The Whole She-bang." *Film Comment* 40 (4): 44–47.

Stoler, Ann Laura. 2006. *Haunted by Empire: Geographies of Intimacy in North American History.* Durham: Duke University Press.

Stoll, Davis. 1999. *Rigoberta Menchú and the Story of All Poor Guatemalans.* Boulder, Colo.: Westview Press.

Sudbury, Julia. 2005. *Global Lockdown: Race, Gender, and the Prison-Industrial Complex.* 1st ed. New York: Routledge.

Sullivan, Paul. 1989. *Unfinished Conversations: Mayas and Foreigners between Two Wars.* Berkeley: University of California Press.

Sundquist, Eric. 1993. *To Wake the Nations: Race in the Making of American Literature.* Cambridge: Harvard University Press.

Swarms, Rachel L. 2004. " 'African American' Becomes a Term for Debate." *New York Times,* 29 August.

Takougang, Joseph, and Bassirou Tidjani. 2009. "Settlement Patterns and Organizations among African Immigrants in the United States." *Journal of Third World Studies* 26 (1): 31–40.

Tang, Eric. 2000. "Collateral Damage: Southeast Asian Poverty in the United States." *Social Text* 18:55–79.

Tapia, Ruby. 2001. "Un(di)ing Legacies: White Matters of Memory in Portraits of 'Our Princess.' " *Cultural Values* 5:261–87.

Tarantino, Quentin. 2003. *Kill Bill: Vol. 1.* Miramax Studios.

——. 2004. *Kill Bill: Vol. 2.* Miramax Studios.

Tate, Claudia. 1995. Introduction to *Dark Princess: A Romance,* by W. E. B. Du Bois. Jackson: University Press of Mississippi.

Tatum, Beverly. 1997. *"Why Are All the Black Kids Sitting Together in the Cafeteria?" and Other Conversations about Race.* New York: Basic Books.

Taylor, Diana. 2003. *The Archive and the Repertoire: Performing Cultural Memory in the Americas.* Durham: Duke University Press.

Tchen, John. 1999. *New York before Chinatown: Orientalism and the Shaping of American Culture, 1776–1882.* Baltimore: Johns Hopkins University Press.

Thomas, Brook. 1997. *Plessy vs. Ferguson: A Brief History with Documents.* Boston: Bedford Books.

Thompson, Lanny. 2002. "Representation and Rule in the Imperial Archipelago: Cuba, Puerto Rico, Hawai'i, and the Philippines under U.S. Dominion after 1898." *American Studies Asia* 1 (1): 3–39.

Turner, Victor. 1989. "Betwixt and Between: The Liminal Period in *Rites de Passage.*" In *The Forest of Symbols: Aspects of Ndembu Ritual,* ed. Victor Turner, 93–111. Ithaca: Cornell University Press.

Urrea, Luis Alberto. 1993. *Across the Wire: Life and Hard Times on the Mexican Border.* New York: Anchor Books.

Van Dijk. 2003. *Dominación etnica y racismo discursivo en España y América Latina.* Barcelona: Gedisa Editorial.

van Gennep, Arnold. 1960. *The Rites of Passage.* Chicago: University of Chicago Press.

Van Hear, Nicholas. 2000. "Locating Internally Displaced People in the Field of Forced Migration." *Norsk Geogr. Tidsskr* 54.

Vega, Ana Lydia. 1994. *Miss Florence's Trunk.* In *True and False Romances: Stories and a Novella,* trans. Andrew Hurley. New York: Serpent's Tail.

Viesca, Victor Hugo. 2004. "The Battle of Los Angeles: The Cultural Politics of Chicana/o Music in the Greater Eastside." *American Quarterly* 56:719–39.

Villanueva, Alma. 1985. "La Chingada." In *Five Poets of Aztlán,* ed. Santiago Daydi-Tolson, 137–63. Binghamton: Bilingual Review Press.

Volpp, Leti. 2001–2. "The Citizen and the Terrorist." UCLA *Law Review* 49:1575–600.

Von Eschen, Penny. 1997. *Race against Empire: Black Americans and Anticolonialism, 1937–1957.* Ithaca: Cornell University Press.

Wallenstein, Peter. 1994. "Race, Marriage, and the Law of Freedom: Alabama and Virginia, 1860s–1960s." *Chi-Kent L. Rev.* 70:371.

Washington, Booker T. 1965. *Three Negro Classics*. New York: Avon Books.

Weinbaum, Alys. 2004. *Wayward Reproductions: Genealogies of Race and Nation in Transatlantic Modern Thought*. Durham: Duke University Press.

———. 2007. "Interracial Romance and Black Internationalism." In *Next to the Color Line: Gender, Sexuality, and W. E. B. Du Bois*, ed. Susan Gillman and Alys Eve Weinbaum. Minneapolis: University of Minnesota Press.

Wells-Barnett, Ida B. 1969. *On Lynchings: Southern Horrors, A Red Record, Mob Rule in New Orleans*. New York: Arno Press.

West, Cornel. 1994. "The New Cultural Politics of Difference." In *The Postmodern Turn: New Perspectives on Social Theory*, ed. Steven Seidman. Cambridge: Cambridge University Press.

Widener, Daniel. 2003. " 'Perhaps the Japanese Are to Be Thanked?' Asia, Asian Americans, and the Construction of Black California." *Positions: The Afro-Asian Century* 11 (1).

Wiegman, Robyn. 1999. "Whiteness Studies and the Paradox of Particularity." *Boundary 2* 26:115–50.

Williams, Brackette F. 1991. *No Stain on My Name, War in My Veins: Guyana and the Politics of Cultural Struggle*. Durham: Duke University Press.

Williams, Patricia J. 1991. *The Alchemy of Race and Rights*. Cambridge: Harvard University Press.

Willis, Sharon. 1997. *High Contrast: Race and Gender in Contemporary Hollywood Film*. Durham: Duke University Press.

Wilmore, Gayraud S. 1998. *Black Religion and Black Radicalism: An Interpretation of the Religious History of African Americans*. Maryknoll: Orbis Books.

Winant, Howard. 2001. *The World Is a Ghetto: Race and Democracy since World War II*. New York: Basic Books.

Wolf, Eric. 1959. *Sons of the Shaking Earth*. Chicago: University of Chicago Press, 1959.

Wolseley, Roland. 1971. *The Black Press, U.S.A.* Ames: Iowa State University Press.

Wright, Richard. 1995 [1956]. *The Color Curtain: A Report on the Bandung Conference*. Cleveland: World Publishing Company.

Young, Cynthia. 2006. *Soul Power: Culture, Radicalism, and the Making of the U.S. Third World Left*. Durham: Duke University Press.

Contributors

VICTOR BASCARA is associate professor in the Department of Asian American Studies at UCLA. He is the author of *Model Minority Imperialism* and other writings on the relationship of U.S. imperialism and Asian American cultural politics.

LISA MARIE CACHO is an assistant professor at the University of Illinois, Urbana-Champaign, in the Department of Latina/Latino Studies and the Asian American Studies Program. Her work has been published in *Cultural Values*, *Latino Studies*, and the anthology *Immigrant Rights in the Shadows of Citizenship*, edited by Rachel Buff. She examines the ways in which communities of color in the United States are relationally criminalized, sexualized, and devalued.

M. BIANET CASTELLANOS teaches in the Department of American Studies at the University of Minnesota. She has worked with Maya communities for over fifteen years. She is the author of *A Return to Servitude: Maya Migration and the Tourist Trade in Cancún* (University of Minnesota Press, 2010) and has published essays in *Frontiers*, *Latin American Perspectives*, *Chicana/Latina Studies*, and the *Journal of Latin American and Caribbean Anthropology*.

MARTHA CHEW SÁNCHEZ is an associate professor in the Department of Global Studies at St. Lawrence University. She is the coordinator of Caribbean and Latin American Studies program. She is the author of the book *Corridos in Migrant Memory* (University of New Mexico Press, 2006) and has published articles in *Third Text Journal, Journal of Family Communication,* and the journal of the International Communication Association. Her entry "Sábado Gigante" was published in *The Encyclopedia of Latina and Latino Popular Culture in the United States,* edited by Cordelia Candelaria, Arturo Aldama, and Peter J. García, and a chapter on Sábado Gigante and the cultural homogenization of Spanish-speaking people was published in the book *Globalization, Media Hegemony and Social Class,* edited by Lee Artz and Yahya R. Kamalipour.

RODERICK A. FERGUSON is associate professor of race and critical theory and chair of the Department of American Studies at the University of Minnesota, Twin Cities. He is the author of *Aberrations in Black: Toward a Queer of Color Critique* and is completing a manuscript titled "The Reorder of Things: On the Institutionalization of Difference."

GRACE KYUNGWON HONG is associate professor of women's studies and Asian American studies at UCLA. She is the author of *The Ruptures of American Capital: Women of Color Feminism and the Culture of Immigrant Labor* (University of Minnesota Press, 2006).

HELEN H. JUN is associate professor of African American studies and English at the University of Illinois, Chicago. Her book *Race for Citizenship: Black Orientalism and Asian Uplift from Pre-Emancipation to Neoliberal America,* examines how the history of U.S. citizenship has situated Asian Americans and African Americans in uneven and interlocking political-economic and social relationships since the mid-nineteenth century. Her current research explores how the seemingly anachronistic discourse of slavery is deployed to address two distinct modes of exploitation under late capitalism: the U.S. prison-industrial complex and global human trafficking.

KARA KEELING is associate professor of critical studies in the School of Cinematic Arts and of African American studies in the Department of American Studies and Ethnicity at the University of Southern California. She is author of *The Witch's Flight: The Cinematic, the Black Femme, and the Image of Common Sense* (Duke University Press, 2007); coeditor (with Colin MacCabe and Cornel West) of a selection of writings by the late James A. Snead, *European Pedigrees/African Con-*

tagions: Racist Traces and Other Writing; and author of several articles that have appeared in *GLQ, Qui Parle, Black Scholar, Women and Performance*, and elsewhere.

SANDA MAYZAW LWIN was most recently a senior fellow at the Rothermere American Institute at Oxford University. She has taught at Yale University, Smith College, Mount Holyoke College, and the University of Massachusetts, Amherst. Her areas of specialization include American literature, Asian American literary and cultural studies, critical race theory, and legal studies. She is completing a book manuscript, "The Constitution of Asian America," which analyzes the legal and cultural formation of Asian America through literary and legal narratives of citizenship, immigration, and exclusion. She currently resides in London.

JODI MELAMED is associate professor of English and Africana Studies at Marquette University. She is the author of the forthcoming book *Represent and Destroy: Liberal Racial Orders, Literary Studies, and Racial Capitalist Globalization* (University of Minnesota Press).

CHANDAN REDDY is the author of a number of essays and articles on the topic of race, sexuality, and late capitalism. He is an associate professor of English at the University of Washington, Seattle, and author of the forthcoming book *Freedom with Violence: Race, Sexuality and the U.S. State* (Duke University Press).

RUBY C. TAPIA is associate professor of comparative studies and women's studies at Ohio State University. She is the author of *American Pietás: Visions of Race, Death, and the Maternal*, University of Minnesota Press (2011), and a coeditor of *Interrupted Life: Experiences of Incarcerated Women in the United States*.

CYNTHIA TOLENTINO is associate professor of English at the University of Oregon. Author of *America's Experts: Race and the Fictions of Sociology* (University of Minnesota Press, 2009), she is at work on a book-length study of representations of U.S. legal categories for the Philippines and Puerto Rico.

Index

Abjection, 9, 213, 247, 249–52, 256, 262; of refugees in *Kelly Loves Tony*, 198

Acosta, Zeta, 252–59. See also *The Revolt of the Cockroach People*

African American studies and history, 3, 17–18, 301–2; African diaspora, 55–56; black migrations and, 120, 123–24; black racial formations and, 122–29; black women and, 12–16; East African migration and, 20, 114–16, 127–29; ideal types in comparison and, 20; marriage plot in literature of, 195; mourning in, 34; *Plessy v. Ferguson* and, 293, 309; slavery and governess novels and, 318–23; social historical narratives of oppressed groups and, 157–72; value and devaluation and, 12–16. See also "Black Orientalism"; Black press in nineteenth century; *Dark Princess*; *Loving v. Virginia*, desire for gay and lesbian marriage rights and

Alarcón, Norma, 247, 249

Alternate imaginings, 15–16; of African American studies, 124, 126; by Chicano and Chicana nationalists, 246, 250, 256, 262, 264–65; of Chinese in Mexico, 221–25; of death and solidarity, 265; of globalization, 69–70; irony and absurdism as critique and, 259–64; of refugees, 199; women of color feminism and queer as color critique and, 2–3

Alternative comparative methods, 18–20, 264–65; need for, 1–2; queer of color and woman as alternative critique of, 8. *See also* Queer of color critique; Strange affinities; Women of color feminism

Alternative modes of coalition, 55

Anderson, Benedict, 242–43, 300

Anti-identitarianism, 78–82

Antimiscegenation. See under *Loving v. Virginia*, desire for gay and lesbian marriage rights and

Antiracisms, 78, 157–58; access to higher education and, 83–90; neoliberal multiculturalism and, 83–89

Appadurai, Arjun, 79

Appropriation, 63–64, 67, 73–74

GRACE KYUNGWON HONG is associate professor of Asian American studies and wom-en's studies at the University of California, Los Angeles. She is the author of *The Ruptures of American Capital: Women of Color Feminism and the Culture of Immigrant Labor* (2006).

RODERICK A. FERGUSON is associate professor and chair of American studies at the University of Minnesota. He is the author of *Aberrations in Black: Toward a Queer of Color Critique* (2004).

Library of Congress Cataloging-in-Publication Data

Strange affinities : the gender and sexual politics of comparative racialization / edited by Grace Kyungwon Hong and Roderick A. Ferguson.
p. cm.—(Perverse modernities)
Includes bibliographical references and index.
ISBN 978-0-8223-4970-9 (cloth : alk. paper)
ISBN 978-0-8223-4985-3 (pbk. : alk. paper)
1. Group identity. 2. Ethnicity. 3. Race. 4. Gender identity. 5. Sexual orientation.
I. Hong, Grace Kyungwon. II. Ferguson, Roderick A. III. Series: Perverse modernities.
HM753.S87 2011
305.42089—dc22
2010054506

www.ingramcontent.com/pod-product-compliance
Lightning Source LLC
Chambersburg PA
CBHW051949270326
41929CB00015B/2585